Designing Central Banks

The activities of central banks are relevant to everyone in society. This book starts by considering how and why in general central banks evolved and specifically the special aspects of the contribution of the Northern European Central Banking Tradition. With that foundation, the book then turns to a series of contemporary themes. Firstly, this book looks at independence, how central banks can actually influence their respective economies, goals, responsibilities and governance.

This collection of papers, selected from the joint conference of the Bank of Finland and the Deutsche Bundesbank in November 2007, will help motivate continuing research into the institutional design of central banks and promote a better understanding of the many challenges central banks are facing today. This volume gives a detailed perspective on the benefits of price stability and central bank independence and, due to the advances in macroeconomic theory, has prompted a substantial rethink on central banks' institutional design.

With contributions from such scholars as Alex Cukierman and Forrest Capie and a foreword by Erkki Liikanen and Professor Axel A. Weber, this volume will be useful reading for monetary economists around the world as well as all those with an interest in central banks and banking more generally.

David Mayes is Director and Adjunct Professor at the Europe Institute, University of Auckland. **Geoffrey Wood** is Professor of Economics at Cass Business School, London.

Routledge international studies in money and banking

1 **Private Banking in Europe**
Lynn Bicker

2 **Bank Deregulation and Monetary Order**
George Selgin

3 **Money in Islam**
A study in Islamic political economy
Masudul Alam Choudhury

4 **The Future of European Financial Centres**
Kirsten Bindemann

5 **Payment Systems in Global Perspective**
Maxwell J. Fry, Isaak Kilato, Sandra Roger, Krzysztof Senderowicz, David Sheppard, Francisco Solis and John Trundle

6 **What is Money?**
John Smithin

7 **Finance**
A characteristics approach
Edited by David Blake

8 **Organisational Change and Retail Finance**
An ethnographic perspective
Richard Harper, Dave Randall and Mark Rouncefield

9 **The History of the Bundesbank**
Lessons for the European Central Bank
Jakob de Haan

10 **The Euro**
A challenge and opportunity for financial markets
Published on behalf of *Société Universitaire Européenne de Recherches Financières (SUERF)*
Edited by Michael Artis, Axel Weber and Elizabeth Hennessy

11 **Central Banking in Eastern Europe**
Edited by Nigel Healey and Barry Harrison

12 **Money, Credit and Prices Stability**
Paul Dalziel

13 Monetary Policy, Capital Flows and Exchange Rates
Essays in memory of Maxwell Fry
Edited by William Allen and David Dickinson

14 Adapting to Financial Globalisation
Published on behalf of *Société Universitaire Européenne de Recherches Financières (SUERF)*
Edited by Morten Balling, Eduard H. Hochreiter and Elizabeth Hennessy

15 Monetary Macroeconomics
A new approach
Alvaro Cencini

16 Monetary Stability in Europe
Stefan Collignon

17 Technology and Finance
Challenges for financial markets, business strategies and policy makers
Published on behalf of *Société Universitaire Européenne de Recherches Financières (SUERF)*
Edited by Morten Balling, Frank Lierman, and Andrew Mullineux

18 Monetary Unions
Theory, history, public choice
Edited by Forrest H. Capie and Geoffrey E. Wood

19 HRM and Occupational Health and Safety
Carol Boyd

20 Central Banking Systems Compared
The ECB, the pre-euro Bundesbank and the Federal Reserve system
Emmanuel Apel

21 A History of Monetary Unions
John Chown

22 Dollarization
Lessons from Europe and the Americas
Edited by Louis-Philippe Rochon and Mario Seccareccia

23 Islamic Economics and Finance
A glossary, 2nd edition
Muhammad Akram Khan

24 Financial Market Risk
Measurement and analysis
Cornelis A. Los

25 Financial Geography
A banker's view
Risto Laulajainen

26 Money Doctors
The experience of international financial advising 1850–2000
Edited by Marc Flandreau

27 Exchange Rate Dynamics
A new open economy macroeconomics perspective
Edited by Jean-Oliver Hairault and Thepthida Sopraseuth

28 Fixing Financial Crises in the 21st Century
Edited by Andrew G. Haldane

29 **Monetary Policy and Unemployment**
The U.S., Euro-area and Japan
Edited by Willi Semmler

30 **Exchange Rates, Capital Flows and Policy**
Edited by Peter Sinclair, Rebecca Driver and Christoph Thoenissen

31 **Great Architects of International Finance**
The Bretton Woods era
Anthony M. Endres

32 **The Means to Prosperity**
Fiscal policy reconsidered
Edited by Per Gunnar Berglund and Matias Vernengo

33 **Competition and Profitability in European Financial Services**
Strategic, systemic and policy issues
Edited by Morten Balling, Frank Lierman and Andy Mullineux

34 **Tax Systems and Tax Reforms in South and East Asia**
Edited by Luigi Bernardi, Angela Fraschini and Parthasarathi Shome

35 **Institutional Change in the Payments System and Monetary Policy**
Edited by Stefan W. Schmitz and Geoffrey E. Wood

36 **The Lender of Last Resort**
Edited by F.H. Capie and G.E. Wood

37 **The Structure of Financial Regulation**
Edited by David G. Mayes and Geoffrey E. Wood

38 **Monetary Policy in Central Europe**
Miroslav Beblavý

39 **Money and Payments in Theory and Practice**
Sergio Rossi

40 **Open Market Operations and Financial Markets**
Edited by David G. Mayes and Jan Toporowski

41 **Banking in Central and Eastern Europe 1980–2006**
A comprehensive analysis of banking sector transformation in the former Soviet Union, Czechoslovakia, East Germany, Yugoslavia, Belarus, Bulgaria, Croatia, the Czech Republic, Hungary, Kazakhstan, Poland, Romania, the Russian Federation, Serbia and Montenegro, Slovakia, Ukraine and Uzbekistan
Stephan Barisitz

42 **Debt, Risk and Liquidity in Futures Markets**
Edited by Barry A. Goss

43 **The Future of Payment Systems**
Edited by Stephen Millard, Andrew G. Haldane and Victoria Saporta

44 **Credit and Collateral**
Vania Sena

45 **Tax Systems and Tax Reforms in Latin America**
Edited by Luigi Bernardi, Alberto Barreix, Anna Marenzi and Paola Profeta

46 **The Dynamics of Organizational Collapse**
The case of Barings Bank
Helga Drummond

47 **International Financial Co-operation**
Political economics of compliance with the 1988 Basel Accord
Bryce Quillin

48 **Bank Performance**
A theoretical and empirical framework for the analysis of profitability, competition and efficiency
Jacob Bikker and Jaap W.B. Bos

49 **Monetary Growth Theory**
Money, interest, prices, capital, knowledge and economic structure over time and space
Wei-Bin Zhang

50 **Money, Uncertainty and Time**
Giuseppe Fontana

51 **Central Banking, Asset Prices and Financial Fragility**
Éric Tymoigne

52 **Financial Markets and the Macroeconomy**
Willi Semmler, Peter Flaschel, Carl Chiarella and Reiner Franke

53 **Inflation Theory in Economics**
Welfare, velocity, growth and business cycles
Max Gillman

54 **Monetary Policy over Fifty Years**
Heinz Herrman (Deutsche Bundesbank)

55 **Designing Central Banks**
Edited by David Mayes and Geoffrey Wood

Designing Central Banks

Edited by David Mayes and Geoffrey Wood

Routledge
Taylor & Francis Group
LONDON AND NEW YORK

First published 2009
by Routledge
2 Park Square, Milton Park, Abingdon, Oxfordshire OX14 4RN

Simultaneously published in the USA and Canada
by Routledge
711 Third Avenue, New York, NY 10017

Routledge is an imprint of the Taylor & Francis Group, an informa business

First issued in paperback 2011

Typeset in Times by Wearset Ltd, Boldon, Tyne and Wear

British Library Cataloguing in Publication Data
A catalogue record for this book is available from the British Library

Library of Congress Cataloging in Publication Data
Designing central banks / edited by David Mayes & Geoffrey Wood.
p. cm.
1. Banks and banking, Central I. Mayes, David G. II. Wood, Geoffrey Edward.
HG1811.D47 2009
332.1'1–dc22

2009004074

ISBN13: 978-0-415-47616-4 (hbk)
ISBN13: 978-0-415-69654-8 (pbk)
ISBN13: 978-0-203-87344-1 (ebk)

Contents

Contributors

Jan Marc Berk, Head of Research, De Nederlandsche Bank

Forrest Capie, Official Historian, Bank of England

Roger Clews, Special Advisor, Bank of England

Alex Cukierman, Professor, Tel Aviv University

Michael Ehrmann, Adviser, European Central Bank

Øyvind Eitrheim, Director of Research, Norges Bank

Marcel Fratzscher, Head of International Policy Analysis, European Central Bank

Hans Gersbach, Professor, ETH Zurich

Már Guðmundsson, Governor, Central Bank of Iceland

Jakob de Haan, Professor, University of Groningen

Volker Hahn, ETH Zurich

Heinz Hermann, Head of Research, Deutsche Bundesbank

Erkki Liikanen, Governor, Suomen Pankki

Ludger Linnemann, University of Dortmund

David Mayes, Director, Europe Institute, University of Auckland

Loretta J. Mester, Senior Vice-President and Director of Research, Federal Reserve Bank of Philadelphia

Mattias Persson, Head of Financial Stability, Sveriges Riksbank

Jan V. Qvigstad, Deputy Governor, Norges Bank

Georg Rich, Honorary Professor, University of Bern

Juha Tarkka, Advisor to the Board, Suomen Pankki

Roland Vaubel, University of Mannheim

Axel A. Weber, President, Deutsche Bundesbank

Geoffrey Wood, Professor, Cass Business School

Mark A. Wynne, Vice President and Senior Economist, Director, Globalization and Monetary Policy Institute, Federal Reserve Bank of Dallas

Foreword

Over the past few decades, lessons learned from economic events combined with advances in macroeconomic theory have prompted a substantial rethink on central banks' institutional design. As a result, there has been considerable convergence globally concerning the guiding principles for central banks. In particular, there is widespread agreement on the substantial benefits of price stability and central bank independence, on the forward-looking nature of monetary policy and its need for credibility. We are now in an era in which central banks in many countries throughout the world have enjoyed notable success in keeping inflation at a low level. Nonetheless, some interesting monetary policy issues remain unresolved.

2007 marked the fiftieth anniversary of the Deutsche Bundesbank. In 2008, the European System of Central Banks, of which both the Bank of Finland and the Deutsche Bundesbank are integral parts, celebrated its tenth anniversary. This has presented a good opportunity to look into the question of how the institutional design of central banks has evolved in the past and of what we should expect in the future. Against this background, a joint conference of the Bank of Finland and the Deutsche Bundesbank was held in Eltville, Germany, on 8–9 November 2007. The two days of the conference were very productive and stimulating with practitioners from central banks and academics from all over the world tackling a variety of issues, ranging from central bank independence and central banks' goals to their responsibilities, communication methods and the issue of what kind of research central banks should pursue.

This collection of papers from the conference will help share this experience with a wider audience. Our hope is that the studies in this volume will motivate continuing research into the institutional design of central banks and promote a better understanding of the many challenges central banks are facing today. Above all, we wish to thank the contributors and editors whose expertise, ideas and efforts have brought this volume to life. Pooling research within the decentralised European System of Central Banks has proved beneficial, and there is no doubt that organising joint conferences, such as this one, is a course that we should, and will, be pursuing more closely in the future.

Professor Axel A. Weber, President of the Deutsche Bundesbank
Erkki Liikanen, Governor of the Bank of Finland

Acknowledgement

The project was undertaken jointly with Heinz Hermann of Deutsche Bundesbank, who looked after all the local arrangements in Eltville and Wiesbaden but unfortunately could not participate in the production of this book.

Introduction

David Mayes and Geoffrey Wood

Introduction

Over the last 20 years a large number of new central banks have come into being in the former Soviet Union and in the former communist Central and East European countries. This has generated an upsurge of interest in how central banks should best be designed for the modern world. This has occurred at the same time that the European System of Central Banks and the European Central Bank have been designed and come into operation. A third force overlays this remarkable period of change. In tandem with the reorganisation of corporate governance and managerial focus of private-sector firms and public-sector organisations, central banks have also been transforming themselves into focused and efficient organisations that deliver the targets required of them in an open and verifiable manner. Gone are the days that central banks were a 'gentleman's club with an interest in finance'. Between them, these factors have led to a considerable consensus on the focus of central banks, how they should be structured and governed, and on how they should operate.

Our task in this book is to explore how this apparent consensus has arisen, how it contrasts with the past, what it contains and how it may develop in the future. To do this we have organised contributions from well-known authorities in the field to put together the various facets of our task. The individual chapters reflect the personal views of the authors but we took the opportunity to bring all the contributors together in a conference held at the Bundesbank's conference and training centre in Eltville to discuss these ideas. Hence the chapters are followed by a discussion, reflecting a wider range of views.

This book is organised very much as the conference was. It starts with two chapters on the origins of central banking, looking both at the Anglo-Saxon model, and at the slightly different history in northern Europe. This prepares the way for chapters on what history reveals to be the two core – indeed, defining – functions of central banks. These are the preservation of monetary and of financial stability. These are considered in that order, the first section incorporating both a most imaginative discussion of the communications strategy of central banks and how that can be used to assist achievement of the price stability objective and an examination of how that objective can in practice be defined.

The book then turns to financial stability matters, particularly the relatively new problems created by having large banks operating across independent nation states (the large British banks of the past operated to a considerable extent across British colonies) and the complications that may arise with regard to money market and capital access (the former at least never troubling the British banks as they had access to London).

The substantial financial dislocation around the world since the sub-prime mortgage market in the United States began to unravel has also had an impact on thinking about the design of central banks. The general trend has been towards 'narrower' central bank mandates but the recent problems have led people to realise that what affects financial stability is far wider and that the financial institutions that are essential to the smooth operation of the financial system are rather more extensive than was previously thought. This implies that the central bank needs to have a role not just in handling emergencies but in the prudential operation of the financial system normally. The trend of having central banks focus on monetary policy and separate financial services agencies focus on financial supervision seems to be halting. Now the emphasis is on a different division, with conduct of business issues still being the preserve of financial supervisory authorities but the prudential functioning of financial institutions being more open. At the least the central bank needs to be better informed but there is now pressure for closer involvement, with the Dutch and Irish models of the central bank also having responsibility for prudential supervision gaining much more support.

Design

By the 1980s it began to become broadly accepted that the primary focus of central banks should be on achieving and then maintaining price stability, although the exact phraseology varies from case to case and some central banks such as the Bundesbank and the Swiss National Bank had already had this as their dominating goal for some time. We can point to a number of landmark events in this process. The decision by the Federal Reserve under Paul Volcker to attack inflation vigorously at the beginning of the 1980s is clearly one of the best known. In Europe, the turning point can perhaps be ascribed to the decision in France in 1983 to follow the policy of the franc fort and thereby seek to emulate West Germany's success in maintaining low inflation. Without this it is unlikely that the impetus towards monetary union would have developed and proceeded as it did. The role of the Thatcher government in the United Kingdom should also be acknowledged in the dramatic change in the aim of monetary policy in 1979. However, this change in policy focus, like the change to the 'franc fort' policy, was implemented by the government and not by the central bank. So by no means was the running made entirely by the central banks themselves. Further afield, the Reserve Bank Act of 1989 in New Zealand probably provided the clearest encapsulation of the purpose of central banks and the idea of a contract between the central bank and society to deliver price stability. This is particularly notable because in the past these duties simply emerged rather than being stated in advance, often being taken for granted as the implicit contract after some years of the promise being delivered. Currently the mandate for producing and maintaining financial stability is solidifying in the same manner.

The assistance in central bank design provided, in the 1990s and more recently, to the transition country central banks came from a relatively modest number of sources and in a sense reflects the normal expectation that advice will tend to be heavily related to the experience of the advisor. An example of this in a previous period of central bank creation or redesign comes from the 1930s, when there was a rash of central bank creations, particularly in the old Commonwealth, and instigated by the Bank of England. It is thus no surprise that the structure of these central banks, including the Reserve Bank of New Zealand, should be similar to that of the Bank of England. In the case of the modern-day transition countries, much of the help came from the IMF and its wide range of consultants, and also from central banks such as the Bundesbank, the Austrian National Bank which was instrumental in setting up the Joint Vienna Institute, the Bank of England, which set up the Centre for Central Banking Studies, and the Bank of Finland, which set up an Institute for the Eastern European transition economies and provided the first advisor in Albania, *inter alia.*

The key to these initiatives was not that they were simply involved with the design of central bank laws and structures but that they involved the detailed training of thousands of central bank employees in the procedures of Western central banks. Thus the whole culture of operation was transferred, and a substantial collegiality built up in the central banking community. It may be that similar communities have been built up in other institutional areas such as the police but the central banking community seems to stand out as one in which this transfer has been pre-eminent. How well this collegiality will hold together in times of international stress is a question raised (implicitly) in the chapter by Mattias Persson (pp. 196–215).

In part this collegiality has been emphasised by monetary union in the EU. Central banks used to be relatively cautious in what they shared with each other. But in Asia-Pacific, for example, there has been a steady development of institutions, with the joint SEACEN training centre in Kuala Lumpur, the SEANZA joint course and more recently EMEAP (the executive meeting for East Asia Pacific central banks). EMEAP has gone beyond its original information-sharing meetings at deputy and governor level to extended general work in particular sectors and generation of swap and other facilities. However, this falls far short of the joint efforts put in not simply to design the European Central Bank through the Delors Committee of central bank governors but through the detailed discussions of the sub-committees on each area of practical concern set up under the European Monetary Institute in the five-year preparation for the ECB. Here each member central bank was able to share its experience and help distil the best aspects of their joint knowledge. Although naturally the largest country central banks had the main influence and the Bundesbank law is often mentioned as a blueprint for the ECB, there was a substantial degree of mutual learning that has of course intensified since the ECB came into being in 1998 and the introduction of the euro in 1999.

There has been increasing international convergence in many areas of central banking, such as monetary policy operations, and not just in the major issues such as objectives, independence and accountability. The combination of the initiative by the IMF to try to ensure that central banks acted as a bulwark against inflationary fiscal policy by governments in the transition economies and the strongly independent position of the Bundesbank in the German economic system helped not just the independence of new central banks but the increasing independence of many of the established ones. Not only was it possible to point to these changes as a source of financial credibility for the countries but it was also possible to show the improved real terms economic performance that appeared to coincide with this structure.

The mechanism of inflation targeting which has been introduced in many countries has helped make the role of those central banks much clearer and to increase transparency of their operations. Inflation targeting gives both an objective and a means of assessing the performance of the bank. However, at the same time central banks realised the importance of credibility in keeping down the 'costs' of monetary policy. In so far as the structure and responsibilities of the bank and its record of action contributed to a belief that whatever would be necessary to achieve price stability would actually be done, then expectations of future inflation will tend also to fall into the target range, and price setters will behave on the assumption that the general price level will move within these bounds. Achieving this change in behaviour and expectations involved central banks in establishing or reinforcing a number of aspects of their credibility. Not only did they have to demonstrate their willingness to set policy in a way which could conflict with short-run political popularity but they had to show their ability and willingness to act in the present so as to overcome the challenges to price stability in the future.[1] This involved the ability to forecast and to develop a credible forward-looking policy. It also required considerable openness. Most central banks could not behave like the Bundesbank and trade on a long history of successful inflation control. They could not wait to establish credibility through their performance, but had to do it through emulation of the structure of their more credible counterparts, and by putting in place an incentive structure which made it appear likely that the objectives would be followed and that the bank would not be diverted by more immediate political pressures.

In one sense the new central banks were better off than their more established counterparts, who had to be able to demonstrate that they had changed the ways of the past even though most of the same staff were still in the organisation and many of the politicians of previous years were still in office. This strong process of borrowing credibility from those central banks that already had it was an important force in bringing about the degree of common understanding among central banks that now exists. Central banks have probably already passed through the period when they had their greatest independence and power. While inflation was being successfully reduced other political concerns could be subservient for a while. Now that inflation performance has worsened a little and central banks have shown themselves unable or reluctant to cope with the full impact of large and persistent external shocks, their political position will have been eroded somewhat. The addition of concerns over the lack of anticipation of the current financial crisis and the quality of the response to it means that their reputation is now likely to be more realistic.

In Chapter 3, Alex Cukierman, one of the pioneers of developing indices to measure the independence, accountability and other structural aspects of central banks governance, reflects on the relationship between legislated powers and actual practice. In the period before the burst of legislation on independence, many central banks were in practice much more independent and influential over public policy than their charters implied. Since that burst of legislation some of them are finding out where the practical limits to their independence lie; these are sometimes inside those laid down in the legal framework. Governments have power over appointments and in many cases still set targets even if central banks have operational freedom in achieving them. When times are difficult central banks may make losses, sometimes up to the point that they require recapitalisation. Negotiations over such matters open up the opportunity for influence, and the fear of them could encourage a less costly and hence easier monetary policy. In this regard the future will show how the very recent developments will affect central banks independence and behaviour.

Financial stability

During the 1990s a second major concern, financial stability, emerged. This was probably expressed most clearly in the United Kingdom, where the Bank of England was given a mandate which included financial stability, but it was also a response to a series of crises that had emerged in the developing world, in the Nordic countries and also in Asia and indeed in Russia. In the Asian case in particular it was clear that countries which seemed well-placed domestically could be heavily hit by external disturbances and hence be unable to maintain their own stability in the manner they had expected. While to some extent this new vulnerability was a straightforward consequence of the increasing globalisation of financial markets, it was also a recognition that more traditional means of maintaining stability in the banking system might no longer be possible. Traditionally commercial banks in effect formed a club so that problems in one would be handled by the others (and in compensation effectively dividing the spoils of restricted entry to the industry in good times). The role of the central bank was very much in bringing the players together and in finding equitable solutions. In a more international world those abilities to control and organise diminished.

It is interesting therefore that the response was to try to get international agreement on how to strengthen banking resilience by joint work through the Basel Committee on Banking Supervision. In this way the central banks did not react by trying to make their individual markets more independent of each other but tried instead to ensure that their banks were strong enough to withstand the increased range of shocks to which they would become exposed.[2] Thus, rather than each central bank deciding its own approach, there has been a great deal of commonality.

In financial supervision, however, there remains one big distinction in central bank operation. Central banks are not necessarily bank supervisors. Some, like the Bank of England, have lost that role, whereas others, such as the Central Bank of Ireland and the Dutch central bank, have acquired it. Similarly clear divisions remain over whether such supervisors should be responsible for both conduct of business regulation and prudential regulation. There is in addition a general trend towards amalgamation of sectoral supervisors, encouraged by the fact that banks themselves are running across traditional boundaries and combining deposit taking with insurance and investment banking.

The recent financial turbulence has sharpened these arguments. In the United Kingdom, for example, the Northern Rock episode has shown up three main issues with regard to the design of central banks. (It has shown up other important issues, particularly in regard to the design of deposit insurance, but they lie outside our ambit here.) The first is that there are problems with emergency lending. Simply put, the scale of lending required to provide adequate liquidity in the market to keep them operating 'normally' has proven larger than anticipated. It has also involved taking collateral, particularly in the United States, of a quality that could expose central banks to credit risk to an extent not previously envisaged. Lending to individual institutions, thought to be solvent though illiquid, has also proved difficult. Even ignoring the possible moral hazard from helping out individual institutions, and the market in general when it has taken on excess risk, such lending has generated a stigma for the institution concerned, when it should rather have been a sign of confidence allowing the institution to get the necessary liquidity from the market.

Second, it has been shown to be necessary to intervene rapidly in institutions while they still have positive capital, to prevent collapses which would otherwise have threatened financial stability (in the eyes of the authorities at least). This has also been true in the United States with the rescue of Bear Stearns. Both Bear Stearns and Northern Rock have shown that the range of institutions thought to qualify for assistance is wider than previously thought. Both have also involved innovative measures, emergency nationalisation in the UK case and lending outside the traditional range of institutions in the US. The need to intervene has extended beyond the banking sector into insurance with the rescue of AIG, as it is a major counterparty for the banking system.[3] Thirdly, the UK experience has shown that there are problems in coordinating the central bank, bank supervisor and the ministry of finance when problems arise – despite there being carefully enshrined procedures for such coordination.

While these problems may well be unique and are certainly not very likely to be repeated in exactly the same form, they do call into question some of the architecture of the financial system in regard to stability, most importantly when the institutions run across borders. Almost all the troubled institutions – Bear Stearns, Fannie Mae, Freddie Mac, AIG, Northern Rock and even Lehman

Brothers – could be handled by a single set of authorities without regard to other countries. Such swift and innovative responses would be difficult in an international environment, even within the European Union where integration is an enshrined purpose. As the crisis has evolved and spread to Europe, the Dutch, Belgian and Luxembourgeois authorities have found it necessary to intervene in Fortis, acting on the parts of the group in their own countries. Although this was initially coordinated, the Dutch authorities found they needed to take more sweeping unilateral action. National authorities are designed for handling national problems and face a conflict of interest when action in one country may be required to preserve financial stability in another. No mechanisms exist for trading off such costs or benefits and no institutions exist to carry out both calculations and actions with the swiftness required.

At the national level, one response appears to be to suggest that the central bank should have increased powers. This seems likely in the case of the Federal Reserve and was proposed by the Parliamentary Enquiry into the Northern Rock episode in the United Kingdom. Indeed in the Bear Stearns intervention in the United States, the Federal Reserve used existing powers in a way that extended its influence in ways that had not been thought of previously. There are strong temptations to follow this route of expansion, as the prudential supervisor tends to be required to be concerned with the health of individual institutions while the central bank has regard for the health of the financial system as a whole. Simply summing the risks faced by individual institutions and assessing the correlations is not equivalent. There is also a greater danger of regulatory capture if the supervisor is simultaneously responsible for rescue operations. This might therefore argue against a simple reincorporation of financial supervision in the central bank.

However, the appropriate solution is likely to be affected by, among other influences, the size of the country. Expecting to have two organisations with the scope to cover economy-wide issues may be over-ambitious. Therefore some countries, such as Finland, have chosen to have a very close relationship between the central bank and the financial system supervisor, even though they have a measure of legal independence. There they share common administrative facilities, a single research department and even a common staff restaurant, so people mix freely even though they have clearly separate jobs. It facilitates joint simulation exercises to try to assess the possible impact of shocks and the ready exchange of information. The Deputy Governor of the Bank is the Chairman of the supervisory authority's Board.

The United States, Canada, Mexico and a number of other countries have a different organisational structure, which includes an explicit 'Resolution Authority' with a clear mandate – normally to resolve a problem institution at minimum cost to the deposit insurance fund. Having a clear objective at least focuses the action. It is, however, arguable that whenever problems threaten financial stability this narrow focus is no longer correct and some wider view of loss to society should be borne in mind. However, what is clearly correct in this set up is that it should be a single organisation's job to sort out problems quickly and efficiently, not just with regard to the individual organisation but also with regard to the spillover costs elsewhere.

Normally in the resolution of problem banks whose structure or size implies that their suddenly ceasing operations would cause financial instability, the conclusion is still that shareholders should bear the first loss, and if their commitment is insufficient then the residual should fall on the unsecured creditors, with the deposit insurer taking the place of the insured depositors in this context. It is thus not surprising that resolution authorities in these countries should be the deposit insurance fund, as it faces the first call on the more widespread loss beyond those who have knowingly undertaken the risk. If the central bank were to take on this role in the United Kingdom or elsewhere it would need a separate department to do so as the skills involved are completely different from those required in the analysis of financial stability and in the supervision of individual institutions. A similar line of argument would apply to such an agency were it to be part of the financial supervisor and in addition then the more direct link to the assessment of the impact on financial stability would be lost.

At the international level the problem is, in the absence of any international agency, much less tractable. The ECB has the power under the Maastricht Treaty to take on such a role for the EU countries.[4] However, a European equivalent of the US FDIC (Federal Deposit Insurance Corporation) could also be created for those cross-border banks that were, in the event that they ceased operating, deemed to pose problems for financial stability in a member state. Even so this would not handle banks that were also important outside the EU. Possibly some more general international architecture through the Basel Committee or the BIS might help, but since there is not even much discussion of the idea at the European level a discussion at the wider international level seems rather far-fetched. This presumably means that the lead country with respect to each bank needs to make sure it is in a position to act effectively, whether it believes it can do that unilaterally or with the support of authorities in other countries. In the second case considerable prior agreement will be required so the leader can act in certain knowledge of the support of the others and indeed compel action by them.

Institutional change is, of course, only part of the answer. The United Kingdom has realised in its most recent proposals that a considerable alteration in the law is required to introduce their Special Resolution Regime. Not merely does general law on bankruptcy need to be replaced by a specific regime for banks but company law does not at present permit the authorities to step in while the shares still have some value. Various ideas have been advanced as to how shareholders might be persuaded to agree to these powers, through the cost of deposit insurance or the ability to access emergency lending.

Most other parts of the international financial system seem to be being handled by the system of national central banks and other national institutions. Thus the supervision of international financial markets such as London and New York covers all clients. International parts of the payment system, such as SWIFT or CLS in the case of foreign exchange have direct arrangements rather than an international umbrella.

While there has been considerable convergence of views on the target for monetary policy, that for financial stability is, like its definition, still more amorphous.

Convergence of goals?

Even within monetary policy, convergence has not been total. While price stability has become pre-eminent, the Federal Reserve has persisted with concern for wider economic goals. Price stability itself has lacked clear definition, with a distinction between behavioural concerns – inflation no longer being important in affecting people's longer-term decision making – and simple numerical definitions, such as inflation targets or 'inflation norms' in the case of the Eurosystem. Nevertheless, even there the initial purity of price stability being zero inflation over the medium term after allowing for bias in the measurement of the consumer price index (as set out in the initial Reserve Bank of New Zealand Policy Targets Agreements) has been replaced by low inflation objectives. It is therefore no surprise that the Bank of Canada should have reopened the issue of whether price stability does not entail targeting the price level over the medium term, rather than simply inflation, as with a target for inflation considerable drift in the price level can occur as the years go past.

The flavour seems to have changed. Ten years ago national central banks were slimming their staffs, concentrating on core activities and wondering whether, with the increasing abilities of the market, they would find their range of activities further reduced and might even find it more difficult to implement monetary policy. Now it appears that there are more problems to handle and that it is difficult to extend the more technical approach of the handling of monetary policy to the handling of financial stability.

The current crisis will no doubt lead to pressure for change in a number of other areas involving central banks, not least in deciding whether the system of emergency lending cannot be recrafted to offer confidence rather than stigma. Furthermore, the Greenspan philosophy of being prepared to allow financial bubbles to emerge (or at least financial expansions to occur without explicit measures to offset the increased risk), provided that the authorities are ready to act rapidly once the bubble has burst so as to prevent entry into the debt–deflation spiral, is likely to be contested. The extent of the intervention in markets and the taking of private-sector risks onto the central bank balance sheet are likely to generate a wish not to have to go so far (or more likely further) next time. Stability involves not merely acting at the bottom of the cycle but also making more preparations on the way up. Whether this will involve a more cyclically adjusted approach to minimum capital requirements or greater liquidity requirements (or indeed both) is open to debate. But the role of the central bank is likely to increase.

The opportunity that the last 20 years have offered to create new central banks is unlikely to be repeated. The experience has resulted both in considerable unification of central banking behaviour but also in a much greater exchange of ideas and experience among central banks, leading to a strong sense of community, which will prove valuable as the problems national central banks have to handle become increasingly international in character.

The papers

What did the papers presented at the Eltville conference contribute to the discussion and resolution of these important current problems? Several touched on the problems, either proposing solutions or showing new aspects of the questions. But two papers suggested the endeavour was not perhaps entirely pointless, but certainly likely to be fraught with major difficulties. These two papers were those which opened the conference, two papers on the origins of central banking. The problem these papers both raised is that they point out, to summarise a somewhat complex message, that central banks were not designed but rather evolved to deal with difficulties as they emerged.

The importance of history

But the complexity of the message has to be stressed. Forrest Capie observes that while *central banking* emerged, *central banks* were very often designed, sometimes with theory involved and sometimes on the basis of experience. The Bank of England did emerge as a central bank, in the sense of having the classic monetary and financial stability functions, but it emerged at times resisting theoretical work that would have furthered its objectives (the work of Henry Thornton in particular). Meanwhile, in the twentieth century, the Federal Reserve was actually hampered by theory. It was designed to solve some particular problems, and it was believed at the time that writing the erroneous real bills doctrine into its constitution would facilitate this.

Capie also notes that experience was often translated directly from one environment to another. When Montagu Norman had central banks designed, he certainly had the British environment very much in his mind, even urging the creation of discount houses and a discount market. (Not necessarily a bad idea, but one based, at any rate according to his statements, on experience not analysis.)

Capie also directs our attention to the importance of personalities – not just in the design of banks, but in their functioning. Constitutions can be subverted and even ignored by powerful personalities. The cases he cites were all to the good; but that need not always be the case. What is to be done about that is a matter not yet examined in the recent burst of central bank design; and the matter is not straightforward. If a central bank governor can be removed for folly, who will define folly?

This 'Hayekian' view emphasises the importance of evolution and the very limited usefulness of design. (Many earlier central banks were essentially copies of an existing model – as noted above, the Reserve Bank of New Zealand was first set up closely modelled on the Bank of England, a compliment which was returned in the 1998 Bank of England Act.)

In his chapter Juha Tarkka reaches somewhat similar conclusions, but on a different set of data and with a somewhat different emphasis in his conclusion. He notes as of particular importance the different kind of collateral that was accepted by these northern European central banks. (That their money was based on silver rather than gold is not of importance in the present context.)

They concentrated on loans on mortgage credit and on trade bills, and focused on the 'solidity' of the credit rather than, as in the Anglo-Saxon tradition, on its liquidity. They were concerned with capital values, and lent on 'real bills'. That this did not lead to inflation, despite the nominal indeterminacy emphasised in the modern interpretation of the real bills doctrine, is explained by the delicate trichotomy that Tarkka discusses. There is the version that there is no risk of inflation if the central accepts real bills; the version that it should accept only real bills; and the modern version which identifies the doctrine with excessive interest-rate pegging. In earlier versions of the doctrine, collateral choice, with the focus on quality, was crucial. His discussant notes that we are still in a world where central banks stabilise interest rates, so therefore in a world descended in at least that respect from the northern European one, but the focus is not on the quality of collateral but on the forecasting and anticipatory skills of central bankers.

Tarkka also notes that, in an anticipation of modern developments, banks were often seen as helpful if not perhaps even crucial to economic development, in that they let manufacturers and landowners realise and use their capital. These banks only moved away from the land- and real-bills-based approach under the twin pressures of the going importance of trade and the growing influence of a political class not based in its wealth and connections on land.

The most important implication of his chapter is one that has been little discussed so far in central bank design, but may become important in considering how to respond to the recent difficulties, discussed above, in maintaining financial stability. Should central banks accept the same kind of collateral in normal, price-stability focused operations as they do for operations concerned with financial stability, or should the category change or be widened for the latter? The historical insights of Juha Tarkka's chapter do not provide an answer to this question, but they raise it in a most interesting and provocative way.

His chapter directs one to how central banks, notably the Bank of England and the Federal Reserve, changed the kind of securities they would accept under pressure of the 2007/2008 financial market difficulties. Both banks broadened the range of collateral substantially, paying heed to its quality rather than its liquidity. For example, the Bank of England accepted securitised mortgages, not liquid but if held to redemption highly secure in capital value.

Another matter to emerge from both chapter is the price-stability target chosen for the central bank. It is generally claimed that a constant price-level target is undesirable. Various assertions are made, primarily focusing on the dangers of deflation – induced recession and the zero bound to nominal interest rates. Both these concerns neglect the experience of the gold standard years, when prices rose and fell, and the price-level trend was close to level. Deflations, so long as they were an understood part of the regime, did not seem to matter for output. This is quite different from more recent experience, when recessions have followed sharp and unexpected monetary contractions. The gold standard experience suggests an additional consideration when choosing an inflation target, a subject considered in some detail in the chapter in this volume by Mark Wynne.

Price stability

Three of the chapters deal with price stability directly. One, by Alex Cukierman, on the importance of central bank independence for achieving it, one on how to define it, and one on the use of measures of the money supply to help achieve it.

It is useful next to consider these chapter in that order. (The chapter by Alex Cukierman has been discussed above (p. 5) so we do not repeat that discussion here.)

How is the price stability which is the objective of (part of) central bank policy to be defined and measured? In his fascinating chapter, which explores the history of economic thought as well as economic theory and statistical evidence, Mark Wynne reviews this question. The answer is of course that the question is not straightforward, and that although a clear-cut target is necessary for monitoring, commitment and communication purposes, central banks may well choose to watch a range of indicators as they all give different, albeit partially overlapping, information. He examines the role of core inflation, which may be interpreted as the persistent component of inflation; and then shows that this tempting interpretation is not particularly consistent with US data, so targeting it, or even being influenced by it, could mislead policy makers quite substantially. Also considered in this chapter is the problem of quality change. Do indices allow for this adequately? The widespread view is that they underestimate for it, so that indices overstate inflation. But although, as he documents, this view is well-established it is not well-supported by evidence. Indeed, some evidence suggests understatement of inflation. What about asset prices? Strong theoretical arguments can be advanced for their inclusion in the central bank's target. There are also practical arguments – Wynne points out the relationship between a bank having a consumer-based inflation target and house price booms over the last decade. But how it could be done is not clear, and the argument not universally accepted. (Although most would be comfortable with at the least having asset prices as something to be monitored as a warning signal.)

Also considered is what level should be set, whatever target is chosen. Should it be zero, to achieve on average price stability as measured by whatever target is chosen? Or should it be a little above that, to avoid the dangers of deflation and the zero bound to interest rates? As Martin Feldstein has shown, moving to zero from even a modest 2 per cent inflation per annum brings benefits. What about these above-mentioned costs? Mark Wynne does not discuss these – his chapter already covers a very substantial area. But there should surely be work on whether deflation is a problem. Recent work by economic historians suggests that it may not be if it is expected as part of the policy regime; and the zero bound only matters if the short-term interest rate is both the only operating instrument of the central bank and crucial to the transmission of monetary policy. Both these are surely not self-evident truths. Mark Wynne's chapter shows very clearly that even when the matter of the central bank's constitution is sorted so that all involved are satisfied that it is at the least workable and likely not to need changing too soon, there are important and difficult problems to be resolved. A workable solution is reasonably easy to attain, but a good one may well not be.

One item that Mark Wynne does not mention that may have a significant effect on the design of the approach to price stability in central banks is that the Bank of Canada is embarked on an extensive project to review its target, part of which involves a review of whether an inflation target should be replaced by a price-level path target. Under inflation targeting, errors are not corrected. In recent years, aided by the increases in energy and food prices, some central banks have exceeded their targets on average. There is therefore no longer a good match over the longer term between a price-level path and an inflation target with positive errors offset by negative errors. It is therefore becoming more debatable whether an inflation target that is frequently not met or subject to upward bias is actually consistent with concepts of price stability. Previously such a price-level target was thought too difficult because of the problems of risking deflation or encountering the zero bound we have just mentioned. With the lower inflation rates and lower volatility experienced as part of 'the great moderation' a price-level target path could be achieved without such problems if there is not too aggressive reaction to shocks. If price expectations can be focused on the price level instead of inflation then such a policy will become more attractive and will help overcome the zero bound problem.

The money supply has slipped out of fashion among central banks; few watch it explicitly, some even try to deny watching it at all. Georg Rich seeks to rehabilitate it, at least for the ECB, but his discussant is sceptical. The ECB's 'Second Pillar' comprises money supply analysis. Many writers have criticised this as being at best unhelpful and quite conceivably misleading. Rich appraises the ECB's defence, and concludes it could do better – there is a better defence available. This, he suggests, would take account of the effects of changes in the ECB's refinancing rate, and in money demand changes. His discussant was not fully persuaded. He argued that some of the changes proposed were easy to make in retrospect, but not so easy to justify at the time they had to be made. The money supply might, it was suggested, be better treated as many central banks treat asset prices, something to watch as a source of information. Roger Clews, the chapter's discussant, in particular suggested that examining all the factors which could shift money demand would prove an illuminating exercise, whether or not – and he inclined to not – one went on to use the adjusted aggregates to guide policy.

With current inflationary pressures and financial stability following a period when money and credit aggregates rose at levels that were inconsistent with many conventional estimates of sustainable growth, perhaps money indicators also are due for a return to fashion. The list of what central banks should take into account in achieving price stability continues to increase. Allowing such an exuberant approach to economic expansions as was permitted in the last 20 years in some countries may come in for reappraisal as the impact on prices is appreciated.

Communication

How should central banks communicate what they are trying to do? This question has at least two aspects. Should central banks give any indication of where they think they might move interest rates next? And what information should be given in speeches (and publications) by the policy maker (or if it is a committee that decides policy, policy makers) about their thinking processes, reflections on the past and thoughts on the future?

The present Governor of the Bank of England has a clear-cut view on the first version of the question: if a central bank knew where the interest rate was to go next, it should move it there now. Announcing an 'inclination' is to give more weight to feelings, intuitions and forecasts than they should properly bear. In their chapter in this volume, Hans Gerbach and Volcker Hahn somewhat qualify this view. Forward guidance may involve the disclosure of private information. If it does, one could very reasonably ask why not just disclose it? But one can imagine circumstances where the information is not sufficiently certain to justify formal announcement, but its existence or the consequences of its existence can be implied by forward guidance. This use, 'cheap talk' to use the authors' term, can help reduce uncertainty.

Forward guidance is also, provided there are costs of some sort in deviating from the guidance, a way of reinforcing commitment. This reinforcement is particularly valuable when there is an inflation bias. But, as will be clear, because the results are of the form they are, depending on such factors as costs of deviation from commitment and credibility of forecasts, the results do not generalise, except to the extent that they show what has to be considered by any central bank considering whether or not to give 'forward guidance'. It should also be remarked that, as central bank's circumstances can change, once a central bank has decided what to do on the basis of the authors' advice, it has a problem: what if circumstances change? How then should it announce and explain its change of behaviour? This chapter opens up a complex, albeit troublesome, area.

The chapter by Ehrmann and Fratzscher is on an aspect of this. Given that there is going to be communication by the central bank other than simply a rate announcement, what benefits can it bring, and how can these be maximised? The authors find that:

> *more active* as well as *more consistent* communication by committee members improves the predictability of monetary policy decisions significantly, and reduces the disagreement among forecasters, both about policy decisions in the short run as well as about the future path of interest rates.

This is a plausible result, and it is reinforced by the conclusions reported on similar work, but with somewhat different statistical methods and a different data set, by the chapter's discussant. Of course, in view of the conclusions of Gersbach and Hahn, whether or not this effectiveness is always a good thing is not clear. The issues here are indeed complex, and admit no general solution.

Several central banks have opted to trace out paths for interest rates over the future that are consistent with achieving their inflation targets (among them Norway, Sweden, Iceland and New Zealand, which started the trend). Whether these represent forward guidance is more debatable. What they help show is the extent of the challenge to monetary policy from present and expected conditions. When coupled with simulations that explore what reactions might be needed if various of the risks to inflation are realised, this approach can assist not simply the credibility of policy but the private sector and government in planning their future actions.

A more worrying facet of Ehrmann and Fratzscher's analysis is the implication that it is in the interests of efficient monetary policy for central banks to 'manage' their communication. The public airing of disagreement among policy makers over what should be done seems to be associated with worse prediction of monetary policy decisions – after allowing for the current level of uncertainty in macroeconomic information – while more communication (as long as it is consistent) seems to be associated with more accurate prediction. An alternative view is that when there is not a general consensus about what to do, having a more informed public debate will assist policy makers in facing the difficulty. New ideas and information may emerge. In the same way, while a very firm steer as to what policy is going to do next will certainly achieve predictability, it may suppress valuable information from the market about the emergence of other risks. Quite how suppressing the existence of debate is consistent with the objective of transparency which many central banks espouse takes us into the realms of sophism.

Stability

The chapter by Mattias Persson examines aspects of the financial stability task of central banks by addressing problems of cross-border banking.

Persson's chapter deals particularly with the EU, but even here the problems are considerable. Central to them is that however much supervisors are in agreement, however well they foresee problems, unless they are so skilled and lucky as to prevent all problems at some point capital must be committed by the government of one country to help the residents of another. This may be just conceivable should the amounts be trivial, but there is no commitment mechanism to guarantee it; and whatever the commitment mechanism one would have to be cautious about its being able to enforce the provision of funds significant by national budgetary standards. The example of Switzerland is perhaps instructive in this regard. Conscious of being a modestly sized country with a large banking sector, and in particular two very large international banks, limits have been announced to the amount of support Switzerland would provide should one of its banks get into difficulties. Though far from trivial, these amounts are certainly unlikely to be sufficient should a major Swiss bank get into difficulties.

Overview

In view of the range of matters discussed above, and of the great uncertainties exposed, it may seem remarkable how satisfactory monetary performance has been, and how episodes of financial instability have not spread with catastrophic consequences for the real economy. But one should observe that getting the inflation rule exactly right is not necessary, and probably not feasible. A workable approximation that is adhered to gets one a long way.

The bigger problems lie with financial stability, which has been heavily tested in the period since the conference took place. Indeed at the time of writing it is not clear when the nadir will be reached and the system turn round. Any remarks we make now can be rapidly overtaken by events. Up until recently financial stability has been preserved by a combination of luck and ad hoc emergency measures. The luck came in because most of the troubled institutions had little significant international exposure. Where they did, domestic concerns for stability in the United States were more than sufficient to motivate the authorities in a way that coincidentally handled the spillover abroad effectively. The ad hoc emergency measures were unprecedented expansions of collateral type, and nationalisation. Neither of these seems the kind of solution on which future reliance should be placed.

In late September and early October 2007 (the time of writing) it looked as if the luck was running out. The crisis spilled over to Europe, with the authorities in Belgium, Germany, Iceland, Ireland, Luxembourg, the Netherlands and the United Kingdom having to step in to protect financial institutions.[5] The United States, after an initial setback, passed a programme to purchase the most difficult financial assets, so as to try to return markets towards normal with extensive inter-institutional trading. Stock markets were heavily hit by uncertainty – bank shares in particular. With some countries entering recession the calls not just for current action but reform of the whole system are strong. Central banks found their role considerably expanded and with the onset of more widespread losses and the need to use taxpayer funds, governmental responses and parliamentary enquiries are to be expected, as demonstrated by the United Kingdom.

There is thus much work on financial stability to be done. This may well lead to further changes in the design of central banks. Views are now changing on the sensible allocation of powers for stability of the financial system, prudential supervision of financial institutions and conduct of business by individual institutions. Australia separated all three after a careful investigation, the United Kingdom combined the second two and the Netherlands the first two, while many other countries, including the United States, have more divisions particularly with regard to sectors. While the pendulum may have started to swing back on the degree of independence central banks may have, it is swinging outwards on their prudential responsibilities in the quest for greater financial stability.

Notes

1 It is noticeable that exactly the same approach is currently being used to establish the conviction that central banks will do whatever is necessary to maintain (collateralised) liquidity in international financial markets. If markets believe that liquidity will be available when they need it in the future then much of the tightness in the present will disappear.
2 Unfortunately, while they pursued the idea of capital buffers enthusiastically they abandoned their efforts on a joint approach to liquidity.
3 Rescues have also extended as far as Fannie Mae and Freddie Mac in the United States. However, as federal housing finance institutions this has been as much an issue of an obligation through implicit ownership as one of financial stability.
4 Article 105§6, but exercising this power requires unanimity in the Council of Ministers. In any case the power does not extend to the insurance sector.
5 To illustrate the speed of movement, in the course of one week the United Kingdom nationalised another mortgage lender, Bradford and Bingley; the German authorities rescued Hypo Real Estate Holdings at a cost of €50bn; Iceland rescued Glitnir and saw its exchange rate slide; the Netherlands, Belgium and Luxembourg have had to intervene heavily in Fortis, France and Belgium in Dexia; Ireland thought it necessary to issue a blanket guarantee; all this in a week when the US Congress passed a $700bn package for liquidating the stock of financial assets that had become largely unsaleable on the open market.

1 Some scattered thoughts from history on evolution and design in central banking*

Forrest Capie

Introduction

My reaction when asked to offer a chapter on the history of central banking was, could there be anything left to say? But there might be, for while the ground is well-trodden and the pattern of development in central banking well-known, people can be relied upon to forget old truths and in any case interpretations differ. First, a caution is needed. Economists almost invariably ask for a model. There is no model in this chapter. There isn't even a strong hypothesis. Rather some thoughts are offered as a contribution to a conversation on the design of central banks and why they are the way they are. Second, the chapter may appear overly Anglocentric. I don't make much apology for that. Apart from the fact that it is what I know most about, there is some justification in that the Bank of England was the first central bank and it was frequently used as a model for others. It was hugely influential. Its story is central to the development of central banking. Finally, there is a vast literature on the subject, much of which I have read and perhaps absorbed but make no attempt to list here.

The pattern in the development of central banking that is commonly accepted is: there was a classical period when central banks were often privately owned and independent – the late nineteenth and early twentieth centuries; that was followed in the mid twentieth century by a period when discretion on monetary policy ruled but the banks were largely dependent; and then there was a return to a concern with price stability and independence in the latter part of the twentieth century. To some extent it is implicit in this that there was an ebb and flow as the banks either adjusted to whatever environmental changes were taking place – evolution – or accepted the direction of the state – design. Charles Goodhart's book with 'evolution' in the title has undoubtedly been influential in encouraging the evolutionary view and the idea of evolution still grips. Goodhart set out to show how central banks 'have evolved naturally over time ... rather than conforming to an initially planned structure'.[1] But it is clear that not all was evolutionary. But if not, then what? Were they consciously designed? One possible title for this chapter was, 'Evolution, design (intelligent or otherwise), or what?' But such a title could have continued: 'or transplant and then back to the drawing board and perhaps some of all these and not necessarily in any particular order', though that would have been a bit long. The chapter suggests that the beginnings of central banking, in the classical period, were evolutionary, and the period that followed was essentially one when design prevailed. It then hints at what evolution and design might suggest for the story of independence and performance that followed.

Definition

First, some definition is needed since there is frequently disagreement over how central banking should be defined, and there is certainly room for discussion. It is sometimes asserted that the Riksbank was the first central bank. That is not the case. Some would want to argue, possibly on stronger grounds, that the Wisselbank, an earlier institution, was the first.[2] One way of approaching the subject might be to list what it is that central banks do, or have done, so that a decision could be made as to whether a particular institution qualifies. Unfortunately, such a list runs to greater length than there is room for in this chapter. The list would range over note issue, all kinds of agency work for government, through the gamut of supervisory and regulatory roles, to advice, to promoting economic development and economic growth, and still not get to what are currently recognised as their two key or core purposes: price stability and financial stability.

For a long time the view was that the lender of last resort was the key defining feature of a central bank – certainly when trying to locate their origins and early activity. But even here care must be taken over what the lender of last resort is. There is mixed use of the term. But the most satisfactory definition of the lender of last resort is: the institution that comes to the aid of the market (and not any single institution) in times of liquidity shortage. The basics involve the role of banker to the banks and the concern with banking stability. It was surely that that led to the lender of last resort, and that that properly defines the origins.[3] That would rule out many institutions at least in their early years when they were the only bank in the country. There were occasions when nascent central banks came to the rescue of one of their customers (a bank) in much the same way as a commercial bank may extend additional loans to one of their customers who is temporarily illiquid, or conceivably by some standards insolvent. They did so when the present expected return from the new loan was itself zero or negative if the wider effects should warrant it. But that is not a lender of last resort. The LLR can be dated from the time when the bank accepted its responsibility for the stability of the banking system as a whole, which overrides any residual concern with its own profitability. So it is the intellectual basis and reasoning that matters rather than any example of rescue action. But shifts in mental perceptions are difficult to identify and date.[4]

Origins and evolution

Equipped with that definition we would conclude that the earlier central banks were essentially late-nineteenth/early-twentieth-century creatures. There are some examples from the nineteenth century, notably the Bank of England, but mostly not. Interestingly, Palgrave's 1896 dictionary has no entry for central banking. And Sayers, the distinguished historian of central banking, notes that central banks *in the main* began to appear around 1900.[5] Where evolution took place, it took a very long time – in the Bank of England's case close to 200 years. There is a good case to be made for evolution, at least for those central banks that made their appearance in the nineteenth century, even if these were few.

The birth of the institutions that became central banks was frequently as banker to their government with a principal task being managing the government's debt. That was the case for the Bank of England, the story of whose origins and development is well enough known not to need repeating here. But there are some elements that can be set down briefly that remind how it evolved as a lender of last resort. In its early years the Bank was a normal commercial bank, though with monopoly joint-stock status; and it was the government's bank. While commercial banks were developing in England in the eighteenth century they were for a long time closer to cloakrooms than modern fractional reserve banks. Although the principles of fractional reserve banking were not only grasped but being acted upon from the seventeenth century, extreme caution prevailed and the money multiplier remained very low.

However, by the time of the Napoleonic Wars or soon after, the banking system had developed to the point where runs on banks became possible, even likely. When the first real crisis struck in England in 1825 it was huge – genuine panic. The Bank had by that time emerged as the centre or pinnacle of the system. It alone was in a position to help but it was handicapped by regulation since the Usury Laws were still in place. These were thereafter relaxed so that when the next crisis struck in 1836/1837 the Bank was in a better position to perform its role of lender of last resort. It was a step forward.

In 1844 legislation further strengthened the Bank's position and gave it a phased-in monopoly of the note issue. And the gold standard was more strictly defined. This latter, however, presented problems when the next crisis broke in 1847 for while it was clear what the Bank should do, it could not do it without breaking the law. The solution was for the Chancellor to permit the Bank temporarily to suspend convertibility.

There are those who would argue that if free banking had been allowed – no regulation at all – as it had been in Scotland for almost 150 years up to 1844, there would have been no need for a central bank, and there would have been greater stability. But that opens up too much territory of a different and wide-ranging kind. The facts were that by the middle of the nineteenth century a system had developed to cope with the conditions such as they were. Discount houses had emerged as intermediaries between the banks and the Bank of England where long-running antagonisms had brought distance. This particular institutional arrangement was to provide a useful additional element in the system since it meant that when banks needed to borrow they would do it through the discount market and not directly from the Bank. What that meant was that if any one was in difficulty, the danger of individual treatment was greatly reduced since the Bank need not know whose paper it was discounting, coming as it did from the discount house – the temporary home of the paper – paying attention only to the quality of the paper.[6]

Two further crises in 1857 and 1866 brought other experiences, and better appreciation of the required behaviour. They showed that the letter from the Chancellor would always be available in these circumstances. The crisis in 1866 brought home the fact that no bank was too big to fail.[7] The Bank could therefore do what was needed. But would it? Bagehot was still critical of the Bank in 1866 for not acting sooner than it did – lending, 'hesitatingly, reluctantly, and with misgiving. In fact to make large advances in this faltering way is to incur the evil of making them without the advantage'.[8] In fact Bagehot went further by suggesting that not only should the Bank act promptly but that it should announce in advance that it would so act. By the 1870s it had not quite done that but to all intents and purposes it was behaving like a mature lender of last resort.[9] Bagehot's advocacy of a clear announcement of what they would do in advance was somewhat in advance of Kydland and Prescott. In the late twentieth century pre-commitment provided a case for the independence of central banks. In the 1870s the Bank of England made no explicit statement to that effect but its behaviour made it implicit.

There were other developments in the system in England and notable among them were changes in the banking system. That became a concentrated structure heavily branched and diversified geographically and industrially or by activity. It had also found its way by learning an appropriate balance sheet structure with sufficient in the way of liquid assets. It is surely no coincidence that for the next 100 years there were no banking/financial crises. All the important lessons had been learned and practices adopted either explicitly or implicitly. So there was a readiness and ability by the Bank to lend to whatever extent was needed. The lending was done anonymously and so greatly reduced or even eliminated moral hazard. So well understood were the arrangements and so great the trust developed among the participants that in themselves these promoted stability.

There would of course still be mishaps or extraordinary or unforeseeable events. In 1890 there was an example of the first when Barings failed. There was no need for the Chancellor's letter for there was no panic. The Bank nevertheless took on another role, that of crisis manager and organised a rescue operation. In 1914 there was an example of the second, when war broke out. Although the years 1890 to 1913 are sometimes characterised as years of growing international tension, there was not much evidence of that in financial market data; the war came as a bolt from the blue to investors. There was no preparation for war in the Bank. But again the Bank put into practice the lessons learned in the nineteenth century, raising Bank Rate sharply and providing liquidity for all with good paper.

All of this can surely legitimately be told as a story of evolution, albeit occasionally affected by regulation. To a considerable degree the evolution was possible in England in a relatively free laissez-faire environment. When that faded and regulation began to grow new problems arose. In England, though, that did not happen until after the Second World War, and it was accompanied by a period of poor performance.

There is also a link with the payment system and this might be seen to be an evolutionary feature. In the early days of banking systems some sort of arrangements for clearing develop, and beyond that for settlement. This was again a feature of the Bank of England's development.[10] A conference held in Frankfurt in November 2007 began from the position that, 'historically, the widely accepted core purposes of central banking, monetary and financial stability, grew out of their role as provider of the ultimate settlement asset in the payments system'. Commercial banks certainly developed means of reducing the cost of transactions among themselves in clearing and settling – an evolutionary process.

In so far as central banks were initially ordinary commercial banks, they were involved in these developments. But how did convergence on their liabilities for settlement take place? Was it a genuine evolutionary process or was it imposed by states capitalising on the benefits of such a development? Again in the early stages of this the evolutionary aspects are likely to dominate, and then after a certain point – perhaps the third quarter of the nineteenth century is the useful dating – new central banks would tend to imitate the existing models. But in the twentieth century other factors are likely to have played a part. One such would be the likelihood that international clearing and settlement would probably be facilitated by domestic convergence on state money.

In the English case the story of clearing is an obvious evolutionary process with clearing houses appearing naturally to perform an obvious function. But settlement is the next stage. This took place initially in the eighteenth century with banks accepting each other's notes and settling bilaterally in specie.[11] It was the 1850s before the London clearing house began settling over deposit accounts on the Bank of England; that is, just a few years after the Bank of England had been given a monopoly of the note issue.

Design and spread

While the origins of *central banking* might be found in evolution, most *central banks* have been designed. And even where an institution originally evolved it has often been redesigned at some point. Many examples of design can be found by looking at the large number that either modelled themselves on the Bank of England or were among those the Bank of England set out, if not quite to design, at least to influence heavily. It could hardly start to do this before it became a central bank itself and that was a late-nineteenth-century event.

Almost by definition theory has a part to play when design is considered. But what ideas get adopted, by what means and at what time? At the beginning of the nineteenth century Henry Thornton set out all that needed to be known on the role of the central bank both in terms of monetary and financial stability.

> to limit the total amount of paper issued, and to resort for this purpose, whenever the temptation to borrow is strong, to some effectual principle of restriction; in no case, however, materially to diminish the sum in circulation, but to let it vibrate only within certain limits; to allow a slow and cautious extension of it, as the general trade of the kingdom enlarges itself; to allow of some special, though temporary, increase in the event of an extraordinary alarm or difficulty, as the best means of preventing a great demand at home for guineas; and to lean on the side of diminution, in the case of gold going abroad, and of the general exchanges continuing long unfavourable; this seems to be the true policy of the directors of an institution circumstanced like that of the Bank of England. To suffer the solicitations of the merchants or the wishes of government, to determine the measure of the bank issues, is unquestionably to adopt a very false principle of conduct.[12]

But the Bank of England for one initially did not accept Thornton's ideas, indeed explicitly rejected them. It adhered instead to the real bills doctrine, something it claimed it had learned from experience – good practical banking. Thornton demonstrated the fallacy of the Bank's position but that was ignored. Real bills became part of the 'banking school' story and, apart from the triumph of the currency school in 1844 in relation to defining the gold standard, it was the banking school's ideas that prevailed for most of the next 100 years. It was accepted that the Bank should protect the gold reserve and the exchange rate. It should also be ready to provide assistance to the banking system in times of panic. And it would accommodate the needs of trade by discounting good (real) commercial paper. The last would be more fully specified as to lend only on good collateral of short-term self-liquidating commercial bills and not government paper. These procedures would guard against inflation.

The lack of conscious use of theory and even its rejection was still in evidence when Montagu Norman was questioned by the Macmillan Committee in 1929. When asked what theory guided him he replied that he went by feel; some say he abjured theory. And it is usually to him that the phrase 'the Bank is a bank and not a study group' is attributed. It was a phrase that continued to be used to guide new recruits as late as the 1970s.

In the history of central banking, the First World War is the turning point. Up until 1914 the Bank of England 'had been governed by men who, as Directors, were uncommonly "sessile"; and served by officers and clerks even more sessile'.[13] They hardly left the Bank, never mind London. In the nineteenth century there had been intermittent contact with the Bank of France and occasional correspondence with some others such as the Reichsbank. A few countries had accounts at the Bank. But during the War and immediately after, new relationships developed and the Governors, Directors and others could be found travelling all over the world. By 1930, 17 leading countries held accounts at the Bank. Part of this activity arose out of the desire to promote the restoration of orderly monetary, financial and trading conditions in the world; part was that under the gold exchange standard there was closer contact with monetary authorities abroad. Furthermore, under the new standard the Bank of England encouraged Empire countries to hold their reserves in London balances rather than in gold and then advised them on the appropriate proportion to hold of Treasury Bills and other government securities and deposits with the Bank. Efforts at cooperation intensified after the collapse of the gold standard at the beginning of the 1930s.

The Bank's long history of encouraging the establishment and development of central banks around the world began almost immediately after the First World War. It worked at the founding and development of central banks in the 'dominions' and other territories in the 1920s and 1930s, and promoted close relations with them. It offered 'friendly authoritative advice' and helped on specific problems as they arose. The inter-war years witnessed the Bank's involvement with the South African Reserve Bank, the Commonwealth Bank of Australia, as well as a more 'passive but opportunist' role in the establishment of the Bank of Canada and the Reserve Bank of New Zealand.[14] Other countries outside the Commonwealth were also shown interest, notably Egypt, Brazil and Argentina. Not only did the Bank's influence spread in this way but it often put them in a strong position when some kind of assistance was needed. While the dominions and Commonwealth were where the early efforts were concentrated, Norman also did what he could in Europe.

When the South African Reserve Bank was founded in 1920 Norman was able to get one of his senior staff, the Chief Accountant Clegg, installed as Governor. Norman told the Committee of Treasury in the Bank of England that 'the policy and methods of the new Bank (SARB) should from the outset accord with those of the Bank of England'.[15] Norman kept in close contact with Clegg thereafter. Since South Africa was the major gold-producing country this was clearly of some value. Perhaps the main benefits would flow at a far later date. The Bank became the agent for the South African Bank in the London gold market and when difficulties arose in the 1960s it was undoubtedly beneficial to the Bank of England that it could exert the right kind of pressure where it mattered.

Following the Genoa Conference in April 1922 Norman turned his attention to other countries such as Australia, Canada and India. In Australia in the 1920s, after the Commonwealth Bank had been given new responsibilities and more nearly approximated a central bank, they recognised they were inexperienced and they were keen to learn. There was no more willing tutor than Montagu Norman. In 1927 he sent out Sir Earnest Harvey, Comptroller in the Bank. (This was a post created in 1918 for a senior administrator. Harvey became Deputy Governor in London in 1929 until 1936.) Harvey spent three months in Australia, 'detailing the basic principles that should be adopted' – the desirability of being privately owned, not to compete with the commercial banks and to supervise informally.[16] These arrangements were not without their tensions and one was present in the humiliation the Australians felt at the beginning of the 1930s when the Bank of England appeared to be sending in the bailiff in the form of Sir Otto Niemeyer. But it was always to the English model that the Australians turned. In the 1930s the Governor of the Australian Bank appealed to the commercial banks in Australia to behave more like the English banks who 'unhesitatingly and loyally follow the lead of the Bank of England'.[17] When the Canadian central bank was established in 1935 it too reflected the influence of the Bank of England.

Norman was not insensitive to local institutional arrangements but he did frequently suggest that a discount market should be established so that short rates could be manipulated in pursuit of the smooth working of the gold standard. That seems to have happened over much of Africa. Norman also resented any influence from anywhere else. 'When a dominion Deputy Governor visited the United States, Norman was concerned lest so inexperienced a traveller might fall into the wrong hands in New York.'[18] By the end of the 1920s the Bank was sending a fortnightly newsletter out to all the new institutions carrying intimations of good practice. Work continued in the 1930s with the Bank influential not simply in planting the idea of the need for a central bank but in placing many of its own people in the banks and in suggesting policy rules (design). When New Zealand was in the process of establishing its reserve bank it sought and was given the Bank's advice on details. A former Chief Cashier in the Bank was installed as the first Governor for a period of seven years. That happened not to be a success – a matter of personality.

The case of India is interesting. In the course of the nineteenth century a monetary system had evolved. Keynes described how India had 'drifted' into a monetary system with neither 'contemplation' nor 'explanation'.[19] He quoted the deputy secretary of the Bank of Bengal, who said that by 'an almost imperceptible process the Indian currency will be placed on a footing which Ricardo and other great authorities have advocated as the best of all currency systems', that was one of notes and cheap token coins convertible into gold. As Keynes said, this provided a main objective of a good currency – cheapness and stability. The system was then imitated across much of Asia.

But Keynes nevertheless felt there was need for improvement in the form of a central bank. India had no 'rediscount market, no elasticity in the note issue, no bank rate policy, and an "Independent Treasury System" in place of a Government banker'. Keynes advanced a proposal for such an institution but it was one that specifically excluded the Bank of England model since those responsible for policy should be appointed by government and be under its ultimate authority. There should, though, be a high degree of independence and at the same time that should be combined with sound banking knowledge. The governor and deputy governor should be from a commercial and banking background. And it would be better if the bank were not situated in Delhi but to be distanced geographically from government in order to lessen government influence. Such an operationally independent bank would allow government to avoid pressure for lending. The proposal was not, however, successful. Neither was a second proposal in 1927 which failed over the issue of public/private ownership and control. It was 1935 before the Reserve Bank was established with Norman's guidance.

Montagu Norman's enthusiasm for international financial 'cooperation' was picked up and developed by his successor Cobbold. In the post-Second World

War period at least up until 1980 the Bank placed staff in central banks, provided training courses at the Bank for overseas central bankers, and offered advice on the establishment and running of the new financial organisations. Whereas in the inter-war years the focus had been on the 'white' dominions, in the 1960s and 1970s the Bank widened its scope of assistance most notably to parts of Africa and was involved in the banks of over 50 countries.[20]

Haslam's history lists nearly 300 overseas posts in new central banks and other financial institutions which were filled between 1945 and 1974 from the Bank.[21] While secondment of Bank staff to overseas posts had existed since the end of the First World War, the numbers involved were relatively small compared to those after the Second World War. The Bank supplied staff ranging from Governor down, with the bulk of them Advisers, Chief Cashiers, or General Managers and Exchange Controllers.[22] As colonies acquired their independence, the old currency boards were seen as symbols of colonialism, but the Bank's expertise was still needed for the creation of a stable financial system. The Bank believed that it was important that newly independent countries should get off to a good start in financial matters and thus exerted themselves to find suitable people to aid the organisations.

It is difficult to judge the overall success of the Bank's work abroad. In the course of the period 1955–1978, they appointed eight governors and six deputy governors to overseas central banks. Haslam's view is essentially a positive one:

> In the limited, practical but nonetheless fundamental areas, of currency provision, management of government funds and short-term debt, bank clearing, exchange control and the provision of basic statistical information and analysis, most of the ventures in which the Bank of England participated produced creditable standards of performance, often in the face of daunting manpower shortages. It must not be thought that the picture lacked highlights even in the areas where general expectations were somewhat disappointed.[23]

Against all that, given that the role of central banking was a diminished one after the 1930s, it may have been that the training was less sound that it once had been. There was also extensive training of overseas central bankers by the Bank at the Bank through visits and a Commonwealth Central Banking Summer School was established at the Bank.[24] As one official expressed it, 'we want to sow the proper central banking doctrine early in Colonial minds'.[25] The courses also gave the Bank an opportunity to lay the foundations for cooperation with the future senior officials of central banks.[26] The range of participants was further extended in 1973 when Italy, France and Germany attended the Central Banking Course.

The Bank also had a role in the origins of the Federal Reserve; or at least it was the main model that was examined. The history of the origins of the Federal Reserve is too familiar to repeat here but one or two points may be worth reflecting on further. A banking/financial system had clearly evolved in the United

States at an early stage; indeed some argue that in every respect it was a system that was in advance of Britain and Europe in the early nineteenth century.[27] But the proximate explanation for the Fed is usually taken to be the 1907 panic and the defects in the system that the panic revealed. Time was then spent considering the experiences of other countries and that, together with the specific problems identified, prepared the way for the blueprint for the new bank. But some of the central concerns were not easily resolved, questions such as the degree of central control or whether it should be publicly or privately owned and controlled.

More than that, the founders disagreed over the main functions. The 1907 panic was the main reason for the new institution being seen as 'a clearing house for clearing houses'. But by the time of the Bill's presentation to Congress in September 1913 something much grander had been developed. It is not surprising that in the United States with its long record of populism and its deep distrust of the moneyed interest that a great deal of heat should have been generated over where control should lie. And yet while it is common to talk of the Fed as being independent (except for the period from 1934 to 1951) the early years have some puzzles, and there are lapses after 1951 too. For example, Carter Glass who introduced the Federal Reserve Bill and had worked on its design became a member of the Board in Washington. But when he was a Board member he was Secretary of the Treasury at the same time. Where once – before the Fed's foundation – he had been opposed to central control, he later – after he became Secretary of the Treasury – favoured it, for as a politician he then wanted low interest rates. And to achieve that he preferred using credit controls and directing credit as the means of containing inflation.

Perhaps more seriously for the long-term performance of the Fed was the fact that the 'real bills' doctrine was written into the constitution of the Federal Reserve. The real bills doctrine says that increases in credit, directed to financing real output, are non-inflationary. Other discounting, for example of government securities, is non-productive and so inflationary. Holders of these views therefore disapproved of open market operations in government paper. The leading monetary economists in the United States at the beginning of the twentieth century supported the doctrine and so it was of little surprise that it was written into the Federal Reserve Act. Henry Thornton had exposed the fallacy of the doctrine more than 100 years before. It failed to distinguish between real and nominal variables, and failed to recognise that controlling quality did not control quantity. It led to pro-cyclical policy. But that lesson was either not learned or it was forgotten.

In the Great Depression in the United States, 1929–1933, part of the dispute within the Fed was over whether open market operations should be used or discounting reflected the 'entrenched "real bills" doctrine'.[28] Benjamin Strong had rediscovered Thornton and would have used open market operations, but he died in 1928. In the Great Depression it was perhaps the failure to distinguish between real and nominal that was of chief importance. (This incidentally was a fault that continued to run through the 1950s and 1960s in the United

Kingdom and elsewhere.) So, as Meltzer argues in his recent history, the Fed followed the wrong model from the outset. Meltzer went further than that in arguing that the model dominated personality (Strong). According to Freidman and Schwartz the structure of the Fed was flawed from the beginning and contributed to its inability to learn.[29]

Independence

For those designing central banks in recent years the argument has seemed straightforward: inflation is a monetary phenomenon; there is no long-run trade-off between output and inflation; price stability has become the primary objective. These all point to central bank independence for achievement. Central bank independence became the great mantra of the late twentieth century. What difference for independence did the origins of a central bank make in terms of evolution or design? Independence does not flow naturally from the origins of the particular central bank. But the likelihood is that where a central bank has evolved – a nineteenth-century phenomenon – there will be greater independence than where it has been designed – more commonly a twentieth-century phenomenon – although it does depend upon the date at which all this happened. And it may also be the case that where it has evolved, elements of independence may be longer lasting.

What is usually considered as independence is in fact fairly limited – instrument or operational independence as opposed to goal independence. That is freedom to use interest rates or money supply or whatever else is deemed necessary to achieve the target they have been given. The goal is defined by government. That has tended to be highly satisfactory to central banks for it is something they have a long history of – the old convertibility model was effectively this. So what has come to be accepted at least implicitly is the idea put forward by Friedman a long time ago.

But how can the degree of independence that actually prevailed be captured? A large number of studies tried to build indices of independence based on factors such as how the board were appointed, what the nature of ownership was, whether the Bank was private or not and so on. Part of the argument of this section will be that it is impossible to do that since there are too many other factors that distort the nature of the condition.

Independence is of little use if governments are profligate. Something that needs to be made explicit for the macroeconomic policy context is the government budget constraint. The phrase may not have been used before the late twentieth century but the concept was at least implicitly understood by many central bankers, particularly on continental Europe. In the Bank it was the basis for the constant nagging by governors of chancellors to try to contain government spending. Just as the individual consumer faces a budget constraint so too does government. The present value of its consumption, current and future, must equal the present value of its income – tax collection current and future.

Government expenditure is equal to tax revenue, plus new borrowing, plus the change in the monetary base. There need not be a direct link between the budget deficit and the monetary base, and to some extent the connection will depend on the degree of independence from government the central bank enjoys, but constant borrowing will almost invariably result in an expanding money supply. The worst experiences of inflation around the world are testament to this. Weak governments, unable to raise taxes or borrow beyond a certain point, buy support or quieten opposition by agreeing to their demands and that means spending, which in turn requires, in effect, printing money.[30] It is now well understood that monetary and fiscal policy must go together.

In developing countries it was often the 'fiscal abuse' of the central bank that severely damaged its independence. In a study of 26 developing countries Max Fry showed how,

> By making central banks responsible for a range of fiscal expenditures, developing countries undermine not only the banks' independence but also monetary policy objectives. Fiscal activities involve expenditures that reduce central bank profits and may even produce losses. If central bank losses are not met from government budget appropriations, they must eventually lead to an expansion in central bank money and the abandonment of any monetary policy goal of price stability.... Governments can tap central bank profits either directly through transfers or indirectly by obliging the central banks to engage in fiscal activities.[31]

Independence is also affected by the way in which central banks are financed and here too there is a difference between evolution and design. There are essentially three ways in which central banks are financed. The first is the retention of seigniorage. The second is out of general taxation. The third is by way of a levy on the most immediate beneficiaries of the public good that is being provided, say monetary or financial stability. The first seems to lack the right kind of incentive. The second presents problems for independence. The third appears to offer the greatest freedom for whatever kind of independence there is. Again, in the history of the Bank of England this was an evolutionary process. For convenience the commercial banks held balances at the Bank, and this is the basis of the system that still obtains.

There was another factor that was important for successful achievement of the monetary policy objective and that was the nature of the personalities of governors and chancellors involved. And that was perhaps supported by the length of the terms that they enjoyed. To stay with the Bank of England example, Montagu Norman is usually the first candidate to spring to mind – an undoubtedly powerful personality who ruled the Bank for almost a quarter of a century. He even seemed to have a hold over Benjamin Strong at the Federal Reserve. It was partly Norman's, still perplexing, weak performance as witness at the Macmillan Committee that damaged his reputation and that of central banking more generally. Nevertheless, he had a powerful 'descendant' in Cameron Fromanteel

Cobbold, Governor 1949–1961. Cobbold was a protégé of Norman and although he did not immediately succeed him, he is often referred to as his successor. Cobbold had seven different chancellors to deal with. Not only had he vast experience compared to them, he had other attributes including great charm. He successfully defended the Bank's 'independence' over a long period and through many difficulties. The independence was weakened when lesser personalities followed.

Personality has a major role to play across the development of central banking. Might the world have been an entirely different place, for example, had Benjamin Strong not died in 1928? Friedman and Schwartz and more recently Meltzer believe so. When Strong died and power within the Fed shifted from New York to Washington, monetary policy was damaged and the Great Depression followed with consequences that are still with us. In Germany in the 1930s Schacht at the Reichsbank oversaw the ending of the hyperinflation and gained a reputation as a financial genius, and greatly strengthened his role and that of the Reichsbank.

Personality can clearly be strong, neutral or weak, and of course much more complex and varied than can be reduced to a few adjectives, let alone some numbers. It can also have negative outcomes. One example is that of Coyne at the Bank of Canada. The relationship between the Bank and the Ministry of Finance in Canada was vague. Coyne was a strong and outspoken critic of government, as was Cobbold, but Coyne made his feelings widely and publicly known to such an extent that he had effectively to be dismissed.

Conclusion

In the 1930s for a variety of reasons, in the United Kingdom in particular but also more generally, monetary policy became completely discredited and central banks were demoted in terms of policy making. It was only the return of fixed exchange rate regimes after the Second World War that gave them back some powers and some prestige. And the fixed-rate regime was generally strongly favoured by central banks for that reason.

Furthermore, given the nineteenth-century origins of the institutions that became central banks and the apparent success of the prevailing international monetary system – the gold standard – it is hardly surprising that central bankers who ran the system remained deeply committed to gold and to sound money and were generally conservative in this sense. It should not be a surprise then to find history and personality coming into play in the years after the Second World War.

The Bank of England in the long period after the Second World War is perhaps a good example. It supposedly lost its independence in 1946 when nationalised. But there are several reasons for believing that in fact little changed. The main point worth making here is that the circumstances were such as to allow a degree of operational independence that has some parallels with the more recent one. In the 1950s and 1960s there was a target set – the exchange rate. The Bank was charged with the task of holding to that rate and given pretty well complete freedom to do that. Given the pressure sterling was under in the period, that involved a number of tasks including seeking international assistance from central banks and the BIS in the form of short-term credits and swaps. It required encouraging belief in London as an international financial centre which, in the Bank's eyes, meant preserving stable conditions. But it also required the use of Bank Rate as a shock and a psychological weapon. It so happened that there was a long-standing belief that dated from the 1930s, and was reinforced by Radcliffe, that interest rates were not important for the domestic economy. So the initiative for Bank Rate changes were expected to come from the Bank and in almost all cases they did. So there was a target and operational independence to achieve it. There is even an element of transparency in that the pound was either convertible into other currencies at a particular rate or it was not, though I would not want to push that line too far. All of that sounds very like the present arrangements. But there was an obstacle to successful achievement of policy and that was the need for appropriate fiscal behaviour. There was no more persistent critic of government expenditure than the Bank's governors in the 1950s and 1960s. The number and intensity of complaints on excessive government expenditure from the governor to the Chancellor grew. And while the strong personalities of Cobbold and Cromer helped to retain a certain amount of independence there were distinct limits to their abilities. In that sense nothing has changed.

It might be tempting to extend this story to the 1970s when monetary targeting was adopted. So another target was given to the Bank. Did this represent another period of such independence? So long as monetary policy was seen as part of demand management then the Treasury would be the central authority and the Bank's role would be subordinate. But once monetary policy changed to being focused on setting the framework and containing inflation, then the Treasury was only involved in setting the target and perhaps agreeing the range of techniques to be used in attaining the target. The rest, operational independence, could be left to the Bank. However, there are several new reasons why this did not work. First, the Bank did not really believe in the target and did little to achieve it. Also there were lesser personalities confronting ever more reckless government expenditure. There were changed views on interest rates; and there was a lack of understanding of the changed circumstances of floating exchange rates.

People engaged in reform or regulation are usually too much dominated by the events of the time. So, for example, in the many Latin American countries whose central banks were designed in the 1930s, their major preoccupation was to cope with deflation. They were generally ill-prepared, 'institutionally or intellectually, to fight the inflation which shortly afterwards was their real problem.'[32] Another danger lies in the fact that financial stability and monetary stability are closely related but that that has been lost sight of or at least until very recently had been. The focus in the nineteenth century was financial stability. The twentieth century has been dominated by inflation of extreme and lasting kinds and the emphasis for central banks has so shifted.

Notes

* I thank Geoffrey Wood and Anna Schwartz for comments on an earlier version, and Marc Flandreau for his comments as discussant at the conference.

1 Goodhart, *Evolution of Central Banking*, p. vii.
2 Quinn and Roberds, 'Bank of Amsterdam', pp. 262–265.
3 Some would wish to argue that a kind of monetary management prevailed from the early nineteenth century. See Flandreau's imaginative paper, 'Pillars of Globalisation'.
4 Capie, Goodhart and Schnadt, *The Development of Central Banking.*
5 Sayers, *Central Banking after Bagehot.*
6 Capie, 'Evolution'.
7 Clapham, *The Bank of England.*
8 Bagehot, *Lombard Street*, pp. 63, 64.
9 Bagehot, *Lombard Street.*
10 But other central banks have often been seen as ways of rationalising payments systems. See Bordo and James, 'From 1907 to 1946', p. 91.
11 Quinn, 'Goldsmith-Banking'.
12 Thornton, *Paper Credit*, p. 259.
13 Clapham, *Bank of England*, p. 420.
14 Sayers, *Bank of England*, pp. 209, 513.
15 Sayers, *Bank of England.*
16 Schedvin, *Australia*, p. 50.
17 Schedvin, *Australia*, p. 138.
18 Sayers, *Bank of England*, p. 208.
19 Keynes, *Indian Currency*, p. 3.
20 Haslam, *Central Banks*, appendix.
21 Haslam, *Central Banks.*
22 Hennessy, *Domestic History*, p. 306.
23 Haslam, *Central Banks*, p. 1109.
24 Watson, 'Commonwealth Central Banking Summer School', 1 October 1956, OV21/26.
25 Bank of England archive, 'Central Banking Course - Colonial Candidates', 1 November 1956, OV21/26.
26 Bank of England archive, O'Brien to Watson, OV21/26.
27 Sylla, Wright, and Cowen, *Alexander Hamilton, Central Banker*, 61–86.
28 Meltzer, *History of the Fed*, p. 288.
29 Friedman and Schwartz, *Monetary History.*
30 For some examples, see Capie, 'Conditions'.
31 Fry, 'Fiscal Abuse', p. 1.
32 Emminger, 'Inflation', p. 58.

References

Bagehot, Walter (1873) *Lombard Street: A Description of the Money Market* (London: Henry S. King & Co.).

Bordo, Michael and Harold James (2007) 'From 1907 to 1946: A Happy Childhood or a Troubled Adolescence?' in Swiss National Bank Centenary Conference collection.

Capie, Forrest (1986) 'Conditions in Which Very Rapid Inflation Has Occurred', *Carnegie-Rochester Proceedings*, 24 (Amsterdam: North Holland), 115–165.

Capie, Forrest (2002) 'The Evolution of the Bank of England as a Mature Central Bank', in P.K. O'Brien and D. Winch (eds), *The Political Economy of British Historical Experience, 1688–1914* (Oxford: Oxford University Press), 295–315.

Capie, Forrest, C.A.E. Goodhart and N. Schnadt (1994) *The Development of Central Banking* (Cambridge: Cambridge University Press).

Clapham, Sir John (1944) *The Bank of England: A History. Vol. 2, 1797–1914: With an Epilogue, The Bank as It Is* (Cambridge: Cambridge University Press).

Emminger, O. (1973) 'Inflation and the International Monetary System', Tenth Lecture of the Per Jacobsson Foundation, Basle, 16 June 1973.

Flandreau, M. (2006) 'Pillars of Globalisation: A History of Monetary Policy Targets, 1797–1997', paper presented at the 4th ECB Central Banking Conference, 9–10 November 2006.

Friedman, Milton and Anna Schwartz (1963) *A Monetary History of the United States 1867–1960* (Princeton, NJ: Princeton University Press).

Fry, Max (1993) 'The Fiscal Abuse of Central Banks', IMF Working paper WP/93/58.

Goodhart, C.A.E. (1988) *The Evolution of Central Banking* (Cambridge, MA: MIT Press).

Haslam, E.P. (1979) *Central Banks in the Making: The Role of the Bank of England 1948–74, Vols 1, 2 and 3* (private circulation).

Hennessey, Elizabeth (1992) *A Domestic History of the Bank of England, 1930–1960* (Cambridge: Cambridge University Press).

Keynes, John Maynard (1913) *Indian Currency and Finance* (London: Macmillan).

Meltzer, Allan H. (2002) *A History of the Federal Reserve. Volume 1, 1913–1951* (Chicago, IL: University of Chicago Press).

Quinn, Stephen (1997) 'Goldsmith-Banking: Mutual Acceptance and Interbanker Clearing in Restoration London', *Explorations in Economic History*, 34 (4) (October), 411–432.

Quinn, Stephen and William Roberds (2007) 'The Bank of Amsterdam and the Leap to Central Bank Money', *American Economic Review*, 97 (2) (May), 262–265.

Sayers, R.S. (1957) *Central banking after Bagehot* (London: Oxford University Press).

Sayers, R.S. (1976) *The Bank of England* (Cambridge: Cambridge University Press).

Schedvin, C.B. (1971) *Australia and the Great Depression: A Study of Economic Development and Policy in the 1920s and 1930s* (Sydney: Sydney University Press).

Sylla, Richard, Robert E. Wright, and David J. Cowen (2009) 'Alexander Hamilton, Central Banker: Crisis Management during the U.S. Financial Panic of 1792', *Business History Review*, 83, 61–86.

Thornton, Henry P. (1802) *An Enquiry into the Nature and Effects of the Paper Credit of Great Britain* (London: Hatchard).

2 The north European model of early central banking

Juha Tarkka

The historical analysis of how central banks emerged and developed is usually presented with the main focus on the countries which were most successful in terms of financial development. Consequently, the development of the Bank of England as a central bank and monetary policy maker is seen as the main case of reference, as the previous chapter by Forrest Capie illustrates. This is of course well justified by the fact that, by the latter half of the nineteenth century, the English type of central banking became an important model which inspired many other countries' financial and monetary reforms. Another important standard of reference has been Banque de France.

In spite of some important differences, the Bank of England and Banque de France, and the way these banks operated during the classical gold standard, can be said to constitute the ideal type of the classical central bank. But what exactly distinguished the classical model of central banking from the other models which were eventually abandoned? What were the alternatives the classical model ultimately superseded, and why?

Capie *et al.* (1994), in their review of the development of central banking, fix the beginning of central banking in various countries by two indicators: the *legal* monopoly of note issue, and the de facto assumption of the responsibilities of the lender of last resort. These criteria seem natural from today's perspective but they were probably not considered by contemporaries as the main parts of the central banking 'revolution' of the late nineteenth century. In order to get a true perspective on what actually was special about the victorious classical model of central banking one has to contrast it with the relevant alternative designs and their performance, and study the reasons which led to the adoption of the classical model. It is the claim of this chapter that the crucial feature which distinguished classical central banking from its predecessors was actually the lending doctrine, especially with regard to collateral policy.

This chapter is about the proto-central banking development of the countries of the Baltic Sea basin. I survey the development of central banking institutions in the area from their beginning roughly until the period when they became fully fledged central banks in the classical sense. The Baltic Sea area is particularly interesting, because there public banks of issue emerged quite early, and also reached a scale which was significant in their day. It is well-known that the

Swedish Stockholm Banco was the first bank in Europe to issue banknotes; and one can note that the value of the banknotes of the Russian Assignat Bank in circulation in the 1830s was clearly larger than that of the Bank of England.

The design of the organisation and the principles of operation of the proto central banks of the Baltic Sea area display a certain underlying unity which enables one to speak about a particular north European model of early central banking. This model was different from the classical model of central banking in some ways which were only changed in the latter half of the nineteenth century, when the classical model was finally adopted in the Baltic Sea area as well.

One may perhaps question the practical relevance for today's central banking of the study of '*wie es eigentlich gewesen*' around the Baltic Sea basin before the adoption of the classical gold standard, with regard to the central banking practices of that period. In addition to the general historical interest, which I believe would in itself certainly warrant the study of the patterns of proto-central banking in the area, a review of alternative models of central banking – even historical ones – may pay off by drawing attention to aspects of central banking currently disregarded (or taken for granted) by theoretical analysis. One such aspect, once very important but now nearly forgotten by theoreticians, is the question of what types of credit are suitable for central banks. However, the question of eligible collateral must be resolved in one way or another by every central bank even of today, and becomes especially topical in times of financial turmoil, when the financial system turns to the central bank for liquidity.

As I demonstrate in this chapter, one of the interesting contrasts between the early north European model and the classical model of central banking is the difference in what forms of credit were considered appropriate for an issuing bank (or more generally, a money-creating bank) to extend. The classical model of central banking *à la* Bank of England or Banque de France was based on what can be called a restrictive form of the real bills doctrine. This emphasised the liquid ('self-liquidating' was the contemporary term) nature of the assets appropriate for the bank of issue. By contrast, the early north European model emphasised another asset criteron, the underlying security (or indeed solidity) of the banks' investments, and was based more directly on the idea of using banks to increase the liquidity of otherwise illiquid assets. The proto central banks were often established to alleviate what was seen as a shortage of liquidity and means of payment in the economies. These concerns led to a lending policy where land credit had a big share. Loans to government were also important in many cases.

In the remaining parts of the chapter, I consider the development of the ideas regarding the suitable lending forms for banks of issue. I contrast the earlier thinking, which was based on the concept of real credit (and led to the land-based and goods-based lending policies of the proto central banks), with the real bills doctrine and the currency principle, which in turn constituted the distinguishing features of the classical model of central banking. After a brief introduction to the monetary and economic structure of the Baltic Sea area in the period of interest, I present an overview of the development of proto central banks in the countries of the area. I also consider the reasons which eventually led to the abandonment of the early north European model and the adoption of the classical central banking principles.

The competing lending doctrines

The particular characteristics of the early north European model of central banking are best presented by comparing them to the two dominant principles of classical central banking, the currency principle and the real bills doctrine. It is well-known how important both of these competing doctrines and the debate between their supporters were for the development of the English model of central banking in the nineteenth century, and they were also an increasingly important influence in the central bank reforms in other countries (culminating in the establishment of the Federal Reserve System in the United States in the spirit of the real bills doctrine; see Meltzer 2003: 70).

The real bills doctrine was famously stated by Adam Smith in 1776 in *The Wealth of Nations* (Smith 1991: 269). Basically, this doctrine says that issuing banks should grant credit only against real (meaning trade-related) bills of exchange. It has been one of the most controversial topics in the history of central banking, and the controversy is not only about the practical value of the doctrine, but also about its precise content. One may distinguish at least three different interpretations of what the real bills doctrine precisely means, or what is best denoted by the term.

One interpretation can be called the 'enabling version' of the doctrine. That can be summarised by the general claim that the central bank cannot over-issue the currency if it discounts only real bills, i.e. short-term paper which has a commercial origin in the trade of goods. I call this 'enabling' because it implies that the issuing bank can extend credit quite freely if it only sticks to the policy of real bills as collateral.

The enabling version identifies the real bills doctrine with the 'antibullionist' position of the directors of the Bank of England in the British parliamentary hearings in 1810, refusing to accept the blame for the decline of the value of the pound sterling vis-à-vis gold (cf. Cannan 1925: 45–48). The enabling version of the real bills doctrine had in fact been refuted quite conclusively by Henry Thornton already before the hearings, in his 'Paper Credit', in which he had pointed out that the supply of 'real bills' to the issuing bank is not necessarily limited by the 'needs of the trade', especially if the interest rate was lower than the rate of profits (Thornton 1802).

Another version of the doctrine can be called 'the restrictive version' of the doctrine. Its content is negative. It says that it is not safe for a note-issuing bank to invest in kinds of assets other than short-term real bills. In particular, the cover of the banknotes in circulation, over any metal reserve, should consist of real bills. This interpretation can be identified with the advocates of the 'banking school' during the controversy in the United Kingdom in the 1830s about the lending policy of the Bank of England (banking school advocates Tooke and Fullarton, in particular; see Schumpeter 1982: 725–731). They limited their argument in favour of the real bills policy to the case in which the conduct of the bank of issue was also constrained by the requirement of convertibility of its notes to specie (coin or bullion, gold or silver). They argued that the bank could not possibly over-issue when convertibility was maintained, since any excess money would then simply flow back to the bank as the demand for discounts would be reduced (this is the 'law of reflux').

The third interpretation of the real bills doctrine to appear in the literature, although much more recently, is the 'interest rate pegging version'. This equates the real bills policy with a passively accommodating supply of reserves, so that a central bank following this version of the real bills doctrine would satisfy any demand for money at the going interest rate. This is the interpretation given to the doctrine by Friedman and Schwartz (1963) and Humphrey (1982), who correctly point out that an interest rate pegging rule, as a sole guiding principle for monetary policy, would not suffice to determine an equilibrium level of prices in the economy. In making this point, they echo the main argument in Thornton's *Paper Credit.*

As much as any doctrine, the real bills doctrine can only be understood in context. It was formulated for a purpose, and, although the subsequent literature might give a different impression, the purpose was not to defend inflationary policies in the United Kingdom or elsewhere during suspension of convertibility. The real bills doctrine makes sense only as an alternative to something it was meant to rule out. As formulated by Adam Smith, and as understood by his followers, not only the famous proponents of the banking school but many central banking reformers and practitioners until the early twentieth century at least, the *real bills doctrine was directed against the idea of issuing banknotes backed by real estate* (or land-based credit). It was meant to be a restrictive doctrine, intended to ensure the liquidity of the banks of issue (and banks taking sight deposits as well). If the demand for banknotes would diminish for any reason, the bank would have to reduce its lending, and needed flexibility to do this. The fact that the antibullionists in the British debate of around 1810, who appealed to the real bills doctrine, obviously did not understand how suspension of convertibility had altered the effects of monetary policy does not refute this point.

The main alternative, that is, the idea of land-based supply of money, was very influential in northern Europe before the real bills doctrine finally superseded it around (as late as) the middle of the nineteenth century. The question of land banks and of money backed by fixed assets was subject to a lot of controversy already in the eighteenth century, starting from John Law's *Money and Trade Considered* (1705), in which he proposed monetising landed property. Despite the spectacular failure of Law's Banque Royale in France, the idea of using land to back banknote issues remained alive in the continental discussion and banking practice.[1] It seems that even the second disastrous French experiment with land-backed money, the assignats of the revolutionary government, failed to decisively discourage the continental (and Scandinavian) statesmen and economists from proposing, establishing and running banks of issue based – directly or indirectly – on agricultural mortgage credit. This will be apparent from the review of the proto-central banking arrangements of the Baltic Sea area which will follow below.

For contemporaries, the idea of land banks had both theoretical and practical merits. The theoretical merits were perhaps best summarised by Sir James Steuart, who had lived on the European continent for a long time and can actually be considered a continental economist (both in terms of the influences on him and the influences which his work had on others). According to Steuart, land credit was the preferable backing to banknotes, because of the greater security and solidity it gives to the banking institution. Following the influential German cameralist J.H.G. von Justi (1760: 652–663), Steuart divided bank credit into real (backed by property), mercantile (backed by 'obligations of merchants or manufacturers') and personal (backed by the capital invested by the banker himself). Steuart considered mercantile credit, which would include trade bills, as the most insecure of these and argued strongly in favour of the more tangible real backing – in effect, mortgages of land. Liquidity he thought was a secondary concern for the rational creditor: 'Coin may be wanting, upon some occasions, to men of the greatest landed property. Is this a reason to suspect their credit?' (Steuart 1767: 479–483).

Steuart's category of real credit would have included, of course, banknotes backed by metallic reserve, or by a pledge of other durable goods. But mostly he refers to real estate, and it is clear that, for him as well as many of his contemporaries, the practical merits of land as collateral for banknotes seemed overwhelming. Among the influential contemporary authorities, the preference for real collateral is shared by von Justi, for instance, who in his *Grundfeste* (1760) writes that 'a bank with complete security is of enormous benefit for the state', but maintains that only properly insured property is secure enough as collateral.[2]

In the United Kingdom, of course, the idea of a land-based bank of issue never took root, and the Bank of England practice developed along the lines of the real bills doctrine (even after the resumption in 1816, and after the Bank Charter Act of 1844, in the sense of the restrictive version of the real bills doctrine). In France, after two disasters with land-bank experiments, the Banque de France was established, in 1800, firmly on banking-school principles and concentrated on the discounting of bills of exchange (see Ramon 1929). This contrasts sharply with the north European developments, where land-based proto central banks of issue were the norm rather than the exception.

The reasons for establishing land-based banks of issue were the scarcity of other types of collateral to monetise, on the one hand, and the advantages which the system seemed to promise to landowners, on the other. Already John Law had complained about the scarcity of monetary metals in the Scotland of his day (Law 1705, chapter 7), and the same concern of the lack of circulating metal is recurrent in the continental discussions of the eighteenth and early nineteenth century. The whole point of banks of issue was to economise on the use of precious metals in monetary circulation and reserves. Another powerful argument for land banks was that they seemed to large landowners, who in many cases were heavily indebted, to be a way to restructure and consolidate their debts into longer mortgages with a lower interest rate than would otherwise have been possible. In the period in which land-based proto central banks were established, in the Baltic Sea area in particular, the landowning gentry was a very powerful political force. This is especially true in Russia and its Baltic provinces, and in Poland, as well as in Prussia, but also the politics of the Scandinavian countries were dominated by landowners until the constitutional (parliamentary) reforms of the mid nineteenth century (in Denmark, 1849; in Sweden, 1865).

A third important ingredient in north European thinking (apart from the competing real bills and land-bank doctrines) was the currency principle, which sought to limit note issues in a way which would ensure convertibility to metal and preserve the self-regulating properties of a full metallic standard. According to the currency principle, the function of banks of issue was not to increase the quantity of money, but merely to reduce the costs of maintaining and using the monetary system. This could be done by backing banknotes by 100 per cent metallic reserves, so that the justification for the use of banknotes would be their convenience, compared to coin, but not the possibility of increasing the money supply by credit operations. Ideally, the backing could be by reserves of bullion, not coin. It was thought that this principle would guarantee the continued convertibility of the banknotes and thus their value in gold.

The famous statement of the currency doctrine is Ricardo's *Proposals for an Economical and Secure Currency* (Ricardo 1819), but, in fact, the conservative statutes of the old continental banks of exchange (Bank of Amsterdam and the Bank of Hamburg, see van Dillen 1934 and Soetbeer 1855: 90–97), are evidence that the currency principle was well-known as an ideal, and heeded, already two centuries before Ricardo's proposal.

Ricardo proposed a complete separation of the issuing institution (a currency board, in more modern terms) from banking activities, but this was not to be. Instead, the reconciliation in the United Kingdom of the currency principle with the practical merits of central banking – i.e. economising on metallic reserves and contributing to the liquidity of the financial system – happened through the famous Bank Charter Act of 1844 (see Horsefield 1944). This divided the bank into two departments, the issue department and the banking department. The issue department backed its issued banknotes with metal, except for a fixed quota of a 'fiduciary issue' which was given to the banking department. The banking business of the Bank of England, in the usual sense of the word, was to be taken care of by the banking department.

On the continent, ideas similar to the currency principle had also been influential, even though the distinction between bank deposits and currency, which was central to the British currency controversy, was not viewed in the same way on the continent. The continental version of the currency doctrine can be seen in the design of the great banks of exchange, which made it a point to at least appear to keep 100 per cent metallic reserve backing for the bank money they created. Adam Smith's description of the Bank of Amsterdam is particularly famous (see Smith 1991: Book IV, Chapter III). As early as 1619, long before the British Bank Charter Act, the Bank of Hamburg was divided into two departments: the bank of exchange, creating the underlying bank money and operating the payment system, and the loan bank, which created credit against appropriate collateral security (pledges of silver, in the case of Hamburg).

The similar two-department structure was repeated in the design of other continental proto central banks, such as the Bank of Sweden, the Royal Bank of Berlin (Prussia) and the Bank of Finland in its early phase. As will be shown below, in some other countries of the Baltic Sea basin, the division into two was effected by establishing two or even three formally different institutions, which, however, operated in close symbiosis (the Russian proto-central banking system until 1860 is an important case in point, as is the early Polish system).

With some simplification, one may characterise the influence of the above-mentioned banking doctrines on the development of the proto central banks of the Baltic Sea area in the following way. In the early stages, there was a strong influence of the idea of land banks; to maintain credibility, the issue of currency and the granting of credit were, however, often separated at least superficially into different departments or institutions. In practice, the activities of these departments or institutions were closely intertwined, and the additional integrity created by the separation of the issuing bank, or department, seems doubtful (even in the Bank of Hamburg, it seems that the good credit enjoyed by the institution was probably more due to the strict collateral policy of the bank than to its two-department structure).

Over time, however, the influence of the real bills doctrine seems to have increased. This is evident from the increased reluctance to cover banknotes with long-term mortgages. By the mid nineteenth century, in most countries of the Baltic Sea area a transition was happening from land-bank-type proto central banks towards classical central banking, based on a combination of the real bills doctrine and stiff cover regulations in the spirit of the currency principle. The part of note issue which was covered by metal was to be covered by trade bills. As is shown, this transition started in the 1840s, and was clearly almost complete when the gold standard was adopted in the area in the 1870s (but later in Russia).

The Baltic Sea area

The countries of the Baltic Sea basin constitute an interesting commercial and financial entity which, despite its apparent cultural and political diversity, actually displays much historical unity as well, especially in terms of trade and finance (see e.g. Kirby 1995 for a broad overview of the history of the region). This Baltic unity probably dates at least as far back as the times of the Hanseatic League when the city of Lübeck acted as the dominant trading centre for the whole region. Later, the predominance of Amsterdam, Hamburg and London, each in turn the leading centre of trade and finance, supported the economic unity of the region.

During our period of interest, the Baltic Sea financial and trading region comprised Denmark, Sweden, Prussia, Russia, its Baltic provinces (of Estonia, Livonia and Courland), Finland and Poland. One can also include Norway, although it has no Baltic coast. Under the period we consider, Norway was in political union first with Denmark and later with Sweden, and these political links were also reflected in its monetary and banking developments. The inclusion of Russia, although geographically far from being a predominantly Baltic Sea country, is sensible, because its trade and financial linkages in the period of interest as well as its monetary developments clearly indicate that it was an essential part of the Baltic world. Finally, the economy of the Baltic Sea area during our period of interest cannot be depicted without including the city-state of Hamburg, even though Hamburg also had its continental and global roles which mean that it cannot be viewed only as the trading hub of the Baltic Sea area.

Our period of interest extends from the emergence of proto central banking in the latter half of the eighteenth century until the breakthrough of classical central banking in around the mid nineteenth century. In that time, the economies of the area were still overwhelmingly agricultural. Apart from the great mercantile centre of Hamburg, the towns in the area lived mostly by exporting primary products of their hinterlands such as grain (from Prussia, Poland and the Baltic provinces), timber and other forestry products such as tar and pitch (from Sweden, Norway, Finland and Russia), iron and copper (from Sweden and Russia), fish (from Denmark and Norway) and flax and hemp (from Russia, Poland and Prussia). Britain was the greatest customer. The imports to the ports of the Baltic Sea consisted of salt, manufactures and luxury articles, wine and some tropical products (Oddy 1807; Kirby and Hinkkanen 2000: chapter 7).

During this period and until the 1870s, the monetary system in the Baltic Sea area was based on the silver standard. The basis of almost all monetary systems of the area can be traced back to the silver reichsthaler (rixdollar), originally regulated by the Holy Roman Empire. The standard for the classic reichsthaler was set by the Diet of Augsburg as early as 1566. Of one Cologne mark of fine silver, nine reichstaler were to be minted, so that one reichstaler would contain 25.97 g of fine silver. This standard coin came to be referred to as reichsthaler specie, to distinguish it from the numerous minor variants which later developed (Rittmann 2003: 62–63). The monetary system was integrated in its silver base and in its common roots in the reichsthaler, but there was also some diversity because of the existence of debased 'courant' (currency) coins, intended for local use, and the circulation of different types of depreciated (below par) banknotes here and there. Moreover, there were different systems of subdividing the reichsthaler into smaller units.

In the late eighteenth century, before the Napoleonic Wars disrupted the monetary systems of the area, the currency systems were roughly as follows.

The city of *Hamburg* had a silver standard based on the reichsthaler, divided into three marks or 48 schillings. This divisional system was called the Lübeck system (*lübische Währung*). For international trade and finance, the most important kind of money was that created by Hamburg's important municipal giro bank, Hamburger Bank. The bank redeemed its deposits with silver at a rate which implied a silver content of 25.40 g for the reichsthaler banco (a third of a reichsthaler banco was called the mark banco). This silver content fixed the value of the Hamburg bank money so that it corresponded exactly to the 'rigsdaler specie' coins minted by the Kingdom of *Denmark* and used there for foreign trade payments and as a standard of value in financial contracts (Sieveking 1934: 149–150; Svendsen and Hansen 1968: 13–16).

However, local circulation in Hamburg and its surrounding areas, including Denmark, Lübeck and *Mecklenburg*, used 'courant' coin, which contained about 19 per cent less silver than the Hamburg bank money or the rigsdaler specie coin minted in Denmark. The coexistence of two parallel monetary standards, a 'hard' or specie standard for finance and foreign trade and a courant standard for daily transactions, was typical of the area in the eighteenth and early nineteenth century (Rittmann 2003: 122–125; World Coins 2002, 2004).

In Denmark, the rigsdaler courant was used as a standard for banknotes which, however, lost most of their value during a period of rapid inflation during the Napoleonic Wars. This led to a monetary reform in 1813 in which a new monetary unit, the rigsbankdaler, was introduced. The continuing power of the hard reichsthaler specie as a monetary unit is well demonstrated by the fact that the silver content of the new Danish rigsbankdaler was defined to be exactly one-half of the old rigsdaler specie. The depreciated courant money was converted to rigsbankdalers at the rate of 6 rd courant to one rigsbankdaler (Svendsen and Hansen 1968: 84–127).

Norway was under Danish rule until 1814 and its monetary system was based on the old Danish rigsdaler specie (the speciedaler). The speciedaler standard was retained when Norway separated from Denmark and united with Sweden in 1814, one of the political changes caused by the Napoleonic Wars. Despite the same basic unit, there was a difference between the Norwegian and Danish divisional systems, however: in Norway, from 1796, the speciedaler was divided into 120 skilling, unlike the Danish system of 96 skilling to one rigsdaler specie (Rygg 1918: 94–97).

After a monetary reform enacted in 1776, *Sweden* too had a silver standard based on the reichsthaler. The Swedish version of the coin, called the riksdaler, contained 25.7 g of fine silver and was thus very close to the Danish rigdaler specie and the Hamburg reichsthaler banco. Following the Lübeck system, which was adopted in the monetary reform, the Swedish riksdaler was also subdivided into 48 shillings. Before the reform of 1776, Sweden had had its own currency unit, the Swedish daler, which moreover existed in two varieties, 'daler silvermynt' and 'daler kopparmynt'. These had depreciated over the decades until their value was only a fraction of the 'hard' international riksdaler. In the reform of 1776, in which a solid monetary standard was sought, the Swedish daler was superseded by the more international, stable and credible riksdaler. The Swedish, Danish and Norwegian monetary systems continued to be based on their respective silver dalers until the countries adopted the gold standard in the early 1870s and formed the Scandinavian currency union (Heckscher 1941).

Prussia had a silver standard based on the Prussian thaler, which was a lighter version of the classic reichsthaler. It was divided into 24 groschen. Since the mid eighteenth century, the standard was such that 14 Prussian thalers were coined from one Cologne mark of fine silver (this was called the Graumann standard; cf. Shaw 1895: 378–383). In modern terms this meant that the silver content of the Prussian thaler was 16.7 g. Parallel to the Prussian thaler, the Prussian government attempted to introduce a separate bank currency, the Prussian pound banco, for domestic bank transactions and bills of exchange. Originally, the plan was to tie the Prussian pound banco to gold. Introduced in 1766, when the Royal Bank of Berlin started operations, the Prussian pound banco failed to gain any significant voluntary use, however, and soon it become just an inconvenient multiple (1.3125-fold) of the Prussian silver thaler. The few remaining accounts denominated in Prussian pounds were finally converted into thalers in 1818 (Kruse 1782; Niebuhr 1854).

Later, as the German unification process gained momentum, the Prussian silver standard was adopted by the Dresden coinage agreement in 1838 as the basis for monetary unification in the German Customs Union, the Zollverein.[3] This development reflected the de facto spread of influence of the Prussian monetary system. On the Baltic coast, the Prussian standard was also adopted by Mecklenburg immediately after the Dresden agreement, despite the fact that Mecklenburg was not a member of the Zollverein. The Prussian thaler was superseded by the German mark only when Germany adopted the gold standard in 1873.

The *Russian* monetary unit was the silver rouble, subdivided into 100 kopecks. The silver rouble was also a descendant of the thaler. Peter the Great had defined the rouble on the basis of the imported thaler-type coins which circulated in Russia in his time. The silver content of the rouble coin remained fairly stable. Since the mid eighteenth century (and until the First World War), 22 roubles and 75 20/36 kopecks were minted from a Russian pound of fine silver, implying that, in modern terms, the silver content of the rouble was almost exactly 18 g fine (see e.g. Parker Willis 1897; Heller 1983).

The monetary system of the Russian Empire was not completely unified, however. In the Baltic provinces of *Livonia* and also *Courland*, which were part of the Russian Empire since 1710, the standard money was the reichsthaler Albertus. This was a type of reichsthaler minted originally in the Netherlands, containing 24.36 g of fine silver. (The Dutch, who minted this coin for use in the Baltic trade, also called it the silver ducaat.) In the albertusthaler system of Livonia, one reichsthaler Albertus was subdivided into 90 groschen. However, the Livonian groschen was an accounting unit which was not actually minted. Instead, a variety of foreign coins was used there as small change, valued at conventional rates (Buchholtz 1899; Stieda 1909).

The use of reichsthalers in Livonia reflected the German dominance in the economic and cultural life of the province, which was self-governed by local nobility and burghers, despite being formally under Russian sovereignty. Another complementary explanation for the use of thalers is trade, in particular the enormous influx of silver from northern Germany and the Netherlands to

Russia through the city of Riga: Riga, the capital of Livonia, was the second most important point of export in the whole Russian Empire and had a large trade surplus, bringing to this city and the Empire large imports of silver (cf. Blanchard 1989).

The peculiar separate monetary system of Livonia was significant because of the position of Riga as a major commercial centre for the Russian Empire. Also, it is evidence of the unity of the Baltic Sea trading area, extending across national borders. The albertusthaler system was ended, however, in the second decade of the nineteenth century when the Russian government at last took effective steps to unify the monetary system of Livonia with the Russian parts of the Empire, about a century after conquering the province. So, in 1810, the rouble was introduced as the legal accounting currency in Livonia, and in 1814 the circulation of albertusthalers and other foreign coins as means of payment was forbidden (Buchholtz 1899: 28).

Poland was another country which was annexed by the expanding Russian Empire but retained its traditional monetary system, at least for a period. The traditional Polish currency unit was the silver zloty (also called the Polish gulden), subdivided to 30 groszy. However, the zloty was in fact also part of the thaler system, since the zloty was defined compatibly with the Prussian system, so that 6 zloty equalled 1 Prussian thaler (Kruse 1782). After the Kingdom of Poland was founded in 1815 as part of the Russian Empire by the Congress of Vienna, the zloty was slightly adjusted, now compatible with the Russian silver rouble so that 1 silver rouble was equal to 6 zloty 20 groszy (that is, 20 zloty = 3 roubles). The silver content of the zloty of the Congress Kingdom of Poland was thus 2.7g, about 3 per cent less than before 1815 (World Coins 2004: 1025–1029).

The internal autonomy of the Kingdom of Poland was strongly reduced after the uprising of 1830, however, and the Polish coins started to be minted with dual inscriptions, in roubles as well as in zloty (this step was facilitated by the relatively simple proportionality between the two currency units). Finally, in 1841, after Russia had resumed the convertibility of its rouble banknotes to silver, the zloty was discontinued as a monetary unit and Poland was integrated to the Russian monetary system (Wójtowicz and Wójtowicz 2005: 139–140).

Finland, which had previously been part of Sweden, was annexed by the Russian Empire in 1809 after a war with Sweden. An autonomous Grand Duchy of Finland was established, with a commitment by the Russian Emperor to keep the old (Swedish) constitution, laws and privileges in force in the country. Formally, the Russian monetary system, based on the silver rouble, was introduced in Finland after the annexation by the Empire. In practice, however, money circulation in Finland remained largely Swedish. Swedish riksdaler-denominated notes continued to be used widely in Finland until 1840, when the Bank of Finland finally unified the monetary circulation in the country by replacing the Swedish notes by its own notes, denominated in and convertible to silver roubles. Later, in 1860, Finland obtained its own monetary unit, the markka, which was then defined as one-quarter of the silver rouble (and thus coincided exactly with the silver content of the French franc; see Pipping 1961).

We can observe the unity of the monetary systems of the region in their basis in the silver reichsthaler. A further interesting feature, which also testifies to the underlying unity of the monetary systems of the countries of the Baltic Sea area, is the similarity of the experience of the countries with the suspension of convertibility of banknotes after the Napoleonic Wars. (In Russia, the banknotes had been in practice inconvertible since the late 1780s.) Soon after the long period of wars was over, in 1815 the countries of the area managed to stabilise the value of their banknotes roughly, but only at rates considerably below par. A return to the silver convertibility of banknotes was achieved only later, but when it was done, the countries of the Baltic Sea area moved in close succession: Sweden resumed convertibility to silver in 1834, Denmark in 1838, Russia in 1839, Finland in 1840 and Norway in 1842.[4]

The development of the north European model of proto central banking

I now turn to examine the development of the proto central banks in the Baltic Sea region from the late eighteenth century until the mid nineteenth century, when their special characteristics started to disappear gradually. The focus is on the asset structure and organisation of these banks, as these are the aspects which are the most characteristic of the early North European models of (proto) central banking.

As discussed above, the roots of the particular features of the North European model of proto central banking can be traced to two sources of influence: the example of the great banks of exchange in Amsterdam and Hamburg, on the one hand, and the cameralist ideas of land banks (as in Steuart), on the other. Of course, the structure and activities of the proto central banks of the Baltic Sea area also reflected the underlying economic structure, its requirements and the kind of collateral which it could supply. It also reflects the interests of different power groups and political constituencies in the respective countries.

However, the development of the banking institutions was not simply passive accommodation to the demands of the real economy, or merely a reflection of rent seeking by the most powerful social groups (such as the landowning gentry). It is clear that there was also an attempt to stimulate the economic development of the countries, especially their agriculture and commerce. The proto central banks were planted as instruments of a kind of development policy, mostly based on imported ideas. There is little if any evidence, however, that these development motives for the establishment of public banks were fulfilled to any great extent. On the contrary, the economic takeoff of the region occurs only in the latter half of the nineteenth century, when the era of proto central banks was already largely over.

We will review the rise of the proto central banks in the countries in the region one by one, before analysing how the early north European model was ultimately abandoned.

Hamburg

Among the proto central banks of the Baltic Sea area, the Bank of Hamburg (Hamburger Bank) is a special case. On the one hand, its example was uniquely important for the development of other banks in the region. Its public ownership and its two-department structure were followed by most other bank projects in the Baltic Sea area. On the other hand, it was special also in its reach and purpose. It was the only one of the proto central banks to have a larger, regional impact extending throughout the whole Baltic Sea area, as it served as the indisputable financial hub for the whole region at least from the 1790s until the 1860s. It was also special in the sense that it did not issue banknotes, creating only a money of account. Because of its very good credit, bills drawn on Hamburg (by the customers of the private bankers of the city, and payable at the bank) were generally accepted means of payment in the whole Baltic Sea area. In this sense, it indirectly created an important means of payment for a larger area than the city itself (Sieveking 1933).

The Bank of Hamburg was established in 1619, soon after its 'older sister', the Bank of Amsterdam (Amsterdamsche Wisselbank). It was a public institution, controlled and guaranteed by the city of Hamburg and managed by trustees appointed from the merchants of the city (Soetbeer 1855: 90–97). Its purpose was to centralise the silver reserves of the Hamburg merchants and to operate an account transfer mechanism among its depositor clients. To enforce the position of the bank, it was ruled that bills of exchange payable in Hamburg were to be paid at the bank.

In textbooks, giro banks such as the banks of Amsterdam and Hamburg are sometimes presented as deposit banks only, which held 100 per cent reserves and operated a payment system based on those reserves. In fact, however, the Bank of Hamburg was divided into two departments from the start, the bank of exchange (wechsel-banco) and the loan bank (lehn-banco). The loan bank financed the City of Hamburg with long-term loans and the merchants of the city with short-term 'Lombard' credit, secured with deposits of silver or silver coin. The loans to the city treasury were, apparently, usually small in comparison to the total balance sheet of the bank, however (Sieveking 1934: 139–141).

Sweden

The Bank of Sweden (Sveriges Riksbank, formerly Riksens Ständers Bank) is well-known for Europe's first banknotes, issued in the 1660s by its predecessor, Stockholms Banco, which, however, soon went bankrupt and was nationalised. The organisation of the Bank of Sweden followed the model of the Bank of Hamburg in that it was divided into two separate departments, the bank of exchange (wäxel-banco) and the loan bank (låne-banco). The practical operations of these two departments were much less restricetd than in the case of the Bank of Hamburg, however.[5]

The bank of exchange did not just manage a deposit transfer system but also issued various kinds of receipts and transferable letters of credit which gradually evolved into fully fledged banknotes. By the mid eighteenth century, the issuing activity became the bank's most important source of funds. There was a period, however, from 1789 to 1803, when the State Debt Office of Sweden (Riksgäldskontoret) issued currency notes in amounts far greater than the Bank of Sweden notes, and effectively crowded out the latter. The reason why debt office notes were issued was the war against Russia in 1788–1790, which increased the financing needs of the state, and the Bank was not willing to comply. The debt office notes depreciated in relation to the bank's own notes until, in a stabilisation measure in1803, the debt office notes were placed under the responsibility of the Bank of Sweden for a reduced value (1 riksdaler in debt office notes was declared to be equivalent to two-thirds dalers banco). The debt office notes continued to circulate, however, until the silver convertibility of notes was resumed in Sweden in 1834 (Ahlström, 1989).

The forms of credit extended by the loan bank department of the Bank of Sweden were much more diverse than in Hamburg. The bank was allowed to lend against a variety of real collateral, such as precious metals, exportable merchandise and real estate. Of these, the real-estate loans were long term; on the other hand, the loans against the pledge of precious metals and mechandise were of less than one year's maturity. In practice, in the last decades of the eighteenth century, the loans on real estate were by far the predominant category of loans to the private sector, but these were often surpassed in magnitude by the bank's loans to the crown and crown enterprises (see Brisman 1931a: 121–135; Sveriges Riksbank 1931: 10–13).

From the start of the nineteenth century, the Bank of Sweden started to increase its short-term private lending through so-called discount offices (Brisman 1924: 17–60). These agencies were first only partly owned and funded by the Bank of Sweden, having private shareholders too, and issuing their own notes, but after they all failed around 1815 after the end of the war, the bank resumed the discount office activities on its own account by establishing semi-independent discount offices under its own umbrella and full ownership.

The purpose of the discount offices was to give short-term commercial and personal credit, of maturities of less than six months (in principle at least). In the early years of their activity, they also issued bonds and notes in their own name (however, drawn on their credit facility in the Bank of Sweden). The significant novelty was that the discount offices could grant loans against personal guarantee, so that pledging physical collateral was not necessary. Despite their name, the discount offices were not allowed to buy bills of exchange, however (Brisman 1931b: 120–144). Their name merely referred to the short-term nature of their lending and the practice of charging the interest on the loan at the time when the loan was disbursed, not when it was paid back.

In the course of the first half of the nineteenth century, the short-term lending of the Bank of Sweden through its discount offices reached a significant share of the total assets of the bank. However, the long-term real-estate loans lingered on as a major activity of the bank itself, as did the traditional export loans on the collateral of merchandise. The difference from the classical model of central banking is clearly visible in the facts that the actual discounting of bills was not practised, and that it was thought necessary to organise the short-term commercial lending separately from the bank itself, in discount offices under separate management from the Bank of Sweden, although financed by the latter (Brisman 1924: 22–30; Brisman 1931a: 117).

Denmark

Of all countries of the Baltic Sea area, Denmark's monetary history of the eighteenth and early nineteenth centuries is perhaps the most turbulent. Denmark was the only country in the area to experience a period of hyperinflation, and its financial system had to be completely reconstructed after the collapse ('state bankruptcy') of 1813.

The Copenhagen Assignat, Exchange and Loan Bank (Den Københavnske Assignations-, Veksel- og Laanebank), usually called the Kurantbank, was established in 1736 in order to support the development of the commercial sector. The bank was given the exclusive right to issue banknotes, assignats, which were denominated in Danish rigsdaler *courant* (whence the nickname of the bank), and which the bank was obliged to redeem with these silver coins at any time. The smallest banknote allowed was 10 rd. The notes were legal tender only in payments to the crown (such as taxes and customs duties).

According to its statutes, the Kurantbank could lend against a broad range of collateral, such as merchandise. The lending was constrained, in theory, to be short-term, that is less than six months' maturity. Most of the constraints which were initially intended to apply to the lending activities of the bank were eventually disregarded, however. Loans were in practice often renewed so they actually became long-term, and were given against real-estate collateral – sometimes even without collateral. By the 1760s, lending by the bank grew strongly and most of it went to the crown (Wilcke 1927: 322–344).

After the British navy attacked Copenhagen in 1807, and Denmark joined the war on the French side, the volume of banknotes put into circulation rapidly increased and their value started to decline. By December 1810, the banknotes were worth only 22 per cent of their nominal value in silver. In 1812–1813, hyperinflation ensued, and in 1813 the Kurantbank was finally closed. A comprehensive monetary and banking reform was enacted and a new monetary unit, the rigsbankdaler, was introduced.

A temporary institution, the State Bank (Rigsbank), was founded to issue and manage the new currency. The measures were extreme. The Rigsbank obtained, by decree, a primary mortgage of 6 per cent to all fixed property in Denmark, which the landowners, however, could redeem in silver. Moreover, the landowners owed annual interest at 6.5 per cent for the mortgages held by the Rigsbank (Svendsen and Hansen 1968: 87–115). The resulting asset structure of the Rigsbank was extraordinary. Not only was it an issuing bank based on land credit but these assets had been obtained by a compulsory levy. It was thus a kind of mixture of the Prussian type of a mortgage society – in the sense of compulsory mortgage – and the French revolutionary assignats (which were, of course, based on confiscated property).

The Rigsbank was only a temporary institution, and in 1818 a new central bank, the Danish National Bank (Danmarks Nationalbank, at first called Nationalbanken i Kjøbenhavn) was established. This bank was organised along the lines of the classical central banking model. It was a private corporation with a royal charter. Despite of its privileged position, including the monopoly right of note issue, the Danish National Bank was independent from the government.

For its initial assets and revenues, the National Bank acquired the forced mortgages of its predecessor, the Rigsbank. Although the bank was established with the classical, banking-school type of central bank in view, it was clear that, with its land-based asset structure inherited from the Rigsbank, it would take time to complete the transition to the classical model, especially as the bank had to conduct a deflationary monetary policy in order to stabilise the value of its banknotes. As a result, during the first two decades of its activity, most resources of the bank were devoted to withdrawing enough notes to ensure that their value was gradually brought to par with silver. This limitation of lending of course prolonged the land-based asset structure of the institution (Svendsen and Hansen 1968: 125–145).

Norway

Norway's central banking history resembles (and stems from) the Danish. The Bank of Norway (Norges Bank) was established in 1818, not long after the separation of Norway from Denmark. It was the bank of issue, inheriting the initial depreciated value of the banknotes of the Danish Rigsbank.

Even though its statutes had not explicitly provided for real-estate lending, in practice loans on mortgages were the clearly predominant form of credit for the Bank of Norway from the start and it turned out to be yet another land-based bank of issue in the region. As a justification for this, it was explained that lending on mortgages was more secure than bills of exchange – an old argument familiar from Steuart. Moreover, the Bank of Norway had to conduct a deflationary policy until convertiblitity of banknotes to speciedaler silver could finally be achieved in 1842. In these circumstances of restrictive policy, it was difficult to expand the lending activities of the bank to new areas (Rygg 1918: 231–241).

Almost all of the bank's lending was on real-estate mortgages in 1830, and ten years later, was still 84 per cent. Originally, one-quarter of the bank's funds had been reserved for discounting of bills, but this came to nothing in practice. The asset structure of the Bank of Norway remained mostly based on long-term loans on real collateral until the late 1850s (Klovland 2004: 208).

Prussia

In Prussia, the Royal Bank (Königliche Bank) was established in 1765 and soon obtained the right to issue banknotes. The head office was in Berlin. Characteristically for a north European proto central bank of the period, the bank was divided into two departments, an exchange bank (Giro-Banque) and a loan bank (Lehn-Banque). The exchange bank was to open transferable giro accounts deposits and issue banknotes against the deposit of coin. However, the exchange bank was not at all successful and even the banknote issues remained very small (Niebuhr 1854; Poschinger 1878: 131).

The loan-bank department of the Royal Bank was in turn divided into two departments, the discount office and the Lombard office. The discount office would discount short-term bills of exchange up to the maturity of two months, whereas the Lombard office would grant credit against collateral, which according to the statutes of 1766 could consist of gold, silver or jewels. The selection was thus a very narrow one, almost as in the Bank of Hamburg. Because of the modest success of the bank of exchange, most of the activities of the loan bank were financed by interest-bearing deposits (Niebuhr 1854: 189–196).

Despite the strict restrictions of lending in its original statutes, the Royal Bank soon expanded its lending to comprise long-term loans to government departments and, after 1794, also into mortgage credit. A large part of the mortgage credit of the Royal Bank was extended partly for political reasons to the parts of Poland which were annexed by Prussia in the partitions of 1793 and 1795. The investment to Polish mortgages and the associated real-estate boom in the conquered areas lasted for about a decade (Niebuhr 1854: 71–76). The outbreak in 1806 of the War of the Fourth Coalition against Napoleon, which ended in defeat for Prussia, caused a financial crisis and proved fatal for the Royal Bank, however. Large parts of its mortgage assets became non-performing and ultimately worthless. The bank had to stop payments and it was practically out of operation from late 1806 until 1817. Even after that, a very large part of its assets were in the process of being slowly liquidated and phased out (Poschinger 1878: 215–219).

The new activities of the Royal Bank after the war (from 1818) were much more cautious than before the war and lending grew only slowly. The bank only discounted bills of exchange and made Lombard loans on collateral, mainly on government paper and precious metals, but also on inventories of merchandise. Mortgage bonds, which had caused the bank large losses when the war broke out, were no longer accepted as collateral.

After the war, the paper money circulation in Prussia was mainly in the form of treasury notes, and the Royal Bank was not very active as a bank of issue. So, interest-bearing deposits continued to be its main source of funds. However, it issued some large-denomination cash notes (*Kassenscheine*) in the 1820s and until 1834, when the note circulation in Prussia was unified and taken completely over by the treasury (Poschinger 1878: 224–226). The issue function was only resumed by the bank in 1847, when the Royal Bank was converted to a new institution, the Prussian Bank (Preussische Bank), which was an issuing bank of the classical type (Poschinger 1879: 15–23; Ziegler 1993).

Russia

The Russian proto-central banking development can be considered to have begun with the simultaneous establishment in 1786 of two banking institutions, called the Assignat Bank and the State Loan Bank. Between themselves, these institutions, which, according to the imperial manifesto by which they were created, were to operate 'as a single entity', actually constituted a typical north European proto central bank. This entity issued banknotes and granted long-term loans on mortgages; moreover, it also gave large loans to the government which was in financial difficulty at the time because of a war with Turkey (PSZ 1830: chapters 13.219 and 16.407). The two-bank entity created in 1786 had some predecessors in Russia, in small-scale government lending offices and issuing of notes backed by copper (see Heller 1983: 33–43), but for practical purposes, founding of the two banking institutions, 'as a single entity', in 1786 marked the start of Russian proto central banking and created its general structure, which would remain almost intact until the 1860s.

After 1786, the amount of banknotes issued by the Assignat Bank increased by leaps and bounds, especially during the several wars which Russia either started or was drawn into. The convertibility of the assignats to metal had to be suspended and their value declined. In the spring of 1812, when Napoleon's invasion of Russia was imminent, the assignats were declared legal tender. This was done in a very particular way, however: they were to be received as legal tender for the value quoted in the St Petersburg bourse, instead of their nominal value. The silver rouble thus remained the legal unit of account and the basis of the monetary system, but assignats became the predominant means of payment, with a fluctuating value in terms of the legal unit of account. It seems likely that this arrangement, which amounted to a kind of dual standard, alleviated the harmful effects of inflation and also weakened the effects of Gresham's law in Russia, thus contributing to the relative durability of the rather complex monetary system of the country in the following decades (Zieliński 1898).

The volume of assignats peaked during Napoleon's invasion of Russia. In 1815, there were 825 million roubles of assignats in circulation. At the same time, their value bottomed out, the assignat rouble being quoted in the St Petersburg bourse as only 20 per cent of the silver rouble. Despite the decline in their value, the total stock of assignats was still worth more than the whole Bank of England circulation at the time.[6]

The activities of the State Loan Bank were broadly typical of an agricultural mortgage bank. It extended 20-year loans to the landowning nobility against the collateral of their land. A particular tsarist Russian speciality was that, as collateral, the property was evaluated according to the number of peasants (serfs) attached to it.[7] To finance its activities, the loan bank took sight deposits, which grew to considerable amounts, especially in the 1850s, and was also financed by the other parts of the state banking system (the Assignat Bank and the State Commercial Bank, of which see below).

The Russian government made attempts to develop short-term commercial credit as well. Discount offices were established in the major Russian ports in 1797, as subsidiaries of the Assignat Bank, to finance Russian merchants, but their activities remained relatively insignificant. The volume of commercial credit started to grow only after 1817, when the discount offices were converted into a State Commercial Bank. This institution took deposits and discounted bills of exchange, and made short-term Lombard loans against the collateral of commercial inventories. However, the volume of credit extended by the Commercial Bank remained quite small compared to the long-term lending by the State Loan Bank, and in fact, the State Commercial Bank transferred a large part of its deposits to the latter for use in agricultural mortgage lending. In practice, then, the state banking institutions of Russia in that period were not really separate from each other but constituted a closely integrated system (Heller 1983).

The structure of the Russian proto-central banking system thus displays all of the main features typical of the early north European central banking model: state ownership and control, emphasis on long-term mortgage credit financed by issuing banknotes (and taking liquid deposits) and a structure in which the issue function and the lending function were formally, but only formally, separated to different departments. The Russian and the Swedish cases are remarkably similar to each other in that both added a third component to the state banking system to finance commercial activities with short-term loans. In the case of Sweden, this was constituted by the discount offices, and in the Russian case, the State Commercial Bank. In both cases, the commercial part of the system was financially closely connected with the bank of issue and the loan bank, however.

Despite the depreciation of the notes, the Russian monetary system did not collapse and the value of the assignat rouble was eventually stabilised. Finance minister Gurev managed first to reduce the amount of assignats in circulation by about 28 per cent by 1823. Thereafter, Count Kankrin, Gurev's successor, completely stabilised the volume of the assignat stock for 20 years. The value of the notes also stabilised to a level of about 27 per cent of the silver rouble (Zieliński 1898; Pintner 1967: 190–197). It might be argued that Kankrin's policy was perhaps the first successful application of quantity theory principles, in the monetarist fashion, to monetary policy.

In 1843, the Russian government completed a monetary reform with the aim of achieving a system in which banknotes would be convertible to metal. Assignats were first made convertible to new silver-backed banknotes (so-called 'credit roubles') issued by the Treasury and then withdrawn from circulation with the conversion rate of 1 silver rouble to 3.5 assignat roubles. As part of the same reform, the old Assignat Bank was converted to the State Credit Note Bureau, which was to assume all the duties and obligations of the former Assignat Bank as the institution of issue in Russia (Pintner 1967: 215; Levicheva 2004: 24–30). The silver reform of 1839–1843 stabilised the Russian monetary system for more than a decade, until the Crimean War caused a crisis which was to prove fatal to the old state-owned banking system of the country and lead to its replacement with a new and more modern one (Zieliński 1898: 32–43).

Finland

The Bank of Finland (whose original name in Swedish was 'Växel- Låne- och Depositions Contoiret in Storfurstendömet Finland', meaning The Exchange, Loan and Deposit Office in the Grand Duchy of Finland) was established in 1811, after the country had been politically separated from Sweden and annexed by Russia, as a Grand Duchy with its own laws and internal administration, and the Russian Emperor as the Grand Duke.

The original tasks of the bank were to provide for the exchange of Russian banknotes and to issue its own small-denomination notes in order to alleviate the shortage of means of payment in the country (almost all silver had disappeared from circulation after both Swedish and Russian banknotes had depreciated during the war). The lending activities of the bank were intended to help Finnish nationals to redeem their debts to Sweden, as well as to promote 'agriculture, commerce and other means of livelihood'. It was also hoped that the bank could help drive out the Swedish money still circulating in Finland, but in this it was not completely successful until 1840 (Schybergson 1914: 24–34, 85–94).

The bank was subordinate to the finance department of the government, which also supplied its starting capital and controlled its most important decisions. Characteristically for a north European public bank at the time, the bank was divided into two departments, called funds, which, however, were under same management. The original fund, consisting of the bank's own capital and retained profits, was to be used for long-term mortgage lending on real estate. The term of these loans was 20 years. The other fund, which was called the banknotes fund, was financed by the bank's own note issue. Apart from cash reserves (originally the reserves[8] were required to cover at least half of the notes in circulation), this fund was to be used for short-term lending, with maturities from six months to one year. Priority was to be given for loans to manufacturers, against the pledge of their unsold inventories.

In practice, the long-term real-estate loans constituted the largest share of the bank's lending until the 1840s when, as a consequence of a monetary reform, the banknote circulation grew rapidly and increased resources thus became available for shorter-term lending. But even then, most of this shorter-term lending was against tangible collateral such as merchandise. Bills of exchange were not mentioned in the original statutes and the bank did not discount any for almost three decades after its establishment (Pipping 1961: tables 2, 3 and 5).

Poland

Bank of Poland (Bank Polski) was founded in 1828 as a part of the financial reconstruction of the Kingdom of Poland, created by the Congress of Vienna in 1815 as a state with its own constitution; however, belonging to the Russian empire, with the Emperor as its king. The Bank of Poland was, from its founding, intimately connected with the other important government-sponsored banking institution in the country, the Land Credit Society (Towarzystwo

Kredytow Ziemskie) founded in 1825. When Bank Polski, the national bank of issue, was founded, as a state institution, half of its capital of 20 million zloty was paid in the form of mortgage bonds of the Polish Land Credit society, 'drawn upon national wealth' (Radziszewski 1910: 508).

The Polish Land Credit society followed a model of a state-chartered mortgage association which was originally a Prussian invention. The idea was to pool the real estates of all landed debtors to a form a collateral pool against which very secure, and hopefully liquid, bonds could be issued for the mutual benefit of all landowners. In some provinces, joining the credit societies (*Landschaften*, in German) was compulsory for all landed gentry, in some areas only those who wished to obtain loans had to join. The first such institution was actually not established in the Baltic Sea basin, but in the province of Silesia (today in south-western Poland) in 1770. However, soon the focus turned to the Baltic shores. Land-credit societies were founded by royal decrees for Prussian Pomerania (1781), West Prussia (1787) and in 1788, East Prussia (Poschinger 1878: 153–154). The Polish Land Credit Society was founded in 1825 (Jasiukowicz 1911: 31–47).

The tasks of the Bank of Poland included the management of the debt which the new kingdom owed to foreign countries and foreign nationals, as well as to support 'the expansion of credit, trade, and national industry' (Radziszewski 1910: 507). The bank could issue banknotes, convertible to silver, up to the value of its own capital (this indicates that the founders, such as Count Drucki-Lubecki, the finance minister of the kingdom, believed in the 'credit theory' of banks of issue, according to which the value – 'credit' – of the banknotes was mainly dependent on the solvency of the issuing bank, as opposed to its liquidity in terms of reserves. See Andréen 1956 for a discussion of these doctrines in the Swedish context). According to its statutes, the Bank of Poland could accept transferable deposits, as well as time deposits, and make loans. It could lend against the security of mortgage bonds (issued by the Land Credit Society), government paper, or the pledge of tangible collateral (such as agricultural products, manufactured articles and other valuables). It could also discount bills of exchange. In practice, the bills of exchange remained a very small part of the balance sheet until the 1860s (according to the balance sheets published in Radziszewski 1910: 522–530).

Livonia

In Riga, Livonia, a short-term lending institution, the Riga Discount Office (Rigische Diskontokasse) was established in 1794 and operated in connection with, and under the guarantee of, a municipal loan fund owned by the Great Guild of the merchants of Riga. In was thus a municipal institution, whose legal status resembled that of the Bank of Hamburg. In 1819, the Diskontokasse obtained some features of an issuing bank as it started to issue cash notes. These cash notes were of rather large denominations, usable mainly in the wholesale trade within the city, as they were intended to alleviate the shortage of means of payment among the merchant community. The Riga Discount Office was entitled to issue these cash notes to twice the value of its own capital. The notes were issued against the collateral of short-term deposit of different securities, such as the mortgage bonds of the Livonian mortgage credit society (called the Livonian Credit System).[9] The obvious purpose of this arrangement was to monetise otherwise illiquid assets, such as land. In practice, the note circulation of the Rigische Diskontokasse remained rather limited, however (Stieda 1909; Engelhardt 1902).

The transition to classical central banking

The north European proto central banks were phased out or transformed around the mid nineteenth century by banking and monetary reforms in countries of the region. There was a lot of country-specific variety in the timing and form of this change, but the direction was the same throughout the whole Baltic Sea area. It was the trend towards the English (or French) model of an independent central bank, mostly concentrating on the discounting of bills of exchange.

In *Prussia*, the Royal Bank was converted to the Prussian Bank (Preussische Bank) by the bank ordinance of 1846. The reason for the reform was that the supply of money, which in Prussia at that point was based on notes issued by the treasury, was seen as too inflexible. Therefore, it was decided to revert to the more conventional system in which notes were issued by a state bank. According to the first paragraph of its statutes, the objective of the Prussian Bank was 'to promote money circulation, to make capital available, to support trade and industry, and to prevent an excessive increase in the interest rate'. As pointed out by Ziegler (1993), the statutes were designed to make the money supply more responsive to the demand for money and credit, and followed the prescriptions of the English Banking School to some extent. Actually, the new system resembled in many respects that of the Banque de France. Silver specie and bills of exchange were now the preferred types of cover for banknotes; in practice, too, the bills of exchange became the predominant form of credit granted by the Prussian Bank (Poschinger 1878: 229–233; Poschinger 1879: 15–48). In 1856, all remaining state paper money in Prussia was finally converted to banknotes of the Prussian Bank.

The Prussian Bank was to be the core of the future German State Bank, the Reichsbank, which was established in 1873 after German unification. As part of the unification of the monetary system, other public banks in Germany were then merged into the Reichsbank. One of the proto central banks which were merged in the Reichsbank in 1875 was the old Bank of *Hamburg*. The Bank of Hamburg had suffered a severe blow in the great commercial crisis of 1857, which hit Hamburg especially hard. A large part of the Hamburg banking houses had had to stop payments, and the Bank of Hamburg itself was criticised for its inability to assist in the liquidity crisis. After that, according to Sieveking, the demands for banking reform in Hamburg could no longer be suppressed. It was obviously felt that the liquidity crisis had proven that the Hamburg application of the currency principle was too inflexible, in the same way as that principle turned out to be unhelpful in the United Kingdom during the great banking crises of the nineteenth century. Although the Bank of Hamburg begun to discount bills of exchange (in a very small scale), in 1856, it was inevitably swept away as an institution by German monetary union and the emergence of private commercial banks (Sieveking 1933: 103–110).

The *Danish* National Bank was fashioned in a 'classical' way from its start in 1818, as far as its new business was considered. The Danish National Bank was also by its form a private company in the manner of the Bank of England and the Banque de France. However, the Danish National Bank, by the act of its foundation, had acquired the mortgage assets and the banknote liabilities of its predecessor, the Rigsbank. In the beginning these constituted the largest part of the new bank's balance sheet and could be phased out only very gradually. Another challenge was that in 1818, the banknote liabilities of the bank stood about 25 per cent below their par value in silver. A long period of transition followed, during which the Danish National Bank conducted a restrictive monetary policy until the value of banknotes rose to par with silver and the mortgage debt had been paid off. These goals were achieved by about 1835, whereafter the National Bank could operate along the lines of a classically constituted central bank (Svendsen and Hansen 1968: 131–134, 220–222).

In *Norway*, an independent mortgage bank was established in 1852, however, and this made it easier for the Bank of Norway to refocus its lending from mortgages (as it had been) to the discounting of bills. The international crisis of 1847 had already demonstrated that the asset structure of the Bank of Norway of that time, still mostly consisting of real-estate mortgages, was not well-suited to a bank of issue. It prevented the bank from using the discount rate as an instrument to regulate the reserve flows and the amount of banknotes in circulation. Also, it made the bank's liquidity position very vulnerable. According to Rygg, the reduction of mortgage-based lending was resisted by the parliament, however. The gradual phasing out of the long-term mortgage loans and the growth of the bills of exchange portfolio took a long time, roughly until Norway joined the gold standard in 1873 (Rygg 1918: 231–237; Rygg 1954: 113–116).

In *Sweden*, the transition from proto central banking to the classical model of central banking was stepwise and took a long time. In the course of the 1860s, loans on fixed property, which were no longer so important, were phased out of the balance sheet of the Bank of Sweden. At the same time, the short-term loans, made through the autonomous discount offices but financed by the Bank of Sweden, were growing in importance.

Finally, steps were taken which recognised the discounting of bills as the normal activity of the Bank of Sweden as a bank of issue. In 1864, the bank itself was allowed to start to discount bills of exchange and the former discount offices were merged into the bank. At first, however, the newly created discount department remained under separate management from the rest of the bank (until 1874). Broadly speaking, it can be said that, in Sweden, the transition to classical central banking was completed almost simultaneously with the adoption of the gold standard (in 1873). However, the share of bills of exchange in the bank's portfolio grew only gradually, so that it did not emerge as the clearly biggest asset category in the balance sheet of the Bank of Sweden before the 1880s (Davidson 1931).

In *Russia*, the old state banking system ran into insurmountable difficulties soon after the international financial crisis of 1857. In November 1857, the exchange rate of the rouble collapsed (the rouble had been floating for some years, after its convertibility to silver had been suspended during the Crimean War), and in the following spring deposits started to flow out of the state banks. The situation was critical, which is apparent from the fact that during the year 1859 alone, deposits in the state banks were down by two-thirds. The old Russian banking system was in danger of actually collapsing. In an attempt to improve the banks' liquidity, all new lending against fixed property was halted and any rescheduling of existing loans was forbidden. Sight deposits were converted to perpetual bonds issued to depositors. As if to make the situation even more complicated, this occurred at the same time as the government was preparing for a huge land reform, the great emancipation of the serfs (Hoch 1991). This reform completely transformed the collateral basis of the Russian banking system, which had developed in the conditions of the serf economy.

The bank reform decided in 1860, which marked an attempt to move to the classical central banking model *à la* Banque de France, merged the former state banking institutions into a new central bank, called the State Bank of the Russian Empire (Gosudarstvennyi Bank Rossiskoi Imperii). This bank succeeded the former State Commercial Bank, the State Loan Bank and the State Credit Note Bureau (which had earlier, in 1843, succeeded the old Assignat Bank), acquiring their assets and obligations (PSZ 1862: chapter 35.847; Zieliński 1898).

The new Russian State Bank was organised along more classical lines than the previous central banking system of the country had been. In particular, the structure of private credit allowed to the bank was completely changed. Land credit on mortgages, previously so important, was no longer permitted. Instead, the bank could extend credit to private parties by discounting bills of exchange of less than six months' maturity. It could also make short-term loans against security of precious metals, or government paper (or private bonds or shares guaranteed by the government). In the typical early north European fashion, it could also lend against the pledge of merchandise, i.e. inventories of export and import goods (Levicheva 2004: 75–106, 173–201).

The transition from agricultural mortgages to short-term commercial credit marked a notable change in the Russian credit policy, since 90 per cent of the lending of the previous state banking institutions had been in agricultural mortgages (Zieliński 1898). On the other hand, for decades after the reform, the government, not the private sector, remained the major debtor of the State Bank. This obviously reduced the significance of the change of the lending doctrine. In many ways, the bank remained 'little more than a treasury bureau' (Conant 1915: 260).

The dependence of the bank on the treasury is apparent from the fact that, at this stage, Russian banknotes remained formally the liability of the Russian treasury, and the State Bank merely redeemed and exchanged them on the account of the treasury. The volume of the notes over and above their metallic cover was simply entered in the balance sheet of the bank as treasury debt. This arrangement was continued until the financial position of the Russian government was improved, and its debt to the central bank was reduced, in the 1890s during the financial administration of Count Witte (Parker Willis 1897).

A major attempt to restore the convertibility of the rouble banknotes to silver, at par, was made soon after the new central bank was established. This failed, however, in late 1863 after a loss of public confidence at least partly due to the Polish uprising and the possibility of its escalation into a European war (Hayward 1973: 165–176). Thereafter, the Russian banknotes remained inconvertible to metal until the adoption of the gold standard in 1897.

In *Poland*, the transition towards classical central banking occurred as part of the process of integrating the Bank of Poland into the Russian central banking system. This started soon after the uprising of 1863.

According to Wójtowicz and Wójtowicz (2005: 139–141), the Bank of Poland refocused its activities on the discounting of bills of exchange in 1864. This can be interpreted as a first step towards 'modernisation', i.e. towards the classical central banking model. In 1870, the control of the Bank of Poland was taken by the Russian ministry of finance and its right to issue banknotes was abolished. Also the right to extend long-term loans was discontinued. The liquidation of the Bank of Poland was initiated in 1885 and in the run-up to the Russian gold standard reform, the Bank of Poland was finally merged with the State Bank of the Russian Empire in 1894. In Poland, as in the other parts of the Empire, the State Bank concentrated its activities on discounting of bills of exchange (Schön 1928: 80–82).

In the Baltic province of *Livonia*, the only locally administered public institution with some resemblance to a bank of issue was the Riga Discount Office, as was discussed above. Its fate was to turn into a normal commercial bank. Its issuing function had never been of a very significant scale. After 1860, when the Russian State Bank was established, and the local branch of the Russian State Commercial Bank became the Riga branch of the State Bank, the traditional functions of the Riga Discount Office became increasingly superfluous. The institution had to be reformed and modernised to fit in its new environment. In 1873, the Riga Discount Office was finally converted into a municipally owned commercial bank, Rigaer Stadt-Diskontobank (Stieda 1909: 149–157, 459).

Whereas the central banking systems of Poland and Livonia were ultimately unified with the central banking structure of the Russian Empire, the development in *Finland* took a different direction. Despite the position of Finland as a part of the Empire, the transition to the classical model of central banking happened on a local basis. The development of the Bank of Finland, initially a quite primitive proto central bank, towards classical operating principles started slowly in 1840, when the discounting of bills of exchange was allowed to it (Schybergson 1914: 96–102). Until that point, long-term agricultural credit on mortgages had been the predominant form of lending by the bank. The share of commercial credit in the activities of the Bank of Finland started to grow, especially in the decade after the end of the Crimean War in 1856. In his study, Pipping (1961: 529) sets the watershed in the year 1859. However, initially the most important form of commercial credit was against the pledge of merchandise, i.e. financing inventories of export goods. The bills of exchange became clearly predominant as a form of credit for the Bank of Finland quite late, in fact, only after Finland joined the gold standard in 1878, after Sweden but before Russia.[10]

In terms of its position vis-à-vis the government, the Bank of Finland was made independent of the economic department of the government in 1863, when it was handed over to the care and responsibility of the Diet (the four-chamber parliament of the Grand Duchy of Finland). This change was made in order to observe the Swedish constitution, which the Russian Emperors had pledged to keep in force in Finland. It also strengthened the position of the Bank vis-à-vis the government. However, it should be noted that, even before this change, the Bank of Finland had not usually given credit to the government so that this increase of institutional independence did not cause a change in the lending policy of the bank (see e.g. Pipping 1961: 484–485).

Conclusions

Above, I have sought to demonstrate some remarkable characteristic similarities of the development of central banking in the area of the Baltic Sea basin in the century before the adoption of the gold standard. We can see how there existed a north European model of early central banking (proto central banking is actually a more appropriate term, because the banking system around these early public banks was mostly quite undeveloped – Hamburg excepted). The north European model can be characterised especially by its reliance on real collateral (land or merchandise), as opposed to bills of exchange which are the preferred type of lending according to the real bills doctrine followed by the classical central banking model. The north European model emphasised solidity and safety (identified with tangibility) of its collateral, whereas the classical model, exemplified by the Bank of England and the Banque de France, put the greatest weight on the liquidity of the collateral.

Another characteristic feature of the north European model was the institutional separation of the different functions to different departments, funds, or even to closely linked separate banks. This was presumably in order to maintain confidence on the part of the general public, that the currency was not going to be over-issued and its value jeopardised. The third characteristic feature of the north European proto central banks is the typically public ownership and control of the banking institutions (as opposed to the formally private corporation which was typical for the classical model of central banking).

It is difficult to pinpoint, with certainty, any single reason which caused the transition from proto central banking to the classical central banking era in the Baltic Sea area. Broadly speaking, this transition took place during the latter half of the nineteenth century, with Germany and the Scandinavian countries proceeding fastest and Russia slowest. But why did this change happen? There are several alternative explanations. The old model failed clearly and spectacularly only in Russia, where financial problems created by the Crimean War (and the financial excesses of the railroad boom after that, which I have not had the space to discuss here) were the proximate reasons for the failure. Of course, the previous Russian mortgage system, underlying the old state banking institutions, was unsustainable and incompatible as such with the emancipation of the serfs.

Among the hypothetical reasons which may have caused the transition to classical central banking in the area, one might propose the following:

- industrialisation and foreign trade liberalisation created new types of collateral, and increased the supply of bills of exchange suitable for the backing of banknote issues. As a result, transition of the classical model became *possible*;
- the political influence of the industrialists and merchants increased at the expense of landowners, a change which redirected the credit policies of state-run credit institutions. This may have triggered a *change in the objectives* of financial policy;
- economic liberalism caused the governments of northern Europe to adopt a less interventionist approach to financial policy, which meant increasing *reluctance* to involve themselves in banking;
- the rise of the private banking sector (and thus the transition to a two-level banking system) made the land-based proto central banks more or less *redundant*;
- the transition to the gold standard and financial integration with London and Paris, as the hubs of the international gold standard, made it *necessary* to emulate the central banking arrangements in these centres, lest the competitiveness of the countries in the international capital market suffer.

It is not possible here to test and discriminate between these (or any other) alternative historical explanations for the change in the central banking landscape of the Baltic Sea area after about 1850. What is evident, however, is that by the final decades of the century, the real bills doctrine had become the universally accepted theory of how banks of issue should be designed, and was to remain so at least until the Great Depression and even later in many countries. It is also evident that the idea of issuing banks based on long-term mortgage credit was seen as outdated by the middle of the nineteenth century.

From today's perspective, the issue of land-based banks of issue vs. the real bills doctrine might seem remote and irrelevant. In monetary theory, the focus has in recent decades been on the supply of reserves, and (what is actually the same thing) on the interest rate policy in terms of some risk-free interest rate. This approach has naturally pushed the older issue of acceptable collateral (or, 'eligible paper') to the background in terms of theoretical research. In practice, however, the central banks of today also pay great attention to their collateral policy. How do they approach the question of security vs. liquidity in their collateral policies, the question which was central in the debates of the eighteenth and nineteenth centuries?

In the practice of central banking, the real bills doctrine in its original form has given way to other principles of central bank collateral choice. Instead of bills of exchange, securities of various kinds are the dominant types of collateral in central banks. It could not be otherwise, of course, as the bill of exchange has lost its former position as an instrument of commercial credit in the course of the last half a century. Open market operations have also replaced the discount window as the main form of central bank credit. What remains of the discount window are the standing credit facilities maintained by central banks to the benefit of commercial banks, but the amount of credit extended through these facilities is now typically small, in normal circumstances, compared to the amount of credit extended through open market operations. The assets accepted as collateral for the credit extended through the standing facilities may or may not be the same as those that are eligible as collateral in open market operations.

The Eurosystem, for example, has a broad list of eligible collateral, recently harmonised across the euro area, which now includes bank loans in addition to tradeable securities of various sorts (the bills of exchange have vanished, of course). In the Eurosystem, the same single list of collateral applies to market operations and to discount window lending through the liquidity credit facility. The Fed, by contrast, distinguishes between what material is used in open market operations (marketable government paper), and what is accepted as collateral at the discount window (ECB 2007).

Today's version of the real bills doctrine might be the idea that central banks should accept only liquid, marketable assets as collateral in their credit operations or outright purchases. That rule is generally followed, but not without exceptions. In addition to marketable securities, the ECB also accepts as collateral some non-marketable credit claims (bank loans) in both its market (repurchase) operations and its liquidity credit facility. The Fed policy has been to accept non-marketable assets only at the discount window but not in its open market operations.

From the theoretical point of view, of course, the trade off between solidity and liquidity of collateral can only arise because of imperfections in the financial markets: in perfect markets, good (secure) collateral is always also liquid. However, the *raison d'etre* of central banks lies, of course, precisely in the fact that financial markets are *not* perfect and the central bank must influence the liquidity creation in the economy in various ways. Interest-rate policy is all about influencing the price of liquidity. On the other hand, central banks are justifiably reluctant to interfere with the pricing of risks in the financial markets, at least in normal times. However, market imperfections are more important in times of distress (as seen after August 2007) than in normal times, and then the demarcation line between the pricing of risk and the pricing of liquidity becomes less obvious.

How should this be taken into account in the design of the collateral policy of central banks? Is this an argument for distinguishing between the kind of collateral accepted in normal steering operations, on the one hand, and at the discount window, on the other? It is evident that these questions continue to be at the heart of the design of central bank policy in pursuit of financial and monetary stability. As my survey of the early north European model of central banking has shown, the issue of the appropriate collateral policy for central banks is not only relevant today, but is also one of the oldest issues in the theory and practice of central banking.

Notes

1 There had been a land-bank proposal in England, competing with the bill-based alternative of the Bank of England, in the late seventeenth century, but it was not adopted, see Murphy (1997: 50–51).

2 For this reason, von Justi thinks it necessary that an insurance institution should be established to operate in connection with the bank (see Justi 1760: 620–635).

3 Later, when the metric system was introduced in 1857, the Graumann standard used in the Zollverein was redefined by specifying that 30 thalers should be minted from 500 g of fine silver. This was practically equivalent to the previous definition.

4 Cf. Brisman (1931a) for Sweden; Svendsen and Hansen (1968) for Denmark; Pintner (1967) for Russia; Pipping (1961) for Finland; and Rygg (1918) for Norway.

5 Heckscher (1934) has shown that the Bank of Amsterdam was used as an example when Stockholms Banco was founded; it is, however, apparent that the structure of the Swedish bank even more closely resembles that of the Bank of Hamburg.

6 Bank of England note circulation in 1815 was £26 million (cf. Bank of England 1967) and the note circulation of the Russian Assignat Bank, converted to pounds sterling was £36 million. This results from applying to the sum of 825 million assignat roubles an exchange rate of 23 roubles to the pound. According to Zieliński (1898: 10), the price of assignats was quoted at approximately 11 pence sterling at the time.

7 This regulation in the statutes of the bank, according to which registered serfs entitled the landowner to cheap credit from the Loan Bank, was to give rise to the brilliant contemporary satire by Nikolai Gogol, *Dead Souls* (1842).

8 The first statutes are silent on the kind of assets which would qualify as reserves. In practice, the reserve consisted of Russian banknotes (assignats) and, later, increasingly of silver.

9 Mortgage institutions of the Prussian type were established both Livonia and Estonia in the beginning of the nineteenth century. In the imperial decree of 1802 allowing the establishment of the Baltic mortgage societies, it was noted, to justify the measure, that the nobility of these provinces had not been able to take advantage of the credit extended by the state banks to other parts of the Russian empire.

10 Compare tables 3 and 5 in Pipping (1961) with table 3 in Pipping (1969).

References

Ahlström, G. (1989) Riksgäldskontoret och Sveriges statsskuld före 1850-talet. In E. Dahmén (ed.), *Upplåning och utveckling*. Stockholm: Allmänna Förlaget, pp. 91–134.

Andréen, P.G. (1956) Det svenska 1700-talets syn på banksedlar och pappersmynt. *Historisk tidskrift*, 76 (1), 9–34.

Bank of England (1967) Bank of England Liabilities and Assets: 1696 Onwards. *Bank of England Quarterly Bulletin*, 7 (2), 159–163.

Blanchard, I. (1989) *Russia's 'Age of Silver'. Precious-Metal Production and Economic Growth in the Eighteenth Century*. London and New York: Routledge.

Brisman, S. (1924) *Sveriges affärsbanker. Grundläggningstiden.* Stockholm: Svenska Bankföreningen.

Brisman, S. (1931a) Tiden 1803–1834. In *Sveriges Riksbank 1668–1924. Bankens tillkomst och verksamhet.* Stockholm: P.A. Norstedt & Söner, pp. 1–163.

Brisman, S. (1931b) Den stora reformperioden 1860–1904. In *Sveriges Riksbank 1668–1924. Bankens tillkomst och verksamhet.* Stockholm: P.A. Norstedt & Söner, pp. 1–226.

Buchholtz, A. (1899) *Geschichte der Juden in Riga.* Riga: Kümmel.

Cannan, E. (1925) *The Paper Pound of 1797–1821. A Reprint of the Bullion Report.* London: P.S. King & Son (1969 reprint, London: Frank Cass).

Capie, F., C. Goodhart and N. Schnadt (1994) The Development of Central Banking. In F. Capie, C. Goodhart and S. Fischer (eds), *The Future of Central Banking.* Cambridge: Cambridge University Press, pp. 1–231.

Conant, C. (1915) *A History of Modern Banks of Issue.* New York: Putnam's Sons.

Davidson, D. (1931) Tiden 1834–1860. In *Sveriges Riksbank 1668–1924. Bankens tillkomst och verksamhet.* Stockholm: P.A. Norstedt & Söner, pp. 1–232.

Dillen, J.G. van (1934) The Bank of Amsterdam. In J.G. van Dillen (ed.), *History of the Principal Public Banks.* The Hague: Martinus Nijhoff (1964 reprint, London: Frank Cass), pp. 79–124.

ECB (2007) The Collateral Frameworks of the Federal Reserve System, The Bank of Japan and the Eurosystem. *ECB Monthly Bulletin,* 10.

Engelhardt, Hermann (1902) *Zur Geschichte der Livländischen adeligen Güterkreditsozietät.* Riga: W.F. Häcker.

Friedman, M. and A. Schwartz (1963) *A Monetary History of the United States, 1867–1960.* Princeton, NJ: Princeton University Press.

Hayward, O. (1973) *Official Russian Policies Concerning Industrialization During the Finance Ministry of M. Kh. Reutern 1862–1878.* Unpublished PhD thesis, University of Wisconsin.

Heckscher, E. (1934) The Bank of Sweden in its Connection with the Bank of Amsterdam. In J.G. van Dillen (ed.), *History of the Principal Public Banks.* The Hague: Martinus Nijhoff (1964 reprint, London: Frank Cass), pp. 161–200.

Heckscher, E. (1941) *De svenska penning-, vikt- och måttsystemen. En historisk översikt.* Publikationer utgivna av Historielärarnas Förening I. Stockholm: P.A. Nordstedt & Söner.

Heller, K. (1983) *Die Geld-und Kreditpolitik des Russischen Reiches in der Zeit der Assignaten (1768–1839/43).* Wiesbaden: Franz Steiner.

Hoch, S.L. (1991) The Banking Crisis, Peasant Reform, and Economic Development in Russia, 1857–1861. *The American Historical Review,* 96 (3), 795–820.

Horsefield, J.K. (1944) The Origins of the Bank Charter Act, 1844. *Economica,* New Series, 11 (44), 180–189.

Humphrey, T. (1982) The Real Bills Doctrine. *Federal Reserve Bank of Richmond Economic Review,* 68 (5), 3–13.

Jasiukowicz, S. (1911) *Der landschaftliche Kreditverein im Königreich Polen 1825–1910.* München: Wolff & Sohn.

Justi, J.H.G. von (1760) *Die Grundfeste zu der Macht und Glückseeligkeit der Staaten; oder ausführliche Vorstellung der gesamten Policey-Wissenschaft. Erster Band.* Königsberg: J.H. Hartungs Erben (1965 reprint, Aalen: Scientia).

Kindleberger, C.P. (1984) *A Financial History of Western Europe.* New York: Oxford University Press.

Kirby, D. (1995) *The Baltic World 1772–1993, Europe's Northern Periphery in an Age of Change*. London: Longman.

Kirby, D. and M.-L. Hinkkanen (2000) *The Baltic and the North Seas*. London: Routledge.

Klovland, J.T. (2004) Monetary Aggregates in Norway 1819–2003. In Ø. Eitrheim, J.T. Klovland and J.F. Qvigstad (eds), *Historical Monetary Statistics for Norway 1819–2003*. Norges Bank Occasional Papers, No. 35. Oslo: Norges Bank, pp. 181–240.

Kruse, J.E. (1782) *Allgemeiner und besonders Hamburgischer Kontorist*. Hamburg.

Law, J. (1705) *Money and Trade Considered. With A Proposal For Supplying The Nation With Money*. Edinburgh: Anderson (1966 reprint, New York: Augustus Kelley).

Levicheva, I.N. (2004) Stanovlenie i razvitie Gosudarstvennogo banka. In Yu.A. Petrov (ed.), *Iz istorii gosudarstvennoj kreditnoj sistemy Rossii*. Moscow: Tsentralnyj bank Rossijskoj Federatsii, pp. 8–74.

Meltzer, A. (2003) *A History of the Federal Reserve. Volume I: 1913–1951*. Chicago, IL: The University of Chicago Press.

Murphy, A.E. (1997) *John Law, Economic Theorist and Policy-Maker*. Oxford: Clarendon Press.

Niebuhr, M. von (1854) *Geschichte der Königlichen Bank in Berlin*. Berlin: Decker (1971 reprint, Glashütten: Detlev Auermann).

Oddy, J.J. (1807) *European Commerce. Vols. I-II*. Philadelphia, PA: J. Humphreys.

PSZ (1830) *Polnoe sobranie zakonov Rossiiskoi imperii s 1649 goda. Tom XVIII. 1767–1769*. St Petersburg.

PSZ (1862) *Polnoe sobranie zakonov Rossiiskoi imperii s 1649 goda. Sobranije vrotoje. Tom XXXV. Otdelenije pervoje 1860*. St Petersburg.

Parker Willis, H. (1897) Monetary Reform in Russia. *The Journal of Political Economy*, 5 (3), 277–315.

Pintner, W.M. (1967) *Russian Economic Policy under Nicholas I*. Ithaca, NY: Cornell University Press.

Pipping, H. (1961) *Paperiruplasta kultamarkkaan. Suomen Pankki 1811–1877*. Helsinki: Suomen Pankki.

Pipping, H. (1969) *Kultakannan turvissa. Suomen Pankki 1878–1914*. Helsinki: Suomen Pankki.

Poschinger, H. von (1878) *Bankwesen und Bankpolitik in Preussen. Erster Band*. Berlin: Julius Springer.

Poschinger, H. von (1879) *Bankwesen und Bankpolitik in Preussen. Zweiter Band*. Berlin: Julius Springer

Radziszewski, H. (1910) *Bank Polski*. Warsaw: Bank Polski.

Raffalovich, A.G. (1918) *Russian Trade and Commerce*. London: P.S. King & Son (2005 reprint, Boston, MA: Elibron).

Ramon, G. (1929): *Histoire de la Banque de France d'apres les sources originales*. Paris: Bernard Grasset.

Reutern-Nolcken, W. (1914) *Die Finanzielle Sanierung Russlands*. Berlin: Reimer.

Ricardo, David (1819) *Proposals for an Economical and Secure Currency; With Observations on the Profits of the Bank of England as They Regard the Public and the Proprietors of Bank Stock*. London: John Murray.

Rittmann, H. (2003) *Deutsche Münz- und Geldgeschichte der Neuzeit bis 1914*. Solingen: Brockhaus.

Rygg, N. (1918) *Norges Banks historie. Förste del*. Kristiania: Centraltrykkeriet.

Rygg, N. (1954) *Norges Banks historie. Annen del*. Oslo: Emil Moestue.

Schön, J. (1928) *Das Polnische Bankwesen.* Katowice: Kattowitzer Buchdruckerei- und Verlags-S.A.

Schumpeter, J. (1982) *History of Economic Analysis.* London: Allen & Unwin.

Schybergson, E. (1914) *Finlands Bank 1811–1911.* Helsingfors: Frenckell.

Shaw, W. (1895) *The History of Currency 1252 to 1894.* London: Wilsons & Milne (2005 reprint, Boston, MA: Elibron).

Sieveking, H. (1933) Die Hamburger Bank 1619–1875. In *Festschrift von Melle.* Hamburg: Augustin, pp. 21–110.

Sieveking, H. (1934): Die Hamburger Bank. In J.G. van Dillen (ed.), *History of the Principal Public Banks.* The Hague: Martinus Nijhoff (1964 reprint, London: Frank Cass), pp. 125–160.

Smith, A. (1776) *Inquiry into the Nature and Causes of the Wealth of Nations* (1991 Everyman edition, New York: Knopf).

Soetbeer, A. (1855) *Beiträge und Materialen zur Beurtheilung von Geld- und Bank-Fragen mit besonderer Rücksicht auf Hamburg.* Hamburg: Voigt.

Steuart, Sir James (1767) *An Inquiry into the Principles of Political Economy. Vols. I–II.* (1966 edition by A. Skinner. Edinburgh: Oliver and Boyd).

Stieda, E. von (1909) *Das livländische Bankwesen in Vergangenheit und Gegenwart.* Leipzig: Deichert.

Svendsen, K.E. and K.A. Hansen (1968) *Dansk pengehistorie 1700–1914.* Copenhagen: Danmarks Nationalbank.

Sveriges Riksbank (1931) Statistiska tabeller. In *Sveriges Riksbank 1668–1924. Bankens tillkomst och verksamhet. Vol. V: Bilagor.* Stockholm: P.A. Norstedt & Söner, pp. 1–221.

Thornton, H. (1802) *An Enquiry into the Nature and Effects of the Paper Credit of Great Britain.* London: J. Hatchard.

Wilcke, J. (1927) *Kurantmønten 1726–1788.* Copenhagen: G. E.C. Gad.

Wójtowicz, G. and A. Wójtowicz (2005) *Monetary History of Poland.* Warsaw: Twigger.

World Coins (2002) *Standard Catalog of World Coins. Eighteenth Century 1701–1800.* Ed. by Chester L. Krause and Clifford Mishler. Iola, WI: Krause Publications.

World Coins (2004) *Standard Catalog of World Coins 1801–1900.* Iola, WI: KP Books.

Ziegler, D. (1993) Zentralbankpolitische Steinzeit? Preussische Bank und Bank of England im Vergleich. *Geschichte und Gesellschaft,* 19 (4), 475–505.

Zieliński, L. (1898) *Die Rubel jetzt und vor 100 Jahren.* Jena: Gustav Fischer.

COMMENTS BY LUDGER LINNEMANN

In this chapter, Juha Tarkka does a tremendous job in at least two respects: the one related to the economic history of early central banking, and the other consisting of a demonstration of the way in which economic thinking influenced the evolution of central bank practice. The chapter accumulates an impressive wealth of information on the specifics of the way in which early central banking began to emerge in the northern European countries and on the principles according to which they operated. It then tracks the developments of central banking arrangements in the nineteenth century, and highlights the role of theory for actual practice. Moreover, the chapter points out possible lessons to be drawn from the interaction of events and ideas for the present and future of central banking.

In these comments, I briefly summarise what appear to me to be some important steps in these developments, and then take the opportunity to connect these, and the theoretical discussion surrounding them, to the present way of thinking about monetary policy and central bank practice.

As the chapter points out, the early northern (proto) central banks shared the common feature of issuing bills against land, or in some cases merchandise, as collateral. This system of mostly land-based credit emerged as a reaction to what was often perceived as a shortage of liquidity. The resulting monetisation of illiquid land-based assets took place with an emphasis on the perceived solidity of the system, in the sense that the requirement of having land as collateral was seen as a safeguard against the possibility of inflationary over-issuance of bills. The later developments, towards the second half of the nineteenth century, then saw a growing influence of the real bills doctrine, and a consequent reduction in the emphasis on the land-based collateral system, which tended to provide insufficient amounts of liquidity to the economy.

As the chapter points out, there are several ways of interpreting the real bills doctrine: Juha distinguishes the enabling version, which holds that there is no risk of over-issuance of liquidity if only trade-related bills are discounted by the central bank, the restrictive version requiring that banks should not go beyond trade bills when exchanging illiquid assets against liquid notes, and the more modern interpretation of the real bills doctrine as being associated with pegging the nominal interest rate. In any case, the characteristic feature of central banking based on discounting bills generated in private trading transactions is that the amount of liquidity available is largely demand determined. While such a system is surely more flexible than the earlier land-based one, it certainly raises the question of what, if anything, could prevent inflationary over-issuance of liquidity.

The position of adherents to the real bills doctrine that inflation will not occur if the collateral is required to be trade-related bills is, of course, from a modern point of view, subject to the problem of nominal indeterminacy: if inflation blows up the nominal value of trade bills, the nominal amount of collateral being eligible for exchange in liquidity providing central bank transactions follows suit, such that there is no nominal anchor, and nothing will prevent inflation from rising further. This leads to an interesting comparison of the views that prevailed in the nineteenth-century early northern European central banks, and the dominant viewpoint of twentieth-century monetary theory, namely monetarism. While the early discussion sought insurance against inflationary tendencies in restrictions on the nature of assets to be posted as collateral in discount operations, monetarism pointed out that it is simply the quantity of liquidity provided that is decisive for nominal stability. In a nutshell, the monetarist view is that it does not matter which particular assets a central bank monetises, just how much of them, since it is control of the quantity of money which is the nominal anchor.

It is not surprising, therefore, that the emphasis on collateral choice that the chapter describes for the early developments has lost its prominence in the aftermath of monetarism. However, if we draw out the historical lines to present-day discussions, there is an interesting irony in the fact that current operating procedures of central banks, which tend to control short-term nominal interest rates, again allow the amount of liquidity circulating to be largely demand determined. In a sense, thus, we have gone full circle around monetarism with its emphasis on money-supply control and are back in a situation which is very similar, in this respect, to the one when the real bills doctrine was taken seriously. The important difference is, of course, that nobody proposes nowadays that the right choice of collateral implies any provision against inflationary tendencies. In contrast, these are under control in the modern system because of the judicious use of interest-rate policy by the central banks, not because of any collateral requirements. The historical change that Juha's chapter makes visible thus can be seen in a shift from objective factors, like collateral choice, to more subjective ones, like the modern reliance of the skills of central bankers in managing inflationary expectations through interest-rate setting in a system where liquidity is demand determined.

3 Central bank independence and monetary policy-making institutions

Past, present and future

*Alex Cukierman**

Two decades ago and earlier most central banks in the world functioned as departments of ministries of finance. By law, custom or both, they were expected to utilise their policy instruments to achieve myriad objectives such as high levels of growth and employment, provision of funds to government for the financing of public expenditures and to address balance of payments problems.[1] They were also expected to maintain financial and price stability but the price-stability objective was one among several other objectives in the charter of the Bank and had no particular status. In some cases like Spain and Norway it did not even appear in the charter. Paralleling this state of affairs, economic theory did not attribute particular importance to central bank independence (CBI) and the concept of credibility of monetary policy was in the early stages of development. Furthermore, a notable legacy of the Keynesian revolution was the belief that a certain amount of inflation is conducive to economic growth.

Although some banks had a reasonable amount of legal independence, the level of actual independence, particularly in developing countries, was usually lower than the one indicated in the law. Except for a few cases central banks did not possess instrument independence and the responsibility for price stability was, at least implicitly, located in the ministry of finance and other economic branches of government. In a few developed economies (such as the United Kingdom, Japan, the United States and West Germany) with wide capital markets, price stability was maintained mainly through the actions of relatively conservative treasury departments or because of de facto independent central banks.[2]

Most other countries that enjoyed reasonable levels of price stability achieved this result by pegging their currencies to the currency of a country with sufficiently conservative aggregate nominal policies. Under the Bretton Woods system most currencies were automatically pegged to the US dollar. Following the breakdown of this system in the 1970s many countries adopted unilateral pegs and, later on, bands. Countries without any of those three commitment devices endured prolonged episodes of high and variable inflation as exemplified by the cases of Argentina, Brazil, Israel, Mexico and Chile, among others.

The contrast of this state of affairs with current practice and academic consensus with respect to CBI cannot be overemphasised. Most central banks in today's world enjoy substantially higher levels of both legal and actual independence than 20 years ago or earlier. CBI and accompanying institutional arrangements, such as inflation targeting, have become widely accepted commitment devices. In spite of some contentious issues, the following broad practical consensus backed by academic work has emerged. The primary responsibility of the central bank (CB) is to assure price stability and financial stability. Without prejudice to these objectives the CB should support the economic policies of government. To achieve its main objective the bank is given instrument independence.[3] Delegation of authority to a non-elected institution should be accompanied by accountability and transparency. It is noteworthy that those two buzz words of modern monetary institutions were hardly heard 20 years ago or earlier. In the absence of independence, accountability was unnecessary and, as political entities, governments and ministries of finance had no incentives to raise questions about their own transparency in the conduct of monetary policy.[4]

This chapter is a selective survey of the vast literature of the last 20 years on CBI.[5] Section 1 quickly reviews the institutional changes that have occurred in the area of central bank autonomy and related monetary policymaking institutions in the world during the last 20 years. It discusses some of the reasons for those developments and provides an overview of accumulated empirical evidence on the relation between CBI and the performance of the economy. Section 2 opens with a discussion of some of the lessons from stabilisation of inflation and proceeds to consider the issue of CBI within the broader context of choice of nominal anchor. It also reviews recent evidence on asymmetric central bank objectives and its consequences. Section 3 briefly reviews recent literature which considers the impact of effective conservatism or independence on economic performance in the presence of labour unions.[6] A main insight of this literature is that, in the presence of large wage setters, CBI affects real variables such as the rate of unemployment, implying that conservatism affects economic performance even in the long run.

Section 4 closes the chapter by considering future challenges facing central banks. Price stability is now a permanent fixture of industrial economies and of many developing economies, and CBI is a well-established feature of the contemporary monetary order. Starting from the presumption that those features are here to stay, the discussion in this part focuses on issues relating to the conduct of monetary policy by independent central banks in an era of price stability. In such times the bank is naturally expected to devote more attention to stabilisation of the output gap. The chapter discusses the risks associated with such a flexible inflation-targeting regime. In some instances a trade off between democratic accountability and CBI may arise. This occurs, for example, when, due to its obligation to maintain financial stability, the CB engages in operations that lead to substantial losses. A closely related issue is the distribution of CB profits and losses between the CB and government and the optimal level of CB capital. The section reviews this, hitherto, relatively neglected issue.

1 The evolution of CBI over the last two decades: evidence, reasons and consequences

1.1 Evolution of CBI

The most widely available indices of CBI refer to the level of independence as specified in the law. It is well known that actual independence may often deviate, quite substantially, from legal independence. Such deviations are more important in developing than in industrial economies. This is probably due to better enforcement of the law in the first group of economies.[7] Other, more behaviourally oriented proxies, have therefore been used. One, used only for developing countries, is the actual, as opposed to the legally mandated, turnover of CB governors and the other is a proxy for the political vulnerability of the CB governor. This index is defined as the frequency of cases in which the governor is replaced within a short period of time following a political transition.[8] None of those indices fully represents the actual independence of the CB. But, taken together, they provide a more complete picture of differences in CBI across countries and over time.

Legal independence

There is mounting evidence that the legal independence of most central banks in the world increased during the 1990s to an extent that appears to be a veritable revolution in central bank legislation. This is particularly remarkable in view of the fact that during the 40 years ending in 1989 there had hardly been any reforms in CB legislation. This statement is based on a number of legal indices, the most comprehensive of which are those in chapter 19 of Cukierman (1992) and in Cukierman *et al.* (1992), on updates and extensions of these indices for some subgroups of countries and on updates of the Grilli *et al.* (1991) index.[9] The Cukierman *et al.* (1992) index has been updated for 26 former socialist economies (FSEs) for the decade of the 1990s by Cukierman *et al.* (2002). A somewhat broader index for 24 Latin American and Caribbean countries was recently developed by Jacome and Vazquez (2005).[10] The Grilli *et al.* index has been reconstructed for a sample of over 40 countries for two points in time; 1991 and the end of 2003 by Arnone *et al.* (2006).

In spite of some differences in coverage, definitions and the fact that not all indices have been updated for all countries, the broad picture that emerges is that legal independence took a quantum upward jump during the 1990s. The most direct evidence for this appears in the Arnone *et al.* (2006) paper that provides data for both 1991 and 2003. In addition, comparison of legal independence of the CB in the FSEs with that of developed economies in the 1980s by Cukierman *et al.* (2002) show a substantially higher level of independence in the former group. Interestingly, table 2 in that paper suggests that in about one-third of the FSEs, legal independence in the 1990s was higher than the legal independence of the highly independent Bundesbank during the 1980s. In line with the Maastricht Treaty the legal independence of the Bundesbank has also been upgraded since the 1980s, along with that of all the countries that joined the Economic and Monetary Union (EMU).

To illustrate the revolution in the level of legal independence during the 1990s, Figure 3.1 shows the evolution of average legal independence in nine Latin American countries during the last 50 years of the twentieth century. The figure combines data from Cukierman *et al.* (1992) with updated data from Jacome and Vazquez (2005). The main lesson from the figure is that, after 30 to 40 years of relative immobility in CB legislation, there was a quantum jump in the level of legal independence in those countries.

A similar picture emerges for the subset of FSEs that had separate central banks prior to the downfall of the Soviet Union (Figure 3.2). The legal reforms they instituted, mainly in the early 1990s, represent about a tripling of the LVAW index developed in Cukierman *et al.* (1992). Eight of the FSEs had two

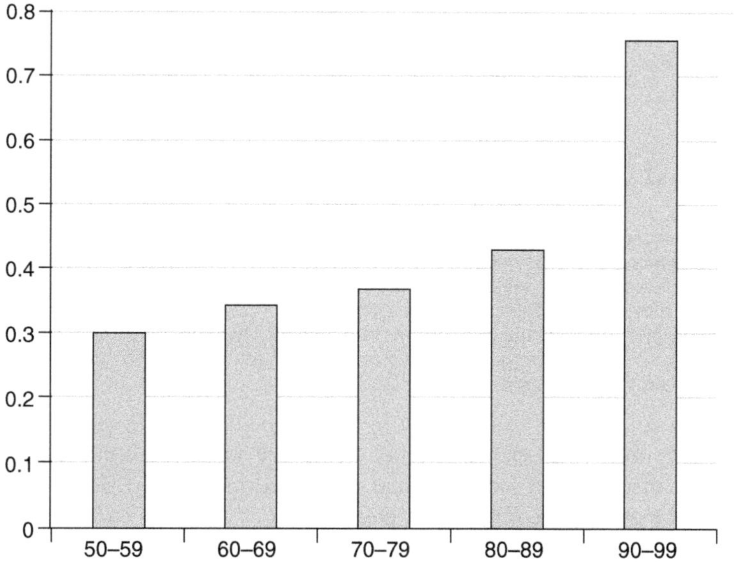

Figure 3.1 The average aggregate index of legal independence over time in nine latin American economies.

Note
The figure combines data on the aggregate index of legal independence, LVAW, from Table A1 in Cukierman *et al.* (1992) for the 40 years between 1950 and 1989 with data on the same index for the decade of the 1990s from Appendix II in Jacome and Vazquez (2005) for nine Latin American countries. The countries are: Argentina, Bolivia, Colombia, Honduras, Mexico, Nicaragua, Peru, Uruguay and Venezuela. The index is defined over the zero to one interval, with zero corresponding to complete dependence and one to the maximum possible level of independence. Each column in the figure represents the average value of LVAQ over these countries in the corresponding period. In the first two subperiods the number of countries is smaller than nine either because some of the central banks have not been created yet, or due to lack of data. For some of the countries Jacome and Vazquez provide a coding for the 1980s as well. In those cases the figures used are averages between their codings and those of Cukierman *et al.* for the 1980s.

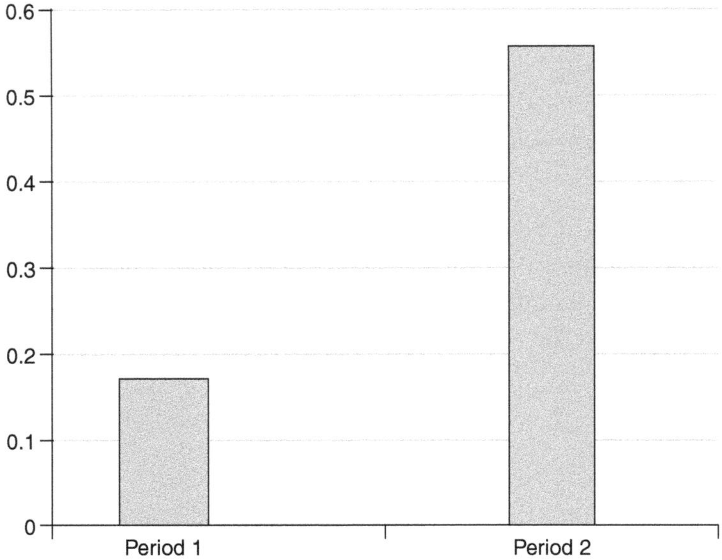

Figure 3.2 The evolution of legal independence in six former socialist economies (source: adapted from Table 1 of Cukierman *et al*., 2002).

Note
The figure shows the average value of the LVAQ index (see note to Figure 3.1 for details) for six former socialist economies which were not part of the Soviet empire and had, consequently, central bank laws prior to the downfall of the Soviet Union. The countries are Croatia, Hungary, Macedonia, Poland, Romania and Slovenia. The figure for period 1 reflects the average level of legal independence in those countries prior to the central bank reforms of the 1990s. The figure for period 2 reflects the average level of legal independence in those countries after the last central bank reform those countries had between the early 1990s and 1997.

CB reforms during the 1990s at intervals of about five years. Figure 1 in that article shows that the levels of independence embedded in second CB laws are substantially higher than those of the first CB laws.

Examination of more detailed information in these and other sources suggests that the trends illustrated by those figures reflect a *worldwide* trend towards substantially higher levels of CB independence. Moreover, the fact that the second CB law in FSEs that had two CB reforms reflects a uniformly higher level of independence than the first law supports the view that the trend towards legal independence intensified during the 1990s. Those conclusions are corroborated by recent updates of the Grilli *et al.* (1991) index of CBI produced by Arnone *et al.* (2006). They update this 1991 index for 18 developed economies, nine emerging economies and four developing countries for legislation outstanding as of the end of 2003. Their index is standardised, as in the Cukierman *et al.* (1992) index to the 0–1 range. They find that the mean levels of legal independence in those three groups of countries rose, respectively, from 0.476, 0.313 and 0.341 in 1991 to 0.774, 0.646 and 0.636 in 2003 (Table 10).

Actual independence and some illustrations of discrepancies between actual and legal independence

Have there also been meaningful changes in the actual level of CBI as proxied by the actual turnover of CB governors and by the index of political vulnerability of the CB during the 1990s? Dreher *et al.* (2007) update and extend the turnover data set to 137 countries. Comparison of this data set with the earlier data from Cukierman (1992) and Cukierman *et al.* (1992) should, in principle, make it possible to examine whether high turnover rates in developing countries are lower today than in the past.[11] Although such a comparison has not been done explicitly, casual evidence for Latin American countries in which turnover and the political vulnerability of the CB were among the highest in the world until the end of the 1980s points to a substantial increase in independence as proxied by both of those indices.

In addition to legal status, actual independence depends on various formal and informal institutional arrangements such as the type of exchange rate regime, the ability of the bank to engage effectively in open market operations, the stance of fiscal policy and the existence of explicit institutional arrangements beyond the law that make the price-stability objective a recognised (mainly by the political establishment) objective of the CB. A prominent example of the latter is the various inflation targeting methods adopted by about 20 countries since this innovation was pioneered at the end of the 1980s in New Zealand and Canada.

Cukierman (2007b) constructs a judgemental index of actual CBI for the Bank of Israel since its creation in 1954 which takes the factors above and several others into consideration. Comparison of this index of actual independence with its legal counterpart suggests that, in spite of relatively limited changes in legal independence, there have been substantial changes in the actual independence of the Bank following the stabilisation of high inflation in 1985. In particular, while actual independence was substantially lower prior to and several years following the 1985 stabilisation, the relation between those two types of independence has been permanently reversed since the mid-1990s.

Until the 1985 inflation stabilisation, one of the main tasks of the Bank of Israel was to channel and extend credit to various sectors of the economy. This was done through an elaborate system of directed credits to various sectors of the economy. The Bank had relatively little influence on the size, composition and the terms of those credits. On top of that, due to other institutional restrictions, the Bank's ability to conduct effective open market operations was severely limited. In addition the capital market was highly segmented and dominated by non-competitive elements. The combination of those factors seriously impeded the actual ability of the Bank to focus on the price-stability objective.

The main factors responsible for increases in the actual independence of the Bank of Israel in the post-1985 stabilisation period (in spite of a relatively immobile charter) were: a gradual reduction, mostly through attrition, of directed credits; a gradual lifting (until their complete elimination at the end of 2001) of restrictions limiting the Bank's ability to issue short-term securities for monetary policy purposes; a gradual process of desegmentation of credit markets; a gradual process of lifting of various controls on capital flows; a gradual flexibilisation of the exchange rate and its gradual replacement by inflation targets since December 1991. Starting in the mid-1990s, substantial increases in the short-term interest rate set by the Bank (in spite of public criticisms by the Treasury and exporters) point to an increase in the relative effective emphasis on price stability. The Israeli experience suggests that substantial changes in the actual independence of the Bank may occur without much change in legal independence.

A similar but less dramatic process occurred during the first half of the 1990s at the Bank of England. Due to changes in monetary policy-making institutions at the end of 1992 the actual independence of the Bank of England rose without any change in CB legislation. Underlying this trend was the disappointing performance of monetary targets during the 1980s and, in the early 1990s, the low credibility of Britain's commitment to the Exchange Rate Mechanism (ERM) which led, in September 1992, to the depreciation of the pound sterling (Bowen, 1995). The poor performance of those two alternative anchors – monetary stocks and the exchange rate – convinced Chancellor Lamont to introduce an anchor based on a final rather than an intermediate target leading to the introduction of inflation targets in the United Kingdom.

Although the final decision regarding the setting of short-term rates and of the inflation target remained in the hands of the Chancellor, the new policy framework increased the involvement of the Bank of England in monetary policy making. The Bank was invited to participate in joint meetings with the Treasury in order to formulate and tender advice on interest rates to the Chancellor. The prompt publication of those minutes made it possible for the Bank to quickly transmit its point of view to the public. To effectively operate the new framework, the Bank was asked to produce forecasts of inflation under the assumption of unchanged interest rates and to produce inflation reports that would explain the reasons for missed targets and convey the uncertainty about the inflation forecast to the public.[12] In addition, after November 1993, the Bank had some limited discretion about the timing of implementation of the interest-rate decision made by the Chancellor. As a consequence of those institutional changes the actual independence of the Bank of England increased already in the early 1990s despite the fact that legal independence followed only during the second half of the decade.[13]

1.2 Why did CBI increase so much during the 1990s?

The evidence surveyed in the previous section supports the conclusion that there has been a sustained worldwide increase in the levels of both legal and actual independence during the 1990s. This trend is due to a combination of global and regional factors. This subsection briefly reviews the main factors.[14] Two main global factors underlie the trend towards higher CBI. One is an increased worldwide quest for price stability triggered by the stagflation of the 1970s and the dismal economic performance of some high-inflation countries, in Latin America and elsewhere. Contrary to the 1960s and the 1970s, the accepted view during the 1980s and the 1990s became that inflation and the associated uncertainties retard growth. The relatively good real performance of some low-inflation countries such as Germany and Japan till the 1980s supported this view.

The second factor is globalisation, the gradual dismantling of controls on capital flows and the associated widening of international capital markets. Those processes reinforced the quest for price stability and raised the importance of CBI as a signal of macroeconomic nominal responsibility to domestic and international investors. As argued by Maxfield (1998), this factor was particularly important in developing countries whose political establishments were anxious to establish smooth access to international capital markets. Relatedly, the IMF embraced the view that a high level of independence is a desirable institutional feature and actively promoted CB reform in many developing economies through conditionality and other means. In addition the intellectual revolution triggered by the KPBG inflation bias story helped cement a consensus that trying to use money to raise output beyond its full information, flexible price value is ineffective and only leads to socially harmful inflation.[15] By offering a relatively simple theory of the prisoner's dilemma aspects of the interaction between monetary policy makers and individuals in the economy, the inflation bias model provided academic credence for the claim that monetary policy should be delegated to a sufficiently independent CB and helped spread this notion internationally.

Among the regional motives for increasing independence are: first, the breakdown of other institutions designed to safeguard nominal stability, such as the European Monetary System (EMS) and the Bretton Woods System, intensified the search for alternative institutions. Second, the good track record of the highly independent Bundesbank demonstrated that CBI can function as an effective device for ensuring nominal stability. Third, the acceptance of the Maastricht Treaty by the European Community implied that, in order to conform with the Treaty, many countries in the Community had to upgrade the independence of their CB as a precondition for membership in EMU. The fact that such a stipulation has been introduced in the Treaty in the first place is related to the good record of the Bundesbank and to the central position of Germany within the Union. Fourth, after recent successful stabilisation of inflation, particularly in Latin America, policy makers were looking for institutional arrangements capable of reducing the likelihood of high and persistent inflation in the future. In view of the experience available at the time, raising CBI was a natural way to achieve this objective. Fifth, the upgrading of CBI and the creation of best-practice Western-type central banks in the former socialist countries was part of a more general attempt by these countries to create the institutional framework needed for the orderly functioning of a market economy. The fact that many of these new central banks were granted substantial *de jure* independence was no doubt motivated by evidence from the industrial economies suggesting that inflation and legal independence are negatively related and that independence and growth are either positively related or unrelated (see next subsection).

The discussion above still leaves open the question why many countries choose to raise their commitment to price stability by upgrading CBI rather than through other means such as unilateral pegs? This question is discussed in subsection 4.2.4 within the context of choice of nominal anchor.

1.3 CBI and economic performance

This subsection briefly surveys existing evidence on the relation between CBI and economic performance in the areas of inflation, growth, investment and the distributions of real and nominal rates of interest.

Inflation

The early evidence in Alesina and Summers (1993), Grilli *et al.* (1991), Cukierman (1992: chapter 19) and Cukierman *et al.* (1992) suggests that, for the industrial economies, inflation and legal independence are negatively related. By contrast, in the group of developing countries neither inflation nor growth are related to legal independence. This is most likely due to the fact that, at least until the early 1990s, there was hardly any link between actual and legal independence within this group of countries. When behaviourally oriented proxies for independence, such as the actual turnover of CB governors and the index of political vulnerability, are used, a negative relation between inflation and independence emerges within the group of developing countries as well (Cukierman, 1992: chapter 19; Cukierman *et al.*, 1992; Cukierman and Webb, 1995).

Using data on the legal independence of freshly created central banks in FSEs during the 1990s, and controlling for cumulative liberalisation, price decontrols and wars, Cukierman *et al.* (2002) find no relation between inflation and legal independence during the initial stages of liberalisation. However, once the process of privatisation and liberalisation of domestic prices and of foreign trade becomes sufficiently large and sustained, a negative relation between inflation and legal independence does emerge. A possible reason is that legal independence is enforced in practice only when the shift to a market economy has become sufficiently important to induce the authorities to seriously engage in law enforcement.

For the Latin American and Caribbean countries during the 1990s, and controlling for international inflation, banking crises and the exchange rate regime, Jacome and Vazquez (2005) find a negative relation between inflation and legal independence. For a similar group of countries and time period Gutierrez (2003) finds that countries that entrench the legal independence of the CB in the constitution have lower inflation than those that do not.

Is there a general lesson from those different empirical investigations? The evidence is consistent with the conclusion that inflation and *actual* CBI are negatively related in both developed and developing countries. But the extent to which this basic relation is also reflected as a negative relation between inflation and *legal* independence depends on several other factors, such as regard for the law and the degree of commitment to CBI, as proxied *inter alia* by whether or not the CB charter is entrenched in the constitution.

One may argue that the negative relation between independence and inflation arises because of reverse causality from inflation to independence rather than from independence to inflation. It is hard to resolve this important question on the basis of existing evidence. Using data on legal independence for the Latin American and Caribbean countries during the 1990s, Jacome and Vazquez (2005) do not find evidence to support causality from legal independence to inflation. Closer examination of their data suggests that in some cases, the stabilisation of high inflation preceded the upgrading of legal CBI. This was the case in Argentina, Peru and Nicaragua in the early 1990s and in Brazil at the end of the 1990s. In such cases inflation was initially quite high and the stabilisation was of the 'cold turkey' type. In other Latin American countries, such as Columbia, Paraguay and El Salvador, legal CBI was granted during the disinflation process which then continued in a gradual fashion. In one case (Venezuela) inflation actually accelerated after legal independence was upgraded in the early 1990s.

Data from Cukierman *et al.* (2002) show that acceleration of inflation following the upgrading of legal CBI was quite common during the early to mid-1990s in the FSE. This was the case following the first CB reform in Kazakhstan, Lithuania and Mongolia, and in Croatia, Belarus, Turkmenistan, Ukraine, Tajikistan, Latvia and the Kyrgyz Republic. Kazakhstan, Lithuania and Mongolia had a second round of CB reform from the mid-1990s onwards, after high inflation has been largely stabilised. From that point onwards low inflation persisted. More generally, Cukierman *et al.* (2002) find that legal independence in the FSE is associated with lower inflation only after the process of liberalisation has gathered sufficient momentum. A possible explanation for this finding is that law enforcement was relatively poor during the early stages of liberalisation and as a consequence legal independence did not translate into actual independence. This and other evidence support the view that CBI functions reasonably well as an inflation-prevention device. However, once high inflation has been allowed to develop CBI alone does not always suffice for the restoration of price stability.[16]

How about the direction of causality between behavioral proxies of CBI and inflation? Using governors' turnover as a proxy for actual (lack of) independence, Cukierman (1992: chapter 20, section 7) finds evidence in favour of two-way causality between turnover and inflation during the 40 years ending in 1989. Dreher *et al.* (2007) produce more recent evidence suggesting that causality runs from inflation to turnover.[17]

Growth, investment and the distribution of nominal and real rates of interest

For developed economies Grilli *et al.* (1991) found that real growth and CBI are unrelated. This led them to label CBI a 'free lunch'. Those results are corroborated in studies by Alesina and Summers (1993) and Cukierman *et al.* (1993).

For developing economies, Cukierman *et al.* (1993) find that, although there is no association between legal independence and the rate of growth of per capita income, the association between growth and actual independence as proxied by the political vulnerability of the CB and related measures of turnover has a positive impact on the rate of growth. More precisely, using data from the 1960s to the 1980s and controlling, *inter alia*, for initial GDP, the change in terms of trade, initial primary and secondary enrolment ratios, it is found that higher political vulnerability of the CB governor and related measures of turnover are negatively associated with per capita growth.

For a subset of developing countries, Cukierman *et al.* (1993) also find, in some cases, a similar negative impact of turnover on the share of investment in GDP. A possible joint interpretation of the last two results is that, under weak central bankers, private investments are reducing the long-run rate of growth.

Alesina and Summers (1993) and Cukierman *et al.* (1993) find that in developed economies the variability of both nominal and real rates of interest is negatively associated with legal independence. The second paper also finds, for the decade of the 1980s, that the average real return to depositors was higher in developed economies with higher levels of legal independence.

For developing countries Cukierman *et al.* (1993) find that the variability of both nominal and real deposit rates of interest is positively associated with the turnover of CB governors.

The broad conclusion from those findings is that the variabilities of both real and nominal rates of interest are lower, and that the average real return to depositors is higher in countries with higher levels of *actual* independence.

2 Remarks on disinflation and the changing structure of nominal anchors

2.1 'Cold turkey' versus gradual stabilisations and the role of the CB

During the last two decades many high-inflation countries the world over stabilised inflation. Some of those stabilisations were of the 'shock' or 'cold-turkey' type and others were gradual. Some involved the ministry of finance and even the entire government while others were implemented mainly by the CB. Two regularities appear to emerge from those experiences. First, by and large, very high inflations at rates over 100 per cent were stabilised using the first method whereas stabilisations of inflation in the two-digit range were implemented gradually. Second, government involvement in the stabilisation of high inflation was usually larger when high inflations were stabilised whereas low inflations were stabilised mainly, or solely, by the CB.

Thus, the stabilisation of low inflation by industrial countries following the oil shocks of the 1970s was done gradually and usually with relatively little involvement of the government. Similarly, the stabilisation of low inflation in Chile since the beginning of the 1990s was done gradually, mainly by the CB. By contrast the stabilisation of high inflation in Bolivia, Argentina and Israel during the 1980s were of the cold-turkey type and featured a substantial involvement of government. Interestingly, Israel went through both types of stabilisations at different times. The cold-turkey 1985 stabilisation that permanently reduced inflation from the three-digit range to between 10 and 20 per cent per annum was led by government to the extent that the minister of finance and the prime minister were personally involved. On the other hand, the next phase of stabilisation, that took place over the decade of the 1990s and reduced inflation to the 0–2 per cent range, was done mainly by the CB in spite of occasional criticisms of the bank's restrictive policy by the minister of finance.

In what follows, I argue that those regularities are not accidental for two reasons. First, under high and persistent inflation the public's belief in the seriousness of policy makers' commitment to price stability is likely to be substantially lower than under low inflations, or using terminology borrowed from Barro (1986) and Cukierman and Liviatan (1991), the initial 'reputation' of policy makers is lower in the second case. Reputation is defined formally in those papers as the probability, β, that the public attributes to the event that the policy maker in office intends to deliver the inflation target that he announces beforehand. When β equals 1, reputation is perfect and when it is 0 reputation is nonexistent. In most real life situations β is strictly between 0 and 1. That is, policy makers have some reputation but it is not perfect.

The model captures imperfect reputation by assuming that the policy maker in office can be one of the following two *exogenously given* types. A dependable type who takes the inflation target as a commitment to set the policy instrument in a way that will make inflation as near to the target as possible, and a weak type who mimics the announcement of his dependable counterpart, but is not really committed, and is therefore subject to the classical KPBG inflation bias problem. Both types share an identical objective function which is increasing in unexpected inflation and decreasing in inflation. One can think of the dependable type as a policy maker who feels that reputation is an important electoral asset whereas the weak (or opportunistic) policy maker believes that reputation is a minor factor in its re-election prospects.

Cukierman (2000a) extends those frameworks to allow for imperfect control of inflation by policy makers. An important consequence of imperfect control is that the opportunistic policy maker can engage in short-term discretionary policies without being revealed as weak with probability one. In such an environment the public adjusts β gradually using Bayes rule. However, when sufficiently extreme rates of inflation occur, reputation takes a jump. In particular, following the realisation of a sufficiently high rate of inflation the policy maker loses all reputation, and following the realisation of a sufficiently low rate of inflation he establishes his credentials as being dependable with probability one. Both policy-maker types aspire towards higher reputation since the impact of the preannounced inflation target is higher when reputation is higher and this raises the value of their objectives.

When in office, the dependable policy maker attempts to raise his reputation by announcing and implementing a sufficiently low inflation target in order to increase the probability that his dependability will be subsequently revealed with probability one. When in office, the weak policy maker attempts to preserve his existing reputation by mimicking his dependable counterpart in the preannouncement of the target and by scaling down his planned inflation to a level below the one period discretionary rate. Thus, the two policy makers have opposite incentives with respect to revelation of their identities. The dependable CB aspires to reveal his type with probability one while the opportunistic policy maker tries to minimise the chances that his type will be revealed. Even if he mimics his dependable counterpart in deeds as well as in words for some time, the opportunistic type will ultimately inflate at the high discretionary rate. As a consequence permanent stabilisation of inflation is achieved only when a dependable policy maker is in office.

Stabilisation of inflation brings with it long-term benefits at the cost of abandoning short-term advantages associated with the creation of unanticipated inflation under discretion. One can therefore think of the onset of a drive for stabilisation as an increase in the concern of policy makers for the future, relative to current objectives, and model it as an increase in the discount factor, δ, common to both types. The framework above implies that when a dependable policy maker is in office and δ goes up, raising the incentive to implement a stabilisation, the type of stabilisation chosen by the dependable type will depend on the initial level of reputation. In particular, a shock treatment is more likely when initial reputation is sufficiently low and gradual stabilisation is more likely when it is sufficiently high (Proposition 6 in Cukierman, 2000b).

The intuition underlying this result is the following. An increase in the discount factor makes the future more important and induces *both* types, when in office, to inflate at lower rates. When reputation is sufficiently low the reduction in planned inflation by the dependable type (D) is larger than the reduction in planned inflation by the weak type (W) because, at a low reputation, D stands to gain relatively more from full separation than W stands to lose from it at the margin. As a consequence the probability of a shock treatment after which D is clearly separated from his weak counterpart is higher than that of gradual stabilisation. When initial reputation is sufficiently high W stands to lose relatively more than what D stands to gain from full separation. Hence, when the future becomes more important, W makes a relatively stronger effort to prevent full separation than the effort made by D to establish his identity beyond any doubt. As a consequence the probability of gradual stabilisation is higher than that of a shock treatment.

A second factor that affects the relative desirability of shock versus gradual stabilisation under moderate versus high inflation is related to the existence of nominal wage contracts and other temporary nominal rigidities. In particular, when initial inflation is sufficiently high, the structure of overlapping sticky wages and prices is very compressed. As a consequence the relative price distortions associated with a shock treatment are relatively small. By contrast, when initial inflation is moderate the structure of overlapping wage contracts and prices is spread out, making the relative price distortions associated with a shock treatment higher and more persistent. Hence gradual stabilisations are relatively more attractive in this case.

Why do governments tend to be more heavily involved in the stabilisation of high inflations whereas low inflations are frequently stabilised mainly by the CB? There are several reasons. First, the root cause of high inflation is usually due to government's fiscal imbalances and the need to finance them through seigniorage. In the presence of limited government access to credit markets such needs often create high inflations (Bolivia in the first half of the 1980s is an example). Since the root cause of the problem resides in government's fiscal needs the solution must involve government.

Second, even when the root cause resides elsewhere, once high inflation has been allowed to develop, it is quite likely that the CB alone will not be able to do the job for several reasons. In such cases, without a clear-cut demonstration of fiscal responsibility by government, the low reputation of policy makers makes it extremely hard for the CB to convince the public that a change in regime is around the corner. This is reinforced by the fact that during high inflation the independence of the CB is low. In addition if, as was the case in countries such as Chile and Israel, indexation is widespread at the outset and a shock stabilisation is implemented, some or all of the indexation arrangements have to be temporarily suspended. Clearly, actions of this type are not within the arsenal of instruments of the CB. They require, instead, the involvement of government and other groups such as labour unions.

2.2 Changes in the transmission process in the aftermath of successful stablisations

Although they are desirable, successful stabilisations temporarily complicate the conduct of monetary policy. The reason is that such stabilisations induce changes in the transmission process of monetary policy through a variety of channels. Wages and prices become more sticky, the degrees of informal and formal indexation go down and the pass-through coefficient and dollarisation go down as well. All those phenomena have taken place in Israel following the success of inflation targeting in reducing inflation to the current standards of Europe and the United States. Schmidt-Hebbel (2004) documents similar trends for Chile.

Those changes lead to a lengthening of the transmission of monetary impulses to inflation and the real effects of monetary policy become more persistent. Since they raise the ability of monetary policy to affect output and employment, those are desirable developments. On the other hand those structural changes make pre-disinflation knowledge about the precise magnitudes of the coefficients of the transmission mechanism somewhat obsolete and raise the CB uncertainty concerning the structure of the economy. As a consequence, during several years following successful stabilisations, monetary policy makers are forced to rely more heavily on various judgemental procedures and on a larger amount of relatively partial signals about the impact of monetary policy.

2.3 The inflation target, asymmetric CB objectives and non-linear reaction functions

During the last decade much of the academic research dealing with CB reaction functions has been cast in terms of Taylor rules. For the most part these rules assume that the CB loss function is quadratic in the output gap and in the deviation of inflation from its target.[18] This formulation leads to nice linear reaction functions and implies that the CB treats losses from being above and being below target with respect to both inflation and output in a symmetric manner. In the absence of uncertainty about future shocks possible asymmetries in losses do not matter. However, when it is recognised that real-life central banks are uncertain about future shocks when they pick their policy instruments, the shape of the objective function over the entire possible range of losses becomes important.

After a period as vice chairman of the Fed, Blinder (1998: 19, 20) suggests that 'in most situations the CB will take far more political heat when it tightens preemptively to avoid higher inflation than when it eases preemptively to avoid higher unemployment'. Although the Fed enjoys a fair amount of actual independence it is not totally insensitive to the reactions of the political establishment and the public. It is therefore likely that, in making policy decisions, the Fed may weight losses from negative output gaps more heavily than losses (if any) from positive output gaps. Cukierman (2000b) formalises this asymmetry by postulating that the CB is concerned with losses arising from negative output gaps but is indifferent to the size of the gap as long as it is positive and shows that, in such a case, there will be an inflation bias even if the bank aims at achieving potential output on average. Using cross-sectional data from industrial economies, Cukierman and Gerlach (2003) find support for this theory. Using a more general specification of asymmetric output gap objectives, Ruge-Murcia (2003) finds that such a specification fits the behaviour of US inflation better than the traditional Barro and Gordon (1983) model which relies on quadratic objectives.

It might appear, at first glance, that there should be no reason for asymmetries in losses from the discrepancies between inflation and the inflation target (the 'inflation gap'). However, in periods of gradual disinflation, in which the CB is anxious to establish a reputation for being committed to the target, it may be more apprehensive of positive than of negative inflation gaps. Hence during such periods the Bank may follow policies which make it more likely that the inflation target will be missed from below than from above. Interestingly, during the gradual Israeli disinflation at the end of the 1990s and the beginning of the twenty-first century, the bank missed the target many more times from below than from above.[19] A similar phenomenon occurred in the United Kingdom during the inflation targeting period.

Essentially, asymmetries in losses from inflation and output gaps reflect inflation avoidance and recession avoidance on the part of the CB with respect to those gaps. Such motives generally lead to non-linear Taylor rules. Cukierman and Muscatelli (2008) investigate the consequences of asymmetric preferences within a New Keynesian framework of the type suggested by Clarida *et al.* (2000) and test for the existence of non-linearities in the interest-rate reaction functions of the United States and the United Kingdom.

In times of stable inflation, as has been the case in the United States since the mid-1980s, recession-avoidance preferences may dominate. In times of inflation stabilisation, due to reputational considerations, inflation-avoidance preferences may dominate. In the presence of both avoidance motives the reaction function may still be linear because the two motives affect the conventional linear Taylor rule in opposite directions. Recession avoidance alone tends to make the Taylor rule concave in both gaps and inflation avoidance alone tends to make it convex in both gaps. Hence, in the presence of both motives, the Taylor rule is non-linear if one of those motives dominates the other.

Cukierman and Muscatelli (2008) develop a criterion for finding the dominant avoidance motive and apply it to the United Kingdom and the United States. They find evidence supporting the existence of asymmetric CB objectives in most periods as well as substantial over-time variations in the identity of the dominant avoidance motive in both countries. In particular, the period between the end of the 1970s and 1990 in the United Kingdom is characterised by a dominant recession-avoidance motive. By contrast, since the introduction of inflation targets in 1992, the UK reaction function is characterised by a dominant inflation-avoidance motive. In the United States there was evidence of a dominant inflation-avoidance motive during the (Vietnam War) inflationary build-up under McChesney-Martin. But during the (stable price level) Greenspan era and, to a lesser extent during the Burns–Miller period, there has been evidence of a dominant recession-avoidance motive.

The more general lesson from those findings is that the objective functions of central banks are likely to adapt over time in order to address the most pressing economic problem of the day.[20]

2.4 CBI cum inflation targets versus exchange rate anchors

Price stability can be achieved through a variety of anchors. Delegation of authority to an independent and sufficiently conservative CB (with or without explicit targeting of inflation) is one type of anchor and some level of commitment to a unilateral peg is another one.[21] Different countries have utilised, or still are utilising, one or the other, or some combination or variation of those anchors. The last 15 years have witnessed a substantial reshuffling of nominal anchors.[22] Some countries in Latin America and elsewhere have gradually shifted from an exchange-rate anchor to effective CBI augmented by explicit inflation targeting.[23] Other countries, such as those joining the euro area, substantially raised their commitment to permanently fixed exchange rates by eliminating separate currencies through the creation of the EMU. China continues to maintain an implicit fixed peg, as do some countries in the Far East.

An argument often advanced in favour of replacing exchange-rate-based anchors by CBI and explicit or implicit inflation targeting is that this makes it possible to utilise monetary policy for domestic stabilisation purposes. However, the flexibility required for stabilisation policy can also be achieved by exchange-rate bands at the cost of occasional abandonment of the band. For a given level of reputation, Cukierman *et al.* (2004) discuss some of the factors that determine the choice of band width and the associated point along the trade off between flexibility and credibility. An analogous, although not quite identical, trade off arises under an independent CB with inflation targets. Here this trade off is determined by the degree of targeting flexibility of the bank which depends on its conservatism. By allowing larger and more sustained deviations of inflation from its target, a less conservative CB leaves more flexibility for stabilisation policy which is analogous to a wider exchange-rate band.

A second argument against exchange-rate anchors is that, in the current era of free capital mobility, the level of foreign exchange reserves needed to defend a fixed peg is likely to be prohibitive more often than before. This was vividly illustrated by the 1998 currency crises. Again, if one wishes to maintain flexibility this can be achieved by widening the band. In spite of this, many developing economies still peg their currencies to some key currency (Calvo and Reinhard, 2002). Those remarks are consistent with the view that different anchors are appropriate for different countries, as well as for the same country in different time periods.

Interestingly, independently of whether they use an exchange-rate anchor, a dirty float, a band, a diagonal peg or a freely floating exchange rate, most countries have upgraded the legal independence of their central banks during the 1990s. Thus, it appears that legal independence of the CB has come to be considered as desirable even if some type of exchange-rate anchor is being used. But the likelihood that this legal independence translates into actual independence is higher the looser the exchange-rate anchor.

3 The role of central bank independence in unionised economies

The literature on credibility and endogenous monetary policy that followed the lead of KPBG implicitly assumes that all markets, the labour market in particular, are competitive. A basic consequence of this assumption is that the conservatism, or effective independence, of the CB affects inflation and the extent of countercyclical policy but not the long run or affects the potential level of output and employment. In other words, in the absence of cyclical shocks, the level of CB independence is neutral with respect to the real economy in the same sense that money is neutral in classical monetary discussions such as that of Patinkin (1963). The last ten years have witnessed the emergence of a new literature that considers the impact of monetary and labour-market institutions on the economy in the presence of large wage setters such as labour unions. This section reviews some of its main ideas very briefly.[24]

An important general message of this recent literature is that, when wage settlements are centralised within a small or moderate number of unions, CBI affects inflation *as well as* real variables such as employment, output and real wages. The basic reason for this dramatic difference in outcomes is that, when setting nominal wages, labour unions act strategically by taking the policy response of the CB into consideration.[25] Since the expected response of the CB depends on its independence, the actions of unions and the level of economic activity come to depend on CBI. This insight and the analytical frameworks that underlie it are particularly relevant for European economies in which the fraction of the labour force covered by collective agreements is large and in which wage-bargaining institutions are often rather centralised.

3.1 Main ideas and analytical frameworks

Most of the literature on the strategic interaction between the CB and unions shares two basic presumptions. First, nominal wages are contractually fixed for a certain period of time which I refer to as the 'contract period'. Second, monetary policy and prices can be adjusted during the contract period. Casual observation supports both presumptions. Union nominal wages are normally fixed for at least one year while prices and the money supply are usually adjusted at frequencies that are higher than one year. Those presumptions lead to the formulation of simple game theoretic models in which unions move first and set nominal wages while the CB moves second and chooses, depending on the model, the rate of inflation or the money supply. Third, union management likes higher real wages for its members but dislikes unemployment among them. Some of the recent literature also assumes that unions are averse to inflation. This is motivated by the observation that in many cases the pensions of union workers are not indexed and that union members, like other individuals, generally dislike inflation.

For the sake of simplicity a good part of the recent literature investigates the strategic interaction between the labour market and the CB for the extreme case of a single, all-encompassing monopoly union. The more recent literature generally considers the case of several unions. Following the lead of the KPBG-type models, much of the literature on unions and the CB assumes that the CB directly controls the rate of inflation. More recent literature recognises that prices are set by firms and that the policy instrument of the monetary authority is the money supply.[26] A basic consequence of this difference in modelling choices is that in the first group of models monetary policy affects the economy only via supply-side channels whereas in the second group it affects it mainly through demand-side channels.

This difference in modelling strategy leads to diametrically opposed conclusions about the real effects of CBI on the economy. In particular, papers which assume that the CB directly controls inflation and that unions are averse to inflation conclude that by alleviating the inflationary fears of unions more conservative central banks induce higher real-wage demands and higher levels of unemployment (Skott, 1997; Cukierman and Lippi, 1999; Lawler, 2000; Lippi, 2003).[27] On the other hand, work by Soskice and Iversen (1998, 2000) which abstracts from unions' inflation aversion and postulates that the monetary authority controls the money supply concludes that less accommodating central banks moderate unions' wage demands by raising the fear of unemployment among their members. This view implies that both inflation and unemployment are lower under less accommodative central banks.[28]

Coricelli *et al.* (2006) propose a framework that integrates those different mechanisms into a unified framework making it possible to identify the conditions under which either of the effects above dominates. The framework features both supply-side and demand-side transmission channels of monetary policy. They find that, for realistic values of the relative aversion of unions to inflation and to unemployment, higher CBI reduces the bargaining power of unions and leads to lower values of unemployment, real wages and inflation. The main features of this framework are as follows. Prices and wages are set, respectively, by monopolistically competitive firms and by labour unions. Prices are fully flexible and wages are contractually fixed. The CB affects the price level and employment indirectly via its choice of money supply. The game now has a third stage in which firms set prices so as to maximise their real profits. This is preceded by the choice of money supply in the second stage and by the choice of nominal wages in the first stage.[29]

4 Future challenges for an era of price stability

In sharp contrast to the 1980s, large parts of the world currently enjoy price stability and central banks have become the guardians of this stability. This, I believe, is a good arrangement since reasonably independent central banks have a comparative advantage in maintaining price stability in comparison to bringing high rates of inflation down.[30]

There are several reasons to believe that this era of price stability is here to stay. First, even moderately independent CBs today find it easier than in the past to insist on delivering price stability because so much of each country's trade is with countries that are also characterised by price stability. This is reinforced by substantially higher freedom in the movement of capital and the associated wider international capital markets. In this new era, nominal and/or financial instability within a single country is much more costly than in the past in terms of limitations on the access to capital markets. Ministries of finance and governments, anxious to maintain unhindered access to borrowing in case of need, understand that letting inflation persistently deviate from the world norm will raise the risk premium on their borrowings and generally limit their ability to borrow. They, consequently, are more willing than in the past to allow central banks to focus on price stability. Similar considerations apply to the maintenance of financial stability. Thus, free and wide capital markets reinforce the incentives of governments to appoint relatively conservative central bankers and to give them enough latitude to maintain a strong focus on the attainment of price stability.

4.1 Monetary policy in an era of price stability and flexible inflation targeting

At the same time, once inflation has been conquered, there is a natural tendency to expect that, when choosing its policy instruments, the central bank will pay more attention to the state of the real economy than during the period of inflation stabilisation. Using Svensson's (1997) terminology, they expect the bank to become a flexible inflation targeter, or if the bank had already been flexible during stabilisation, they expect it will become even more flexible once inflation had been conquered.[31] Such expectation arises first because politicians and the public generally expect policy-making institutions to deal with the current main problem. Once inflation has been eradicated from the system, they take this fact for granted and expect the bank will pay more attention to other pressing problems of the day.

But there is also a deeper, welfare-based reason to justify more flexibility (or less conservatism) on the part of the CB. It is related to the fact, discussed in subsection 4.2.3, that the policy trade off between inflation and economic activity changes after the permanent stabilisation of inflation. In particular, a unit change in the policy instrument, such as the interest rate for example, has a relatively stronger and more sustained impact on economic activity in comparison to inflation than prior to the stabilisation of inflation. It can be shown that, under such circumstances, a higher degree of flexibility in monetary policy is indicated. The intuition is that, since the policy trade off between economic activity and inflation is now 'better', it pays on welfare grounds to let monetary policy focus, relatively more than during disinflation, on stabilisation of the output gap.[32]

Obviously flexible inflation targeting requires an operational measure of the output gap. Since the output gap is defined as the deviation of actual output from potential output, implementation of flexible inflation targeting requires an operational measure of the output gap. Although central banks have been using various smooth versions of actual output to proxy for potential output for quite a while this procedure may at time cause serious policy mistakes. In addition it is not grounded in theory. The next subsections briefly review the origins of those problems.

4.2 The perils of output gap stabilisation

Nobody knows with certainty what the time path of potential output is. Although part of this uncertainty is resolved with the benefit of hindsight there is normally substantial uncertainty about the current and near-future expected level of this variable at the time monetary policy choices are made. A major implication of this observation for the choice of monetary policy procedures is that, due to poor real-time knowledge about the output gap, flexible inflation targeters condition their policy on a variable that is measured with a substantial amount of error.

In an important paper, Orphanides (2001) shows that during the second half of the 1970s and part of the 1980s the Fed systematically overestimated potential output leading to substantial overestimation of the magnitude of the recession at that time. Since the Fed behaved as a flexible inflation targeter, those forecast errors induced a monetary policy stance which came to be considered, with the benefit of hindsight, as excessively loose, thus contributing to the inflationary bulge of the second half of the 1970s in the United States. The fact that there was a substantial decrease in output during the second half of the 1970s is well known and is not under dispute. What is at issue here is how much of this decrease was due to cyclical elements over which monetary policy has some temporary impact versus how much was due to changes in potential output over which monetary policy has little or no impact.

Since errors of forecast are sometimes positive, at other times negative, and normally not persistent, one may think at first blush that policy errors induced by poor measurement of the output gap should not inject persistent errors into the choice of monetary policy. Unfortunately, this is not the case with the output gap. Cukierman and Lippi (2005) show that errors in forecasting potential output and the output gap are generally serially correlated. The intuitive reason is that, unlike forecasts of many variables whose true values become known with a lag of one period, the true values of potential output and of the output gap are not revealed with certainty, even after the fact. As a consequence monetary policy errors of flexible inflation targeters become serially correlated as well. In periods in which potential output does not deviate much from its trend, the measured persistence in policy is small and may not constitute a serious problem for growth targeting. But in periods with large deviations of potential output from its trend, policy errors may be quite persistent over time. Thus, in the presence of flexible inflation targeting, the inherent unobservability of the output gap is particularly dangerous for nominal stability around and following turning points in the path of potential output.

4.3 A new conception of the output gap

An intriguing recent innovation of New Keynesian economics is to conceptualise potential output as the level of output that would have been produced in the economy under flexible wages and prices and perfect competition in all markets. Woodford (2003: chapter 6) shows that, provided those conditions are satisfied, economic welfare is maximised when output is equal to this concept of potential output.[33] On this basis he suggests that monetary policy should be directed at minimising the gap between actual output and this New Keynesian potential output concept.

This notion of potential output has two attractive features. First, it is welfare based. Second, it is particularly suited as a target for monetary policy since it directs attention to the distortion that monetary policy can handle relatively more efficiently (temporary distortions of relative prices). But its practical applicability is limited by the fact that there currently are no empirical measures of the flexible price and wage equilibrium.[34] In addition most real-world markets are imperfectly competitive. Once this is recognised the level of output that maximises welfare no longer necessarily equals the flexible wage and price equilibrium (Benigno and Woodford, 2005; Cukierman, 2005). On top of that the flexible price/wage equilibrium is often more volatile than the sticky price/wage equilibrium implying that policy makers should aim at making the level of output more, rather than less, volatile. My reality judgement is that, even if reliable measures of the flexible price/wage equilibrium had been available, most central bankers would resist such a policy. Cukierman (2005) provides a partial rationalisation for such resistance by showing that, in the presence of monopolistic competition on product markets, the sticky price/wage equilibrium may well dominate its flexible counterpart.

4.4 Capital market inflationary expectations as a guide to monetary policy

Since prices are determined by the decentralised decisions of many sellers the rate of inflation is ultimately determined by the aggregation of their decisions. An important insight of New Keynesian economics is that, due to temporary price and wage stickiness, the aggregate rate of inflation depends on inflationary expectations. The central bank can therefore affect the rate of inflation by influencing inflationary expectations. Importantly, this implies that a current credible change in CB policy may affect the rate of inflation immediately and not only with a lag, as is the case in backward-looking models.[35]

Countries such as Israel and Chile in which the joint availability of nominal and indexed bonds makes it possible to obtain up-to-date information on inflationary expectations can therefore use this information as a leading indicator of inflation and partially base monetary policy on it. The Bank of Israel has actually done that to various extents during the last decade with reasonable success. One advantage of inflationary expectations from the capital market as an indicator of monetary policy is that when, due to unanticipated adverse shocks, credibility declines, the bank can act quickly to restore credibility before the decline has had a serious impact on inflation. During periods following the successful stabilisation of inflation in which the uncertainty about structural economic parameters is high, the availability of such an indicator is particularly attractive.

Bernanke and Woodford (1997) point out that, if conventionally defined rational inflationary expectations are used as the sole indicator for policy, the price level may become indeterminate and the rate of inflation may diverge. This is sometimes referred to figuratively as the problem of 'the monkey in the mirror'. However, in spite of occasional substantial reliance on inflationary expectations from the capital market, no such instability had been recorded in Israel. Possible reasons for this divergence between theory and outcomes are that the Bank of Israel has relied on other indicators as well and generally deviated from precise adherence to the mechanical rule postulated in Bernanke and Woodford. My gut feeling is that, although the problem of the monkey in the mirror may become a real possibility under high inflation, it is very unlikely in the current generally very-low-inflation environment.

4.5 Central bank capital, distribution of profits and independence

The issue of CB capital and of rules for the distribution of profits and their impact on the bank's independence is a relatively neglected institutional aspect of central banking. It appears, at first blush, to bear strong similarities to such questions for private corporations. Formally central banks and private firms are incorporated within a similar legal structure and utilise similar accounting principles. However, this resemblance in formal procedures hides several important differences. Unlike private corporations, CBs are set up to achieve aggregate policy objective(s) rather than to maximise profits. Unlike a private corporation, a negative net worth (or capital) at the CB does not imply that the bank will go bankrupt and cease to operate. Finally, the main owner of the CB is the government rather than private individuals implying that any distribution of profits increases the spending power of government and that CB losses ultimately translate into revenue losses or additional expenditures for the central government.

When the level of CB capital becomes negative and drops below some threshold there is a danger that the political establishment might be successful in preventing the bank from following policies that lead to additional losses, limiting the independence of the bank through its balance-sheet position. In such cases, the more capital a CB possesses, the better its ability to conduct policy independently from fiscal authorities. This consideration is particularly important when the public interest requires the CB to adopt policies that create further losses for the bank. Such situations may arise for a variety of reasons such as when achievement of an inflation target necessitates contractionary policies, when financial stability considerations require the bank to assume the losses of failed financial institutions in order to reduce the risk of a systemic crisis or due to a costly defence of a peg or band.

The point is not that negative capital always limits the policy options of the bank. Thus, the Banco Central de Chile managed to stabilise inflation in spite of negative capital on its balance sheet. In the Chilean case the negative capital was not a constraint because government was committed to maintain a budgetary surplus. But there obviously are other cases in which the negative capital of the bank seriously limited independence. Examples are provided in Stella (2005).

Does that imply that in order to ensure CBI, government should always cover all CB losses? The answer is not clear cut since such an arrangement allows a non-elected institution (the CB) to make fiscal policy decisions. This is obviously questionable on grounds of democratic accountability. Consequently, there is a trade off between democratic accountability and CBI. This trade off may become particularly important when the occurrence of large economic or political shocks force the CB to engage in policies that have substantial adverse fiscal implications. When endowed with sufficient legal independence and positive levels of capital, it is quite likely that most Western CBs will be able to engage in loss-creating policies when such policies are required. However, if at the time those policies are needed the bank already has a substantial amount of negative capital, it is likely that the political establishment will have the ability, and often the incentive, to stop, delay or severely limit them.

This risk is important mainly in developing countries in which the association between actual and legal independence is loose. In such cases the relation between independence and the level of CB capital is likely to be discontinuous in the sense that below a certain threshold of negative capital the CB will be seriously limited by political authorities even if it enjoys a high level of legal independence. But above this threshold the ability of the bank to conduct policy independently will not depend, to a first approximation, on the level of CB capital. It follows that maintenance of a sufficiently high level of capital is basically a (partial) insurance against states of nature in which the bank's ability to resist the pressures of political authorities is weakened.[36]

Similar considerations apply to rules and regulations for the allocation of CB profits to government. Such rules are often not very transparent and biased towards larger distributions to government opening the door for evasion of deficit limits. Clear and transparent rules about the distribution of profits as well as about procedures for rebuilding negative levels of central bank capital enhance the bank's independence and its credibility as a guardian of price stability. An enlightening discussion of those issues appears in Stella (2005).

Notes

* I thank an anonymous referee, Jakob de Haan, Roland Vaubel and David Archer for useful comments on previous drafts. Earlier versions of the chapter were presented as a distinguished lecture at the September 2005 meeting of the Chilean Economic Association in Vina del Mar Chile, at the November 2006 Second Economic History Panel on the Evolution of Central Banks (Bank of England), at the September 2007 Bocconi University Conference on Central Bank Independence and at the November 2007 joint Bundesbank–Bank of Finland Conference on Designing Central Banks in Eltville, Germany.

1 In the case of many developing countries the central bank often functioned as a development bank that provided subsidised loans to various sectors of the economy.

2 Partly because of the US wide capital markets, the de facto independence of the Federal Reserve was higher than its legal independence. At the time the German Bundesbank was unique, in that it enjoyed both *de jure* as well as de facto independence and generally used its independence to promote public support for price stability. In spite of this long-term position the Bundesbank's policy occasionally responded to the electoral cycle. Vaubel (1997) shows that monetary expansion accelerated at the beginning of pre-election periods when the German government had a political majority at the Bundesbank council and that it decelerated when the reverse was true.

3 In a few cases such as the ECB and the Banco Central de Chile, the bank is even given some limited goal independence in the sense that it is free to determine its own inflation target.

4 For reasons of space I do not discuss the fast-expanding literature on those topics. The March 2007 issue of the *European Journal of Political Economy* is devoted to CB transparency and communications.

5 Previous surveys appear in Eijffinger and de Haan (1996) and in Berger *et al.* (2001).

6 Although related independence and conservatism are not quite the same. Independence refers to the ability of the bank to implement the policies it desires without political interference. Conservatism refers to the importance that the bank assigns to price

stability in comparison to real objectives like high levels of economic activity and employment. Obviously, effective conservatism, which determines policy choices, depends both on the bank's conservatism, as well as on its independence. For the purposes of this survey there is no need to distinguish between those two concepts. I therefore use the terms conservatism and independence interchangeably to mean 'effective conservatism'. However, there are contexts in which it is useful to keep conservatism and independence apart (Eijffinger and Hoebericht, 1998).

7 Using data till the end of the 1980s Cukierman (1992: chapter 19) documents a negative correlation between inflation and legal independence in developed economies but no significant relation between those two variables in developing countries. More recent evidence surveyed below suggests that the difference between actual and legal independence may also vary over time within a given country.

8 The turnover variable was originally introduced in chapter 19 of Cukierman (1992) and in Cukierman *et al.* (1992). De Haan and Kooi (2000) and Dreher *et al.* (2007) have updated this index and extended it to a wider sample of countries. The index of political vulnerability appears in Cukierman and Webb (1995).

9 This index is based on a coding of 16 different characteristics of CB charters that pertain to the allocation of authority over monetary policy, procedures for resolution of conflicts between the CB and government, the relative importance of price stability in CB objectives as stated in the law, the seriousness of limitations on lending by the CB to government, and procedures for the appointment and dismissal of the governor of the CB. Cukierman *et al.* (1992) present a weighted index of those 16 characteristics (LVAW) and Cukierman (1992) presents an unweighted version of the same characteristics (LVAU). Both indices refer to a sample of over 60 countries.

Other indices that appeared until the beginning of the 1990s such as those used by Bade and Parkin (1988), Alesina (1988, 1989), Alesina and Summers (1993), Grilli *et al.* (1991) and Eijffinger and Schaling (1993) can, for the most part, be approximated by subsets of the components of the LVAW (or of the LVAU) index.

10 The additional features included in the Jacome–Vazquez index involve procedures for appointment and dismissal of the entire CB board rather than just the governor, the extent to which the CB has a say with respect to exchange-rate policy, the obligations of the CB as a lender of last resort, the existence of provisions for the preservation of CB capital and the existence of legal provisions relating to the accountability and transparency of the CB.

11 Dreher *et al.* (2007) focus on the impact of political instability, elections and inflation on the probability that a CB governor is replaced rather than on the evolution of turnover over time.

12 Compared to a money stock target that may be only loosely related to inflation, an inflation target has the advantage that it focuses on the final objective of policy. But, unlike sufficiently narrow monetary targets, inflation is less controllable. Some of the consequences of this trade off for monetary policy are discussed in Cukierman (1995).

13 By contrast, inflation targets in New Zealand were introduced, concurrently with a substantial upgrading of legal independence, in 1989. But they have not been embedded in the Reserve Bank of New Zealand law. The 1989 law only requires that the Governor and the Minister of Finance agree (in a Policy Targets Agreement) on some target or targets for monetary policy. This was done expressly because nobody knew at the time whether the inflation targeting framework will succeed in delivering price stability.

14 A more extensive but older discussion appears in Cukierman (1998).

15 KPBG stands for Kydland and Prescott (1977) and Barro and Gordon (1983).

16 Using cross-sectional data from 11 EMU countries, Vaubel (1997) shows that, when a measure of the public's sensitivity to inflation is added to a regression of inflation on legal independence, the first variable is negative and significant whereas legal inde-

pendence is not significant. Further details appear in Vaubel's comment on this survey.

17 Relatedly, de Haan and Kooi (2000) present evidence supporting the view that the relation between inflation and turnover is driven mainly by data from high-inflation countries.

18 See, for example, Taylor (1999) and, for Latin America, Loayza and Schmidt-Hebbel (2002).

19 This even led some critics of the Bank to claim that the Bank was aiming at an inflation target that was lower than the one assigned to it by government (Sussman, 2007).

20 Alternatively one can think of those objective functions as being time invariant but dependent on the long-run state in which the economy happens to be. To my knowledge, existing literature did not attempt to model or estimate such dependence explicitly.

21 In some isolated cases price stability has been achieved without either of those anchors by having sufficiently conservative treasuries conduct monetary police. This was the case in Japan during the second half of the twethieth century.

22 The two ways in which changes that have occurred, worldwide, in the use of exchange-rate-based anchors during the 1990s are discussed in Fischer (2001).

23 Corbo (2002) discusses the reasons for these changes for Latin American countries.

24 Some of the earlier work in this area was carried out by political scientists. Hall (1994) and Hall and Franzese (1998) are examples. A recent survey that focuses mainly on the subsequent economic literature appears in Cukierman (2004).

25 In more technical terms they act as Stackelberg leaders vis-à-vis the CB.

26 By using money equilibrium the analysis in those models can be recast, equivalently, in terms of an interest rate instrument instead of a money stock instrument.

27 In the extreme case of a monopoly union this view implies that (abstracting from stabilisation policy) a populist or ultra-liberal CB that cares only about unemployment is best for a society that dislikes both inflation and unemployment.

28 Accommodation and conservatism are distinct concepts. However, empirical evidence presented in Cukierman *et al.* (1998) suggests that more conservative central banks are less accommodative. Such an association is also implied by theory.

29 An extension of this framework designed to capture strategic interactions between fiscal and monetary policies in the presence of unionised labour markets appears in Cukierman and Dalmazzo (2006).

30 Cukierman *et al.* (2002) show that high levels of legal CBI in the newly created central banks of the FSEs did not stop the substantial inflationary impact of price decontrols during the 1990s.

31 According to these definitions, a CB is a flexible inflation targeter if its loss function penalises the output as well as the inflation gaps. By contrast a bank is a strict inflation targeter if it cares only about the inflation gap. Obviously there can be only one kind of strict targeter but many types of flexible targeters depending on the weight of the output gap in comparison to that of the inflation gap in the bank's loss function. The higher this weight, the more flexible, or less conservative, is the bank. In practice, CBs that target only inflation will also appear 'flexible' if they seek to bring it back on target after a shock with a lag rather than at the first opportunity.

32 This point is developed more fully in Cukierman (2007b).

33 An early formulation of this principle appears in Goodfriend and King (1997) and Rotemberg and Woodford (1997).

34 To a first approximation there is no connection between traditional measures of potential output based on various smoothers of output and the flexible wage and price equilibrium under perfect competition.

35 A survey appears in Clarida *et al.* (1999).

36 A fuller discussion appears in Cukierman (2006).

References

Alesina, A. (1988) 'Macroeconomics and Politics', *NBER Macroeconomics Annual*, 3, 13–52.

Alesina, A. (1989) 'Politics and Business Cycles in the Industrial Democracies', *Economic Policy*, 8, 57–98.

Alesina, A. and L. Summers (1993) 'Central Bank Independence and Macroeconomic Performance: Some Comparative Evidence', *Journal of Money, Credit and Banking*, 25, 151–162.

Arnone, M., B.J. Laurens and J.-F. Segalotto (2006) 'Measures of Central Bank Autonomy: Empirical Evidence for OECD, Developing and Emerging Market Economies', IMF Working Paper 06/228, October.

Bade, R. and M. Parkin (1988) 'Central Bank Laws and Monetary Policy', University of Western Ontario, manuscript.

Barro, R.J. (1986) 'Reputation in a Model of Monetary Policy with Incomplete Information', *Journal of Monetary Economics*, 17, 3–20.

Barro, R.J. and R. Gordon (1983) 'A Positive Theory of Monetary Policy in a Natural Rate Model', *Journal of Political Economy*, 91, 589–610.

Benigno, P. and M. Woodford (2005) 'Optimal Stabilization Policy When Wages and Prices are Sticky: The Case of a Distorted Steady State', in J. Faust, A. Orphanides and D. Reifschneider (eds), *Models and Monetary Policy*, Washington, DC: Federal Reserve Board.

Bernanke, B. and M. Woodford (1997) 'Inflation Forecasts and Monetary Policy', *Journal of Money, Credit and Banking*, 29 (4), 653–684.

Berger, H., J. de Haan and S. Eijffinger (2001) 'Central Bank Independence: An Update of Theory and Evidence', *Journal of Economic Surveys*, 15 (1), February, 3–40.

Blinder, A.S. (1998) *Central Banking in Theory and Practice*, Cambridge, MA: MIT Press.

Bowen, A. (1995) 'British Experience with Inflation Targetry', in L. Leiderman and L. Svensson (eds), *Inflation Targets*, London: CEPR.

Calvo, G. and C. Reinhart (2002) 'Fear of Floating', *Quarterly Journal of Economics*, 117, 379–408.

Clarida, R., J. Galí and M. Gertler (1999) 'The Science of Monetary Policy: a New Keynesian Perspective', *Journal of Economic Literature*, 37, December, 1661–1707.

Clarida, R., J. Galí and M. Gertler (2000) 'Monetary Policy Rules and Macroeconomic Stability: Evidence and Some Theory', *Quarterly Journal of Economics*, 113, February, 147–180.

Corbo, V. (2002) 'Monetary Policy in Latin America in the 90s'. In N. Loayza and K. Schmidt-Hebbel (eds), *Monetary Policy: Rules and Transmission Mechanisms.*, Santiago: Central Bank of Chile, pp. 117–166.

Coricelli, F., A. Cukierman and A. Dalmazzo (2006) 'Monetary Institutions, Monopolistic Competition, Unionized Labor Markets and Economic Performance', *Scandinavian Journal of Economics*, 108, March, 39–63. Available online: www.tau.ac.il/~alexcuk/pdf/ccd-SJE-final-03-05-2.pdf.

Cukierman, A. (1992) *Central Bank Strategy, Credibility and Independence – Theory and Evidence*, Cambridge, MA: MIT Press.

Cukierman, A. (1995) 'Towards a Systematic Comparison between Inflation Targets and Monetary Targets', in L. Leiderman and L. Svensson (eds), *Inflation Targets*, London: CEPR, pp. 192–209.

Cukierman, A. (1998) 'The Economics of Central Banking', in Wolf Holger (ed.), *IEA, Contemporary Economic Issues – Macroeconomics and Finance*, vol. 5, London: Macmillan Press (IEA conference volume 125), pp. 37–82. Also published in Spanish in E. Aguirre, R. Junguito and G. Miller (eds) (1997) *La Banca Central en America Latina*, Tercer Mundo Editores, Bogota, Columbia, and in Portuguese in *Revista Brasileira de Economia*, 50, October–December 1996.

Cukierman, A. (2000a) 'Establishing a Reputation for Dependability by Means of Inflation Targets', *Economics of Governance*, 1, February, 53–76. Reprinted in L. Mahadeva and G. Sterne (eds) (2000) *Monetary Frameworks in a Global Context*, London: Routledge. Available online: www.tau.ac.il/~alexcuk/pdf/TARGT-Published-Version.pdf.

Cukierman, A. (2000b) 'The Inflation Bias Result Revisited', unpublished manuscript. Available online: www.tau.ac.il/~alexcuk/pdf/infbias1.pdf.

Cukierman, A. (2002) 'Are Contemporary Central Banks Transparent about Economic Models and Objectives and What Difference Does it Make?', *Federal Reserve Bank of St. Louis Review*, 84 (4), July–August, 15–45. Available online: www.tau.ac.il/~alexcuk/pdf/FRBStL.pdf.

Cukierman, A. (2004) 'Monetary Institutions, Monetary Union and Unionised Labor Markets: Some Recent Developments', in R. Beetsma, C. Favero, A. Missale, V.A. Muscatelli, P. Natale and P. Tirelli (eds), *Monetary Policy, Fiscal Policies and Labour Markets: Key Aspects of Macroeconomic Policymaking in EMU*, Cambridge: Cambridge University Press, pp. 299–326.

Cukierman, A. (2005) 'Keynesian Economics, Monetary Policy and the Business Cycle – New and Old', *CESifo Economic Studies*, 51 (4), 697–728. Available online: www.tau.ac.il/~alexcuk/pdf/CES-ifo-ES-12-05.pdf.

Cukierman, A. (2006) 'Central Bank Finances and Independence – How Much Capital Should a Central Bank Have', manuscript.

Cukierman, A. (2007a) 'Should the Bank of Israel Have a Growth Target? – What Are the Issues?', *Israel Economic Review*, 4 (2), April, 1–18. Available online: www.tau.ac.il/~alexcuk/pdf/%E0%EC%F7%F1_%F6%E5%F7%F8%EE%EF-%E7%E3%F9.pdf.

Cukierman, A. (2007b) 'De Jure, De facto, and Desired Independence: The Bank of Israel as a Case Study', in N. Liviatan and H. Barkai (eds), *The Bank of Israel, Vol. II: Selected Topics in Israel's Monetary Policy*, Oxford: Oxford University Press. Available online: www.tau.ac.il/~alexcuk/pdf/V2_BI_ch01-Reprint.pdf.

Cukierman, A. and A. Dalmazzo (2006) 'Fiscal – Monetary Policy Interactions in the Presence of Unionized Labor Markets', *International Tax and Public Finance*, 13, 411–435.

Cukierman, A. and S. Gerlach (2003) 'The Inflation Bias Revisited: Theory and Some International Evidence', *The Manchester School*, 71 (5), September, 541–565.

Cukierman, A. and F. Lippi (1999) 'Central Bank Independence, Centralization of Wage Bargaining, Inflation and Unemployment: Theory and Some Evidence', *European Economic Review*, 43, 1395–1434. Available online: www.tau.ac.il/~alexcuk/pdf/Lippi1EER.pdf.

Cukierman, A. and F. Lippi (2005) 'Endogenous Monetary Policy with Unobserved Potential Output', *Journal of Economics Dynamics and Control*, 29, 11, November, 1951–1983. Available online: www.tau.ac.il/~alexcuk/pdf/Lippi-III-2-05-JEDC-final.pdf.

Cukierman, A. and N. Liviatan (1991) 'Optimal Accomodation by Strong Policymakers under Incomplete Information', *Journal of Monetary Economics*, 27 (1), January, 99–127.

Cukierman, A. and A. Muscatelli (2008) 'Non Linearities in Taylor Rules and Asymmetric Preferences in Central Banking – Evidence from the UK and the US', *The B.E. Journal of Macroeconomics*, 8 (1) (Contributions), Article 7. Available online: www.bepress.com/bejm/vol. 8/iss1/art7.

Cukierman, A. and S.B. Webb (1995) 'Political Influence on the Central Bank: International Evidence', *The World Bank Economic Review*, 9 (3), September, 397–423.

Cukierman, A., P. Kalaitzidakis, L. Summers and S. Webb (1993) 'Central Bank Independence, Growth, Investment and Real Rates', *Carnegie-Rochester Conference Series on Public Policy*, 39, Autumn, 95–145.

Cukierman, A., G.P. Miller and B. Neyapti (2002) 'Central Bank Reform, Liberalization and Inflation in Transition Economies: An International Perspective', *Journal of Monetary Economics*, 49, March, 237–264.

Cukierman, A., P. Rodriguez and S. Webb (1998) 'Central Bank Autonomy and Exchange Rate Regimes: Their Effects on Monetary Accommodation and Activism', in S. Eijffinger and H. Huizinga (eds), *Positive Political Economy: Theory and Evidence*, Cambridge and New York: Cambridge University Press, pp. 78–120.

Cukierman, A., Y. Spiegel and L. Leiderman (2004) 'The Choice of Exchange Rate Bands: Balancing Credibility and Flexibility', *Journal of International Economics*, 62 (2), March, 379–408.

Cukierman, A., S. Webb and B. Neyapti (1992) 'Measuring The Independence of Central Banks and Its Effect on Policy Outcomes', *The World Bank Economic Review*, 6, September, 353–398.

de Haan, J. and W. Kooi (2000) 'Does Central Bank Independence Really Matter? New Evidence for Developing Countries Using a New Indicator', *Journal of Banking and Finance*, 24, 643–664.

Dreher, A., J.E. Sturm and J. de Haan (2007) 'Does High Inflation Cause Central Bankers to Lose Their Job? Evidence Based on a New Data Set', CESifo Working Paper No. 2045.

Eijffinger, S. and J. de Haan (1996) 'The Political Economy of Central Bank Independence', *Special Papers in International Economics, No. 19, International Finance Section*, Princeton University.

Eijffinger, S. and M. Hoeberichts (1998) 'The Trade-off between Central Bank Independence and Conservatism', *Oxford Economic Papers*, 50, 397–411.

Eijffinger, S. and E. Schaling (1993) 'Central Bank Independence in Twelve Industrial Countries', *Banca Nazionale del Lavoro Quarterly Review*, 184, March, 64–68.

Fischer, Stanley (2001) 'Distinguished Lecture on Economics in Government: Exchange Rate Regimes: Is the Bipolar View Correct?', *Journal of Economic Perspective*, 15, 3–24.

Goodfriend, M. and R. King (1997) 'The New Neoclassical Synthesis and the Role of Monetary Policy', *NBER Macroeconomic Annual*, 231–282.

Grilli, V., D. Masciandro and G. Tabellini (1991) 'Political and Monetary Institutions and Public Financial Policies in the Industrial Countries', *Economic Policy*, 13, 341–392.

Gutierrez, E. (2003) 'Inflation Performance and Constitutional Central Bank Independence: Evidence from Latin America and the Caribbean', IMF Working Paper, March.

Hall, P.A. (1994) 'Central Bank Independence and Coordinated Wage Bargaining: Their Interaction in Germany and Europe', *German Politics and Society*, 31, 1–23.

Hall, P.A. and R.J. Franzese (1998) 'Mixed signals: Central Bank Independence, Coordinated Wage Bargaining, and European Monetary Union', *International Organization*, 52, 505–535.

Jacome, L.I. and F. Vazquez (2005) 'Any Link between Legal Central Bank Independence and Inflation? Evidence from Latin America and the Caribbean', IMF Working Paper 05/75, April.

Kydland, F.E. and E.C. Prescott (1977) 'Rules Rather Than Discretion: The Inconsistency of Optimal Plans', *Journal of Political Economy*, 85, 473–492.

Lawler, P. (2000) 'Centralized Wage Setting, Inflation Contracts, and the Optimal Choice of Central Banker', *Economic Journal*, 110, 559–575.

Lippi, F. (2003) 'Strategic Monetary Policy with Non-Atomistic Wage Setters', *Review of Economic Studies*, 70, 1–11.

Loayza, N. and K. Schmidt-Hebbel (eds) (2002) *Monetary Policy: Rules and Transmission Mechanisms*, Santiago: Banco Central de Chile.

Maxfield, S. (1998) *Gatekeepers of Growth: The International Political Economy of Central Banking in Developing Countries*, Princeton, NJ: Princeton University Press.

Orphanides, A. (2001) 'Monetary Policy Rules based on Real-Time Data', *American Economic Review*, 91 (4), 964–985.

Patinkin, D. (1963) *Money, Interest and Prices*, 2nd edn, New York: Harper and Row.

Rogoff, K. (1985) 'The Optimal Degree of Commitment to a Monetary Target', *Quarterly Journal of Economics*, 100, 1169–1190.

Rotemberg, J. and M. Woodford (1997) 'An Optimization Based Econometric Framework for the Evaluation of Monetary Policy', in B. Bernanke and J. Rotemberg (eds), *NBER Macroeconomic Annual*, 297–346.

Ruge-Murcia, F.J. (2003) 'Does the Barro-Gordon Model Explain the Behavior of US Inflation? A Reexamination of the Empirical Evidence', *Journal of Monetary Economics*, 50, 1375–1390.

Schmidt-Hebbel, K. (2004) 'Toward Floating and Inflation Targeting in Chile', paper presented at a research workshop, Bank of Israel, December.

Skott, P. (1997) 'Stagflationary Consequences of Prudent Monetary Policy in a Unionized Economy', *Oxford Economic Papers*, 49, 609–622.

Soskice, D. and T. Iversen (1998) 'Multiple Wage-Bargaining Systems in the Single European Currency Area', *Oxford Review of Economic Policy*, 14 (3), 110–124.

Soskice, D. and T. Iversen (2000) 'The Non Neutrality of Monetary Policy with Large Price or Wage Setters', *Quarterly Journal of Economics*, 115, 265–284.

Stella, P. (2005) 'Central Bank Financial Strength, Transparency and Policy Credibility', *IMF Staff Papers*, 52, 2, 355–365.

Sussman, N. (2007) 'Monetary Policy in Israel, 1986–2000: Estimating the Central Bank's Reaction Function', in N. Liviatan and H. Barkai (eds), *The Bank of Israel: Volume II, Selected Topics in Israel's Monetary Policy*, Oxford, New York: Oxford University Press, pp. 46–66.

Svensson, L.E.O. (1994) 'Why Exchange Rate Bands? Monetary Independence in Spite of Fixed Exchange Rates', *Journal of Monetary Economics*, 33, 157–199.

Svensson, L.E.O. (1997) 'Inflation Forecast Targeting: Implementing and Monitoring Inflation Targets', *European Economic Review*, 41, June, 1111–1146.

Taylor, J.B. (ed.) (1999) *Monetary Policy Rules*, Chicago and London: The University of Chicago Press and NBER.

Vaubel, R. (1997) 'The Bureaucratic and Partisan Behavior of Independent Central Banks: German and International Evidence', *European Journal of Political Economy*, 13, 201–224

Woodford, M. (2003) *Interest and Prices: Foundations of a Theory of Monetary Policy*, Princeton, NJ: Princeton University Press.

COMMENTS BY ROLAND VAUBEL

I shall address three major problems associated with central bank independence which the paper does not consider:

1 Is low inflation really due to central bank independence or rather to the inflation aversion of the country's electorate? (This is, of course, a very German concern.)
2 Are independent central banks at the same time politically neutral, i.e. non-partisan, in their monetary policies over the electoral cycle?
3 Does central bank independence lead to bureaucratic waste?

In answering these three questions, I shall draw on my own empirical research.

1 The role of inflation aversion

Central bank independence does not have a significant effect on inflation once the inflation aversion of the electorates is taken into account. This is shown in Table 3.1 which reports the results of a cross-section analysis for the 11 original members of the European Monetary Union. If inflation is solely regressed on central bank independence (equation 1), the regression coefficient is significantly negative. If the electorate's sensitivity to inflation is added, the coefficient of central bank independence becomes insignificant, while the coefficient of the sensitivity to inflation is significant at the 1 per cent level. Sensitivity dominates independence.

How is the sensitivity to inflation measured? The data are from Hayo (1998). For each country separately, he regressed the share(s) of respondents mentioning inflation as their primary or second concern among four possible concerns[1] on the current rate of inflation (π_t):

$$s_t = a + b\pi_t \tag{1}$$

The regression coefficient b is the conditional sensitivity to inflation. Table 3.2 shows that it is highest in Germany, Austria and the Netherlands (in that order). It is strongly correlated with the inflation aversion of central banks which Lippi and Swank (1999) have estimated from policy reaction functions (r = +0.91). The sensitivity to inflation can be well explained by the experience of (hyper-) inflation between 1900 and 1940 (π_{t-n}):

$$b_{i,t} = \underset{(4.55^{***})}{1.57} + \underset{(4.22^{***})}{0.069}\, \pi_{i,\,t-n} \qquad R^2 = 0.66 \quad n = 11 \tag{2}$$

Equations 3 to 7 of Table 3.1 indicate that the effect of central bank independence on inflation remains insignificant if independence is interacted with the exchange-rate regime (which it ought to be, but hardly ever is, in studies of

Table 3.1 Cross-section analysis of inflation in EMU-11 and EU-15 (ln), 1976–1993

Equation	*Intercept*	*Conditional sensitivity to inflation ln* b	*Central bank independence ln* I	*Independence without pegging ln* $I^{(1-f)}$	*Pegging ln* $e^f = f$	*Imports/GDP ln* m	R^2 R^2 *adj.*	*n*
1	2.158 (17.59***)		–1.120 (–4.44***)				0.69 0.65	11
2	2.230 (27.18***)	–0.522 (–3.66***)	–0.297 (–1.07)				0.88 0.85	11
3	2.225 (25.14***)	–0.664 (–5.54***)		+0.063 (0.25)			0.87 0.83	11
4	2.337 (19.76***)	–0.527 (–3.45**)		–0.220 (–0.69)	–0.300 (–1.35)		0.90 0.85	11
5	2.387 (18.16***)	–0.606 (–3.54**)		–0.019 (–0.05)	–0.214 (–0.81)		0.81 0.76	15
6	3.422 (9.88***)	–0.593 (–5.80***)		–0.136 (–0.64)	–0.009 (–0.05)	–0.337 (–3.21**)	0.96 0.94	11
7	3.680 (6.89***)	–0.698 (–4.77***)		+0.095 (0.33)	+0.105 (0.41)	–0.399 (–2.47**)	0.88 0.83	15

Source: Vaubel (2003).

Notes
*** significant at 1 per cent level.
** significant at 5 per cent level.
* significant at 10 per cent level.

Table 3.2 Conditional sensitivity to inflation in opinion surveys and inflation aversion estimated from reaction functions

Country	*Conditional sensitivity to inflation (Hayo, 1998)*	*Inflation aversion (Lippi and Swank, 1999)*
Portugal	0.33	0.68
Ireland	0.92	0.11
Italy	1.28	0.39
Spain	1.35	0.51
Finland	1.60	0.20
France	2.05	0.79
Belgium	2.06	1.56
Luxembourg	2.84	1.56
Netherlands	3.59	1.23
Austria	3.95	4.55
Germany	5.81	3.51

central bank independence) or if a dummy for pegging to the deutschemark or the import/GDP ratio are added or if the sample is extended from EMU-11 to EU-15. Other control variables like universal banking or political instability (Posen, 1993) do not have a significant effect on inflation.

Central bank independence and the sensitivity to inflation are highly and positively correlated, i.e. collinear.[2] Probably, they affect each other. If the electorate is very sensitive to inflation, it tends to vote for parties supporting central bank independence and, if the central bank is independent, the latter will probably try to influence public opinion with the aim of strengthening the voters' aversion to inflation.

As the estimates of Table 3.1 are based on very small samples, I replicate the analysis with a sample of 48 countries in 1980–1991 for the purpose of this comment.[3] The source for the sensitivity to inflation is the World Values Survey (1990). It measures the share of respondents who mentioned 'fighting rising prices' as their main concern among four.[4] I call this the 'absolute sensitivity to inflation'. Once more, the regressions are estimated in logarithms, i.e. with constant elasticities. As Table 3.3 shows, neither legal central bank independence (LVAU from Cukierman, 1992) nor the absolute sensitivity to inflation have a significant effect on inflation at conventional levels regardless of whether they are taken separately or combined. However, as Hayo's coefficient measures the concern about inflation relative to the current inflation, the absolute sensitivity to inflation may have to be divided by the inflation rate which the country has experienced in the 1980s. This ratio, which I call the relative sensitivity to inflation, has a highly significant negative effect as predicted. Once more, the coefficient of central bank independence is completely insignificant. If the five countries experiencing inflation rates of more than 100 per cent on average (Argentina, Brazil, Israel, Peru, Uganda) are excluded, the coefficient of central bank independence turns negative but remains insignificant at the 10 per cent level ($t = -1.34$), while the negative effect of the relative sensitivity becomes even more significant. The econometric drawback of this test is that the relative

Table 3.3 Cross-section analysis of inflation (ln) in 48 countries, 1980–1991

Equation	*Intercept*	*Central bank independence (ln)*	*Absolute sensitivity to inflation (ln)*	*Relative sensitivity to inflation (ln)*	R^2
1	2.76 (4.91***)	0.146 (0.34)			0.00
2	1.28 (1.41)		0.454 (1.47)		0.04
3	1.43 (1.48)	0.420 (0.95)	0.569 (1.82*)		0.06
4	4.81 (10.00***)	–0.142 (–0.60)		–1.804 (–7.40***)	0.68

Sources: inflation: Cukierman (1992), Table 19.3; legal independence of central bank: Cukierman (1992); LVAU, Table 19.3; absolute sensitivity to inflation: World Values Survey (1990), University of Michigan; relative sensitivity = absolute sensitivity relative to inflation experienced.

Note
Robust standard errors
*** significant at 1 per cent level
** significant at 5 per cent level
* significant at 10 per cent level
Sample: Countries listed in Cukierman (1992), Table 19.3 except for the following which were not covered by the World Values Survey (1990): The Bahamas, Barbados, Bolivia, Botswana, Costa Rica, Ethiopia, Ghana, Honduras, Kenya, Malaysia, Malta, Nepal, Nicaragua, Panama, Qatar, Thailand, Western Samoa, Yugoslavia, Zaire, Zambia.

sensitivity to inflation may be correlated with the dependent variable simply because the dependent variable is at the same time in its denominator.

The results of both tests are consistent with the view that inflation-averse people choose central bank independence because they hope it will lead to lower inflation but that in fact central bank independence does not have this effect and that inflation is rather determined by the country's 'stability culture' which reflects the voters' preferences and the country's history. But the evidence is also consistent with the alternative interpretation that central bank independence lowers inflation, that for this reason it is preferred by inflation-averse voters and that, in addition, their inflation aversion strongly affects inflation via public opinion. The problem is that we do not know which of the two interpretations is correct. In any case, it seems to be easier to attain price-level stability in conditions of high sensitivity and low independence than in conditions of low sensitivity and high independence.

2 Are independent central bankers non-partisan?

In two independent studies, McGregor (1996) for the United States and Vaubel (1993, 1997a) for Germany have tested the hypothesis that, before elections, central bankers vote for monetary policies favourable to the party or parties that have appointed them. We found that the null hypothesis cannot be rejected at the 1 per cent level. Since partisan majorities in the Bundesbank changed within quarters rather than between quarters quite frequently, I conducted a non-parametric test of four hypotheses with the following results:

Hypothesis 1. During a pre-election period, monetary expansion is faster than during the preceding post-election period ('dependency or opportunist hypothesis').
Yes: 53, 65, 69, 76, 87, 94; $\Sigma = 6$
No: 57, 61, 80, 90; $\Sigma = 4$

The alternative hypothesis cannot be rejected at the 5 per cent level.

Hypothesis 2. If the political regime at the Bundesbank council changes in favour of the federal government, monetary expansion accelerates; if the regime change is unfavorable to the government, monetary expansion decelerates.
Yes: (53), 53, 56, 57, 61, 74, 85, 87, 89, (89), 90; $\Sigma = 11$
No: 52, 60, 65, 75, 77, 78, (79), 80, 82, (90); $\Sigma = 10$

Once more the result is not significant.

Hypothesis 3. If the federal government has a political majority in the Bundesbank council at the beginning of the pre-election period or if the political regime at the council changes in favour of the government during the pre-election period, monetary expansion accelerates; it decelerates if the opposite is the case ('party preference hypothesis').
Yes: (53), 53, 56, (57), (61), 65, (79), 80, 85, 89, (89), 90, 94; $\Sigma = 13$
No: 75, (90); $\Sigma = 2$

The alternative hypothesis can be rejected at the 1 per cent level.

Hypothesis 4. If the political regime at the Bundesbank council changes in favour of the Christian Democrats, monetary expansion decelerates; if it changes in favour of the Social Democrats, monetary expansion accelerates ('partisan theory').
Yes: 52, 60, 65, 74, (90); $\Sigma = 5$
No: (53), 53, 56, 57, 61, 75, 77, 78, (79), 80, 82, 85, 87, 89, (89), 90; $\Sigma = 16$

The alternative hypothesis cannot be rejected.
Once more, two caveats are in order.

1 Subsequent time-series regressions with quarterly data for a more limited time span did not yield a fully significant effect of partisan central bank majorities on inflation (e.g. Berger and Woitek, 1997; Lohmann, 1998). But

since the regime changes do not coincide with ends of quarters, my non-parametric test may well be superior. Besides, there are several other problems with these studies which I have pointed out elsewhere (Vaubel, 1997b, 1998).

2 Partisan leanings may not always have been correctly classified in the case of right–left coalition governments. However, in these cases, I consulted a panel of five 'Bundesbank watchers', and they never contradicted each other. In any case, the empirical result for Hypothesis 3 is so overwhelming that it would probably survive one or two reclassifications.

What are the implications of these findings for the design of central banks? In my view, independent central bankers ought to be subject to sanctions if they do not attain the goal which the elected representatives of the people have set in the central bank's charter. I doubt that fines, as proposed by Walsh (1995), are very promising but I think that parliament ought to be able to dismiss the leading central banker(s) if a moving average of inflation exceeds a critical threshold. The European Constitutional Group (Bernholz *et al.*, 2004: 464) makes this proposal for the European Central Bank. As is well-known, a similar scheme was introduced in New Zealand in 1989, although in this case it is the Minister of Finance who can effect the dismissal.

3 Bureaucratic inefficiency

Alex Cukierman argues that central bank independence should also relate to the central bank's capital. Such independence may have a cost: bureaucratic waste. To test for this possibility, I have conducted a cross-section analysis of central bank staff for 21 industrial countries in 1993. I obtained the following estimate:

$$\begin{aligned} \ln L = 4.39 + &\; 0.965 \ln N + 0.476 \ln PBN + 0.602 \ln QC + 0.665 \ln DIS \\ (4.50^{***}) &\; (10.84^{***}) \quad (1.81^{*}) \quad (2.41^{**}) \quad (0.67) \\ + 0.362 \ln I &- 0.064 \ln E - 0.098 \ln Y \\ (0.45) &\quad (-0.24) \quad (-0.32) \\ R^2 &= 0.91 \end{aligned}$$

where L is central bank staff, N is the number of inhabitants (as the best-fitting proxy for output demand), PBN is a dummy which is equal to 1 if the central bank prints the banknotes itself and 0 otherwise, QC indicates the extent to which the central bank actively controls the quality of the currency in circulation, DIS measures the extent to which the central bank discounts private bills of exchange and other commercial paper, I is degree of central bank independence, E is a dummy for exchange-rate pegging and Y is GNP (or GDP) per capita.

Since an average of six indices of legal central bank independence (Masciandaro and Spinelli, 1994) does not have a significant effect on central bank staff, I tried de facto independence as measured by the turnover rate of central bank governors (Cukierman, 1992). As Table 3.4, columns 1–3, indicate, the coefficient is still insignificant in both industrial and less developed countries. The

Table 3.4 Central bank staff, international cross-section analysis, 1991–1993

Explanatory variables	*(1) Ics* n = *19*	*(2) LDCs* n = *26*	*(3) all* n = *45*	*(4) all* n = *19*	*(5) all* n = *19*
Intercept	9.35 (2.42**)	4.32 (3.19***)	4.11 (6.28***)	3.59 (4.59***)	4.07 (7.43***)
Population (ln *N*)	0.82 (8.77***)	0.70 (6.10***)	0.73 (10.61***)	0.76 (9.01***)	0.73 (10.35***)
Turnover rate of governors (ln *I*)	–0.19 (–0.56)	–0.20 (–0.62)	–0.15 (–0.76)		
Budgetary independence (ln *I*)				0.60 (1.32)	
Salary independence (ln *I*)					0.67 (2.84**)
Pegging (ln *E*)	0.35 (1.08)	0.35 (–0.64)	0.058 (0.24)	0.28 (1.01)	0.19 (0.81)
Income per capita (ln *Y*)	–0.44 (–1.02)	0.11 (0.85)	0.13 (1.83*)	0.17 (2.53**)	0.13 (2.31**)
R^2	0.87	0.71	0.76	0.86	0.90
$\overline{R}^2$	0.83	0.66	0.74	0.83	0.88

Source: Vaubel (1997).

Notes
*** significant at 1 per cent level.
** significant at 5 per cent level.
* significant at 10 per cent level.

same is true for budgetary independence (also from Cukierman, 1992) in column 4. However, column 5 reports a significant effect for salary independence (Cukierman, 1992) which probably reflects independence in all personnel matters.

Does this indicate bureaucratic waste? If staff had been shown to be higher in central banks enjoying monetary policy autonomy, one might have argued that policy-independent central banks need more staff to convince the public that their independence ought to be maintained. But there is no reason why central banks which are independent in matters of personnel need more staff than the others. Are the others understaffed? Do politicians have an incentive to keep the size of bureaucracy below the optimal level? There is one piece of good news, however: it is possible to have monetary policy independence without excess staff if the size and salaries of central bank staff are set by law. The effect of capital independence on bureaucratic waste – notably capital expenditure – is a topic for future research.

Notes

1 The other three concerns were threats to public order, democracy and the freedom of speech. This is the so-called Ingleheart Index published by Eurobarometer. Hayo (1998) reports a significantly negative simple (rank) correlation between inflation and the conditional sensitivity to inflation.

2 Thus, it is not surprising that central bank independence, too, bears a significantly positive correlation with the historical experience of (hyper-)inflation (de Haan and van't Hag, 1995).

3 Computational assistance from Ugurlu Soylu is gratefully acknowledged.

4 The other concerns were 'maintaining order in the nation', 'give people more say' and 'protecting freedom of speech'.

References

Berger, Helge and Ulrich Woitek (1997) 'How Opportunistic are Partisan German Central Bankers: Evidence on the Vaubel Hypothesis', *European Journal of Political Economy*, 13, 807–821.

Bernholz, Peter, Friedrich Schneider, Roland Vaubel and Frank Vibert (2004) 'An Alternative Constitutional Treaty for the European Union', *Public Choice*, 91, 451–468.

Cukierman, Alex (1992) *Central Bank Strategy, Credibility and Independence: Theory and Evidence*, Cambridge, MA: MIT Press.

de Haan, Jakob and Gert Jan van't Hag (1995) 'Variation in Central Bank Independence across Countries: Some Provisional Empirical Evidence', *Public Choice*, 85, 335–351.

Hayo, Bernhard (1998) 'Inflation Culture, Central Bank Independence and Price Stability', *European Journal of Political Economy*, 14, 241–263.

Lippi, Francesco and Otto H. Swank (1999) 'Policy Targets, Economic Performance and Central Bank Independence', in F. Lippi (ed.), *Central Bank Independence, Targets and Credibility*, Cheltenham: Elgar, pp. 121–148.

Lohmann, Susanne (1998) 'Federalism and Central Bank Independence: The Politics of German Monetary Policy, 1957–92', *World Politics*, 50, 401–446.

McGregor, Roy Rob (1996) 'FOMC Voting Behavior and Electoral Cycles: Partisan Ideology and Partisan Loyalty', *Economics and Politics*, 8, 17–32.

Masciandaro, Donato and Franco Spinelli (1994) 'Central Banks' Independence: Institutional Determinants, Rankings and Central Bankers' Views', *Scottish Journal of Political Economy*, 41, 434–443.

Posen, Adam (1993) 'Why Central Bank Independence Does Not Cause Low Inflation: There Is No Institutional Fix for Politics', in Richard O'Brien (ed.), *Finance and the International Economy*, Oxford: Oxford University Press, pp. 53–84.

Vaubel, Roland (1993) 'Eine Public-Choice-Analyse der Deutschen Bundesbank und ihre Implikationen für die Europäische Währungsunion', in Dieter Duwendag and Jürgen Siebke (eds), *Europa vor dem Eintritt in die Wirtschafts- und Währungsunion*, Berlin: Duncker & Humblot, pp. 23–80.

Vaubel, Roland (1997a) 'The Bureaucratic and Partisan Behaviour of Independent Central Banks: German and International Evidence', *European Journal of Political Economy*, 13, 201–225.

Vaubel, Roland (1997b) 'Reply to Berger and Woitek', *European Journal of Political Economy*, 13, 823–828.

Vaubel, Roland (1998) Comment on Susanne Lohmann 'Federalism and Central Bank Independence: The Politics of German Monetary Policy, 1957–92'. Available online: http://vaubel.uni-mannheim.de/publications/index.html.

Vaubel, Roland (2003) 'The Future of the Euro: A Public Choice Perspective', in Forrest H. Capie and Geoffrey E. Wood (eds), *Monetary Unions: Theory, History, Public Choice*, London: Routledge, pp. 146–181.

Walsh, Carl E. (1995) 'Optimal Contracts for Central Bankers', *American Economic Review*, 85, 150–167.

4 How should central banks define price stability?[1]

Mark A. Wynne

It is now widely accepted that price stability should be a (if not the) primary objective of central banks. Even for central banks with dual mandates, such as the Federal Reserve, the achievement of price stability is often seen as a key prerequisite to the attainment of other mandated objectives such as maximum employment. In this chapter I look at how central banks should define price stability, starting with current practices. I consider three questions. First, should price stability be defined in terms of a relatively broad price index, such as the deflator for Gross Domestic Product, or in terms of a narrower measure, such as a Consumer Price Index (CPI)? Second, should price stability be defined in terms of a headline measure of inflation, or in terms of a core measure that routinely excludes or down-weights the prices of certain goods and services? And third, should price stability be defined as no change in the chosen price index, or as a positive rate of increase in the chosen price index? The choice of the horizon over which price stability is to be maintained is arguably as important as the manner in which price stability is defined, but I will not address that question here. I will touch briefly on the question of how asset prices should figure in the definition of price stability, but I will not visit the well-trodden ground of how monetary policy should respond to asset price developments.

The Federal Reserve is perhaps unique among the major central banks in that it does not have an explicit numerical price objective. Former Federal Reserve Chairman Alan Greenspan famously defined price stability in qualitative terms as a situation in which 'households and businesses need not factor expectations of changes in the average level of prices into their decisions' (Greenspan, 1994a).[2] However, as Table 4.1 shows, many central banks, even those that would eschew the label of 'inflation targeter' do have explicit numerical price objectives. In all cases, these price objectives are specified in terms of a measure of consumer price inflation. Furthermore, almost all are defined in terms of the headline rather than a core measure, although that was not always the case. The Reserve Bank of New Zealand (RBNZ), which pioneered inflation targeting, switched from defining its target in terms of core to headline CPI in 1997.[3] In 1998, the Reserve Bank of Australia's inflation target was also changed from referring to 'underlying inflation' (which removed volatile components of the CPI such as the prices of unprocessed food, as well as prices that were heavily

Table 4.1 Numerical definitions of price stability

Country	*Target definition*	*Target index*
Australia	2–3	CPI
Brazil	4.5±2	CPI
Canada	2±1	CPI
Chile	2–4	CPI
Colombia	3–4.5	CPI
Czech Republic	3	CPI
Hungary	3	CPI
Iceland	2.5±1.5	CPI
Israel	1–3	CPI
Mexico	3±1	CPI
New Zealand	1–3	CPI
Norway	2.5	CPI*
Peru	2±1	CPI
Philippines	4–5	CPI
Poland	2.5±1	CPI
South Korea	3±1	CPI
South Africa	3–6	CPI
Sweden	2±1	CPI
Thailand	2±1	CPI core
United Kingdom	2	CPI (HICP)
Euro area	< 2	CPI (HICP)
Japan	0–2	CPI
Switzerland	< 2	CPI

Sources: Berg (2005), Truman (2003) and national central bank websites.*

Notes
Definitions as of mid-2007. The legislation defining Norway's inflation targets states that 'In general, the direct effects on consumer prices resulting from changes in interest rates, taxes, excise duties and extraordinary temporary disturbances shall not be taken into account'. Many countries have changed their target definition over time. Canada: 1991 – 3, 1992 – 2.5. Chile: 1990–1999 – unknown, 2000 – 3.5. Colombia: 2000 – 9, 2001 – 8, 2002 – 6, 2003–2004 – 5–6, 2006 – 4–5. Czech Republic: 1998 – 5.5–6.5, 1999 – 4–5, 2000 – 3.5–5.5, 2001 – 2–4, 2002–2005 – 3–5 to 2–4 (rolling band). Hungary: 2001 – 7±1, 2002 – 4.5±1, 2003–2004 – 3.5±1, 2005 – 4±1, 2006 – 3.5±1. Iceland: 2001 – 2.5±3.5, 2002 – 2.5±2. Israel: 1992 – 14–15, 1993 – 10, 1994 – 8, 1995 – 8–11, 1996 – 8–10, 1997–1998 – 7–10, 1999 – 4, 2000 – 3–4, 2001 – 2.5–3.5, 2002 – 2–3. Mexico: 1995–2003 – unknown. New Zealand: 1990–1995 – 0–2, 1996 – 0–3, 1997–1998 – 0–3 (indexed to CPIX), 1999–2001 – 0–3. Peru: 2002–2006 – 2.5±1. Philippines: 2002 – 5–6, 2003 – 5.5–6.5, 2004 – 4.5, 2005 – 5–6. Poland: 1998 – 9.5, 1999 – 8–8.5, 2000 – 5.4–6.8, 2001–2002 – 6–8, 2003 – below 4. South Korea: 1998 – 9±1, 1999 – 8–8.5, 2000 – 2.5±1, 2001 – 3±1 2002 – 2.5, 2003–2006 – 2.5–3.5. United Kingdom: 1992–1994 – 1–4, 1995–1996 – equal to or below 2.5, 1997–2002 – 2.5 (RPIX until 2003).

influenced by non-market developments, such as tobacco prices) to headline CPI inflation (but again excluding mortgage interest costs). The switch was made following changes to the construction of the CPI. And of course the Bank of England's inflation target, which was originally defined in terms of the Retail Price Index excluding mortgage interest payments (the RPIX, a core-like measure) was redefined in terms of the headline CPI or HICP in 2003. Perhaps the only central bank (that I am aware of) to have gone from targeting a headline measure to targeting a core measure is the Bank of Korea. After adopting inflation targeting in 1998, and targeting a headline measure of the CPI for two years, the Bank of Korea switched to a core measure (CPI inflation excluding non-cereal agricultural products and petroleum-based products) in 2000. In 2006 the target was redefined in terms of headline CPI inflation.

While almost all inflation-targeting central banks define their objective in terms of a headline measure of inflation, many if not all also assign an important role to measures of core inflation in their deliberations and communications with the general public. The importance assigned to core measures varies across countries. Some central banks, such as the Federal Reserve System, which does not have a formal definition of price stability, regularly publish forecasts of core inflation. Others, such as the Bank of England, which has a formal inflation target expressed in terms of a headline measure of inflation, completely eschew the publication of core measures in the regular communications.[4] Yet others such as the Sveriges Riksbank, which has a formal inflation target defined in terms of a headline measure, publish a wide variety of core measures in its regular *Monetary Policy Report*.[5]

The last point to note from Table 4.1 is that all of the central banks listed define price stability as prevailing at a positive measured rate of inflation. Usually some reference is made to measurement problems in justifying this choice, but there are often additional reasons, such as the desire to provide some safety margin against the risks of deflation.

1 Broad versus narrow measures

In practice, the debate over whether central banks should define price stability in terms of a broad or a narrow measure of inflation often comes to down to the choice between using a broad measure such as a GDP deflator to quantify the price objective, or a somewhat narrower measure such as a consumer price index. None of the central banks listed in Table 4.1 defined price stability in terms of a GDP deflator.[6] The reasons for this may well differ across countries but one fundamental argument against defining price stability in terms of a GDP deflator is the fact that, due to its definition, the GDP deflator could rise even as all prices are falling, since import prices enter the GDP deflator with a negative weight (Diewert, 2002). It is worth noting that this is not just a hypothetical concern: in the third quarter of 2007, inflation in the United States, as measured by the GDP deflator, was 1.04 per cent on an annualised basis, its lowest level in nine years, due in no small part to a 47.48 per cent (annualised) increase in the price of imports of petroleum and petroleum products during the quarter. It is possible to define price stability in terms of more of the components of final demand than consumption expenditures but in practice central banks seem to limit themselves to final consumption expenditures. The deflator for consumption expenditures in the national accounts is conceptually distinct from the cost-of-living-based CPI but the two tend to track each other fairly closely in most countries. The attractiveness of the cost-of-living-based CPI as a price objective is due in part to the fact that it has a solid welfare theoretic basis (although a surprising number of national statistical agencies seem to go out of their way to claim that the CPIs they produce are *not* intended to measure changes in the cost of living). Consumption is the final objective of all economic activity, so why not use a measure of the cost of consumption as the objective for monetary policy? In practice many governments and central banks seem to have settled on the consumer price index as the preferred price objective for very practical reasons: it tends to be the measure which is produced with the greatest frequency, gets the most attention and with which most voters are most familiar.[7]

The issue of how best to combine individual prices in a single measure of the price level has been addressed by many economists over the years (see the excellent review by Diewert (2001) or the discussion in Afriat (2005)). The early literature vacillated between the objectives of measuring prices for the purposes of assessing changes in living standards, and measuring prices for the purposes of monetary policy. (Although of course at the time many of these early contributions were made, much of the world was on a commodity standard and monetary policy, to the extent that it existed, was rule based.) One of the clearest statements about the appropriate domain of measurement for monetary policy purposes was made by Irving Fisher in his treatise on *The Purchasing Power of Money*:

> We are brought back ... to the conclusion that on the whole the best index number for the purpose of a standard of deferred payments in business is the same index number which we found the best to indicate the changes in prices of all business done; – in other words, it is the P on the right hand side of the equation of exchange.
>
> (Fisher, 1920, p. 225)

Arguing from a classic quantity theory of money perspective, Fisher was suggesting that for the purposes of monetary policy, the prices of *all* goods and services exchanged through monetary transactions ought to be included in the price index. However, he then went on to note

> It is, of course, utterly impossible to secure data for all exchanges, nor would this be advisable. Only articles which are standardized, and only those the use of which remains through many years, are available and important enough to include. These specifications exclude real estate, and to some extent wages, retail prices, and securities, thus leaving practically nothing but wholesale prices of commodities to be included in the list of goods, the prices of which are to be compounded into an index number. These restrictions, however, are not as important as might be supposed.
>
> (Fisher, 1920, pp. 225–226)

Here Fisher was anticipating the measurement problems posed by quality adjustment and the arrival of new goods in measuring aggregate inflation. His solution was to focus simply on a very narrow set of goods, arguing that these standardised commodities should give us a good sense of where the overall price level was headed. Note that Fisher is here arguing against the inclusion of real estate and financial asset prices on very practical grounds rather than on the basis of any a priori economic theory. Anticipating the later contributions of Bryan and Pike (1991) and Bryan and Cecchetti (1994), Fisher then went on to note that

> For practical purposes the median is one of the best index numbers. It may be computed in a small fraction of the time required for computing the more theoretically accurate index numbers, and it meets many of the tests of a good index number remarkably well.
>
> (1920, p. 230)

However, even if one is reluctant to embrace the quantity theory perspective that informed Fisher's argument, a case can perhaps be made for looking at a wider range of prices when thinking about inflation measurement for the purposes of monetary policy. Consider the following basic identity:

Units of numeraire per unit of good = Units of numeraire per unit of basket × Units of basket per unit of good (1)

Mathematically we can write this in terms of rates of change as

$$\pi_{i,t} = \pi_t + \varepsilon_{i,t} \quad (2)$$

where $\pi_{i,t}$ denotes the rate of change in the (numeraire denominated) price of good *i*, π_t denotes the rate of change in the overall price level (units of numeraire per unit of the basket of goods) and $\varepsilon_{i,t}$ captures the idiosyncratic (relative) movements in the price of good *i*. The raw data generated by a monetary economy are the $\pi_{i,t}$. The object that is of interest to the central bank and ultimately controlled by it is π_t.

To measure the rate of change in the numeraire, π_t, some identifying assumptions must be made. The simplest is to assume that the relative price changes are all uncorrelated with each other and have a mean value of zero. Then it is straightforward to show that a simple average of individual price changes will be a maximum likelihood estimator of the rate of change of the numeraire.[8] This was the measure of general inflation proposed by Jevons (1865). Of course, the assumption of independent relative price changes strains credulity, as Keynes (1930) pointed out. In recent years, more elaborate identifying assumptions have been proposed. Bryan and Cecchetti (1993) proposed specifying simple time-series processes for π_t and $\varepsilon_{i,t}$, while Reis and Watson (2007) use a somewhat more elaborate set of identifying assumptions.[9]

It is worth noting that the recent attempts to estimate the rate of change of the numeraire have limited the domain of measurement to consumer prices, components of the CPI in the case of Bryan and Cecchetti (1993), components of the deflator for personal consumption expenditure in the case of Reis and Watson

(2007).[10] Of course, if we are interested in changes in the value of the numeraire, there is no reason to limit attention to just consumer prices. The logic of measuring changes in the value of the numeraire suggests that one should include *all* prices that are denominated in terms of the numeraire: consumer prices, producer prices, intermediate goods prices, even asset prices.[11,12] This way of thinking about inflation measurement also suggests some important differences with the traditional cost-of-living perspective that underlies the calculation of consumer price indexes. For example, for the purposes of measuring changes in the value of the numeraire, one might want to look at the prices of houses, and not try to impute the value of the service flow from owner-occupied housing. Second, whereas the cost-of-living perspective provides a natural way to deal with the arrival of new goods (due to Hicks (1940)), the numeraire or monetary approach does not. The dynamic factor models are usually estimated using data from the subcomponents of an aggregate consumer price index with new goods simply linked in. Third, it is not clear how one ought to deal with quality changes. This applies to the prices of goods and services that are routinely included in a consumer price index, but also to the prices of assets that might also be included in calculating the value of the numeraire.

2 Headline versus 'core'

According to Table 4.1, few central banks define their price objective in terms of a measure of core inflation. Nevertheless, the contemporary literature on the theory of monetary policy argues that a core measure of some sort is the appropriate objective for monetary policy. However, the concept of core inflation that the recent literature suggests is the appropriate target for monetary policy is slightly different from the concept as it is currently commonly used. I start by reviewing some of the arguments for traditional measures of core before proceeding to a discussion of the more recent literature.

2.1 The traditional case for core inflation

One argument that is occasionally made to support the use of traditional measures of core inflation in monetary policy deliberations is that the central bank does not control the price of energy or the price of food, and therefore should not be charged with stabilising food or energy prices, or at least measures of inflation that include these prices. But just as central banks do not control the price of food or energy, nor do they control the price of clothing, entertainment, furniture or indeed any other individual component of the CPI. The most widely used measures of core inflation simply exclude the prices of specific goods, usually the prices of food and energy, on the grounds that these prices tend to be very volatile and convey little information about underlying inflation trends.[13] However, as many authors have pointed out, it is not always the case that food or energy prices are the most volatile or least informative about underlying trends. Not infrequently, large changes in monthly inflation rates occur that can be attributed to one-time shocks associated with tax changes, or other obviously transitory events. A common response is to simply discard these price changes and report the change in the index without them. Part of the motivation for the limited influence estimators of core inflation proposed by Bryan and Cecchetti (1994) is to put some discipline on the process of deciding which price signals to discard each month in computing core inflation. Indeed, this work has been very influential, and many central banks have explored the usefulness of trimmed mean or weighted median measure of core inflation.

However, these measures are not without their shortcomings. One of the most obvious is their inability to distinguish between transient and persistent extreme price movements. For example, the prices of electronic goods are routinely excluded from trimmed mean measures of core inflation, as the prices of these goods almost always show the largest declines every month. Dolmas (2005) finds that, after the prices of fresh vegetables and eggs, the prices of computers and peripherals are the ones most frequently excluded from his (optimally) trimmed mean measure of PCE inflation. Also included in the 20 most-often-excluded components are the prices of software, video equipment and TVs. Arguably these prices should not be excluded to the extent that they are persistent and likely to occur the following month, and by excluding them the trimmed mean measures of core arguably overstate the true trend rate of inflation.[14]

There are other good reasons why traditional measures of core inflation are unattractive for monetary policy purposes. To begin with, the traditional approaches lack a clear theoretical framework. As has been noted elsewhere, there are almost as many measures of core inflation as there are authors who have written on the topic. What criterion should be used to choose between them? One commonly used criterion is the ability to predict future headline inflation.[15] But if this is the objective of core inflation measurement, why limit oneself to the information in the cross-section distribution of prices or the time-series properties of prices. Why not use all available information? For example, Giannone and Matheson (2006) show that while their proposed new core inflation indicator (based on a dynamic factor model applied to disaggregated consumer price data) for New Zealand outperforms traditional measures in terms of its ability to predict future headline inflation, it is dominated by forecasts generated using a wider array of information. I would venture to suggest that this finding holds more generally.

Alternatively it is sometimes argued that measures of core inflation are intended to give real-time estimates of the underlying trend of headline inflation. But again we might ask, why are such estimates of interest to policy makers? Perhaps a discrepancy between the headline rate of inflation and the underlying trend gives us a signal of where headline inflation might be headed in the future: headline inflation that is above trend might be expected to fall in the future. But again, why not use all available information to asses the outlook for future headline inflation?

Finally, there is the problem that households consume the entire basket of consumer goods and not just some subset. There is the very real risk that a central bank that focuses on a measure of core inflation can be perceived as being out of touch, especially at times when there are large and persistent movements in the prices of the commodities that are excluded from the core measure.

In short, I would argue that there is little to support the use of traditional measures of core inflation as targets for monetary policy. There may be some merit in using them as part of central bank communications but even there the case is less than overwhelming.[16] The best available measures are the cost-of-living-based measures of inflation at the consumer level, although it is worth exploring alternative rationales for measures designed for monetary policy purposes. The Harmonized Index of Consumer Prices (HICP) that is used by the European Central Bank to quantify its mandate for price stability goes some of the way in this direction by taking as its measurement objective the cost of household final monetary consumption, although it too is not without problems.[17]

2.2 The newer case for core inflation

The literature on optimal monetary policy that has emerged in the past decade or so has produced a new set of rationales for monetary policy to focus on a measure of core inflation, albeit a measure that is quite distinct from the traditional measures. One of the more succinct statements of this view is in Woodford's (2003) *Interest and Prices*:[18]

> The prices that monetary policy should aim to stabilize are the ones that are infrequently adjusted and that consequently can be expected to become misaligned in an environment that requires these prices to move in either direction. Large movements in frequently adjusted prices – and stock prices are among the most flexible – can instead be allowed without raising such concerns, and if allowing them to move makes possible greater stability of the sticky prices, such instability of the flexible prices is desirable ... central banks should target a measure of 'core' inflation that places greater weight on those prices that are stickier. Furthermore, insofar as wages are also sticky, a desirable inflation target should take account of wage inflation as well as goods prices.
>
> (Woodford, 2003, pp. 13–14)

A natural question to ask, therefore, is: How well do existing measures of core inflation measure the concept of core implicit in the new literature on monetary policy? The best known and most widely used measures of core inflation are the so-called exclusion measures, such as the CPI 'Ex. Food & Energy' measure in the United States. Almost all national statistical agencies compute a core measure of this type, with the details differing slightly from country to country. It is instructive, therefore, to compare these traditional measures of core with measures constructed so as to give greater weight to prices that change less frequently.

Our understanding of the frequency of price changes has been greatly enhanced in recent years by the work of Bils and Klenow (2004) and the various researchers associated with European Central Bank's inflation persistence network whose work is summarized by Dhyne *et al.* (2005, 2006). Bils and Klenow (2004) report statistics on the frequency of price changes for a large fraction of the US CPI at the level of Entry Level Items (ELIs) for the years 1995–1997. The 350 ELIs they report on cover 68.9 per cent of consumer spending.[19] Examination of their Table A1 reveals that, sure enough, the ELI with the greatest frequency of price changes is 'Regular unleaded gasoline' (ELI 47014), with a frequency of price change of 78.9 per cent. Changes in the prices of gasoline are excluded from the traditional 'Ex. Food & Energy' measure of core consumer price inflation. The ELI with the lowest frequency of price change was 'Coin-operated apparel laundry and dry cleaning' (ELI 44012), with a frequency of price change of just 1.2 per cent. Such prices are routinely included in the traditional 'Ex. Food & Energy' measure of core consumer price inflation. And indeed inspection of Bils and Klenow's Table A1 reveals that many of the ELIs with the most frequent price changes are in the food or energy categories that would be discarded by a traditional 'Ex. Food & Energy' measure of core inflation, while many of the ELIs with the least frequent price changes would be included.

However, further inspection of the same table also reveals that the traditional measure of core would include the prices of a lot of items for which price changes are quite frequent, such as 'Airline fares' (ELI 53011), with a frequency of price changes of 69.1 per cent, 'Automobile rental' (ELI 52051), with a frequency of price change of 56.8 per cent and 'Girls dresses and suits' (ELI 39012), with a frequency of price change of 55.1 per cent. Likewise, the prices of many items that are typically discarded by the traditional 'Ex. Food & Energy' measure of core change relatively infrequently, such as 'Breakfast or brunch' (ELI 19032), 'Lunch' (ELI 19011) or 'Dinner' (ELI 19021), all components of the 'Food away from home' component of the CPI, the components of which are well known to change infrequently.

Similarly detailed information on the frequency of price changes in the euro area has been compiled as part of the Eurosystem's Inflation Persistence Network. Dhyne *et al.* (2005, 2006) summarise the results of that research. The level of detail is not as great as in Bils and Klenow (2004) but the features of the data are similar to what was found in the United States, namely that some, but not all, food and energy prices do change quite frequently. According to data presented in Table A8 of Dhyne *et al.* (2005), the three components of the euro area HICP with the greatest frequency of price changes are 'Fuel type 1' (representative of COICOP 0722011100), 'Fuel type 2' (representative of COICOP 0722013100) and 'Lettuce' (representative of COICOP 0117110100). All are products that would typically be excluded from a traditional measure of core inflation. However, the same table also shows that a traditional measure of core would include the prices or a number of goods whose prices change almost as frequently as some of the excluded items, such as 'Fax machines', 'Television sets' and 'Men's shirts'.

Using the data from Bils and Klenow (2004) and Dhyne *et al.* (2005), we can construct alternative measures of core inflation that weight prices by the (inverse of the) frequency with which they change and compare the performance of these measures with traditional measures of headline and core inflation. Specifically, we construct a measure of core price level defined as follows:

$$\tilde{P}_t = \frac{1}{\omega_1} / \sum_{i=1}^{I} \frac{1}{\omega_1} p_{i,t} \qquad (3)$$

where ω_i is the frequency with which the prices of good i change, and $p_{i,t}$ is the price of good i at date t. We then use this measure of the core price level to compute measures of core inflation at the one- and 12-month horizons. Table 4.2 reports the weights we use for the United States, along with the weights (relative importances) of the eight major expenditure categories in the US CPI. We see that weighting prices by the frequency with which they change leads to a significant decline in the weight attached to Housing and Transportation, and a significant increase in the weights assigned to Medical Care and Education and communication.[20] Figure 4.1 shows 12-month inflation rates for the headline CPI, the traditional core CPI excluding food and energy and the frequency weighted measure of core. Sticky price inflation in the United States (labelled in figure as single-weighted) is somewhat different from the traditional 'Ex. Food & Energy' measure of core inflation.[21] The pairwise correlation between the two series is only 0.52 at the 12-month horizon. Both measures appear to be about equally volatile, and both are less volatile than headline inflation (Table 4.4). Figure 4.1 certainly suggests that a monetary policy rule that responded to sticky price inflation would look quite different from one that responded to a traditional measure of core.

Table 4.2 Alternative weights for measures of US inflation

	CPI-U	*Frequency weighted measure*
Food and beverages	0.16	0.06
Housing	0.41	0.10
Apparel	0.04	0.07
Transportation	0.17	0.07
Medical care	0.06	0.21
Recreation	0.06	0.15
Education and communication	0.06	0.18
Other goods and services	0.04	0.15

Notes
Weights for CPI-U are averages of the relative importances of the expenditure category over 1997–2007. Frequency weights are based on the frequency of price changes reported in Table A1 of Bils and Klenow (2004).

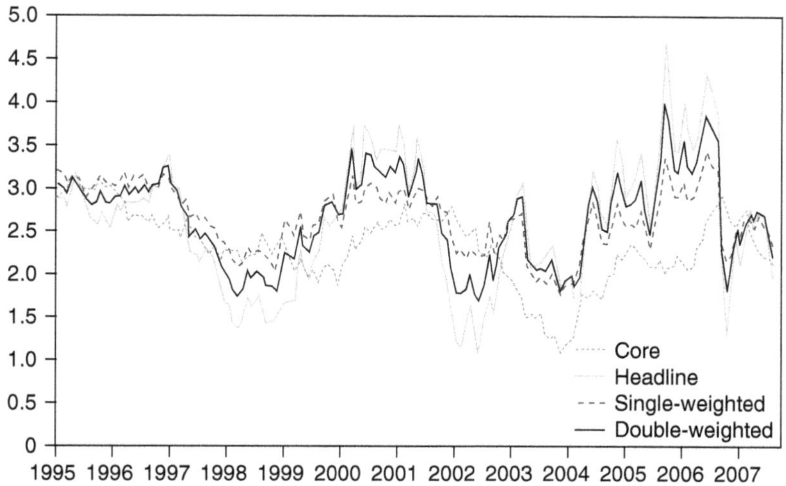

Figure 4.1 Alternative measures of United States inflation.

Table 4.3 reports the same weights for the 12 major expenditure categories of the euro area HICP, and Figure 4.2 plots the time series of the 12-month inflation rates along with the headline and traditional core measures. For the euro area there appears to be a much higher correlation between sticky price inflation and the traditional core measure than is the case in the United States[22] (Table 4.5). Sticky price inflation is about as volatile as headline inflation in the euro area but the differences between both measures and the traditional measure of core are not that great, and one would have to conclude that a monetary policy

Table 4.3 Alternative weights for measures of euro-area inflation

	HICP weight	*Frequency*
Food and non-alcoholic beverages	0.17	0.03
Alcohol and tobacco	0.04	0.06
Clothing	0.08	0.12
Housing	0.16	0.05
Household equipment	0.08	0.14
Health	0.03	0.00*
Transport	0.16	0.03
Communications	0.03	0.07
Recreation and culture	0.10	0.15
Education	0.01	0.00*
Hotels and restaurants	0.09	0.20
Miscellaneous	0.07	0.14

Note

Frequency weights based on the data reported in Table A8 of Dhyne *et al.* (2005). *No data on the frequency of price changes for the Health or Education expenditure categories are reported by Dhyne *et al.* (2005).

Table 4.4 Alternative measures of US inflation, descriptive statistics

	Core	*Headline*	*Inverse-frequency weighted*	*Inverse-frequency and CPI weighted*
Mean				
12 month	2.20	2.56	2.56	2.60
1 month	0.18	0.21	0.21	0.21
Std Dev.				
12 month	0.40	0.84	0.37	0.57
1 month	0.08	0.25	0.14	0.18
AR (1)				
12 month	0.95	0.89	0.85	0.88
1 month	–0.02	0.25	0.01	0.18
Correlation with inverse-frequency weighted				
12 month	0.52	0.84		
1 month	0.41	0.79		
Correlation with inverse-frequency and CPI weighted				
12 month	0.28	0.98		
1 month	0.25	0.96		

Note
Sample period: 1990:01 to 2007:08. Core defined as CPI-U less food and energy.

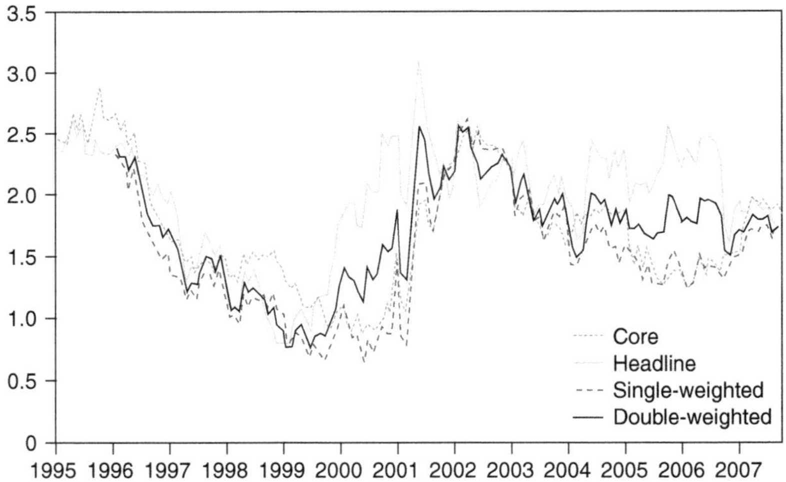

Figure 4.2 Alternative measures of euro-area inflation.

rule based on sticky price inflation would probably not look too different from one based on a traditional measure of core.

These calculations are indicative of how one might go about constructing a measure of sticky price core inflation and can certainly be improved upon. It would be worth exploring how the results change if we use more disaggregated

Table 4.5 Alternative measures of euro-area inflation, descriptive statistics

	Core	*Headline*	*Inverse-frequency weighted*	*Inverse-frequency and CPI weighted*
Mean				
12 month	1.63	1.93	1.49	1.68
1 month	0.14	0.16	0.13	0.14
Std Dev				
12 month	0.44	0.49	0.49	0.44
1 month	0.29	0.23	0.37	0.30
AR (1)				
12 month	0.96	0.92	0.94	0.93
1 month	–0.01	0.08	–0.13	–0.05
Correlation with inverse-frequency weighted				
12 month	0.94	0.59		
1 month	0.98	0.84		
Correlation with inverse-frequency and CPI weighted				
12 month	0.78	0.87		
1 month	0.95	0.92		

Notes
Sample period: 1995:01 to 2007:09. Core defined as HICP excluding food, energy, alcohol and tobacco.

data rather than the major expenditure categories, and if we included wage data as suggested by Woodford (2003).

3 Zero or …?

Table 5.1 shows that no central bank that has formally quantified its price-stability objective has defined price stability as prevailing at a zero measured rate of inflation. If one had to pick an average rate of inflation that most central banks see as being consistent with price stability, 2 per cent or something very close to it would be the obvious choice. One of the arguments most commonly made for defining price stability as prevailing at some positive measured rate of inflation is the possibility or probability that measured inflation rates overstate the true rate of inflation due to the failure of price statisticians to properly correct for improvements in the quality of goods over time, the arrival of new goods and the substitution of cheaper goods and services (and retail outlets) for more expensive ones.[23]

The interest of the economics profession in the issue of measurement bias in price indexes seems to wax and wane. One of the earliest reviews of the accuracy of price statistics in the United States was produced by the so-called Stigler Commission in 1961 (Price Statistics Review Committee (1961)). Introducing the discussion of the problems posed by quality changes, the Commission noted:

> If a poll were taken of professional economists and statisticians, in all probability they would designate (and by a wide majority) the failure of the price indexes to take full account of quality changes as the most important defect in these indexes. And by almost as large a majority, they would believe that this failure introduces a systematic upward bias in the price indexes – that quality changes have on average been quality improvements.
>
> We have very little evidence at our disposal with which to support – or deny – the belief in progressive quality improvement. Indeed we are impressed with how little empirical work has been done on so widely held a view and potentially so important a problem. Changes in buyer's tastes will lead to the appearance of new goods – an uncontroversial example would be fashionable apparel – which are not improvements judged by either previous or subsequent tastes, and the line separating taste changes from quality improvements will depend on the time span invoked.
>
> (Price Statistics Review Committee, 1961, p. 35)

The Stigler committee's characterisation of the prior beliefs of many economists remains as true today as when it was written nearly half a century ago. The prior beliefs of many economists seems to be predicated on a view that statistical agencies do not make *any* adjustments for quality changes when computing inflation statistics which in many, if not all, cases is simply not true. The real issue has to do with how adequately the procedures the statistical agencies employ correct for quality changes. We do know a bit more about the potential biases in measures of inflation today than was the case 45 years ago, but despite the progress there is arguably more that we do not know.

In the 1990s there was something of a resurgence of interest in the issue price measurement. The extraordinary rates of decline in the prices of high-tech goods that accompanied the information technology revolution highlighted the problems associated with the use of fixed-weight indexes for the measurement of prices and quantities in the US national income and products accounts and ultimately led to the adoption of the Fisher chain-weighted indexes in the national accounts in 1996. Federal Reserve Chairman Alan Greenspan drew the attention of US lawmakers to the measurement problems posed by rapid innovation.[24] Questions about the accuracy of the CPI generated more interest when it was pointed out that, due the widespread use of the CPI for indexation of taxes and benefit payments, measurement error had potentially significant fiscal implications. The consequence was the creation of the Boskin Commission, which issued its final report in December 1996 (Boskin *et al.*, 1996), concluding that the CPI as then constructed overstated the rate of increase in the true cost of living index by about 1.1 percentage points a year, with a range of plausible values between 0.8 and 1.6 percentage points a year.

Subsequent to the publication of the Boskin report there were a number of improvements to the US CPI, including more frequent updating of upper-level weights, a change in lower-level weights and the introduction of the chained CPI (C-CPI-U) series. The debate over the accuracy of the US CPI also led the

Federal Reserve to shift away from the CPI to the deflator for personal consumption expenditures (PCE) as its preferred measure of inflation. The shift occurred with the publication of the February 2000 *Monetary Policy Report to the Congress*.[25,26]

The publication of the Boskin Commission report in the United States prompted similar reviews of the accuracy of measures of consumer price inflation in other countries. Wynne and Palenzuela (2004) summarised the state of knowledge for the countries of the European Union as of the early 2000s, and concluded that there was not much hard evidence to base an assessment on one way or another. Indeed, many of the reviews of the accuracy of price statistics in countries other than the United States seemed to reach surprisingly sanguine conclusions, given the limited amount of research available. Since Boskin and the mini-literature it spawned, the issue of measurement bias in price statistics seems to have declined. One recent contribution is Broda and Weinstein (2007), who critically assess the accuracy of the Japanese CPI and argue that the measurement problems are a lot more severe than previous studies have suggested, on the order of magnitude of 2 percentage points a year relative to a true cost of living index, that is, more than twice the 0.9 per cent estimate of Shiratsuka (1999).

Nevertheless, the fact remains that our knowledge of the extent of measurement bias in measures of consumer price inflation is at best limited. Research has shown that the widespread perception that the biases are all in one direction (causing measured inflation always to overstate the true rate of inflation) is simply wrong. Work by Gordon (2004) and Gordon and vanGoethem (2004) found evidence of significant *downward* biases in major components of the US CPI. Røed Larsen's (2007) application to Norwegian data of Hamilton's (2001) approach to estimating bias using Engel Curve estimates led him to conclude that the CPI in Norway understates the rate of increase in the cost of living.[27] Of course it only makes sense to talk about measurement bias when there is a well-defined theoretical ideal which the measured index is supposed to approximate: in the case of the US CPI, the measurement objective is the cost of living index, but many statistical agencies explicitly eschew this as the measurement objective, the HICP being one of the more prominent examples.[28]

Finally, it is worth asking just how costly it might be for a central bank to tolerate a long-run measured inflation rate of 2 per cent per annum if there was no measurement error. Feldstein (1997) estimated the net benefits of going from 2 per cent inflation to zero inflation, and found that they were substantial. The benefits for the United States were on the order of magnitude of 1 per cent of GDP a year, against which one has to offset one-time costs on the order of magnitude of 5 per cent of GDP. The present discounted value of gains equal to 1 per cent of GDP in perpetuity is equal to 38.5 per cent of initial GDP (if we discount using an average growth rate for GDP of 2.5 per cent and a discount factor of 5.1 per cent) so the benefits clearly outweigh the costs. Subsequent research employing Feldstein's methodology by Tödter and Ziebarth (1999), Dolado *et al.* (1999) and Bakhshi *et al.* (1999) found that the benefits of going from 2 per cent to zero inflation were on the order of 1.4 per cent of GDP for Germany, 1.7 per cent of GDP for Spain but only 0.2 per cent of GDP for the UK.[29]

4 Asset prices again

Finally, I want to return to the issue of whether the prices of assets should be included in the measure of inflation used to define price stability. There are well-known differences of opinion among leading central bankers on whether monetary policy should respond to changes in asset prices, whether the prices of financial assets or real assets such as housing. Woodford (2003), for example, argues against the inclusion of asset prices in the measure of inflation targeted by central banks:

> The near-optimal policy stabilizes an inflation measure that puts more weight on prices in the sector where they are stickier ... this provides theoretical justification for a policy that targets core inflation rather than the growth of a broader price index, and offers a theoretical criterion for the construction of such an index. It also explains why it is not appropriate to target an inflation measure that includes 'asset-price inflation' along with goods-price increases, as is sometimes proposed: even if asset prices are also prices and can also be affected by monetary policy, they are among the prices that are the most frequently adjusted in response to new market conditions, and so their movements do not indicate the kind of distortions that one seeks to minimize.
>
> (Woodford, 2003, pp. 440–441)

Others argue against the inclusion of asset prices on the grounds that it can be difficult when movements in such prices are excessive or not justified by fundamentals (a variant of the quality adjustment problem). The counterargument is that rapid growth in asset prices can be indicative of loose monetary conditions and should be responded to by monetary policy.[30] I am not going to resolve that debate here, but I do want to offer a provocative hypothesis.

As noted above all central banks with explicit numerical price objectives have defined price stability in terms of a measure of inflation at the consumer level. In some cases, the measure of consumer price inflation does not include the cost of owner-occupied housing (for example, the euro area and the United Kingdom). In those countries where the cost of owner-occupied housing is included in the measure of inflation at the consumer level, it is only the cost of the service flow. The question I want to pose is: Have asset price booms (and busts), and, in particular, house-price booms, been more common in countries that have focused on inflation (as measured by a conventional CPI) over the past decade than elsewhere? For example, in the United Kingdom home prices are estimated to have tripled over the past 15 years, during which time the Bank of England has been practising orthodox inflation targeting. A number of countries in the euro area, such as Ireland and Spain, have also experienced large increases in house prices in recent years. Is it possible that by focusing on *too narrow* a measure of inflation, central banks have contributed to these booms?

In Table 4.6 I report the results of a simple least squares regression of the average annual increase in house prices on real GDP growth, the share of trade in GDP, a measure of long-term real interest rates and a dummy variable for the presence of an inflation target. Real GDP growth is included as a key fundamental variable driving house prices: faster income growth is usually associated with faster house price appreciation, other things being equal. Indeed the elasticity of house prices with respect to real disposable income is often estimated to be greater than 1 (Girouard *et al.*, 2006). However, over the past decade we have seen a growing number of countries experiencing extraordinarily rapid increases in house prices. Girouard *et al.* (2006) show the number of countries in their 17-country sample experiencing house price increases in excess of 25 per cent over the previous five years steadily increasing since the mid-1990s. Over that same period, globalisation has emerged as a major influence on inflation dynamics, and inflation targeting has become increasingly popular as a framework for monetary policy. Is it possible that the favourable supply shock that globalisation represented (at least until recently) acting in conjunction with an emphasis on inflation measures at the consumer level in many countries helped spark a house-price boom that might not otherwise have occurred had central banks taken a broader perspective on inflation? The simple results in Table 4.6 suggest that there may be something to this. While the coefficient on the importance of foreign trade is not significant, the coefficient on the inflation-targeting dummy is. That is, house-price inflation appears to have been greater in countries with formal inflation targets or explicit numerical

Table 4.6 Inflation targeting and house price inflation

	Coefficient	*Std. Error*	*t-Statistic*	*Prob.*
Constant	−2.681909	1.352301	−1.983219	0.0517
GDP growth	2.083364	0.315563	6.602049	0.0000
Inflation target	2.878636	0.865352	3.326550	0.0015
Trade share	0.009643	0.015066	0.640074	0.5244
Interest rate	−0.600004	0.224206	−2.676132	0.0095
R-squared	0.558238	Mean dependent var.		2.455882
Adjusted R-squared	0.530190	S.D. dependent var.		4.743523
S.E. of regression	3.251339	Akaike info criterion		5.266697
Sum squared resid.	665.9861	Schwarz criterion		5.429896
Log likelihood	−174.0677	Hannan-Quinn criter.		5.331362
F-statistic	19.90268	Durbin-Watson stat.		2.188279
Prob (F-statistic)	0.000000			

Notes

Dependent variable: Average annual increase in house prices. Countries included: US, Japan, Germany, France, Italy, UK, Canada, Australia, Denmark, Finland, Ireland, Netherlands, New Zealand, Norway, Spain, Sweden, Switzerland. Data from Box I.3 of OECD Economic Outlook 79, June 2006, which are in turn updated series from Girouard *et al.* (2006). Data averaged over 1970–1990, 1990–1995, 1995–2000, 2000–2005. Inflation target dummy is 1 for periods during which countries have an inflation target or explicit numerical price objective.

price objectives, even when we control for the rate of growth and the level of real interest rates. Perhaps house-price appreciation would have been more in line with overall inflation developments if central banks in these countries adopted a more comprehensive definition of price stability.

5 Conclusions

Central banks ought to be leaders in the area of price measurement, given the importance of the issue to their objectives. It behoves the staff of central banks around the world to have a better understanding of how the measures of inflation which guide theory policy decisions are constructed and to be engaged in an ongoing constructive dialogue with the statisticians who produce these indexes to find ways to improve them. It is probably going too far for central banks to take a lead role in the production of the price statistics by which their performance will be judged, although if they were to be sufficiently transparent about what they do this need not pose a major conflict of interest.

The accurate measurement of inflation for monetary policy purposes will continue to be a challenge going forward. Measures of headline inflation at the consumer level that take as their measurement objective the cost of living are probably the best for defining price stability, given the current state of knowledge but there are potential alternatives. Ideally, price stability should be defined in terms of the price index that best captures the cost of inflation to society. The cost of living index is a welfare- based measure but it could conceivably be too narrow for monetary policy purposes. The proposed approach of Reis and Watson (2007) deserves further examination. But even within the cost of living framework, there will be significant challenges going forward. The accurate measurement of service prices will grow in importance, as will the need to figure out how best to deal with the costs of owner-occupied housing.[31] The proper treatment of the gains from the arrival in the marketplace of new goods, whether domestically produced or imported, will continue to pose challenges. And these challenges have to be addressed. Defining price stability at a positive measured rate of inflation is costly to society if measurement error is not as significant as some believe.

I have argued that it is inappropriate for central banks to target measures of core inflation for a variety of reasons. However, the modern theory of monetary policy suggests that central banks should target sticky price inflation, which some have interpreted as being the same as core inflation. Above I presented some preliminary estimates of sticky price inflation using the data on the frequency of price changes in Bils and Klenow (2004) and Dhyne *et al.* (2005). For the United States at least, there seem to be some notable differences between sticky price inflation, at least as I calculated it, and a more traditional measure of core inflation. There is clearly scope for further exploration of the concept of sticky price inflation. My simple estimates only used data on the frequency of price changes. Some argue that the appropriate index should also include wages, but the relevant data on the frequency of wage changes is not readily available.

Recent experience underlines the need for a better understanding of how asset prices ought to be treated in defining price stability. One of the central challenges facing statisticians is coming up with an appropriate treatment of the cost of the service flow from owner-occupied housing in measures of consumer price inflation. But there might be grounds for taking a broader perspective on what constitutes price stability. I reported some simple statistical results that suggest that house-price booms have been greater in countries that have explicit numerical price objectives. It is worth exploring further whether this is a robust result, and if so, what explains it.

Notes

1 I thank David Mayes for his comments on an earlier version of this chapter. Jenny Solomon and Janet Koech provided excellent research assistance. The views expressed in this chapter are those of the author and do not necessarily reflect the views of the Federal Reserve Bank of Dallas or the Federal Reserve System.

2 Greenspan's definition echoed the earlier definition of Paul Volcker:

> A workable definition of reasonable 'price stability' would seem to me a situation in which expectations of generally rising (or falling) prices over a considerable period are not a pervasive influence on economic and financial behavior. Stated more positively, 'stability' would imply that decision-making should be able to proceed on the basis that 'real' and 'nominal' values are substantially the same over the planning horizon – and that planning horizons should be suitably long.
>
> (Volcker, 1983)

3 Note that the measure of headline that RBNZ targets excludes mortgage interest rates, and thus might under some definitions be considered a measure of core inflation.

4 The last mention of 'core inflation' in a Bank of England *Inflation Report* was in the November 2000 *Report*.

5 The UND1X measure of core inflation (which excludes mortgage interest expenditure and the direct effects of changes in indirect taxes and subsidies) is the one that receives the most attention in the Riksbank's *Report*. Other measures of core that appear in the Report include UNDINHX (which excludes the price of imports), UND1X excluding energy, UND24 (an Edgeworthian measure that weights prices by the (inverses) of their historical standard deviations) and TRIM85 (which excludes the price changes in the top and bottom 7.5 per cent of the distribution.

6 To the extent that the indexes that the members of the FOMC forecast twice a year in the *Monetary Policy Report to the Congress* might be construed as the Fed's price objective, the Fed had an implicit GNP deflator objective until 1989. The *Monetary Policy Report to the Congress* submitted in February 1989 switched from reporting projections of the implicit GNP deflator to reporting projections of the CPI. And it is worth recalling that the original specification of the Taylor Rule was stated in terms of a GDP deflator rather than a measure of consumer price inflation, although almost all subsequent variants have employed a measure of inflation at the consumer level (Taylor, 1993).

7 See, for example, Svensson (1999) or Issing (2001).

8 See the discussion of the stochastic approach to index numbers in chapter 16 of International Labour Office *et al.* (2004).

9 See also Cecchetti and Wynne (2003) for an application of this approach to euro-area data and an interpretation of the inflation series thus estimated as 'monetary inflation'.

10 Another point that should be kept in mind when using this approach to estimate changes in the value of the numeraire is that it is very important that the raw price series measure pure price changes only and not some combination of price changes and shifts in expenditure patterns. This is not an issue when actual price data are used, which is almost never the case. Rather, indexes of individual price changes are used, and this may pose a problem: fixed weight indexes will capture pure price changes, but chain-weighted or superlative indexes generally will not.

11 There are a few papers that take this more comprehensive approach to measuring inflation. One early example is the unpublished paper of Dow (1993). See also the Bryan *et al.* (2001, 2002). Bryan *et al.* (2001) extend the earlier dynamic factor model of Bryan and Cecchetti (1993) to include the prices of houses, stocks and bonds. Bryan *et al.* (2002) include in addition the prices of commodities, money and gold.

12 But to the extent that all prices (or their rates of change) tend to move together over long periods of time, as Becsi (1994) suggests, focusing on a narrow set of well-measured prices might not be misleading.

13 It goes without saying that measures of core inflation that simply exclude the prices of food and energy cannot be interpreted as providing an answer to the counterfactual question 'What would inflation have been if the prices of food and energy had not increased?'

14 A number of refinements of the trimming approach have been suggested in recent years to try to get around this problem. Pedersen (2005) suggests trimming the most volatile components of the cross-section distribution of prices rather than just the extremes. While this may address the immediate problem, it makes the core measure even more complex and difficult to explain to the general public.

15 For example, Khettry and Mester (2006) evaluate several measures of core in terms of their ability to predict future headline CPI inflation and find that the traditional 'Ex. Food & Energy' measure performs better than other measures. Rich and Steindel (2005) also find substantial predictive power for measures of core inflation but only within sample. Out of sample they find that no single measure of core outperforms the others.

16 Issing (2001) argues against the use of core measure on the grounds that such measures are 'less transparent and more remote from the prices actually paid by the general public' and comes down strongly in favour of the traditional consumer price index as 'being familiar to the average consumer, easily understood, published regularly and in a timely fashion and infrequently revised' (p. 193).

17 See the excellent review by Diewert (2002).

18 See also Goodfriend and King (1997) and Mankiw and Reis (2003).

19 The major omissions are owner's equivalent rent and household insurance (which together had a relative importance in the CPI in December 1996 of 20 per cent), renters' costs (residential rent and other costs, which had a relative importance of 8 per cent), used cars (which had a relative importance in the CPI in December 1996 of 1.3 per cent).

20 While Bils and Klenow's dataset does not include information on the owner's equivalent rent or household insurance components of housing, it does include information on other components of housing costs, such as fuel and utilities, and household furnishings and operation.

21 The double-weighted series in the figures weight the components of the CPI using both the expenditure share weights and the weights reflecting the frequency of price changes.

22 Eurostat publishes several measures of core inflation for the euro area. Here I use the HICP excluding food, energy, alcohol and tobacco but the result seems robust to the use of other measures.

23 Other arguments commonly advanced for defining price stability as prevailing at some positive rate of inflation include the existence of downward rigidities in labour

markets and the desire to avoid the zero bound on nominal interest rates. I will not touch on these arguments here, but instead focus on the measurement issues.

24 See Greenspan (1994b, 1995).

25 In explaining the switch the Board of Governors noted

> The chain-type price index for PCE draws extensively on data from the consumer price index but, while not entirely free of measurement problems, has several advantages relative to the CPI. The PCE chain-type index is constructed from a formula that reflects the changing composition of spending and thereby avoids some of the upward bias associated with the fixed-weight nature of the CPI. In addition, the weights are based on a more comprehensive measure of expenditures. Finally, historical data used in the PCE price index can be revised to account for newly available information and for improvements in measurement techniques, including those that affect source data from the CPI; the result is a more consistent series over time. This switch in presentation notwithstanding, the FOMC will continue to rely on a variety of aggregate price measures, as well as other information on prices and costs, in assessing the path of inflation.
>
> (Board of Governors of the Federal Reserve System, 2000)

26 In July 2004, the FOMC again changed its preferred measure of inflation to the so-called core PCE deflator (i.e. the price index for personal consumption expenditures excluding food and energy) on the grounds that the Committee believed it was 'better as an indicator of underlying inflation trends than … the overall PCE price measure previously featured' (Board of Governors of the Federal Reserve System, 2004).

27 Beatty and Røed Larsen (2005) apply the same approach to the Canadian CPI and find that it overstates the rate of increase in the cost of living.

28 As noted by the European Commission 'The HICPs can all be said to meet their purpose of "measuring inflation faced by consumers" to a degree which is unknown (and perhaps unknowable) because there is no reference by which to determine the extent of any bias' (Commission of the European Communities, 1998, p. 11).

29 Our confidence in the estimates of the size of the benefits of going from 2 per cent to zero is enhanced by the fact that Abel (1997, 1999) arrives at very similar estimates using a very different (general equilibrium model) approach.

30 See, for example, Cecchetti *et al.* (2000).

31 McCarthy (2007) documents the problems posed by the treatment of owner-occupied housing in the Irish CPI.

References

Abel, Andrew B., 1997. 'Comment'. In Christina D. Romer and David H. Romer (eds), *Reducing Inflation: Motivation and Strategy*. Chicago, IL: University of Chicago Press, pp. 156–166.

——, 1999. 'Comment on Chapters 2, 3, and 4'. In Martin S. Feldstein (ed.), *The Costs and Benefits of Price Stability*. Chicago, IL: University of Chicago Press, pp. 156–166.

Afriat, Sydney N., 2005. *The Price Index and Its Extension: A Chapter in Economic Measurement*. New York: Routledge.

Bakhshi, Hasan, Andrew Haldane and Neal Hatch, 1999. 'Some Costs and Benefits of Price Stability in the United Kingdom'. In Martin S. Feldstein (ed.), *The Costs and Benefits of Price Stability*. Chicago, IL: University of Chicago Press, pp. 133–180.

Beatty, Thomas K.M. and Erling Røed Larsen, 2005. 'Using Engel Curves to Estimate Bias in the Canadian CPI as a Cost of Living Index'. *Canadian Journal of Economics*, 38, 482–499.

Becsi, Zsolt, 1994. 'Indicators of the General Price Level and Inflation'. *Federal Reserve Bank of Dallas Economic Review*, fourth quarter, 27–39.

Berg, Claes, 2005. 'Experience of Inflation-Targeting in 20 Countries'. *Sveriges Riksbank Economic Review*, 1, 20–47.

Bils, Mark and Peter J. Klenow, 2004. 'Some Evidence on the Importance of Sticky Prices'. *Journal of Political Economy*, 112 (5), 947–985.

Board of Governors of the Federal Reserve System, 2000. *Monetary Policy Report to the Congress Pursuant to the Full Employment and Balanced Growth Act of 1978, February 17, 2000.* Washington, DC: Board of Governors of the Federal Reserve System.

——, 2004. *Monetary Policy Report to the Congress, July 20, 2004.* Washington, DC: Board of Governors of the Federal Reserve System.

Boskin, Michael J., Ellen R. Dulberger, Robert J. Gordon, Zvi Griliches and Dale Jorgenson, 1996. *Toward a More Accurate Measure of the Cost of Living: Final Report to the Senate Finance Committee from the Advisory Commission to Study the Consumer Price Index*, Washington, DC: Social Security Administration.

Broda, Christian and David E. Weinstein, 2007. 'Defining Price Stability in Japan: A View from America'. NBER Working Paper 13255.

Bryan, Michael F. and Stephen G. Cecchetti, 1993. 'The Consumer Price Index as a Measure of Inflation'. *Federal Reserve Bank of Cleveland Economic Review*, 15–24.

——, 1994. 'Measuring Core Inflation'. In N. Gregory Mankiw (ed.), *Monetary Policy.* Chicago, IL: University of Chicago Press, pp. 195–215.

Bryan, Michael F. and Christopher J. Pike, 1991. 'Median Price Changes: An Alternative Approach to Measuring Current Monetary Inflation'. *Federal Reserve Bank of Cleveland Economic Commentary*, 1 December.

Bryan, M.F., S.G. Cecchetti and R. O'Sullivan, 2001. 'Asset Prices in the Measurement of Inflation', DNB Staff Reports no. 62, Netherlands Central Bank.

Bryan, M.F., S.G. Cecchetti and R. O'Sullivan, 2002. 'Asset Prices in the Measurement of Inflation', NBER Working Papers no. 8700.

Cecchetti, Stephen G. and Mark A. Wynne, 2003. 'Inflation Measurement and the ECB's Pursuit of Price Stability: A First Assessment'. *Economic Policy*, 37, 397–434.

Cecchetti, Stephen G., Hans Genberg, John Lipsky and Sushil Wadhwani, 2000. *Asset Prices and Central Bank Policy.* Geneva Reports on the World Economy, No. 2, International Center for Monetary and Banking Studies and Centre for Economic Policy Research, July 2000.

Commission of the European Communities, 1998. *Report from the Commission to the Council on the Harmonization of Consumer Price Indices in the European Union.* Catalogue number: CB-CO-98-133-EN-C.

Dhyne, Emmanuel, Luis J. Álvarez, Hervé Le Bihan, Giovanni Veronese, Daniel Dias, Johannes Hoffman, Nicole Jonker, Patrick Lünnemann, Fabio Rumler and Jouko Vilmunen, 2005. 'Price Setting in the Euro Area: Some Stylized Facts from Individual Consumer Price Data'. ECB Working Paper, No. 524.

——, 2006. 'Price Changes in the Euro Area and the United States: Some Facts from Individual Consumer Price Data'. *Journal of Economic Perspectives*, 20 (2), 171–192.

Diewert, W. Erwin, 2001. 'The Consumer Price Index and Index Number Theory: A Survey'. Discussion Paper No. 01-02, Department of Economics, University of British Columbia.

——, 2002. 'Harmonized Indexes of Consumer Prices: Their Conceptual Foundations'. *Schweiz Zeitschrift für Volkwirtschaft und Statistik*, 138 (4), 547–637.

Dolado, Juan J., José M. González-Páramo and José Viñals, 1999. 'A Cost-Benefit Analysis of Going from Low Inflation to Price Stability in Spain'. In Martin S. Feldstein (ed.), *The Costs and Benefits of Price Stability*. Chicago, IL: University of Chicago Press, pp. 95–132.

Dolmas, Jim, 2005. 'Trimmed mean PCE inflation'. Federal Reserve Bank of Dallas, Working Paper 0506.

Dow, James P., Jr, 1993. 'Measuring Inflation Using Multiple Price Indexes'. Paper presented to the 68th Annual Conference of the Western Economic Association, Lake Tahoe, NV.

Feldstein, Martin S., 1997. 'The Costs and Benefits of Going from Low Inflation to Price Stability'. In Christina D. Romer and David H. Romer (eds), *Reducing Inflation: Motivation and Strategy*. Chicago, IL: University of Chicago Press, pp. 123–156.

Fisher, Irving, 1920. *The Purchasing Power of Money: Its Determination and Relation to Credit Interest and Crises* (new and revised edition). New York: Macmillan.

Giannone, Domenico and Troy Matheson, 2006. 'A New Core Inflation Indicator for New Zealand'. Reserve Bank of New Zealand DP 2006/10.

Girouard, N., M. Kennedy, P. van den Noord and C. André, 2006. 'Recent House Price Developments: The Role of Fundamentals'. OECD Economics Department Working Paper, No. 475.

Goodfriend, Marvin and Robert G. King, 1997. 'The New Neoclassical Synthesis and the Role of Monetary Policy'. In Ben Bernanke and Julio Rotemberg (eds), *NBER Macro Annual*. Cambridge, MA: MIT Press, pp. 231–295.

Gordon, Robert J., 2004. 'Apparel Prices and the Hulten/Bruegel Paradox'. Manuscript, Northwestern University, Department of Economics.

Gordon, Robert J., and Todd vanGoethem, 2004. 'A Century of Downward Bias in the Most Important Component of the CPI: The Case of Rental Shelter, 1914–2003'. Manuscript, Northwestern University, Department of Economics.

Greenspan, Alan, 1994a. *Testimony before the Subcommittee on Economic Growth and Credit Formation of the Committee on Banking, Finance and Urban Affairs*, US House of Representatives, 22 February 1994.

——, 1994b. *Statement by Alan Greenspan before the Commerce, Consumer, and Monetary Affairs Subcommittee of the Committee on Government Operations*, US House of Representatives, 10 August 1994.

——, 1995. *Testimony by Alan Greenspan before the Committee on Finance, United States Senate*, 13 March 1995.

Hamilton, Bruce, 2001. 'Using Engel's Law to Estimate CPI Bias'. *American Economic Review*, 91, 619–630.

Hicks, John R., 1940. 'The valuation of the social income'. *Economica*, 7, 105–124.

International Labour Office, International Monetary Fund, Organization for Economic Cooperation and Development, Statistical Office of the European Communities, United Nations and The World Bank, 2004. *Consumer Price Index Manual: Theory and Practice*. Geneva: International Labour Office.

Issing, Otmar, 2001. 'Why Price Stability?'. In Alicia García Herrero, Vítor Gaspar, Lex Hoogduin, Julian Morgan and Bernhard Winkler (eds), *Why Price Stability?* Frankfurt am Main: European Central Bank, pp. 179–202.

Jevons, W.S., 1865. 'Variations in Prices and the Value of Currency since 1762'. *Journal of the Royal Statistical Society*, 28, 294–325.

Keynes, J.M., 1930. *A Treatise on Money*. London: Macmillan.

Khettry, N. Neil K. and Loretta J. Mester, 2006. 'Core Inflation as a Predictor of Total Inflation'. Federal Reserve Bank of Philadelphia Research Rap Special Report.

McCarthy, Colm, 2007. 'Owner-Occupied Housing Costs and Bias in the Irish Consumer Price Index'. *ESRI Quarterly Economic Commentary*, Autumn, 83–98.

Mankiw, N. Gregory and Ricardo Reis, 2003. 'What Measure of Inflation Should a Central Bank Target?'. *Journal of the European Economic Association*, 1 (5), 1058–1086.

Pedersen, Michael, 2005. 'An Alternative Measure of Core Inflation'. Danmarks Nationalbank Working Papers, 2005-33.

Price Statistics Review Committee of the National Bureau of Economic Research, 1961. *The Price Statistics of the Federal Government.* New York: National Bureau of Economic Research.

Reis, Ricardo and Mark W. Watson, 2007. 'Measuring Changes in the Value of the Numeraire'. Manuscript, Princeton University, Department of Economics, May.

Rich, Robert and Charles Steindel, 2005. 'A Review of Core Inflation and an Evaluation of its Measures'. Federal Reserve Bank of New York Staff, Report No. 236.

Røed Larsen, Erling, 2007. 'Does the CPI Mirror the Cost of Living? Engel's Law Suggests Not in Norway'. *Scandinavian Journal of Economics*, 109 (1), 177–195.

Shiratsuka, Shigenori, 1999. 'Measurement Errors in Japanese Consumer Price Index'. Federal Reserve Bank of Chicago, Working Paper WP-1999-02.

Svensson, Lars E.O., 1999. 'Price Stability as a Target for Monetary Policy: Defining and Maintaining Price Stability'. Sveriges Riksbank Working Paper Series, No. 91.

Taylor, John B., 1993. 'Discretion Versus Policy Rules in Practice'. *Carnegie-Rochester Conference Series on Public Policy*, 39, 195–214.

Tödter, Karl-Heinz and Gerhard Ziebarth, 1999. 'Price Stability Versus Low Inflation in Germany: An Analysis of Costs and Benefits'. In Martin S. Feldstein (ed.) *The Costs and Benefits of Price Stability*. Chicago, IL: University of Chicago Press, pp. 47–94.

Truman, Edwin M., 2003. *Inflation Targeting in the World Economy*. Washington, DC: Institute for International Economics.

Volcker, Paul A., 1983. 'We Can Survive Prosperity: Remarks at the Joint Meeting of the American Economic Association'. *American Finance Association*, 28 December, 1983.

Woodford, Michael, 2003. *Interest and Prices: Foundations of a Theory of Monetary Policy*. Princeton, NJ: Princeton University Press.

Wynne, Mark A. and Diego Rodriguez-Palenzuela, 2004. 'Measurement bias in the HICP: What do we know and what do we need to know?'. *Journal of Economic Surveys*, 18 (1), 79–112.

COMMENTS BY DAVID MAYES

A great deal has been written on the appropriate definition of price stability but Mark Wynne offers some interesting new insights on four issues:

- narrow or broad measures of inflation?
- headline or core?
- zero or positive inflation?
- should asset prices be included?

I shall tackle all of these but some ground-clearing is in order first.

There is a basic distinction to be made between how central banks should go about defining price stability in order to achieve the objectives they set (or are set for them) and what the objective should be. The public objective needs to be very straightforward but the definition or indeed definitions of price stability used by the central bank in trying to achieve that objective can be very sophisticated and indeed may be purely internal and not communicated for fear of confusing the reader.

This distinction can be illustrated from New Zealand, which was the first inflation-targeting country. The original inflation target in New Zealand was effectively set by politicians – it had to be simple so it could be understood by ordinary people and price setters in particular; it had to be clearly measurable so that people and in particular the minister of finance could see whether it was being achieved. The governor is personally accountable for achieving the target and there is effectively an enforceable contract between the minister and the governor to that end – on appointment of the governor, both parties sign a Policy Targets Agreement covering his five-year term of office.[1] The CPI (consumer price index) was the only index in widespread usage as a measure of inflation. The annual inflation objective was set as 0 to 2 per cent at the beginning. This was intended as a constant price level with the smallest simple achievable fluctuation round that. I shall come back to the distinction between a price-level target and an inflation target later.

However, illustrating the relevance of Mark Wynne's remarks, Clause 2 of the original March 1990 'Policy Targets Agreement' between the Minister of Finance and the Governor of the Reserve Bank is headed 'Measurement of Inflation' and it explains the deficiency of the CPI with respect to the measurement of housing costs and requires the RBNZ to compute an externally verifiable series on a more suitable basis. Second, a series of caveats is listed under which inflation could deviate from the target without it being treated as a failure by the governor to fulfil his contract. This is formulated much more clearly in the December 1990 agreement (the minister of finance changed). These led to the development of a measure of underlying inflation, which was a better reflection of the impact of the RBNZ's policy. It was not the operating target, which was of course forward-looking – forecast headline inflation some specific number of quarters into the future. I shall also return to this later.

Mark Wynne wisely avoids some of the old conundrums. He does not discuss whether some inflation target would be optimal or whether we would have any way of defining that optimality. Although he mentions the idea advanced by Alan Greenspan that stability is achieved if people do not factor the change in the average level of prices into their decisions, this does not quite capture what is involved for decision making by households or firms or indeed governments. The New Zealand regime was set up with the long term in mind. It is a disaster for people if they find that, despite careful planning, their purchasing power gets eroded in retirement, at a stage when there may be little or anything they can do about it. They can only rely on others either directly or through the state. However, what a typical pensioner basket of goods and services might be like

20–40 years in the future is very difficult to assess. Search costs have fallen markedly, an area where pensioners typically had a comparative advantage. Certainly, looking at monetary policy in much of the period 1967–1987 would not have been a good guide as to what to expect.

Broad versus narrow measures

Mark Wynne begins with broad versus narrow measures but the main issues he raises in this and the introductory section are rather wider. The simple issue is decided in practice: all central banks that have adopted inflation targeting have a CPI target and the Eurosystem also follows the same route. There is no debate, except about including asset prices, which he turns to later in his discussion. The first issue, with which no one will disagree, is that we need to get better measurement of many prices if we are really going to maintain price stability in the sense of the purchasing power of money or some other welfare concept. This is becoming clearer with incorporating quality improvements and to some extent with services so that some of the upward biases in measured inflation are being reduced. It is becoming easier to detect and include new goods and services. There is no matching tendency to lower inflation targets, if anything the reverse, and as Wynne points out this will be imposing unintended costs on society.

Headline versus core

As I have already mentioned, targets tend to be headline measures, especially when anomalies have been removed. However, it remains that accountability will be in more qualified terms. Central banks are not normally held responsible for climate variations and hence sharp changes in seasonal food prices. In the same way they are usually absolved from changes in prices that stem from government action, whether administered prices or indirect taxation and from external shocks. What they are not absolved from is second-round effects or the failure to set in place a sensible policy to control the reaction to shocks. Clearly, therefore, central banks talk about these factors in explaining their policy actions both to the public and to parliament/government.

However, there is a problem of symmetry here. If the flow of shocks is symmetric then measures of inflation that exclude them will still follow the same path as the headline over the longer term. Here the distinction between inflation targeting and price-level targeting becomes important. Not only did the original New Zealand system assume that outcomes inside the policy target of 0–2 per cent inflation would cancel out but that any errors would also be symmetric. Practice has not been quite like that, although Gaspar *et al.* (2007) suggest that in Canada and the United Kingdom, for example, the drift in the price level has been small. The RBNZ website has a handy inflation calculator (www.rbnz.govt.nz/inflationcalculator/showcalculator.do). To be as kind as possible – inflation since the beginning of 1990 has been 2.2 per cent per year but the first two years were a period when inflation was being brought down into the range. Over 1992 to the end of 1996 when the range was broadened to 0–3 per cent, inflation was 2.2 per cent a year. Over 1997 until the third quarter of 2002 when the target was raised to 1–3 per cent, inflation was 1.8 per cent per year. Since then it has been 2.6 per cent a year. Clearly the aim of protecting purchasing power has not really been achieved.

Up until 1995 the aim of the RBNZ was to keep inflation in the target range. Since then the aim has been to bring inflation into the middle of the range – the time horizon increased quite quickly from four quarters ahead to 6–8 quarters ahead. What we require from our targeting arrangement is a reasonably forecastable measure that will result in target inflation over an extended period being roughly where we want it. This does not necessarily mean that trying to forecast the target directly (except over short horizons) is the way to go.

Mark Wynne is quite critical of core measures as a guide for policy. Certainly in New Zealand the median was a biased measure, something like the sixty-fifth percentile was needed to track headline inflation over the medium term. He also criticises the use of trimmed means or exclusion of so-called 'erratic' items for giving both biased measures and for being rather poorly correlated along the way. In my experience, policy makers tend not to look at a single measure but consider a range of them and a discussion of how the components of inflation are moving in forming a view about what inflation is likely to be and how it might be affected in the particular circumstances by monetary policy. Excluding items like seasonal food that are likely to revert and items that are highly unpredictable is likely to assist policy making in the sense of discouraging it from being over active. There is thus no search for a single index that will do the job unaided.

However, what I do find very instructive is the new index that Wynne constructs for both the euro area and the United States, weighting prices by the inverse of the frequency with which they change. The hypothesis is that it is the rarely changing prices that are more impervious to policy and contribute more to the persistence of inflation. In the United States this is an unbiased measure of the headline and closely correlated with it. How easily it is forecastable is a different issue. In the euro area the correlation is weaker and the bias greater. Indeed these measures perform fairly similarly to the exclusion approach to estimating core inflation. More work is needed here but coming up with some sort of measures of the underlying path of inflation surely lies at the heart of policy.

Zero or ?

It is implicit from my earlier remarks that I favour price-level or medium-term targets, such as that in Australia and the euro zone, as otherwise inflation targets can drift. Furthermore, price-level targets need to be low enough to protect purchasing power after measurement error. There are other routes for protecting people on fixed nominal incomes, which are viable for low levels of inflation. Wynne mentions that even with 2 per cent inflation there are noticeable costs to the economy according to Feldstein (1997), which are only eliminated if nominal inflation is zero. These costs can cumulate considerably. Normally inflation-targeting central banks have rules for how quickly they would bring inflation back on target if it goes outside the acceptable range. With a price-level target, presumably one would still be keen not to see inflation go outside some acceptable range along the way. It is not quite clear from the Australian experience what that range might be[2] but actual inflation in the euro area has not diverged much from the medium-term target.[3]

However, Mark Wynne does not address some of the well-known arguments for having a small positive rate as a target. One is that it cuts down the chance of having deflation – or needing it in the case of a price-level or medium-term target. The second is that it reduces the chance of encountering the 'zero bound' for nominal interest rates. The third is that nominal wages may be sticky downwards and hence operating at a general level of inflation that implies that many people may need a nominal wage cut could be a problem.

None of these arguments is very persuasive. Falling prices are not necessarily undesirable. Productivity gains can easily be sufficient to justify them and in an open economy the main source of falling prices may be the exchange rate (Siklos, 2005; Wood and Mills, 2007). It is the debt–deflation spiral that needs to be avoided. Other measures exist to counter the zero bound on the central bank's policy rate, especially in an open economy (Bernanke, 2003). Lastly it is not clear that nominal wages in the economy cannot fall sufficiently through less overtime, shorter working hours, job loss and re-employment and retirement and replacement without any need to try to reduce the nominal wage rate of any employee.

With any index, however ideal, there tends to come a point when the statisticians suggest that it can be improved. Hence, in addition to any revisions to policy that may be needed because the price level has diverged from the target, there will be occasions when history is effectively rewritten and a new series, extended backwards, shows that the change in the price level over quite a large number of years is not what it was thought to be. Should monetary policy adjust because the goal posts have been moved, to use Mervyn King's memorable phrase. Normally such 'errors' are accepted and policy recalibrated looking forward from that point. Ensuring 'zero' *ex post* thus seems an unlikely ambition.

Asset prices

It is, however, Mark Wynne's Table 4.6 and the analysis underpinning it which is the principal challenge of his chapter. There is a long-standing debate on whether asset prices should be included in the price-stability target or whether they should simply be information variables. The current balance of opinion favours the latter although there are well-known dissenters (Goodhart, 2001). Using a sample of 17 OECD countries over the period 1970–2005, Wynne shows that after allowing for openness and the rate of economic growth, a dummy variable indicating inflation targeting is clearly positive and significant in explaining the rate of growth of house prices. There are many reasons why this may be the case rather than that the other countries put a heavier weight on asset-price inflation and hence have less of it. A simple one is that the inflation-targeting countries in the main had more problem controlling inflation in the past which is what led them to inflation targeting in the first place. They have therefore seen a bigger regime change as inflation fell and the reduction in servicing costs from low-interest-rate mortgages have been greatest. There is no clear model or theory behind this. However, in joint work with Matti Virén, I have shown that house prices have a clear feed-through effect onto monetary policy in the European Union, irrespective of what is in the target (Mayes and Virén, 2005).

As this and the other sections in Mark Wynne's work suggest, there are many fruitful areas here for future work. While many may have thought that the issue of defining price stability had been thoroughly addressed, there is plenty more that can be done.

Notes

1 The contractual nature of this is emphasised by the fact that new ministers of finance have felt obliged to sign a new contract with the governor on their appointment even if this is identical to that in force at the time.
2 Since inflation targeting started there have been three quarters when the annual inflation rate was negative and six when it has been more than 5 per cent.
3 Since Eurosystem policy has been affecting inflation there have been just two months when inflation has been outside a band of 'below but close to 2 per cent' +/−1 per cent and then only very slightly.

References

Bernanke, B.S. (2003) *An Unwelcome Fall in Inflation?*, Economics Roundtable, University of California, San Diego, La Jolla, California, 23 July.

Feldstein, Martin S. (1997) 'The Costs and Benefits of Going from Low Inflation to Price Stability', in Christina D. Romer and David H. Romer (eds), *Reducing Inflation: Motivation and Strategy*. Chicago, IL: University of Chicago Press, pp. 123–156.

Gaspar, V., Smets, F. and Vestin, D. (2007) 'Is Time Ripe for Price Level Path Stability?', ECB Working Paper No. 818, October.

Goodhart, C.A.E. (2001) 'What Weight Should Be Given to Asset Prices in the Measurement of Inflation?', *Economic Journal*, 111 (472), 335–356.

Mayes, D.G. and Virén, M. (2005) 'Monetary Policy Problems for Currency Unions: Asymmetry and the Problem of Aggregation in the Euro Area', *Economic Modelling*, 22 (2), March, 219–251.

Siklos, P. (2005) *The Economics of Deflation*, Cheltenham: Edward Elgar.

Wood, G.E. and Mills, T.C. (2006) 'Policy Rules and Price Level Flexibility', *Indian Economic Journal*, 45 (3), December, 104–118.

5 A proposal for extracting policy information from the ECB's second pillar

Georg Rich[1]

1 Introduction

The European Central Bank employs a two-pillar approach to setting monetary policy. Under the first pillar, it monitors a wide range of data and relies on various econometric models in order to forecast real growth and inflation of the euro area. Under the second pillar, it considers specifically monetary developments, which, in its view, play a crucial role in determining the future course of inflation. According to the ECB, it uses the second-pillar analysis largely for 'cross checking' the policy information drawn from the first.

While the first pillar conforms to the approaches followed by other leading central banks, the ECB's emphasis on the second pillar is unusual. Numerous central banks, including the US Federal Reserve, no longer pay much attention to money. The relationship between inflation and money growth, they maintain, is not sufficiently stable to allow policy makers to forecast future price movements from monetary developments. Other central banks such as the Swiss National Bank still treat the monetary aggregates as important policy variables. Nevertheless, they do not follow the example of the ECB by placing money on a separate pillar.

New Keynesian models looming large in the current macroeconomic literature also tend to discount the usefulness of money. In these models, money does not play any role in the transmission of monetary policy disturbances to the real economy and the price level. Instead, the central bank is assumed to fix a credible inflation target, which serves as the nominal anchor for the real economy. The central bank influences real activity and the price level by setting a rate of interest consistent with its inflation target. It is of course possible to add a money-demand equation to such New Keynesian models. However, money demand is not essential for determining the nominal values of the variables, as both the level and rate of change in prices are tied down to the inflation target. Woodford (2007a, b) and Svensson (2007) are prominent macroeconomists supporting New Keynesian models without money. They fail to see a need for monitoring money, let alone for placing money on a separate pillar. They deny that the ECB is able to extract useful policy signals from money growth and favour abolishing its second pillar altogether. They take the ECB to task for using monetary indicators that – in their view – are unhelpful in gauging its policy course properly.[2]

The development of the euro-area money stock M3 since the introduction of the common currency tends to nourish doubts about the usefulness of the second pillar in setting monetary policy. The ECB has fixed a reference value of 4.5 per cent for M3 growth. Provided real GDP is near its potential level, the reference value equals the rate of increase in M3 that the ECB considers to be consistent with its objective of keeping HICP inflation slightly below 2 per cent. As indicated by Figure 5.1, M3 growth since 2001 has continuously exceeded its reference value in the past three years by an ever-increasing margin. Despite the excessive growth in M3 during much of the period 2001–2007, inflation has hovered about 2 per cent since 2002, contrary to what one would expect if the deviations from the reference value were to contain useful policy information.

Despite the difficulties of extracting policy signals from aggregate M3, the ECB continues to emphasise the usefulness of its second pillar. It expends considerable efforts in explaining the analysis underlying its second pillar to the public. Nevertheless, I do not find the ECB's defence of its second pillar entirely convincing. Although the ECB's analysis leaves something to be desired, I do not wish to go as far as Woodford and Svensson and to reject money as a policy indicator. Rather, I sketch an alternative procedure the ECB could employ for extracting policy signals from the monetary aggregates. The procedure presented in this chapter could usefully supplement the ECB's arsenal of analytical tools, as it is immune to some of the critical arguments raised against the ECB's second-pillar analysis.

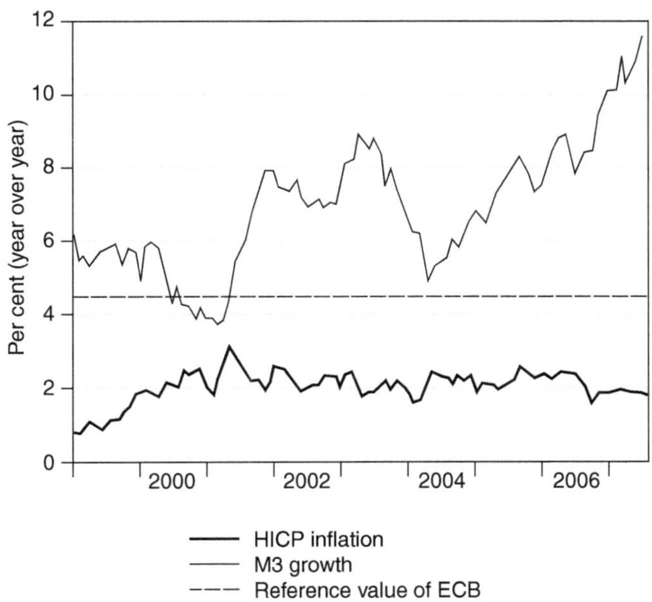

Figure 5.1 Euro-area inflation, growth in the money stock M3 and reference value of ECB (source: ECB data bank).

My procedure draws on information derived from econometric estimates of money demand. It rests on the assumption that the ECB sets its key policy variable, the refinance rate, largely on the basis of its first-pillar analysis. Under the first pillar, the ECB is assumed to employ models and forecasting techniques that tend to disregard money. However, under the second pillar, the ECB monitors monetary variables with the aim of cross-checking the information derived from the first. To this end, it regularly estimates long-run money-demand equations. For my procedure to yield reliable policy signals, nominal money demand should be reasonably stable and determined by just a few key variables such as the price level, real GDP and interest rates. Provided the ECB is able to estimate simple and stable money-demand equations, it constructs reference lines for the respective monetary aggregate. These reference lines are both similar to and different from the ECB's reference value of 4.5 per cent displayed in Figure 5.1. They are similar in the sense that they trace the evolution of the respective monetary aggregate consistent with the ECB's inflation objective and its assumption about potential real growth. However, they differ from the ECB's reference value in three respects:

- They define levels, rather than rates of change in the respective monetary aggregate.
- They shift up or down in response to revisions in the parameter values, as the ECB re-estimates its money-demand equations.
- Most importantly, they shift up or down in response to changes in monetary policy, i.e. to adjustments in the ECB's refinance rate.

Thus, the reference lines not only incorporate information about the ECB's inflation objective and potential real growth. They also take account of changes in monetary policy and in the estimated parameters of the money-demand equations.

Next, the ECB compares the actual development of the respective monetary aggregate with the reference lines. Substantial deviations from the reference lines imply that the ECB should review the policy conclusions drawn from its first pillar. I should note that the procedure presented here for cross-checking the ECB's first-pillar analysis would yield meaningful results even if New Keynesian models were to provide a realistic description of the monetary transmission process in modern economies. Provided money demand is stable, it contains important policy information regardless of whether it serves merely as a residual or plays an active role in the transmission process. Forecasts based on models without money suppress a potentially important piece of information: they ignore the income elasticity of money demand, i.e. a parameter establishing a link between money and economic activity. Because of this link, money may contain information on future inflation. Economists, including Woodford and Svensson, agree that central banks should utilise all available information shedding light on future inflation. Thus, one should not ignore a priori monetary indicators in setting monetary policy.[3]

In the following, I explain my procedure for extracting policy information from money demand. Section 2 offers a critical discussion of the ECB's second-pillar analysis. This is followed by a brief review of existing research on euro-area money demand. In Sections 4 and 5, I apply my procedure to the aggregates M3 and M2 respectively. The chapter ends with a summary and conclusions.

2 The ECB's second pillar: a critical review

In an address to the ECB Watchers Conference of 2007, Jürgen Stark (2007), Member of the ECB's Executive Board, emphasised that the ECB's monetary analysis embodies three main elements:

- The ECB does not focus exclusively on headline M3, but follows a broad-based approach exploiting a full set of monetary, financial and economic information. In particular, the ECB analyses the components and counterparts of M3 and other monetary and credit aggregates.
- The ECB employs a wide range of empirical models, comprising money-demand equations, time-series indicator models and structural general equilibrium models. These models are used for explaining developments in money and credit, for identifying innovations in these variables and for exploring the broader outlook for inflation and real growth.
- The models are supplemented by informed judgement about prospective structural changes in the euro area's monetary and financial sector.

Relying on its monetary analysis, the ECB (2004, pp. 45–49; 2005, pp. 13–16; 2007, pp. 55–61) has repeatedly argued[4] that the surge in M3 growth during the period 2001–2003 did not jeopardise price stability, while a similar expansion since 2004 has threatened to fuel inflation. In the first period, the ECB attributed the acceleration of M3 growth to portfolio shifts into liquid monetary assets, due to public concerns about an uncertain economic and financial outlook. Such portfolio shifts were considered to have little impact on future inflation. Therefore, the ECB decided to cut interest rates despite the surge in money growth. In the second period, by contrast, the ECB found the surge in M3 growth to be correlated with a strong credit expansion driven by easy financing conditions and financial innovations designed to boost bank lending. The ECB came to the conclusion that such developments called for tightening of monetary policy. Otherwise, they would stimulate inflation in due course.

Although the 2001 spike in M3 growth indeed did not cause inflation to pick up significantly, the ECB's analysis raises a number of questions. Even if M3 is adjusted for portfolio shifts (henceforth called 'adjusted M3'), that aggregate still exceeded the ECB's reference value by 1 to 1.5 percentage points during the period 2001–2003 (see Chart F in ECB, 2005, p. 16). Thus the inflation trend should have accelerated from 2 to 3 or 3.5 per cent had adjusted M3 emitted correct monetary policy signals. Furthermore, only the future will tell whether the ECB's distinction between portfolio- and credit-based expansions in M3 growth will pass the test of time and will be helpful in improving inflation forecasts.

Another approach followed by the ECB consists in developing monetary indicators of inflation risks. In as much as such indicators tend to lead inflation, they may be used for assessing the risks to price stability arising from the ECB's current policy course. The ECB has explored the leading indicator role of a wide range of variables. It has not only forecast inflation from a bivariate relationship with unadjusted and adjusted M3 (ECB, 2004, pp. 56–57), but has also examined other indicators such as M1 and M2, loans of financial institutions to the private sector and P* measures of excess liquidity based on adjusted and unadjusted M3 (ECB, 2006, pp. 22–25; 2007, p. 70). In general, the ECB feels that these indicators act as useful warning signals of future inflation.

As far as the indicator role of M3 is concerned, the ECB (2006, p. 25) argues that M3 growth, adjusted for portfolio shifts, provides relatively unbiased forecasts of future inflation. In a critical assessment of the second pillar, the ECB researchers Fischer *et al.* (2006) explore various real-time bivariate forecasting models used by the ECB in its monetary analysis. They find that unadjusted M3 overpredicts trend inflation. Adjusted M3, by contrast, yields forecasts matching average actual inflation. However, the forecasts based on adjusted M3 are much more volatile than those derived from the unadjusted variant. Furthermore, forecasts resting on M3 manage to capture the inflation trend, whereas forecasts relying on the ECB's first pillar are able to trace the fluctuations around the average.

The recent academic literature (Gerlach, 2004; Neumann and Greiber, 2004; Von Hagen and Hofmann, 2007; Assenmacher and Gerlach, 2007) has emphasised the importance of low-frequency movements in M3 for future inflation, a view also endorsed by the ECB (2003, p. 87). Assenmacher and Gerlach favour a modified version of a standard Phillips curve, with inflation decomposed into high-frequency and low-frequency components. High-frequency movements in inflation are determined by the output gap and various cost–push factors, while the low-frequency movements depend on the low-frequency components of M3 growth, output growth and the rate of change in M3 velocity, with the latter assumed to be related to the first difference in long-term interest rates. Assenmacher and Gerlach conclude that their modified Phillips curve fits the data well, i.e. money is useful for forecasting low-frequency movements in inflation. However, they qualify their conclusions somewhat by pointing out that their results rest on data drawn to a large extent from the pre-euro period, a problem to be discussed below.

In a thorough study, Hofmann (2006) assesses the performance of various monetary-indicator models in out-of-sample forecasts of inflation. He considers standard bivariate forecasting models, forecasts based on the common factors contained in a group of monetary indicators, forecast combinations and the modified version of the Phillips curve proposed by Assenmacher and Gerlach. He finds the bivariate models for M3 growth, adjusted for portfolio shifts, to provide better inflation forecasts than all the other models considered in his paper.

However, he also qualifies his conclusions to some extent as his results suggest that the forecasting powers of M3 have deteriorated in recent years.

In a more recent paper, Berger and Österholm (2007) apply a mean-adjusted Bayesian VAR approach to forecasting euro-area inflation from M2 and M3 growth. They find that out-of-sample forecasts of inflation are improved considerably if money growth is included. This result not only holds for bivariate but also trivariate and fourvariate BVARs. Nevertheless, they warn against overemphasising the importance of money. Like Assenmacher/Gerlach and Hofmann, they conclude that the forecast performance of money is substantially lower for the most recent sample periods than for the distant past.

In its 2007 economic survey of the euro area, the OECD (2007, Annex 2.A2) too finds that the predictive ability of M3 has declined. The OECD splits the forecasting period into two halves: 1995 to 2000 and 2000 to 2005. Like Hofmann, the OECD considers a variety of monetary indicators: growth in M1, M2, adjusted and unadjusted M3; and in private lending, a measure of the monetary overhang (difference between M3 and the value estimated from a long-run money-demand equation), a P* indicator, various gap and capacity indicators, and several other indicators. The forecasts provided by these indicators are compared with those derived from a base-line model. For the first period, several monetary indicators indeed contain useful information on future inflation, with M2 able to improve short-horizon forecasts, while M1, M3 and the P* model perform better at longer horizons. Credit growth, by contrast, contains little predictive power. The gap, capacity and other real indicators work well at short horizons. However, the results are different for the second period. The performance of the monetary indicators worsens considerably, except for the P* model, while several real variables outperform the monetary aggregates. Thus, while money was useful for long-horizon forecasts until 2000, it is uncertain whether its predictive power is still intact today.

Even if stable demand equations for the euro-area monetary aggregates were to exist, forecasting inflation from money growth would run up against a fundamental obstacle. Suppose that the ECB is successful in achieving its inflation objective and manages to keep inflation slightly below 2 per cent over an extended period of time. It reacts correctly to any shock threatening to jeopardise its inflation objective by adjusting monetary policy. Suppose further that M3 grows at the reference value of 4.5 per cent. Now the ECB faces a negative shock to aggregate demand, opening up the prospect of deflation. To offset the deflation threat, the ECB responds to the shock by lowering its refinance rate. The drop in the interest rate will stimulate growth in demand for M3, while the business cycle contraction will have the opposite effect. If money demand is strongly sensitive to changes in interest rates, M3 growth is likely to accelerate and surpass its reference value. However, the positive deviation from the reference value does not imply that the ECB is pursuing an inflationary monetary policy. On the contrary, it signals a correct response of policy makers to the deflationary shock. Only if the ECB were to overreact to the shock and to stimulate money growth excessively would the positive deviation from the reference value herald a surge in inflation. Therefore, it is important to distinguish between stabilising and destabilising movements in money growth. Stabilising movements occur so long as the ECB manages to keep inflation close to its objective. The ECB correctly alters its refinance rate in response to destabilising shocks. Money growth also fluctuates substantially about the ECB's reference value, while the variance of inflation is small. In these circumstances, the ECB would waste valuable research resources by trying to forecast changes in inflation from movements in past money growth. Since inflation would remain more or less constant at slightly less than 2 per cent, while money growth would fluctuate considerably, the ECB could not possibly detect a statistically significant relationship between these two variables even it confined its analysis to low-frequency movements in money growth.[5]

For these reasons, the predictive power of money growth is likely to dissipate gradually provided the ECB continues to keep inflation near 2 per cent as it has done quite successfully since 2002. In this case, forecasting inflation from money growth would become an exercise in futility even if money demand in the euro area were to remain stable. Considering the pitfalls of forecasting inflation from money growth, I propose an alternative procedure for extracting policy signals from the monetary aggregates. This procedure rests on estimates of money-demand equations for the euro area. If money demand is sufficiently stable, my procedure may be employed for cross-checking the policy information derived from the ECB's first pillar.

My procedure bears some similarities to an approach proposed by Reynard (2007). Relying on data for the United States, the euro area and Switzerland, he argues that money is a reliable predictor of future price movements if it is adjusted for changes in velocity and potential output. His adjusted measures of money are derived from estimated money-demand equations. Therefore, his approach is also immune to the criticism raised above. However, in contrast to my procedure, Reynard's approach does not take account of the ECB's actual policy stance. He relates money demand to the low-frequency filtered components of interest rates, rather than their actual levels.

3 Euro-area money demand: a brief review

The ECB has long emphasised that euro-area money demand is sufficiently stable to serve as a useful policy device. It has investigated extensively money demand, employing both aggregated and disaggregated approaches.[6] Researchers outside the ECB have also produced a variety of studies on euro-area money demand.[7] According to these studies, money demand was reasonably stable until the introduction of the euro. However, if the sample period is extended beyond 1999, researchers have had less success in uncovering stable money-demand equations, at least so long as simple specifications, relating real demand for M3 to real GDP and interest rates, are tested. Some researchers have been able to restore stability by introducing additional explanatory variables of money demand such as measures of uncertainty capturing the portfolio shifts between

2001 and 2003, proxies for wealth such as house and stock prices, or the inflation rate as a proxy for the opportunity cost of holding money. The ECB (2007, pp. 64–68) admits that simple models explaining the dynamics of M3 are unsatisfactory because this aggregate 'also includes assets that are held for saving and portfolio reasons and therefore are influenced by a richer set of variables' (p. 64). The ECB mentions as additional factors influencing M3 new financial instruments such as structured products limiting downside risk, borrowing to finance M&A activity, the rapid growth in the M3 deposits of non-monetary financial intermediaries, strong capital inflows to the euro area boosting M3 growth, and the influence of wealth on money demand.

In general, existing studies suggest that stability obtains only for complex specifications of M3 demand. The need for complex specifications poses a dilemma if my procedure is applied to M3 demand. My procedure involves forecasts of money demand consistent with the ECB's inflation objective, real potential growth and the ECB's current policy stance. It is easy to derive such forecasts from simple equations relating real demand for M3 to real GDP and interest rates. However, if real demand for M3 is influenced by a host of additional variables, the forecasting exercise becomes tricky because the future evolution of these additional variables must also be taken into account. Some of these additional variables are highly elusive and difficult to predict. Therefore, it is an empirical question of whether simple or complex specifications of money demand yield the most reliable policy signals. I do not explore this question in this chapter, but I admit that it would have to be investigated thoroughly if my procedure were to be applied in practice. For the time being, I limit myself to simple specifications of M3 demand even though the resulting parameter estimates may suffer from instabilities complicating the signal extraction problem.

4 An alternative procedure for extracting policy signals from money growth: the case of M3

In extracting policy information from M3 demand, I assume that the ECB proceeds as follows: at the beginning of each year it estimates simple long-run money-demand equations, relating the level of M3, deflated by the HICP consumer price index, to the level of real GDP and to various interest-rate variables. All the variables, except interest rates, are seasonally adjusted and expressed in logs. The ECB is assumed to compute these equations from rolling samples covering the past 40 quarters. A sample period of 40 quarters appears to be reasonable. It is long enough to yield meaningful results. Likewise, it is not overly long and precludes using information from the distant past that may be irrelevant for current policy decisions. Sensitivity analysis suggests that the results do not alter much if the rolling sample period is shortened by one or two years.

The estimated parameter values of the money-demand equations are shown in Table 5.1. For reasons of data availability, the first sample period ending in 2000Q4 only covers 38 quarters. The estimates are based on co-integration analysis. One of the estimated co-integration equations may be treated as a long-run

Table 5.1 Values of elasticity and semi-elasticity of real demand for M3

Sample periods	*Log M3 with respect to*			
	Log real GDP	*Interest rate difference**	*10-year bond yield*	*Constant*
1991Q4 – 2000Q4**	1.26 (6.92)	0.0035 (0.79)	0.0014 (0.29)	–2.63
1992Q1 – 2001Q4	1.47 (14.06)	0.0083 (2.60)	0.0023 (0.65)	–5.63
1993Q1 – 2002Q4**	1.77 (13.62)	0.0098 (0.96)		–9.80
1994Q1 – 2003Q4	2.15 (7.26)	–0.1089 (–3.96)		–15.40
1995Q1 – 2004Q4**	1.71 (6.02)	–0.1749 (–5.06)		–9.29
1996Q1 – 2005Q4	1.71 (4.84)	–0.2343 (–5.49)		–9.35
1997Q1 – 2006Q4	0.76 (0.72)	–0.5632 (–4.74)		3.80
1997Q2 – 2007Q1	1.42 (2.52)	–0.2935 (–4.87)		–5.14

Notes

Numbers in parentheses are t values. Data on M3 are deflated by the HICP index. Data sources: Real GDP from 1995Q1 onwards: ECB, for earlier data Eurostat (data adjusted to make them comparable with those of the ECB), M3 and interest rates: ECB.

* Difference between 3-month Euribor rate and 10-year bond yield.

** Co-integration equations not statistically significant.

money-demand function, as displayed in Table 5.1. However, the estimates obtained for M3 are not entirely satisfactory. The Johansen test suggests that in three out of the eight sample periods covered by Table 5.1 no statistically significant co-integration equation exists.

In as much as we may trust the estimated equations, they point – with one exception – to a statistically significant relationship between real money demand and real GDP, but the corresponding elasticity, drifting up from 1.3 in the first sample period to over 2 in 1994Q1–2003Q4 and down again to 1.4 in the last sample period, is not very stable. As to interest rates, I employ the differential between the three-month Euribor interest rate and the ten-year government bond yield as an independent variable. I include the interest-rate differential because in other studies it was found to exert a statistically significant impact on euro-area demand for M3. Note that the sign of the semi-elasticity with regard to the interest differential turns from positive to negative as we advance in time. However, it has become statistically significant in the most recent past even though its stability still leaves something to be desired.[8] In the first two equations, I also consider the bond yield – taken by itself – but it fails to explain much of the movements in M3 demand. Inclusion of the bond yield in the equations for the subsequent sample periods tends to generate absurd estimates for the income elasticity of money demand. Similar problems arise if the three-month Euribor rate is substituted for the bond yield. Therefore, I generally confine myself to the differential as the sole interest-rate variable included in the money-demand equations.

Next, I assume that the ECB, from these estimated money-demand equations, derives reference lines describing the evolution of the nominal values of M3, likely to be consistent with its objective of keeping inflation slightly below 2 per cent. Moreover, I take account of the fact that the ECB is prepared to accommodate the increase in the demand for M3 arising from potential real growth in the euro-area economy.

To determine such a reference line, say, at the beginning of 2007, the ECB estimates the money-demand equation displayed in Table 5.1 for the sample period 1997Q1–2006Q4. It then constructs a reference line for nominal M3, covering the five-quarter period from 2007Q1 to 2008Q1. To this end, the ECB derives a corresponding reference line for real M3. It inserts an expansion path for potential real GDP in the equation for real M3 demand, which is assumed to match the long-run trend in the actual values. Thus, potential real GDP equals the estimated values derived from the following regression equation:

$$\underset{}{\text{Logrgdp}} = \underset{(4185.7)}{14.11} + \underset{(58.4)}{0.0052}\, \textit{trend},\ R^2 = 0.98, \text{ sample period. 1991Q1–2007Q2}$$

Since the data for the actual level of real GDP are known only for the period up to 2007Q2 (as of the time of estimation), the values of the potential level for 2007Q3 onwards are extrapolated from the estimated trend. The ECB is also assumed to take account of the policy-induced portion of the interest-rate variables and to set that portion equal to the values estimated from the following regression equations:

$$\text{indiff} = \underset{(-9.37)}{-2.743} + \underset{(5.10)}{0.485}\, \textit{ref},\ R^2 = 0.45$$

$$\text{by} = \underset{(9.78)}{2.906} + \underset{(5.40)}{0.521}\, \textit{ref},\ R^2 = 0.48, \text{ sample period: 1991Q1–2007Q2}$$

where *indiff*, *by* and *ref* denote the interest-rate differential, the bond yield and the ECB's refinance rate respectively.[9] The ECB in turn plugs into the real money-demand equation the policy-induced portion of the interest-rate variables. It derives the reference lines on the assumption that it will leave the refinance rate unchanged in the period 2007Q1–2008Q1. Thus the reference line indicates how real M3 should evolve if the ECB were to keep its policy rate of interest unchanged. Of course, the ECB will update its reference line in the course of the period 2007Q1–2008Q1, as it adjusts its refinance rate. The reference lines displayed in Figure 5.2 constitute such updated versions, incorporating the refinance rates actually set by the ECB up to 2007Q2. Lastly, the ECB determines analogous reference lines for nominal M3 by multiplying the quarterly reference values for real M3 with its objectives for the HICP index. These quarterly objectives are assumed to lie on an expansion path for the HICP index consistent with its aim of keeping inflation slightly below 2 per cent per year. For simplicity, the expansion path for the HICP index is derived on the assumption that the ECB is willing to tolerate an increase in consumer prices of exactly 0.5 per cent per quarter from 2007Q4 to 2008Q1.

As indicated earlier, the location and shape of the reference lines depend not only on the ECB's inflation objective and its assumption about potential growth, but also on its policy rate of interest and the estimated parameters of the money-demand equations. In this chapter, the ECB is assumed (what I am sure it is doing in practice) to set its refinance rate at levels that – in its view – will help achieving or safeguarding its inflation objective in the longer run. Thus, the procedure presented here does not yield any information on the appropriate levels of the ECB's refinance rate. Instead, the ECB must rely on its first pillar in order to determine the levels of its refinance rate that are in sympathy with its inflation objective. Since my proposed procedure exploits information drawn from the first pillar, it cannot serve as a stand-alone approach to setting monetary policy. However, it can be employed to cross-check the results of the ECB's first-pillar analysis.

The reference lines emerging from my procedure are displayed in Figure 5.2. They cover the period 2001Q1 to 2008Q1 and extend from the first quarter of each year to the same quarter of the following year. Furthermore, I compare the reference lines with the actual development of M3. Major deviations in M3 growth from its reference lines imply that the signals extracted from money growth are at variance with those obtained from the ECB's first pillar, as the actual development of M3 is inconsistent with the inflation objective and the assumption of potential growth. In the case of major deviations, the ECB would have to assess the situation in order to find out which of the two pillars – if at all – is likely to emit the correct policy signals.

A comparison of the actual evolution of M3 with the reference lines does not point to major deviations up to the beginning of 2006. If the estimated money-demand equations can be trusted at all, my analysis at best suggests that the ECB's policy course may have been a bit too easy in 2001–2003 and a bit too

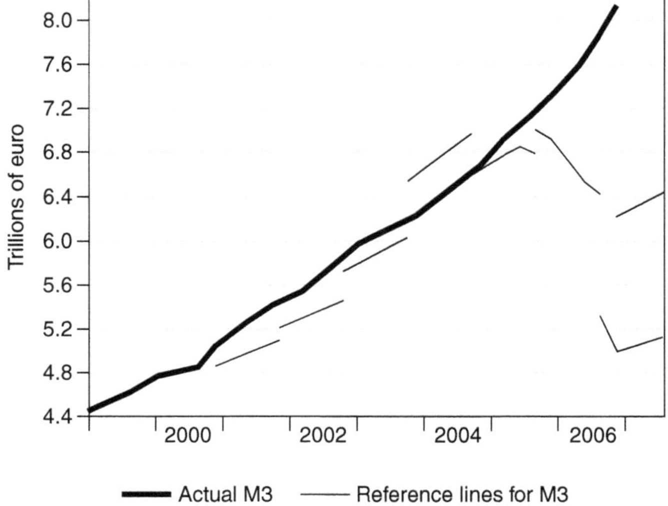

Figure 5.2 Actual levels of M3 and reference lines.

restrictive in 2004. Thus, in downplaying the inflationary effects of portfolio-based money growth, the ECB may not have paid sufficient attention to the surge in M3 growth in 2001 and overreacted, at least initially, to the renewed acceleration in 2004. However, I do not wish to read too much into the information extracted from M3 demand. As may be seen from Figure 5.2, the reference lines derived for 2006 and 2007 move about erratically. According to Table 5.1, both the income elasticity of M3 demand and semi-elasticity with respect to the interest-rate differential are highly sensitive to even a slight advance of one quarter in the sample period 1997Q1–2006Q4. Considering the instabilities in the parameter estimates for the most recent sample periods, I doubt that Figure 5.2 yields useful policy conclusions for 2006 and 2007. Currently, trying to extract reliable policy signals from M3 growth appears to be fruitless. In my view, the ECB should not pay much attention to the aggregate M3, at least not at the present moment.

5 An application to M2

Considering the difficulties arising from M3, I also apply my procedure to an alternative aggregate, i.e. the money stock M2.[10] Figure 5.3 shows that there was a fairly close positive correlation between the growth in the aggregates M2 and M3. Nevertheless there were significant deviations at times even though the two aggregates generally moved in tandem. Therefore, demand for M2 may be more stable than demand for M3.

In line with the analysis for M3, the ECB, say, at the beginning of 2007, estimates a demand equation for real M2, covering the sample period 1998Q2 to

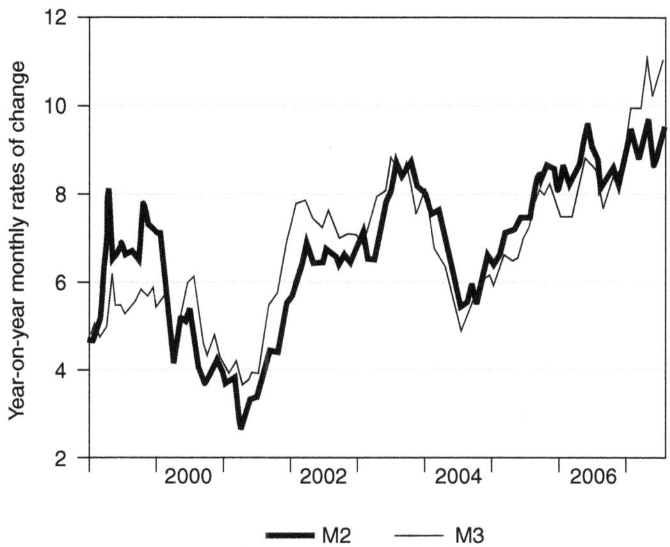

Figure 5.3 Growth in the euro-area aggregates M2 and M3.

2006Q4. The starting date of the sample period is determined by the availability of data. Real M2 is defined in the same manner as real M3. The log of real demand for M2 is related to the log of real GDP and the interest-rate differential. As in the case of M3, the estimates presented in Table 5.2 are based on co-integration analysis. The Johansen co-integration test suggests that the three variables considered in the analysis are co-integrated in all the sample periods. There exists at least one co-integrating equation, which I interpret as a long-run money-demand function.

The estimates in Table 5.2 raise a number of problems requiring discussion. First, the results are sensitive to the choice of the interest-rate variable in the money-demand equation. If the interest differential is replaced by the Euribor rate, the Johansen procedure does not point to any co-integration among the variables. Therefore, I reject this specification. By contrast, if the interest-rate differential is replaced by the bond yield, co-integration exists, but the coefficient for real GDP becomes unstable and tends to assume implausibly low values in the sample periods ending with 2003Q4 and 2004Q4. Figure 5.4 shows why econometric studies are likely to underestimate the influence of real GDP on M2 demand in the early part of the period under consideration if the bond yield is employed as an interest-rate variable. Figure 5.4 relates the velocity of M2 (nominal GDP divided by nominal M2) to the Euribor rate and the bond yield. Velocity clearly tended to decrease from 1997 to 2007. The downward trend in velocity could be explained by two factors: (1) The income elasticity of money demand exceeds unity, i.e. real money demand rises proportionally more than real GDP or (2) the downward trend in velocity reflects the decline in the bond yield over much of the sample period, i.e. real money demand rose relative to real GDP because of falling bond yields. Although the decrease in interest rates no doubt tended to boost money demand, it is implausible to attribute the downward trend in velocity to movements in the bond yield alone. The bond yield ceased to decline in 2005 and rose again substantially thereafter. Yet, velocity continued to proceed on its downward course. If velocity had responded mainly to movements in the bond yield, it should have rebounded after 2005. For this

Table 5.2 Values of elasticity and semi-elasticity of real demand for M2

Sample Periods	*Log M2 with respect to*		
	Log real GDP (income elasticity)	*Interest rate difference*	*Constant*
1998Q2 – 2003Q4	1.50 (21.8)	–0.048 (–9.5)	–6.29
1998Q2 – 2004Q4	1.52 (10.4)	–0.074 (–7.4)	–6.53
1999Q2 – 2004Q4	2.30 (11.9)	–0.046 (–6.1)	–17.73
1998Q2 – 2005Q4	1.88 (11.4)	–0.063 (–5.0)	–11.69
2000Q2 – 2005Q4	2.50 (14.2)	–0.047 (–8.0)	–20.52
1998Q2 – 2006Q4	1.94 (19.5)	–0.036 (–3.9)	–12.56
2001Q2 – 2006Q4	2.43 (19.0)	–0.047 (–9.0)	–19.58

Source: ECB.

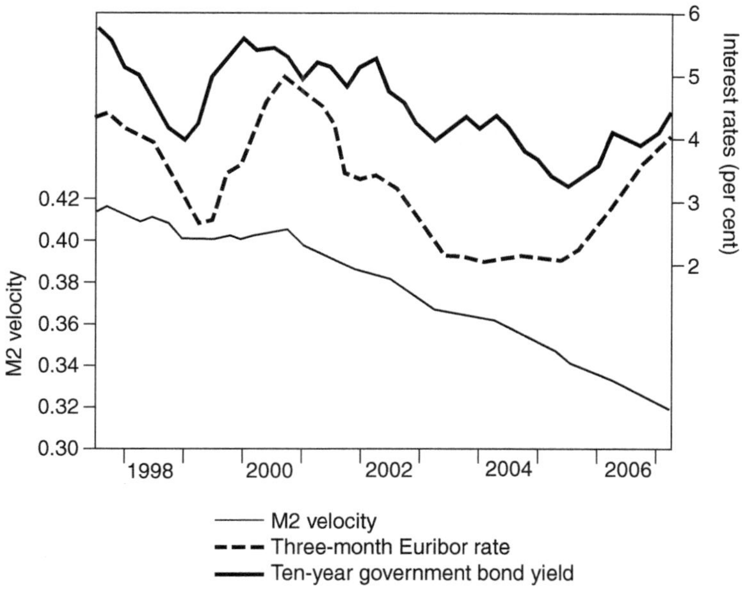

Figure 5.4 Velocity of M2 and interest rates.

reason, I suspect that equations including the bond yield provide misleading estimates of the income elasticity of money demand. A better bet is to use the interest-rate differential. As Table 5.2 clearly indicates, this specification yields estimates of the income elasticity exceeding unity, which in turn accounts mainly for the downward trend in velocity.

Second, the estimates provided in Table 5.2 suggest that the income elasticity of M2 demand increased gradually over the period 1998–2006. It rose from about 1.5 in 1998Q2–2003Q4 to almost 2 in 1998Q2–2006Q4 provided the sample periods always start with 1998Q2. The gradual increase in the income elasticity suggests that its estimates may be sensitive to the choice of sample period. To explore this problem, I assume that the ECB estimates its money-demand equations also from sample periods of fixed length. At the end of each year, it estimates money-demand equations from data based on the past 22 quarters. The estimated coefficients based on sample periods of fixed length are shown in the table too, which reveals a jump in the estimated income elasticity from about 1.5 to 2.3–2.4 from the first sample period to the subsequent periods with a fixed length of 22 quarters. To deal with the uncertainties arising from the size of the income elasticity, I assume that the ECB – at the beginning of each year – derives two versions of the money-demand equation: one estimated from data based on a sample period with a fixed length of 22 quarters and the other one from data based on a sample period of varying length but always starting with 1998Q2.

In a next step, the ECB constructs a pair of reference lines for nominal M2 for the five-quarter period from 2007Q1 to 2008Q1. It derives this reference line in the same manner as those for M3. The reference lines emerging from my procedure are displayed in Figure 5.5. They are not only derived for the period 2007Q1–2008Q1, but also for the three preceding five-quarter periods. The reference lines for the period 2004Q1 to 2007Q2 are based on the refinance rates actually set by the ECB. As already indicated, the reference line for 2007 is based on the assumption that the ECB will keep its refinance rate at the current level of 4 per cent until the beginning of 2008.

The reference lines may be compared with the actual development of M2 for the period up to 2007Q2. As indicated by Figure 5.5, the actual development of M2 more or less conformed to the reference lines until the beginning of 2006. However, since then, the actual levels have moved substantially above the reference values. The uncertainties about the size of the income elasticity do not appear to matter much as this conclusion holds regardless of the sample period chosen for estimating the money-demand equations. Thus, my analysis suggests that the ECB's current monetary stance is still too expansionary, a view probably shared by key officials at the Frankfurt institution. If the ECB has abstained from raising its refinance rate since 13 June 2007, this reflects, in all likelihood, concerns about the current turmoil in financial markets and the attendant risks of a global recession, calling for a great deal of caution in tightening further monetary policy.

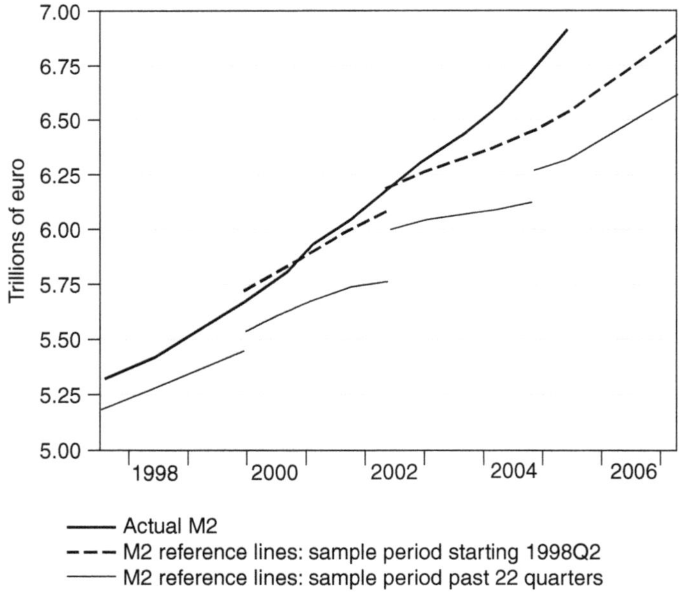

Figure 5.5 Actual levels of M2 and reference lines.

6 Summary and conclusions

This chapter presents a procedure the ECB could employ within the framework of its second-pillar analysis. My procedure involves extracting from estimated money-demand equations for the euro-area policy information suitable for cross-checking the signals obtained from the ECB's first pillar. Specifically, my procedure yields reference lines describing the evolution of the aggregates M2 and M3 consistent with the ECB's inflation objective and potential growth in euro-area real GDP. However, the reference lines based on my procedure differ from the ECB's reference value for M3 in several respects. Above all, my reference lines do not imply a fixed growth rate for the respective aggregate. Rather, they move up or down in response to changes in the ECB's refinance rate, its key policy variable. Furthermore they are updated to shifts in the estimated parameters in the money-demand equations. For these reasons, my procedure is immune to some of the objections to the ECB's fixed reference value. Since 2001 actual M3 growth has exceeded – most recently by an ever-increasing margin – the ECB's fixed reference value (Figure 5.1). Despite persistent M3 growth in excess of the ECB's reference value, it does not necessarily follow that the ECB has pursued an overly expansionary policy course. To interpret correctly the growth patterns revealed by Figure 5.1, we must distinguish between stabilising and destabilising fluctuations in money growth. If M3 growth moves above its reference value because the ECB has rightly lowered its refinance rate in response to an incipient deflationary shock, this does not herald an impending acceleration of inflation. My procedure takes account of this problem by allowing for the reference lines to move up or down in response to changes in the ECB's refinance rate. My procedure rests on the assumption that the ECB, under its first-pillar, uses all available information to set its refinance rate at levels consistent with its inflation objective. In these circumstances, the reference lines derived from my procedure are also likely to be consistent with the ECB's inflation objective. Therefore, by comparing actual growth of the respective aggregate with the reference lines, the ECB may cross-check the policy signals derived from its first pillar. Of course, my procedure yields sensible results only if demand for the respective aggregate is reasonably stable.

Such cross-checking exercises suggest that the ECB since its inception has pursued monetary policies largely consistent with its inflation objective. According to the reference lines derived for M3, the ECB could have pursued a slightly more restrictive course over the period 2001–2003 and a slightly more expansionary course in 2004. However, the results for M3 should be treated with caution. Demand for that aggregate – at least for the simple specifications chosen in this chapter – is not very stable, notably not for the most recent sample periods. Therefore, the ECB, in my view, should not pay too much attention to M3. By contrast, the results for M2 are more encouraging than for those M3. The development of M2 was largely in sympathy with the reference lines derived in my chapter, except for the period since the beginning of 2006, when M2 growth started to move above its reference lines. This implies that European monetary policy at present is still too expansionary, a view probably shared by key ECB officials. Nevertheless, the ECB is reluctant to tighten further monetary policy in the face of the current turmoil in financial markets and the risks of a global recession.

Notes

1 Honorary professor at the University of Bern and private consultant. Contact information: Georg Rich, Parkweg 7, CH-5000 Aarau, Switzerland, phone: +41 62 822 2945, email: g.rich@richcons.ch. I am indebted to Katrin Assenmacher-Wesche and Samuel Renard for very constructive comments.
2 De Grauwe and Polan (2005) are other vocal critics of the ECB's second pillar.
3 Woodford (2007b, p. 29) admits that '[t]here is no *a priori* reason to exclude monetary variables from the set of indicators' to be monitored by central banks.
4 See also Stark (2007).
5 Svensson (2007) makes a similar point.
6 See Coenen and Vega (2001), Bruggemann *et al.* (2003), and Calza and Sousa (2003) for studies on euro-area demand for M3. Recently, the ECB has presented research on sectoral models of money demand (Von Landesberger, 2007).
7 See OECD (2007, pp. 66–67) and Dreger and Wolters (2006), and the literature cited there.
8 Economic theory suggests that the relationship between real demand for M3 and the interest-rate differential may be positive or negative. In the case of a positive sign, an increase in the differential causes funds to move from non-monetary assets into deposits that are part of M3 and yield a market-related return. In the case of a negative sign, funds move from deposits without a market-related return to monetary and non-monetary assets with a market-related return.
9 I calculated quarterly values of the refinance rate as follows: for example, in 2007Q2 the ECB changed its refinance rate once on 13 June from 3.75 to 4 per cent, that is, on the 74th day of the second quarter. Therefore, the average is given by $(3.75\times73+4\times18)/91=3.80$.
10 Reynard (2007) considers euro-area M2 to be a better policy indicator than M3.

References

Assenmacher-Wesche, Katrin and Stefan Gerlach (2007) 'Interpreting Euro Area Inflation at High and Low Frequencies', mimeo.

Berger, Helge and Pär Österholm (2007) 'Does Money Growth Granger-Cause Inflation in the Euro Area? Evidence from Out-of-Sample Forecasts Using Bayesian VARs', Working Paper 2007:30, Department of Economics, Uppsala University, December.

Bruggeman, Annick, Paola Donati and Anders Warne (2003) 'Is the Demand for Euro Area M3 Stable?', European Central Bank, Working Paper Series, No. 255, September.

Calza, Alessandro and João Sousa (2003) 'Why has Broad Money Demand Been More Stable in the Euro Area Than in Other Economies? A Literature Review', European Central Bank, Working Paper Series, No. 261, September.

Coenen, G. and J.-L. Vega (2001) 'The Demand for M3 in the Euro Area', *Journal of Applied Econometrics*, 16, 727–748.

De Grauwe, Paul and Magdalena Polan (2005) 'Is Inflation Always and Everywhere a Monetary Phenomenon?', *Scandinavian Journal of Economics*, 107, 239–259.

Dreger, Christian and Jürgen Wolters (2006) 'Investigating M3 Money Demand in the

Euro Area – New Evidence Based on Standard Models', DIW Berlin, Discussion Paper No. 561, March.
European Central Bank (2003) *Monthly Bulletin*, June.
European Central Bank (2004) *Monthly Bulletin*, October.
European Central Bank (2005) *Monthly Bulletin*, January.
European Central Bank (2006) *Monthly Bulletin*, June.
European Central Bank (2007) *Monthly Bulletin*, July.
Fischer, B., M. Lenza, H. Pill and L. Reichlin (2006) 'Money and Monetary Policy: The ECB Experience 1999–2006', second draft of paper presented at the 4th ECB Central Banking Conference, Frankfurt am Main, 9–10 November.
Gerlach, Stefan (2004) 'The Two Pillars of the European Central Bank', *Economic Policy*, 40, 389–439.
Hofmann, Boris (2006) 'Do Monetary Indicators (Still) Predict Euro Area Inflation?', Deutsche Bundesbank, Discussion Paper 18/2006.
Neumann, Manfred J.M. and Claus Greiber (2004) 'Inflation and Core Money Growth in the Euro Area', Deutsche Bundesbank, Discussion Paper 36/2004.
OECD (2007) *Economic Surveys. Euro Area*, 2006/16, Paris, January.
Reynard, Samuel (2007) 'Maintaining Low Inflation: Money, Interest Rates and Policy Stance', *Journal of Monetary Economics*, 54, July, 1441–1471.
Stark, Jürgen (2007) 'Enhancing the Monetary Analysis', presentation at The ECB and its Watchers IX Conference, Frankfurt am Main, 7 September.
Svensson, Lars E.O. (2007) 'What Have Economists Learned about Monetary Policy over the Past 50 Years?', presented at the Monetary Policy over Fifty Years Conference, on the occasion of the fiftieth anniversary of the Deutsche Bundesbank, Frankfurt am Main, 21 September.
Von Hagen, Jürgen and Boris Hofmann (in press) 'Monetary Policy Orientation in Times of Low Inflation', in David Altig and Ed Nosal (eds), *Monetary Policy in Low-Inflation Economies*, Cambridge: Cambridge University Press.
Von Landesberger, Julian (2007) 'Sectoral Money Demand for Models for the Euro Area Based on a Common Set of Determinants', European Central Bank, Working Paper Series, No. 741, March.
Woodford, Michael (2007a) 'Does a "Two-Pillar Phillips Curve" Justify a Two-Pillar Monetary Policy Strategy?', revised from a paper presented at the Fourth ECB Central Banking Conference 'The Role of Money: Money and Monetary Policy in the Twenty-First Century', Frankfurt am Main, 9–10 November 2006, version 26 March.
Woodford, Michael (2007b) 'How Important is Money in the Conduct of Monetary Policy?', NBER Working Paper Series, No. 13325, August.

COMMENTS BY ROGER CLEWS[1]

For me this is rather a nostalgic chapter. It reminds me of the debates that were had in the United Kingdom 20 and more years ago on the usefulness of monetary aggregates as a guide to monetary policy. And also of the somewhat similar debate ten or so years ago when the Eurosystem was being designed. It is a little sad perhaps that the debate has not yet been resolved.

I thought in the past and still think that there are limitations on the use of simple monetary aggregates, whether as main policy targets or as cross-checks on other analysis. But on the other hand, the activities of the banking system can be very important. I come from an institution that tries very hard not to put all its faith in one model but believes rather in having a suite of models including monetary models. So the idea of cross-checking different sources of information, different theoretical approaches is part of the culture. Cross-checking is not the issue. The issue arising from this chapter is whether it is sensible to try to summarise all the information in the monetary quantities in one number. That may not be doing justice to the information.

Central banks have in practice always gone behind the aggregates and delved into counterparts, sectoral decompositions and so on, and that is surely true of the ECB today – looking as it were behind its second pillar. There is, it is true, an issue of presentation if aggregates are given special status. But what matters most, surely, is that thorough and far-reaching analysis, including monetary analysis, is conducted before policy decisions are taken.

Broad money is endogenous. We are a long way from models in which the governor of the central bank has a lever in his room labelled 'money'. As with any endogenous variable, if money moves in some unexpected way, policy makers have to think about why it has moved. What is the source of the shock? It may in practice be difficult to tie down the source of the shock. But surely in principle it is to the underlying shock that policy makers should respond and not to its reflection in this or that endogenous variable. There is some recognition of this in the chapter, towards the end of Section 1, where the separate effects of a recession and of policy reaction to a recession are identified. But the point is more general. Broad money is largely created by commercial banks and so understanding broad money entails understanding commercial bank behaviour. For example, the banking system may become more competitive and the cost of bank intermediation may fall. Bank balance sheets may expand at the expense of assets and liabilities elsewhere in the economy. That may indeed have implications for inflation that policy makers should consider. But central banks should not *assume* that this particular expansion of banks' balance sheets is to be regarded in exactly the same light as if balance sheets had expanded because the economy was already in a boom.

So although the chapter does refer to 'stabilising' and 'destabilising' fluctuations in money growth, actually it has rather narrowly focused examples of each. A lot of the other analysis of monetary quantities that in practice goes on in central banks can be thought of as a search for other examples of benign or malign monetary developments. At the Bank of England we tend to couch this in terms of distinguishing between shocks to the demand for and supply of money, and there may be subcategories within those broad headings worth looking at. And the Bank of England has quite recently followed the example of other central banks and now conducts its own formal survey of credit conditions. This is another tool for trying to understand the forces at work behind the monetary quantities.

Demand for money equations are reduced forms. If they need to be re-estimated from year to year is that really because some deep parameter of taste or technology has changed? Is it not more likely to be because the results have been affected by some influence not captured by the equation? The fact that the 'reference lines' in this chapter are based on updated equations is not really a source of strength. The fact that they need to be frequently re-estimated is surely a sign of something to worry about.

Another worrying feature for me is that the interest-rate terms are chosen simply on the basis of what works in an equation, without any proper structural stories as to what the mechanism is through which they have their influence. If there is a shock, policy makers will surely want to think about just what that mechanism is. If the equation includes an interest-rate spread which has moved a lot, why has it moved and what are the implications on this occasion? Average relationships over the past, based on possibly quite different shocks, may not help, or not help enough.

Generally speaking, is it not dangerous to base policy on empirical relationships that have something of the black box about them? They seem to have worked up to now but we do not really understand why. Such relationships tend to break down just when you most need them to work. And I do not think it is an answer to say that they can be re-estimated.

An issue with monetary aggregates is of course that they *are* aggregates and the components may behave differently. The chapter has perhaps a nod in this direction in its separate 'reference lines' for M2. But again I think the point is more general. Some of my colleagues have worked on the impact of sectoral money and sectoral bank lending – looking for the separate influence of households' 'disequilibrium' money on consumption and of companies' disequilibrium money on fixed investment. This work is used as a cross-check on other forecasts of these variables, in which monetary quantities are not used. These colleagues have also been particularly concerned with the growth of money holdings and bank borrowing of non-bank financial institutions. Growth of both of these has been particularly fast in recent years. Do non-bank financial institutions' holdings have the same significance as those of 'real economy' sectors? Should their holding of money count as money at all? In this context there are certainly tricky questions of definition around the border between banks and some non-bank institutions closely related to banks.

I have one personal and idiosyncratic concern in this area. It is that we assume too readily that the T in $MV = PT$ are transactions related to the generation of GDP. Actually a huge value of transactions in the economy is trades in assets, particularly financial assets. It may be that this 'financial circuit' is particularly efficient in its use of transactions balances. But that should be established rather than assumed.

In the distant past, when I was a young bank clerk, some of the apparently robust relationships between monetary quantities and economic activity probably had to do with rigidities in the financial system – cartel-like behaviour and regulatory constraints on competition between banking institutions. As these constraints broke down and competition increased, the monetary quantities seemed to lose some of their usefulness. The more extensive payment of interest on money was important there. But over the years as more and more things have become tradable, policy makers have had a far richer set of financial prices from which to extract information. Financial market prices are forward looking and so are policy makers. Markets and policy makers are forming judgements on many of the same things. Options, that give a view on risks, may have a certain appeal for policy makers who think in terms of fancharts. Models based on wide range of financial prices can also be used as a cross-check on the output of forecasting models that treat financial prices less fully. I confess that I had thought that this process would proceed to the point where information from financial market prices would overwhelm that from monetary quantities. But this year we have seen that market prices may not be well founded, that there may be limits to the things that can be traded and that some of the reasons for the existence of banks may be reasserting themselves. So perhaps monetary quantities will have a larger role for longer than I would once have imagined.

So where does this leave us? The chapter attempts to improve the second pillar by taking explicit account of a small subset of the factors that affect the assessment of monetary quantities. But the author acknowledges that there may be other adjustments to be made. It seems to me not to matter very much whether all these other factors can be successfully combined into one super 'reference line'. What matters is that the factors are studied and that policy makers have in their minds the results of that study when they form their policy judgements.

It is understandable that the ECB should have given itself something like the second pillar given the Bundesbank's experience. Presentationally it may be awkward to have to explain that sometimes deviations from the reference rate indicate inflationary risk and sometimes not. But what really matters is that the analysis underlying such statements has been undertaken and absorbed.

Note

1 The views expressed are those of the discussant and not necessarily those of the Bank of England.

6 Forward guidance for monetary policy

Is it desirable?*

Hans Gersbach and Volker Hahn

There is substantial disagreement among both policy makers and academics about the merits of forward guidance for monetary policy. Consequently, practice regarding forward guidance varies significantly across central banks and over time. Many central banks divulge nothing about the future actions they are likely to take. As documented by Geerats *et al.* (2008), the ECB currently uses a traffic-light system with different code words in order to signal its likely decisions in the near future. The Federal Reserve has experimented with different practices. In May 1999 it started publishing a policy bias or policy tilt, but this was discontinued after one year.[1] In 2003 the Fed embarked on a new attempt to issue forward guidance. The central banks of Iceland, New Zealand, Norway and Sweden are much more explicit and publish numerical values for the future path of interest rates.

In this chapter we summarise the arguments for and against the desirability of forward guidance put forward in the literature and assess their validity in the context of various frameworks. We focus on forward guidance through interest-rate projections. Forward guidance can serve two purposes, representing either a commitment device or a means of communication. We point out that there are limits to the communication of private information through forward guidance. If forward guidance represents cheap talk, the precision of the information transmitted by the central bank is limited by credibility problems. If forward guidance is used as a commitment device, a trade off arises between gains from commitment and losses in flexibility.

The chapter is organised as follows: in the next two sections we summarise the main arguments in favour of and against forward guidance. We provide an assessment of these arguments for different scenarios in Section 3. Section 4 concludes.

1 Arguments in favour of forward guidance

The main argument in favour of publishing information on future policy interest rates runs as follows:[2] Aggregate spending, for example firms' investment spending, is affected by long-term interest rates, which only depend on current policy rates to a negligible extent. However, long-term interest rates are crucially affected by expectations about the future path of policy rates. Thus by publishing forward guidance for its monetary policy the central bank may be more successful in affecting aggregate spending in the desired way.

At a deeper level, the value of the forecasts can be twofold. First, the interest-rate forecasts might reveal information that has not already been disclosed by other means of communication. This information may relate to the central bank's objectives or its assessment of economic shocks and the functioning of the economy. Second, in the face of possible time-inconsistency problems, forecasts might be valuable if they enabled the central bank to affect the public's expectations in a favourable manner. This argument requires the central bank to commit to its policy announcements to some extent. How the central bank can commit to a future course of policy will be taken up in the next section. For the moment we assume that some commitment is possible.

Why might commitment be desirable? Several potential areas have been identified in the literature. First, the classic inflation-bias framework of Kydland and Prescott (1977) and Barro and Gordon (1983) involves the central bank targeting a level of output that exceeds the natural level. As a consequence, the central bank's *ex ante* optimal policy is different from its *ex post* optimal policy, therefore commitment is desirable. Second, faced with the danger of deflation it may be optimal for a central bank to convince the public that it will adhere to expansionary monetary policy for some time. However, if inflation gains momentum, the central bank has an incentive to renege on its promise and pursue a less expansionary policy than previously announced.[3] Third, in the New Keynesian framework presented by Clarida *et al.* (1999), gains from commitment are also possible. The central bank would benefit from a commitment to vigorous shock stabilisation in the future. This cushions the impact of shocks on inflation expectations and thus in turn on current inflation. However, once the public has formed its expectations, the central bank may be reluctant to actually pursue the announced policy. Again there are potential gains from commitment.

2 Arguments against forward guidance

To put the arguments against forward guidance into perspective, we begin with a discussion of complete contingent commitment. If it were possible to commit to an entire interest-rate path for all future contingencies, the gains from commitment could be reaped without cost. However, this is not a realistic option for a central bank.[4] First, future shocks cannot be described with sufficient precision to announce a shock-dependent interest-rate path.[5] Second, at the time when a contingent interest-rate path is executed, it might be difficult to identify which shock has actually occurred. Third, it may be difficult to agree on a contingent future path for interest rates if monetary policy is conducted by a committee. Fourth, if decision makers are approaching the end of their term, it is hard to see how they could forecast the future decisions of their successors, especially if they do not know who they will be.

What if the central bank settled for less and provided simple non-contingent policy guidance? Then the first and second objections no longer apply, while the third and fourth remain valid. Moreover, non-contingent forecasts on the central bank's future policy have one additional drawback: central banks may become boxed in and lose some of their flexibility in responding to unforeseen shocks.

Why might deviations from interest-rate projections be costly? First, the central bank needs to explain forecast deviations caused by unforeseen events. Some shocks (for example, those affecting the natural rate of output) may be very difficult to explain. Then it may be necessary to devote substantial resources to the search for hard-to-find evidence explaining a forecast deviation convincingly. If deviations cannot be made plausible to the public and if forecasts are actually valuable for the conduct of monetary policy in the future, then current forecast deviations may involve future costs because the forecasts will be deemed irrelevant by economic agents. Second, frequent forecast deviations may impair the central bank's prestige. They may induce scepticism about the central bank's competence and may also endanger the reappointment of monetary policy committee members.

However, it is important to note that the costs of forecast deviations, while reducing the central bank's flexibility in responding to unforeseen developments, also enable the central bank to pre-commit to a future policy course. If the optimal policy is not time-consistent, this is desirable. Accordingly, forward guidance for monetary policy involves a trade off between gains from commitment and losses in flexibility.

3 Assessment

In this section we compare the costs and benefits of forward guidance on policy interest rates for the scenarios where forward guidance is potentially desirable.

3.1 Commitment in an inflation-bias framework

In the framework set out in Kydland and Prescott (1977) the central bank targets an output level that is higher than the level sustainable in the long run. As the central bank cannot commit credibly to a low inflation rate, inflation is inefficiently high. Several ways of alleviating this problem have been proposed in the literature, including delegation of monetary policy to a conservative central banker (Rogoff, 1985) and reputation-building Barro and Gordon (1983). Forward guidance represents another option for avoiding an inflation bias.

In the Appendix we consider an inflation-bias framework in which a central bank announces future values of the monetary policy instrument. The central bank's forecast on its future policy serves as a future intermediate target and thus alleviates the central bank's credibility problem.[6] We show that for sufficiently small costs from forecast deviations and thus a low degree of commitment, the gains from commitment make forward guidance desirable. If, however, these costs are very large, the central bank cannot respond optimally to shocks, so forward guidance is detrimental.

3.2 Commitment in a New Keynesian model

Gersbach and Hahn (2008) examine the trade off between gains from commitment and losses in flexibility that may be caused by forward guidance in a dynamic New Keynesian framework. They consider four scenarios. First, the central bank publishes a projection about the interest rate in the next period (short-term interest-rate forecast). Second, the central bank announces its interest-rate projection for the next period but one (medium-term interest-rate forecast). Third, the central bank publishes a forecast of inflation in the next period (short-term inflation forecast). The fourth scenario centres on inflation projections for the next period but one (medium-term inflation forecast).

Gersbach and Hahn (2008) show that short-term projections are always harmful. As forecasts concerning the next period do not affect current expectations about inflation in that period, no gains from commitment arise. But in the subsequent period the central bank is boxed in by its announcement and is less willing to respond to shocks in a socially optimal manner.

Medium-term interest-rate and inflation forecasts are potentially more favourable, as the forecasting horizon is extensive enough for inflation expectations to adjust. Gersbach and Hahn (2008) show that gains from commitment never outweigh losses in flexibility where interest-rate forecasts are concerned. By contrast, medium-term inflation forecasts are desirable if the degree of commitment to these announcements is not too high.

3.3 Commitment in a liquidity trap

Many authors have noted that in the presence of deflation or a liquidity trap it may be necessary for the central bank to commit to expansionary policy in the future.[7] This will increase inflation expectations and thus reduce the real interest rate, which is necessary to avoid a deflationary spiral. However, it is unclear whether a commitment to zero interest rates for some time is actually sufficient to increase inflation expectations and thus to induce a low level for long-term real interest rates.[8] Commitment to an unusually high inflation or price-level target[9] maintained for a considerable time (and perhaps achieved by unconventional policy measures) seems more appropriate.

3.4 Revelation of information through forward guidance

Forward guidance may also be interpreted as a means of communicating private central bank information. From a social perspective the question arises whether the central bank should in fact communicate its private information. Though the theoretical findings on the welfare effects of central bank transparency are not unanimous, we assume for the rest of our discussion that transparency is desirable.[10] The next question is whether forward guidance on the future path of interest rates is an appropriate way of revealing information.

If forward guidance is used to reveal information on the central bank's objectives or the state of the economy, we have to remember that information about future policy decisions and the central bank's estimate of future economic shocks will usually be non-verifiable. Accordingly, an important issue is whether the information will be credible.

Why might forward guidance used to reveal the central bank's private information not be credible? First, if current inflation depends on expected future inflation (as in standard forward-looking models), the central bank has an incentive to choose forward guidance suggesting that inflation will be on target in the future, as this will have a beneficial effect on current inflation. Second, the central bank may be reluctant to reveal a future inflation path that leads the public to conclude that a financial crisis is likely. Third, the central bank may not be willing to reveal a high weight on the output target or an output target that exceeds the natural level. These credibility problems severely limit the use of forward guidance as a means of disclosing information.[11]

Nevertheless, it is possible for some information to be transmitted. First, forward guidance may represent cheap talk, i.e. the central bank is not committed at all to previous announcements and incurs no costs if it deviates. In this case, a transmission of precise information is impossible if there are incentives for the central bank to misrepresent its information. However, cheap talk could be used to reveal some vague information (see Stein (1989), who applies the mechanism developed by Crawford and Sobel (1982) to central bank communication).[12]

Second, for the reasons discussed earlier, forecast deviations could be costly, which would make the forecasts credible to some extent. Then two problems would arise. The central bank loses some of its flexibility in responding to unforeseen developments in the future, as it will find it costly to deviate substantially from previous announcements. In addition, signalling costs will occur. Such costs arise because the interest-rate path desired by the central bank may not signal the information the central bank wants to reveal. The central bank thus needs to adjust the interest-rate projection. If it is committed to these projections to some extent, this will lead to suboptimal policy in the future. In this case it would be desirable to announce the private information directly,[13] provided this is feasible.

To sum up, if forward guidance represents cheap talk, then it may convey useful information. However, its precision is limited by credibility problems. If the central bank is somewhat committed to its forecasts, then a direct publication of the central bank's information would be preferable.

4 Conclusions

We have argued that forward guidance regarding the future path of policy interest rates can be either viewed as a means of commitment or as a means of communicating private information. If forward guidance is used to disclose private information and represents cheap talk, imprecise forward guidance, like the ECB's use of code words, may be informative.

If forward guidance is used to create commitment, costs of forecast deviations are a necessary prerequisite for making forward guidance credible to some extent. The central bank then faces a trade off between gains from commitment and losses in flexibility. We show that in an inflation-bias framework, the gains from commitment are sufficient to make the publication of future interest rates worthwhile, unless the deviation costs are very high. By contrast, in a New Keynesian framework Gersbach and Hahn (2008) show that interest-rate projections are detrimental.[14]

In the Appendix we have shown, for a simple inflation-bias framework, that the desirability of forward guidance depends on the deviation costs and hence on the degree of commitment to forecasts. The different practices of central banks with respect to forward guidance and changes therein can be associated with different degrees of commitment. For example, by attaching large error bands to forecasts, a central bank can attempt to reduce its commitment to forecasts over and against the case where only point forecasts are made public. The ECB's traffic-light system can also be interpreted as a system with a low value in deviation costs. While this enables central banks to retain flexibility, they may also forgo some of the gains from commitment.

It is crucial to note that the socially optimal degree of commitment may not be constant over time. If the future economic development is highly uncertain, i.e. shocks are very large, then the losses from less flexibility in responding to shocks may be severe. Therefore a low level of commitment may be desirable. In a similar vein, there may be times when commitment is particularly valuable, for example in the presence of a liquidity trap. Hence the optimal disclosure practice will vary over time and across central banks. These considerations may explain why different central banks choose very different approaches to forward guidance, and why their communication policies have changed substantially in the past.

Appendix: forward guidance and the classic time-inconsistency problem

A.1 Set-up

We consider a very simple model with a neoclassical Phillips curve

$$y = y_0 + \pi - \pi^e + \varepsilon \qquad (1)$$

where we use π and y to denote inflation and output. Inflation expectations are denoted by π^e. Parameter y_0 represents the natural rate of output and ε is a normally distributed supply shock with mean zero and variance σ^2_ε.

The IS curve is given by

$$y = y_0 - (i - \pi^e - \bar{r}) + \mu, \qquad (2)$$

where i is the interest rate chosen by the central bank; $\bar{r} > 0$ is the natural real rate of interest. Variable μ represents a normally distributed demand shock with mean zero and variance σ^2_μ. It is uncorrelated with ε.

Moreover, we assume a quadratic function for social losses

$$\mathrm{L} = \pi^2 + a(y - y_0 - \Delta)^2, \tag{3}$$

where $a > 0$ represents the relative significance of the output target. In the tradition of Kydland and Prescott (1977) and Barro and Gordon (1983), we assume $\Delta > 0$. As a consequence the socially optimal level of output, $y_0 + \Delta$, is higher than its natural level y_0.[15]

The central bank publishes a forecast of its policy instrument, i.e. the interest rate i. We use i^P to denote this projection. Following Gersbach and Hahn (2008), we introduce a new component into the central bank's loss function. We assume that the central bank faces quadratic costs incurred by forecast deviations. Formally, the central bank's losses can be written as

$$L^{CB} = \pi^2 + a(y - y0 - \Delta)^2 + b(i^P - i)^2. \tag{4}$$

If a central bank announces a forecast value i^P, it faces the quadratic costs b $(i^P - i)^2$, which increase in the size of forecast deviations. The size of these costs depends on parameter b ($b \geq 0$), which can be interpreted as the degree to which the central bank is committed to its forecasts. For $b = 0$ we obtain the standard case because announcements represent cheap talk when deviations are costless.

The sequence of events is as follows:

1 The central bank announces the forecast i^P.
2 The public forms rational inflation expectations π^e.
3 Nature chooses the shocks ε and μ.
4 The central bank chooses the interest rate i.

A.2 Solution

We solve the model by backward induction. As a first step, we compute the central bank's optimal choice of i, for given π^e and i^P. Inserting (1) into (4) yields

$$L^{CB} = (y - y_0 + \pi^e - \varepsilon)^2 + a(y - y_0 - \Delta)^2 + b(i^P - i)^2.$$

Using (2), we obtain

$$L^{CB} = (-(i - \pi^e - \bar{r}) + \mu + \pi^e - \varepsilon)^2 + a(-(i - \pi^e - \bar{r}) + \mu - \Delta)^2 + b(i^P - i)^2.$$

Maximisation with respect to i gives

$$-(\mathrm{i} - \pi^e - \bar{r}) + \mu + \pi^e - \varepsilon + \mathrm{a}(-(i - \pi^e - \bar{r}) + \mu - \Delta) + b(i^P - i) = 0.$$

This equation can be easily solved for i

$$i = \frac{\pi^e + \bar{r} + \mu + \pi^e - e + a(\pi^e + r + \mu - \Delta) + bi^P}{1 + a + b}. \tag{5}$$

Now we turn to the public's inflation expectations as a function of the interest-rate projection i^P. Using $i^e = \pi^e + \bar{r}$, we can solve (5) for the public's inflation expectations as a function of i^P

$$\pi^e = \frac{a\Delta - b(i^P - \bar{r})}{1 - b}. \tag{6}$$

Using (1), (2), (5), and (6), we obtain[16]

$$y = y_0 + \frac{b}{1 + a + b}\mu + \frac{1}{1 + a + b}\varepsilon, \tag{7}$$

$$\pi = \frac{b}{1 + a + b}\mu - \frac{a + b}{1 + a + b}\varepsilon - \frac{b}{1 - b}(i^P - \bar{r}) + \frac{a}{1 - b}\Delta, \tag{8}$$

$$i = \frac{1 + a}{1 + a + b}\mu - \frac{1}{1 + a + b}\varepsilon - \frac{b}{1 - b}i^P + \frac{1}{1 - b}\bar{r} + \frac{a}{1 - b}\Delta. \tag{9}$$

Equation (7) represents the expression for y given in the main text. By inserting (8), (9) and (7) into (4), taking expected values, and computing the derivative with respect to i^P, we obtain the first-order condition with the solution

$$i^P = \bar{r} + \frac{2a}{1 + b}\Delta. \tag{10}$$

Combining (8), (9), (7) and (10) yields

$$y = y_0 + \frac{b}{1 + a + b}\mu + \frac{1}{1 + a + b}\varepsilon, \tag{11}$$

$$\pi = \frac{b}{1 + a + b}\mu - \frac{a + b}{1 + a + b}\varepsilon + \frac{a}{1 + b}\Delta, \tag{12}$$

$$i = \bar{r} + \frac{1 + a}{1 + a + b}\mu - \frac{1}{1 + a + b}\varepsilon + \frac{a}{1 + b}\Delta. \tag{13}$$

A.3 Forward guidance and welfare

Expected social losses can be computed by inserting (11) and (12) into (3) and taking expected values. We obtain

$$\mathrm{E}L = \frac{(1+a)b^2}{(1+a+b)^2}\sigma_\mu^2 + \frac{a+(a+b)^2}{(1+a+b)^2}\sigma_\mu^2 + \left(1+\frac{a}{(1+b)^2}\right)a\Delta^2. \tag{14}$$

The first two summands represent the losses incurred by shocks. These terms are increasing in b. Intuitively, announcing a projection for the future interest rate reduces the central bank's flexibility in responding to these shocks. The third term on the right-hand side of (14) can be split into two components, namely $a\Delta^2$ and $\frac{a^2}{(1+b^2)}\Delta^2$. First, $a\Delta^2$ stands for the unavoidable losses caused by the fact that the central bank cannot boost output above its natural rate. Second, $\frac{a^2}{(1+b^2)}\Delta^2$ are additional losses arising because the central bank produces an inefficiently high rate of inflation in its ultimately futile attempt to boost output above its natural level. These losses could be avoided if the central bank targeted the natural level of output. Interestingly, the term $\frac{a^2}{(1+b^2)}\Delta^2$ is decreasing in b. Hence higher levels of b imply that the central bank can commit more effectively to keeping inflation low. As a consequence, it can overcome the time-inconsistency problem to some extent.

To sum up, the publication of monetary policy inclinations involves a trade off. It diminishes the central bank's flexibility in responding to shocks, which is socially detrimental. However, it provides the central bank with a means of committing itself, which may be socially desirable.

It is readily verifiable that

$$\left.\frac{d\mathrm{E}L}{db}\right|_{b=0} = -2a^2\Delta^2 < 0. \tag{15}$$

We thus arrive at the important observation that for sufficiently small values of b the announcement of policy forecasts is socially desirable. It is relatively easy to see that for high values of b losses caused by lower flexibility may outweigh gains from commitment. In such cases, announcing information on the future course of monetary policy is harmful.

Notes

* We thank Alex Cukierman, Stefan Gerlach, Oliver Grimm, Heinz Hermann, Anne Sibert and participants at the Deutsche Bundesbank/Bank of Finland Conference 'Designing Central Banks' in Eltville, 8–9 November 2007, for many valuable comments and suggestions.

1 Cf. *Financial Times*, 20 January 2000, 'Fed to No Longer Adopt Policy Bias Toward Rates'. See also Poole (2003).

2 See, for example, Rudebusch and Williams (2006) and Woodford (2007). The arguments in favour of and against the publication of forward guidance are neatly reviewed in Geerats *et al.*

3 See, for example, Krugman (1998).

4 Goodhart (2001) notes that 'the idea of trying to choose a complete time path by discretionary choice seems entirely fanciful and counterproductive'. See also Blinder (2004) and Mishkin (2004).
5 Gabaix (2005) argues that idiosyncratic movements of large firms are central to understanding aggregate fluctuations. This may make it particularly difficult to describe shocks.
6 Other models where the central bank is committed to previous announcements include Cukierman and Liviatan (1991) and Cukierman (2000). Gersbach and Hahn (2006) compare monetary targeting and inflation targeting if the central bank is committed to the respective targets. Rogoff (1985) examines whether interest rates are desirable as intermediate targets.
7 See Krugman (1998), among others.
8 See Orphanides and Wieland (2000).
9 For an extensive discussion, see Svensson (2006).
10 Gersbach (1998) first showed that transparency in monetary policy may involve losses in terms of welfare. For surveys of this literature, see Geraats (2002) and Hahn (2002).
11 Although we have assumed that a general adoption of transparency would be socially beneficial from an *ex ante* perspective, this does not imply that revealing information truthfully will be in the central bank's interest in every possible situation in the future.
12 For an interesting discussion of the instances where cheap talk can be used to transmit information, see Farrell and Rabin (1996).
13 For example, the central bank's projections of future shocks will be credible to some extent if future deviations of these shocks from their projected values are costly to the central bank.
14 However, their framework can be used to support the publication of inflation projections.
15 For example, in the presence of distortionary taxation the socially optimal level is higher than the level sustainable in the long run.
16 Note that the interest rate chosen by the central bank, which is given by (7), is decreasing in i^P for $b < 1$. A similar finding has led Rogoff (1985) to the conclusion that an intermediate interest target is not advantageous. However, (5) implies that i is an increasing function of i^P for a given level of π^e. The apparently implausible equation (7) can be understood in the following way: an increase in the projected inflation rate can be interpreted as a commitment by the central bank to fight inflation. This reduces inflation expectations, which does not make high interest rates necessary.

References

Barro, Robert and David Gordon (1983) 'Rules, Discretion, and Reputation in a Model of Monetary Policy', *Journal of Monetary Economics*, 12: 101–121.

Blinder, Alan (2004) *The Quiet Revolution: Central Banking Goes Modern*, New Haven, CT: Yale University Press.

Clarida, Richard, Jordi Gali and Mark Gertler (1999) 'The Science of Monetary Policy: A New Keynesian Perspective', *Journal of Economic Literature*, 37: 1661–1707, December.

Crawford, Vincent P. and Joel Sobel (1982) 'Strategic Information Transmission', *Econometrica*, 50 (6): 1431–1451, November.

Cukierman, Alex (2000) 'Establishing a Reputation for Dependability by Means of Inflation Targets', *Economics of Governance*, 1 (1): 53–76, March.

Cukierman, Alex and Nissan Liviatan (1991) 'Optimal Accomodation by Strong Policymakers under Incomplete Information', *Journal of Monetary Economics*, 27 (1): 99–127, January.

Farrell, Joseph and Matthew Rabin (1996) 'Cheap Talk', *Journal of Economic Perspectives*, 10 (3): 103–118.

Faust, Jon and Eric M. Leeper (2005) 'Forecasts and Inflation Reports: An Evaluation', mimeo, December.

Gabaix, Xavier (2005) 'The Granular Origins of Aggregate Fluctuations', mimeo, December.

Geraats, Petra M. (2002) 'Central Bank Transparency', *Economic Journal*, 112: 532–565.

Geraats, Petra, Francesco Giavazzi and Charles Wyplosz (2008) *Transparency and Governance, Monitoring the European Central Bank 6*, London: CEPR.

Gersbach, Hans (1998) 'On the Negative Social Value of Central Banks' Transparency', working paper, University of Heidelberg.

Gersbach, Hans and Volker Hahn (2006) 'Signaling and Commitment: Monetary versus Inflation Targeting', *Macroeconomic Dynamics*, 10 (5): 595–624.

Gersbach, Hans and Volker Hahn (2008) 'Monetary Policy Inclinations', CEPR Discussion Paper 6761.

Goodhart, Charles A.E. (2001) 'Monetary Transmission Lags and the Formulation of the Policy Decision on Interest Rates', *Federal Reserve Bank of St. Louis Review*, 83 (4): 165–186, July.

Hahn, Volker (2002) 'Transparency in Monetary Policy: A Survey', *ifo Studien*, 3: 429–455.

Krugman, Paul (1998) 'It's Baaack! Japan's Slump and the Return of the Liquidity Trap', mimeo.

Kydland, Finn and Edward Prescott (1977) 'Rules Rather than Discretion: The Inconsistency of Optimal Plans', *Journal of Political Economy*, 85 (3): 473–492.

Mishkin, Frederic S. (2004) 'Can Central Bank Transparency Go too Far?', NBER Working Papers 10829, October.

Orphanides, Athanasios and Volker Wieland (2000) 'Efficient Monetary Policy Design near Price Stability', *Journal of the Japanese and International Economies*, 14 (4): 327–365, December.

Poole, William (2003) 'Fed Transparency: How, Not Whether', *Federal Reserve Bank of St. Louis Review*, 85 (6): 1–18, November/December.

Rogoff, Kenneth (1985) 'The Optimal Degree of Commitment to an Intermediate Monetary Target', *Quarterly Journal of Economics*, 100 (4): 1169–1189, November.

Rudebusch, Glenn D. and John C. Williams (2006) 'Revealing the Secrets of the Temple: The Value of Publishing Central Bank Interest Rate Projections', Federal Reserve Bank of San Francisco, Working Paper Series 2006-31.

Stein, Jeremy C. (1989) 'Cheap Talk and the Fed: A Theory of Imprecise Policy Announcements', *American Economic Review*, 79 (1): 32–42, March.

Svensson, Lars E.O. (2006) 'Optimal Inflation Targeting: Further Developments of Inflation Targeting', Working Papers Central Bank of Chile 403, December.

Woodford, Michael (2007) 'The Case for Forecast Targeting as a Monetary Policy Strategy', *Journal of Economic Perspectives*, 21 (4): 3–24.

COMMENTS BY HEINZ HERMANN

In their chapter, Gersbach and Hahn (GH) discuss an aspect of central bank strategy and publication policy which is highly relevant today: how transparent central banks should be in presenting their forecasts to the public. In particular, there is an ongoing and heated debate as to whether central banks should announce their future interest path. GH summarise some of the existing arguments and add new ones to this debate. The chapter comes to several conclusions.

A publication can aim either to reveal private information of the central bank or to signal commitment by the central bank. Both aspects are important when analysing the implications of the publication strategy of a central bank.

The publication of a forecast may make sense for some variables but not for others. Specifically, GH are more sceptical of the wisdom of publishing a future interest rate than with regard to a future inflation rate.

The framework used to analyse these questions is important. In a classic time-inconsistency framework, publication of a future inflation rate may be helpful, as demonstrated in the chapter, whereas GH assure that, in a New Keynesian framework with some stickiness in price formation, the publication of such a forecast is detrimental.

A central argument in the existing literature on why central banks should reveal interest-rate forecasts (or forecasts for other variables) is that they can guide the expectations of the private sector and thereby improve the welfare of the economy. The validity of this argument depends on several preconditions, which are extensively discussed in the literature. GH particularly emphasise the credibility of such an announcement. (This argument may be less relevant with regard to announcing future inflation but becomes much more of an issue if, for example, a central bank makes forecasts about the future stability of the financial system.) However, there are many other preconditions which have to be fulfilled in order to make such a publication successful. For example, Dale *et al.* (2007) stress the importance not just of the fact that the central bank owns information that the private sector does not have but also that the central bank is able to communicate the conditionality and quality of its forecast to the private sector. Usually, central bankers are much more sceptical in this respect than academics (with King (2007) on the one hand and Woodford (2005) on the other as a case in point).

However, GH's main argument is one which was less prominent in the discussion about the publication of interest-rate forecasts (although it is not new in the more general debate on the merits of a rule-based versus a discrete monetary policy). The publication of an interest-rate forecast can be seen as an instrument to commit the central bank. Seen from this angle, the publication may be welfare-improving under certain conditions yet negative under other conditions. In particular, it will reduce the willingness of a central bank to react flexibly to future shocks which were not known when the central bank made its announcement. To make this argument, GH have to assume that deviating from the announced forecast comes at a cost to the central bank.

How convincing this argument is depends on whether we believe that deviating from the forecasts is really a problem for the central bank. GH take the view that missing the forecast will raise credibility problems. This argument may be less convincing if a central bank can make clear that its forecast is conditional (as they usually do) and can clearly spell out the conditions under which the forecast has been made (what is probably more difficult to do). GH mention in this respect that even if it is basically possible to convince the public, analysing and explaining shocks and their consequences to the public comes at a high cost to central banks. (However, one may ask whether central banks which do not publish their forecasts are less careful when analysing shocks.)

The relevance of the commitment argument is open to dispute. After all, we know from the previous literature that conservative and independent central bankers and other contract solutions have been offered as solutions of circumventing the commitment problem. In that respect, it is an open question whether the argument made by GH is really central to the publication debate.

References

Dale, S., A. Orphanides and P. Österholm (2007) 'Imperfect Central Bank Communication: Information Versus Distraction', mimeo.

King, M. (2007) 'The MPC Ten Years on', *BIS review*, 43/2007.

Woodford, M. (2005) 'Central Bank Communication and Policy Effectiveness', NBER Working Paper 11898.

7 Designing a central bank communication strategy

Michael Ehrmann and Marcel Fratzscher[1]

1 Introduction

Communication plays a central role for monetary policy making. Central banks have direct control only over a single interest rate, usually the overnight rate, while their success in achieving their mandate – whether the focus is on price stability or on economic activity – requires that they are able to influence asset prices and interest rates at all maturities. Effective communication as much as credible policy actions are thus of fundamental importance for achieving these objectives.

We start from the conjecture that central bank communication pursues a central goal, namely to enable a better understanding about the goals and strategies of the central bank as well as about its assessment of the current economic situation and the policy stance by the public. In turn, this should allow financial markets to anticipate better the policy decisions as well as the future path of monetary policy, and with reduced uncertainty. Of course, this does not imply that it may not be necessary at times to surprise markets with policy decisions, but in principle a high degree of predictability and a low degree of uncertainty are important elements for the credibility and effectiveness of monetary policy.

But how should central banks communicate? This question is of key importance for all central banks, and it contains many facets for the design of communication strategies. In particular regarding the communication of the central bank's assessment of the current economic conditions and the monetary policy stance, more communication need not always be beneficial, in particular if more communication endangers clarity. A central element is therefore whether central banks should communicate in a collegial manner, by conveying the consensus or majority view of the committee, or in an individualistic way, by stressing and conveying the diversity of views among the committee members. This issue continues to be highly controversial as some policy makers have argued that it is important to communicate this diversity among individual committee members because it helps markets understand the risks surrounding policy decisions and anticipate monetary policy decisions (e.g. Bernanke, 2004). By contrast, others have argued that such a communication strategy may not necessarily provide greater clarity and common understanding among market participants and thus that it may be important for central banks to communicate 'with one voice' (e.g. Issing, 1999, 2005).

This chapter analyses which elements of communication strategies are effective in achieving the objectives of raising predictability and reducing market uncertainty. For this purpose, we analyse the communication strategies pursued by the Bank of England and the European Central Bank (ECB), for the period from May 1997 (January 1999 for the ECB) until May 2004. These two central banks have been shown to have fundamentally different communication strategies, with the members of the ECB's Governing Council being substantially more active than the Bank of England's MPC members, for instance (Ehrmann and Fratzscher, 2007). There may be various reasons for the adoption of such fundamentally different communication strategies, and to some extent the differences may reflect the various political and institutional environments the two central banks operate in.

In our analysis we distinguish between several distinct elements of communication strategies. The chapter's primary objective is to analyse the effect of communication dispersion, i.e. the degree of disagreement among committee members – as well as the disagreement with committee statements – about the future path of monetary policy. In particular we ask whether communication dispersion affects the predictability of monetary policy decisions, with respect to (1) the extent to which financial markets are surprised, and (2) the disagreement among forecasters. We also analyse whether the frequency and the information content of communication affect the predictability of decisions and forecaster disagreement. Moreover, we study and control for the effects of several other factors, such as the degree of uncertainty created by the release of macroeconomic data and other sources of uncertainty.

The empirical results are compelling by showing that more *dispersed* communication among committee members about policy inclinations worsens the ability of financial markets to anticipate future monetary policy decisions. This finding is highly robust and significant across both central banks. The second key result is that more *active* communication (controlling for its dispersion) improves markets' anticipation of future monetary policy decisions significantly. This evidence is suggestive that markets may take some time to fully incorporate information and communication by central banks, and thus that frequent statements may enable markets to better anticipate policy decisions.

Third and finally, we find that lower dispersion and higher frequency of communication not only improve the predictability of monetary policy decisions, but also significantly synchronise central bank watchers' views of the subsequent policy decision as well as the future path of monetary policy.

The findings of the chapter suggest a number of policy implications. Overall, the results imply that communication indeed plays a central role for helping markets anticipate monetary policy decisions as well as for reducing market uncertainty. However, it is important for central banks to provide a consistent message to markets, as the communication of dispersed individual views lowers predictability, both in the short run and in the long run.

The chapter is organised in the following way. Section 2 offers a brief discussion of the communication strategies of the two central banks and a brief review of the related literature on central bank communication. Section 3 outlines the measurement of communication and its dispersion in the two central banks. The hypotheses, the underlying data and the methodology for the empirical analysis are presented in Section 4. Section 5 then provides the empirical analysis of the effects and effectiveness of communication, as well as several robustness tests. Section 6 offers conclusions and draws some policy implications.

2 Central bank communication and committees

Central bank communication regarding the assessment of current economic conditions and the monetary policy stance in principle occurs through two channels: by the policy-making committee and by its individual members. The former may include statements commenting and explaining decisions on meeting days but also publications in the inter-meeting period such as minutes of past meetings or Inflation Reports and Monthly Bulletins. However, the communication by individual committee members – such as through speeches and interviews – is highly influential as it may provide more detailed information, in particular about the diversity of views and the discussions in the committee, and is usually far more flexible in its timing and content than the statements by the committee itself.

Two important choices central banks need to make relate to the amount of information they may wish to provide to the public as well as on the extent to which they reveal diversity of views in the committee. Each of these two choices is important and can be highly sensitive. To the former, many central banks provide some information about the likely future path of monetary policy and the economic outlook. But how explicit should a central bank be in this regard? Many central banks publish their staff projections about key economic variables, and some also reveal explicit inflation projections. Others have even gone so far as to provide an explicit forecast of their likely path of future monetary policy rates. While more and more explicit information may help guide financial markets, there are several risks behind such communication strategies. In particular, such information may be falsely understood by financial markets as implying explicit commitments on behalf of central banks, rather than conditional commitments that may have to be altered, sometimes even radically if underlying economic conditions change.

The second choice for a communication strategy is how much of the diversity of views in the committee a central bank may wish to provide to the public. Forward-looking information is generally surrounded by a substantial degree of uncertainty, which may change over time and be dependent on a variety of economic factors. A central bank must decide to what extent it wants to provide the public with information about the uncertainty it sees, to provide an assessment of the risks and the degree of uncertainty of the economic environment surrounding monetary policy making and to allow market participants to hedge against these risks. But how much of this information should central banks communicate? And in particular, how much of the diversity of views and the disagreement among committee members should be provided to the public?

Several studies in the literature imply that communication, and communication dispersion in particular, may not necessarily be desirable. Amato *et al.* (2002), based on the conceptual work in Morris and Shin (2002), suggest that central bank communication may at times lead markets away from equilibrium, though Svensson (2006) argues that the validity of this argument is based on rather strong assumptions regarding the signal-to-noise ratio of central bank communication. Others (e.g. Winkler, 2002) underline that more information, in particular if it reveals dispersion among committee members, may be undesirable if it reduces the degree of clarity and common understanding among market participants. Moreover, there is a limit to how much information individuals can digest (e.g. Kahneman, 2003). Thus communication, and underlying transparency of central banks, may not be an end itself, but merely a means that allows the central bank to fulfil its mandate more effectively (Mishkin, 2004).

On the empirical side, a number of recent studies have analysed the effect of communication on asset prices. Kohn and Sack (2004) find that statements by the FOMC had a sizable effect on the volatility of various asset prices. In their analysis of different types of communication by the FOMC, Reinhart and Sack (2006) also find that markets are primarily affected by committee-wide communication. Ehrmann and Fratzscher (2007) compare the effects of communication between the Federal Reserve, the Bank of England and the ECB. They find that communication about the monetary policy inclination of committee members exerts substantial effects on financial markets for all three central banks, whereas statements about the economic outlook leads to significant market reactions only for the case of the FOMC.

Other papers that have focused on the content and dispersion of communication are Jansen and de Haan (2006) who have found that the degree of dispersion in the ECB's communication about the outlook for monetary policy was higher in the initial period after its start in 1999 and has declined over time. Gerlach (2007), Heinemann and Ullrich (2007) and Jansen and de Haan (2005) analyse the content of the introductory statements of the ECB's Monthly Bulletin, Introductory Statements to the press conference and speeches by Governing Council members, respectively, and conclude that they can explain well the overall interest rate setting of the euro area. In a related analysis, Jansen and de Haan (2008) also show that dispersed communication by ECB Governing Council members affects predictability negatively, in particular related to statements about euro-area inflation, thus confirming the results presented in this study.

Blinder (2007) analyses the functioning and set-up of different central bank committees, distinguishing between collegial and individualistic committees and central banks where decisions are taken by individuals. The study relates to a literature that has analysed the role of committees in the decision-making process. This literature broadly agrees that decision making in committees helps to improve the overall quality of decisions. This effect arises on the one hand because it allows for learning and pooling of information (Blinder and Morgan,

2005; Lombardelli *et al.*, 2005), and on the other hand because it enhances the flexibility of policy to respond to shocks of different magnitude and nature (Sibert, 2003; Mihov and Sibert, 2006).

In this chapter, we attempt to combine the literature on central banking committees with the one on central bank communication. Given the controversy around how active central banks should communicate, and around the extent to which the diversity of views should be communicated to the public, we aim to assess how both dimensions of central banks' communication strategies affect the predictability of policy decisions and of the path of future interest rates as well as the degree of market uncertainty surrounding policy decisions.

3 Measuring communication and its dispersion

We now turn to the issue of measuring communication by the policy-setting committees and its members. In particular, for the purpose of the analysis we want to identify a measure of communication dispersion or disagreement among the committee members.

3.1 Communication

Central bank communication occurs through two principal channels: statements by the committee as a whole, and statements by the individual committee members. There may be various motivations for central banks to choose their communication strategies and to balance their communication between statements of the committee and those by the individual committee members. Many central bank committees, including those of the Bank of England and the ECB, in general make statements at pre-announced dates, usually using a standard format in terms of language and structure. The Governing Council of the ECB provides an introductory statement followed by a press conference, where the President and Vice-President answer additional questions from the media. The MPC of the Bank of England usually does not provide any explanatory statements when it announces decisions that monetary policy rates remain unchanged, except if that decision would have come as a surprise to markets.

Both committees provide some additional information during the inter-meeting period: the MPC publishes the Minutes and the quarterly Inflation Report, the ECB its Monthly Bulletin and the Annual Report. By contrast, the communication by the individual committee members – such as testimonies, speeches and interviews – occur much more frequently and tend to be more flexible in their timing and content. Although some of these statements, in particular testimonies to the legislatures, tend to be at predetermined dates and have a fixed content in terms of topics, the great majority of statements by committee members are discretionary in nature and thus give the central banks a substantial degree of flexibility and the ability to communicate virtually at any time and on any topic it chooses.

Our empirical measure of communication events is taken from Ehrmann and Fratzscher (2007), where also a more detailed description is provided. The dataset aims to cover all communication events that contain statements about monetary policy inclinations, by the two committees as such as well as by their individual members. This is achieved by extracting all statements by the committee members reported upon by the newswire service *Reuters News*, noting the day on which they occurred. The identification of relevant statements is based on a set of search words, including the name of the policy maker and the words 'interest rates', 'monetary policy' or 'inflation', following the examples of Guthrie and Wright (2000) and Kohn and Sack (2004).

After a thorough reading of all extracted statements, only those with a forward-looking content are kept. Duplicated reported of the same statements are dropped from the database. Furthermore, all statements are classified as to the implications of their content for future monetary policy decisions. Statements that warn about rising inflation pressures, for instance, will be classified as containing a tightening inclination. Overall, this results in the following classification:

$$C_t^{MP} = \begin{cases} +1 & \textit{tightening inclination} \\ 0 & \textit{no inclination.} \\ -1 & \textit{easing inclination} \end{cases}$$

In doing so, we tried to follow the rules advised by content analysis (e.g. Holsti, 1969). The statements have been double-checked by the authors and independently by the research analyst. In case of disagreement, a classification was reached by means of checking other reports. If no agreement could be reached, a statement was discarded. However, the classification of the bulk of all statements was unanimous, and only a relatively small number of statements got excluded from the analysis.

The upper panel of Table 7.1 provides an overview of the communication data in our database for the two central banks. Even though the sample period is longer for the Bank of England, the number of statements by MPC members is considerably smaller than by the ECB's Governing Council members. Partly, this reflects the larger size of the Governing Council, which had 18 members over the sample (17 members through the end of 2001, until Greece joined the

Table 7.1 Summary statistics communication

	Bank of England	*European Central Bank*
Number of statements by committee members		
Total	76	185
Tightening	18	27
Neutral	42	118
Easing	16	40
Communication dispersion		
Among committee members	0.061	0.145
With committee releases	0.095	0.103

euro area), compared to nine members in the MPC of the Bank of England. It is interesting to note that most statements (55 per cent in the case of the Bank of England, 64 per cent for the ECB) are neutral, i.e. provide no inclination for monetary policy.

As an alternative classification of communication, we use the reaction of three-month interest rates on the day of the statement, or more precisely the difference of the closing quote with that of the previous day, as a proxy for the content of each statement. For instance, a statement on monetary policy inclinations on a day when interest rates rise is classified as a tightening statement. This same classification is used for the releases of statements by the committee as a whole (i.e. the Minutes and the Inflation Report of the Bank of England, and the Monthly Bulletin and the Annual Report by the ECB). Clearly, such a classification procedure may be imprecise as several other pieces of relevant news may occur on the day when a statement is made. However, we use this classification mainly as a robustness check in our analysis. In fact, given the importance of central bank communication for interest rates it turns out that both classification procedures provide very similar classifications of the statements and the empirical results below are robust to using either one.

3.2 Communication dispersion

For the purpose of this chapter, we need to measure the degree of disagreement or dispersion of communication across committee members, as well as between statements by individual committee members and those by the committee. An important starting point is the question of which time span to choose for measuring communication dispersion. The inter-meeting period between two monetary policy meetings seems a natural choice of data frequency because it is surrounded by two policy decisions by the committee. Each meeting provides a decision on monetary policy rates, and subsequently market participants have to start anew to form their expectations about the subsequent policy decision. Market participants use the communication provided by the committee and by individual members, as well as other types of information such as macroeconomic news, to shape their expectations about the future policy decisions.[2] To measure the degree of dispersion in each inter-meeting period, we use the dispersion measure used in Jansen and de Haan (2006) and Ehrmann and Fratzscher (2007), which is defined as follows:

$$\Omega_t^{MP} = \frac{\sum_{i=1}^{N-1}\sum_{j=i+1}^{N}\left|C_i^{MP} - C_j^{MP}\right|}{\frac{1}{2}\cdot(N^2 - D)} \tag{1}$$

with N as the number of statements in the inter-meeting period t, C^{MP} the statements on monetary policy inclinations classified as $\{-1,0,+1\}$, as outlined above, and a dummy D with $D = 0$ if N is an even number and $D = 1$ if it is odd. This normalisation allows us to obtain a dispersion measure that lies strictly between zero and one, with $\Omega_t = 0$ if no dispersion is present and all committee members provide statements with the same inclination about monetary policy. $\Omega_t = 1$ if there is a maximum of degree of dispersion across statements within an inter-meeting period *t*. An analogous definition of dispersion is used for statements between committee members and that of the committee as a whole in the inter-meeting period.[3]

The lower panel of Table 7.1 shows some summary statistics of these different communication dispersion measures for the two central banks. The degree of dispersion is much higher for communication of Governing Council members than for those of the MPC. However, compared to the same measure for the US Federal Reserve (Ehrmann and Fratzscher, 2007), it is evident that while the latter pursues a highly individualistic communication strategy, communication at the Bank of England and the ECB is considerably more collegial.

4 Hypothesis, data and methodology

If central bank communication succeeds in making the central bank's goal, strategy and assessment of current conditions understood by the public, financial markets should be able to anticipate well the future path of monetary policy, and there should be little disagreement between forecasters about these expectations. Of course, this does not imply that it may not be necessary at times to surprise markets with policy decisions, but in principle a high degree of predictability is an important element for the credibility and effectiveness of monetary policy. This section discusses the key hypothesis and the data definitions and sources used (Section 4.1), and then outlines the empirical methodology (Section 4.2).

4.1 Hypothesis and data

A successful communication strategy should imply that monetary policy decisions are anticipated well by financial markets. An open question relates to the relevant horizon at which this is desirable, however. Predictability at short horizons can be relevant for financial markets, as surprising monetary policy decisions necessitate a repositioning of market participants. With regard to the real economy, predictability at the long horizon is likely to be more relevant as, for instance, investment decisions take into account the entire future path of interest rates over an investor's planning horizon. For that reason, we will attempt to analyse predictability at both horizons.

At the short horizon, we make use of a poll about market participants' expectations about upcoming monetary policy decisions conducted by Reuters a few days before the meetings of the interest-rate-setting bodies. The surprise component contained in an interest rate decision is then derived as the absolute value of the difference between the actual decision and the mean of the survey expectations conducted by Reuters.[4] To probe deeper into the market's understanding of upcoming monetary policy decisions, we also analyse forecaster disagreement by means of the standard deviation of the responses across individual forecasters.

For a measure of monetary policy predictability at longer horizons, we similarly use data obtained in the Reuters polls, which ask survey participants also about their expectations about the level of policy interest rates at the end of the current and the subsequent years.[5] We refrain from calculating forecast errors over such a long horizon, as it is understood that all central bank communication is conditional on the incoming macroeconomic data. A large forecast error at a given point in time can therefore either reflect the arrival of new information that was unforeseen by the central bank as well as market participants, or it could reflect that central bank communication was not able to convey the central bank's views to the public. As we will not be able to disentangle these two alternatives, we restrict ourselves to analysing the standard deviation of the responses across individual forecasters. This will allow us to understand the extent to which central bank communication can lead to a common understanding among financial market participants about later decisions.[6]

What explains the predictability of monetary policy decisions, or the disagreement about them? There are several factors that may have an influence. The main variables of interest to us here are the ones of central bank communication. The communication variables include the dispersion measures across committee members and vis-à-vis the committee as a whole, as discussed in Section 3, but also the frequency of communication and the size of communication effects. The frequency is measured as the number of central bank statements by the committee and its members, while the size variable is the cumulated change in three-month interest rates on communication days in the inter-meeting period. The reasoning for including these variables is that it may not only be the dispersion of communication, but also the relevance and importance of the statements that influence the predictability of decisions.

Of course, communication is only one factor determining the predictability of monetary policy decisions. Policy decisions may be hardest to predict when there is a high degree of underlying economic uncertainty. In such an environment, it is more likely that items of economic news are contradictory and do not provide a unanimous message about the path of the economy. We proxy such market uncertainty in two separate ways. A first measure is to analyse the uncertainty and conflicting messages emanating from the release of macroeconomic news in the inter-meeting period. We use ten of the most relevant macroeconomic news releases for each of the three countries and areas to construct a *macro news dispersion* measure similar to those for communication dispersion defined in (1).[7]

As for communication, the classification of macro news surprises is done in two ways: a first one by classifying them according to the expected impact on interest rates, for example, a positive GDP surprise should lead to higher interest rates, while a rise, for example, in unemployment should induce lower rates. The second proxy is similar to the alternative one for communication dispersion as we use the actual reaction of interest rates on the day of the release as a proxy for whether the news was perceived by the markets as a positive or as a negative signal about the economy. Both proxies produce very similar measures of macro news dispersion. Moreover, similar to that for communication also the frequency and overall market impact of macro news are included as controls.

Second, other factors apart from the measurable macroeconomic news may also influence the degree of market uncertainty and thus the perception of the outlook for monetary policy and the economy. As a second measure for the underlying uncertainty, we use the *volatility of short-term (three-month) interest rates* in the inter-meeting period. In other words, a larger degree of interest-rate volatility is likely to reflect a larger extent of uncertainty, which in turn may make it more difficult to anticipate monetary policy decisions. In order to avoid a potential endogeneity that communication or macro news may cause more interest-rate volatility, we measure interest-rate volatility as the standard deviation of its daily changes before the first communication event in a given inter-meeting period occurs.

Finally, we control for the potential role of past monetary policy decisions by including a dummy for whether monetary policy rates were changed at the previous meeting. Moreover, we include an additional dummy that measures whether the MPC had published an Inflation Report in the current inter-meeting period.

4.2 Methodology

For the formulation of the model, we need to take into account that our dependent variables – the absolute size of the surprise component of subsequent monetary policy decisions, and the standard deviation of responses about the subsequent or later decisions – are censored to lie at or above zero. In fact, in a number of cases policy decisions are predicted perfectly, or the survey reports no degree of uncertainty, so that a number of observations lie on the lower limit of the distribution at zero. This requires estimating a censored regression or tobit model, which is formulated as follows:

$$y_t^* = x_t'\,\beta + \varepsilon_t \tag{2}$$

where

$$y_t = \begin{cases} y_t^* & \text{if } \; 0 \leq y_t^* \\ 0 & \text{if } \; y_t^* < 0 \end{cases}$$

with y^* as the latent, i.e. unobservable variable, y_t the observable variable measuring the surprise component of monetary policy decisions, x_t the vector of independent variables, and t as the time dimension of the inter-meeting periods. The marginal effect of a change in x_t with regard to the observable variable y_t is

$$\frac{\delta\, E[y_t|x_t]}{\delta x_t} = \beta \cdot prob\,[0 < y_t^*] = \beta\Phi\left(\frac{\beta'\,x_t}{\sigma}\right) \tag{3}$$

under the condition that the disturbance $\varepsilon_t \sim N(0, \sigma^2)$, and with β as the marginal effect of x_t with regard to the latent variable y^*. All results shown below refer to this marginal effect of x_t with regard to the observable variable y_t. The model is estimated via maximum likelihood estimation of the log-likelihood function for the censored regression at $y_t = 0$:

$$\ln L = \sum_{y_t > 0} - \frac{1}{2}\left[\log(2\pi) + \ln \sigma^2 + \frac{(y_t - x_t'\beta)^2}{\sigma^2}\right] + \sum_{y_t = 0} \ln\left[1 - \Phi\left(\frac{x_t'\beta}{\sigma}\right)\right]$$

which is a mixture of a continuous distribution – for the linear regression of the non-limit observations, and a discrete distribution – for the limit observations at $y_t = 0$, again under the condition that ε_t is normally distributed.

Before proceeding to the empirical analysis, a word of caution is in order, referring to the potential endogeneity of communication dispersion. There might be times when interest-rate decisions are difficult to predict, for example due to macroeconomic uncertainty, which in turn may raise the degree of disagreement and thus communication dispersion in the inter-meeting period. We have therefore decided to instrument our variable for communication dispersion through various factors that may influence communication dispersion, but at the same time are truly exogenous to communication dispersion as well as to monetary policy decisions. For instance, macro news dispersion can be considered strictly exogenous because releases of macroeconomic data – which are for economic developments of previous months – are usually influenced neither by communication nor by the current or the last monetary policy decisions. The aim is to use such instruments for determining communication dispersion and then to employ the instrumented communication dispersion variable in model (2) to see whether the findings are sensitive to those shown in Table 7.2. We therefore estimate a tobit model for communication dispersion x_t as a function of several exogenous instruments z_t:

$$x_t^* = \rho + \lambda z_t + \mu_t \qquad (4)$$

where

$$y_t = \begin{cases} 1 & if x_t^* > 1 \\ x_t^* & if \quad 0 \leqslant x_t^* \leqslant 1 \\ 0 & if x_t^* < 0 \end{cases}$$

with x^* as the latent, i.e. unobservable variable, and x_t the observable communication dispersion variable. This follows the same logic as explained for model (2), and under the condition that $\mu_t \sim N(0, \sigma^2)$. The difference is that communication dispersion, by construction, is censored to lie between zero and one, hence the estimated model is a two-limit tobit.

What induces disagreement in communication among committee members? Table 7.2 shows the results for both central banks, using both the tobit estimator of (4) and the OLS estimator.[8] The main driver for dispersion is the frequency of communication. It is therefore important to use an instrumented version of the

Table 7.2 Explaining dispersion in communication about monetary policy inclinations

	Bank of England				*European Central Bank*			
	Tobit		*OLS*		*Tobit*		*OLS*	
	Coef.	*Std err.*	*Coef.*	*Std err.*	*Coef.*	*Std err.*	*Coef.*	*Std err.*
Macro news dispersion	0.021	0.078	–0.001	0.071	–0.012	0.040	–0.024	0.054
Pre-event interest rate volatility	–0.067	0.055	–0.110	0.068	0.006	0.024	–0.005	0.039
Frequency of communication	0.069***	0.014	0.093***	0.019	0.041***	0.008	0.062***	0.013
Monetary policy surprise last meeting	0.027	0.045	0.037	0.045	0.086*	0.049	0.152**	0.065
Interest rate change next meeting	0.004	0.039	0.043	0.045	0.085	0.050	0.137**	0.066
Number of observations	84		84		97		97	
(Pseudo) R-squared	0.362		0.271		0.262		0.278	

Note
Using the tobit model (equation 4), the table shows the marginal effects of a change in the independent variables z_t with regard to the observable variable x_t, which is the communication dispersion on monetary policy inclinations among committee members. The independent variables z_t are defined as explained in the text.
***, **, * indicate significance at the 1%, 5% and 10% levels, respectively.

dispersion variable, which will allow us to disentangle the effects of more active from more dispersed communication. Finally, for the ECB also an interest-rate change in the next meeting and a large monetary policy surprise in the previous meeting induce larger communication dispersion.

5 The effectiveness of communication and its dispersion

We now turn to the main empirical analysis. The central objective is to assess the effect of communication, its intensity and dispersion on different normative dimensions of monetary policy: on the predictability of the subsequent policy decision (Section 5.1), and the robustness to various extensions (Section 5.2), and on the disagreement about the subsequent decision as well as about the future path of interest rates (Section 5.3).

5.1 The predictability of subsequent monetary policy decisions

How do central bank communication and its dispersion affect the predictability of subsequent monetary policy decisions? Apart from communication dispersion, as discussed in detail in Section 4.1, we control for other relevant factors influencing the predictability of decisions. These factors include those that create market uncertainty, as proxied by macro news dispersion and interest-rate volatility, as well as the frequency and size of communication and macro news. Moreover, we control for whether an MPC Inflation Report was issued in the respective inter-meeting period, as well as for whether monetary policy rates had been changed at the previous meeting.

Table 7.3 shows the results using three specifications: starting from a simple model (1) that includes only the communication dispersion and macro dispersion variables, and leading to a more extensive model (3) that includes all sets of variables discussed above.

The key result is that dispersed communication among committee members lowers the predictability of policy decisions significantly, i.e. it raises the market surprise of policy decisions. By contrast, communication dispersion with committee releases does not matter for predictability.

Also the frequency of communication shows some systematic impact on policy predictability for the Governing Council and the MPC. The empirical finding is interesting as it suggests that each additional statement by committee members – on average and controlling for the dispersion of the committee communication – improves the predictability of decisions by around 1 basis point or more. As we have seen earlier, the number of statements made by the committee members of the two central banks varies considerably, being substantially larger in the case of the ECB than for the Bank of England. Accordingly, it appears intuitive that more communication is particularly beneficial for central banks that communicate less on average, whereas the marginal effect of one additional statement becomes smaller with the number of statements already made.

Table 7.3 Explaining the predictability of subsequent monetary policy decisions

	Bank of England						*European Central Bank*					
	(1)		*(2)*		*(3)*		*(1)*		*(2)*		*(3)*	
	Coef.	*Std err.*	*Coef.*	*Std err.*	*Coef.*	*Std err.*	*Coef.*	*Std err.*	*Coef.*	*Std err.*	*Coef.*	*Std err.*
Communication dispersion												
Among committee members	0.023	0.048	1.530***	0.283	1.649***	0.288	0.063	0.029	0.313***	0.059	0.388***	0.062
With committee releases	0.166	0.139	0.157	0.124	0.156	0.123	0.075	0.102	–0.020	0.088	–0.043	0.081
Market uncertainty												
Macro view dispersion	0.020	0.017	0.011	0.017	0.018	0.017	–0.004	0.009	0.004	0.008	0.005	0.007
Pre-event interest rate volatility			–0.003	0.014	0.006	0.016			0.003	0.005	0.002	0.005
Frequency and size												
Frequency of communication			–0.134***	0.025	–0.148***	0.025			–0.020***	0.004	–0.024***	0.004
Frequency of macro news			0.001	0.003	0.001	0.003			–0.002	0.002	–0.002	0.002
Size of communication effects					0.284	0.291					–0.049	0.060
Size of macro news effects					–0.137	0.114					0.033	0.095
Committee decisions and communication												
Interest rate change last meeting					–0.016*	0.008					–0.026***	0.005
Inflation report (MPC)					0.011	0.009						
Number of observations	84		84		84		97		97		97	
Likelihood ratio chi^2	2.84		30.91		36.39		5.09		32.16		48.17	

Note

Using the tobit model (equation 2) with communication dispersion instrumented as explained in the text, the table shows the marginal effects (as defined in equation (3)) of a change in the independent variables x_t with regard to the observable variable y_t, i.e. the absolute value of the monetary policy surprise. Positive parameter estimates do therefore imply lower predictability of monetary policy decisions. The independent variables x_t are defined as explained in the text.

***, **, * indicate significance at the 1%, 5% and 10% levels, respectively.

The only other variable that shows any significance is the dummy for an interest-rate change in the previous meeting: once a change had occurred, the subsequent decisions are less surprising.

5.2 Extensions and robustness

As the next step, we conduct several sensitivity tests to check for the robustness of our results. Beyond the potential endogeneity of communication dispersion, which we attempt to address by means of instrumenting, another issue to be addressed relates to the possibility of an omitted variable bias. The reasoning goes as follows: the fact that we find a significant effect of communication dispersion on predictability in Table 7.3 may simply reflect the possibility that communication dispersion is influenced and determined by other factors that are not included in the model. For instance, high communication dispersion may merely reflect the large degree of macroeconomic uncertainty caused by conflicting or unclear signals coming from macroeconomic or other news, which in turn lead to lower predictability of policy decisions.

We deal with this issue in a number of ways. First, we include as broad a set of control variables as possible in our model. Hence our preferred specification is the one shown in columns (3) in Table 7.3 as here we can control for several other factors. However, as a comparison of the various specifications ranging from a more minimalist specification (1) to a more extensive one in (3) shows, the results with regard to communication are overall robust. We also tested for other definitions of the various variables, including the alternative measures of dispersion discussed in Section 4. The results are robust to these tests, but for brevity reasons are not shown.

Further variables that were added to the regression and tested, but did not alter results, are (1) dummy variables indicating whether the balance of views expressed by the committee is in line with the balance of views expressed by the head of the committee, (2) a variable that captures different degrees of policy activism by summing the number of times interest rates had been changed at the last ten meetings prior to the current meeting, and (3) a variable capturing the voting dispersion in the case of the Bank of England through the variation ratio, both for the current and the preceding meeting.

For another robustness test, we are interested in seeing whether the results obtained depend on the judgemental, and thus subjective, classification of the content of communication. Whereas the benchmark results reported in Table 7.3 are based on the classification explained in Section 3.1, Table 7.4 shows results based on an alternative classification of communication, whereby statements are categorised based on the reaction of interest rates on the day of the statement. For instance, a statement is classified as a tightening statement if interest rates rise on the same day. Such a classification procedure may be imprecise as several other pieces of relevant news may occur on the day when a statement is made, and because it allows only for very few neutral statements. However, it is interesting to note that such an agnostic procedure delivers results that confirm the

Table 7.4 Robustness test: explaining the predictability of subsequent monetary policy decisions – alternative classification of statements

	Bank of England						*European Central Bank*					
	(1)		*(2)*		*(3)*		*(1)*		*(2)*		*(3)*	
	Coef.	*Std err.*	*Coef.*	*Std err.*	*Coef.*	*Std err.*	*Coef.*	*Std err.*	*Coef.*	*Std err.*	*Coef.*	*Std err.*
Communication dispersion												
Among committee members	0.023	0.048	1.530***	0.283	1.649***	0.288	0.007	0.014	0.182***	0.062	0.351***	0.076
With committee releases	0.166	0.139	0.157	0.124	0.156	0.123	–0.568	0.783	0.024	0.757	–0.146	0.685
Market uncertainty												
Macro view dispersion	0.020	0.017	0.011	0.017	0.018	0.017	–0.003	0.009	0.003	0.009	0.007	0.008
Pre-event interest rate volatility			–0.003	0.014	0.006	0.016			0.007	0.006	0.004	0.006
Frequency and size												
Frequency of communication			–0.134***	0.025	–0.148***	0.025			–0.028***	0.010	–0.053***	0.012
Frequency of macro news			0.001	0.003	0.001	0.003			–0.001	0.002	–0.001	0.002
Size of communication effects					0.284	0.291					–0.061	0.069
Size of macro news effects					–0.137	0.114					0.059	0.106
Committee decisions and communication												
Interest rate change last meeting					–0.016*	0.008					–0.034***	0.006
Inflation report (MPC)					0.011	0.009						
Number of observations	84		84		84		97		97		97	
Likelihood ratio chi^2	2.84		30.91		36.39		0.78		14.34		33.31	

Note

Using the tobit model (equation 2), the table shows the marginal effects (as defined in equation (3)) of a change in the independent variables x_t with regard to the observable variable y_t, i.e. the absolute value of the monetary policy surprise. Statements are classified based on the reaction of three-month interest rates on the day of each statement. Positive parameter estimates do therefore imply lower predictability of monetary policy decisions. The independent variables x_t are defined as explained in the text.

***, **, * indicate significance at the 1%, 5% and 10% levels, respectively.

importance of communication for the predictability of monetary policy decisions.

In summary, the results suggest that communication dispersion among committee members is an important determinant of the predictability of monetary policy decisions, both for the Bank of England and the ECB. Moreover, we find that more communication, i.e. a higher frequency of statements by committee members in the inter-meeting period, also induces a significant improvement in the predictability of decisions. These findings are robust to several robustness tests, including a market-based procedure to classify the content of communication.

5.3 Disagreement among forecasters

A high degree of predictability of policy decisions implies not only that the market consensus view about upcoming policy decisions should be well aligned with the actual decision, but should also lead to a common understanding among central bank watchers. In this section, we test whether communication and its dispersion by the two central banks influences the extent to which forecasters disagree about the upcoming as well as later policy decisions. As mentioned above, we measure the disagreement about monetary policy decisions as the standard deviation of the responses across individual forecasters; for the short horizon based on the Reuters poll about the subsequent decision, for a medium-term horizon based on the poll about policy rates at the end of the current or the subsequent year.

Turning first to the short horizon, Table 7.5 shows that the results for the market surprise carry over also to the disagreement among forecasters. Communication dispersion on policy inclinations – in particular among committee members, and partially also with committee communication – reduces the common understanding of forecasters as to what the next interest-rate decision will be, for both the Bank of England and the ECB alike.

The other relevant factor is again the frequency of communication. For both central banks, more frequent communication lowers disagreement about upcoming decisions. This is very much in line with the findings of the previous subsection that more communication also improves the predictability of policy decisions on average. Moreover, as before (albeit significantly so only for the case of the ECB), if there has been a change in policy rates at the preceding meeting, forecasts for the subsequent decision are more synchronised. This should not be too surprising, given that policy rate changes have been relatively infrequent in the sample period under consideration. Once a rate change has occurred, it has therefore in most cases not been too difficult to predict that no change would occur at the subsequent meeting.

So far, we have taken a short-term perspective on the effectiveness of communication by focusing on the role of communication in improving the predictability of the subsequent policy decision. But communication frequently has a much longer time horizon by not only conveying views of policy makers and

Table 7.5 Explaining the heterogeneity in forecasts of subsequent monetary policy decisions

	Bank of England						*European Central Bank*					
	(1)		*(2)*		*(3)*		*(1)*		*(2)*		*(3)*	
	Coef.	*Std err.*	*Coef.*	*Std err.*	*Coef.*	*Std err.*	*Coef.*	*Std err.*	*Coef.*	*Std err.*	*Coef.*	*Std err.*
Communication dispersion												
Among committee members	0.053	0.051	0.746***	0.329	0.727**	0.334	0.103	0.034	0.346***	0.077	0.407***	0.082
With committee releases	0.221	0.142	0.217	0.139	0.231*	0.135	0.026	0.117	–0.042	0.109	–0.065	0.101
Market uncertainty												
Macro view dispersion	0.001	0.020	0.006	0.022	0.011	0.02	0.009	0.010	0.015	0.011	0.019	0.010
Pre-event interest rate volatility			0.011	0.018	0.021	0.020			0.006	0.007	0.002	0.007
Frequency and size												
Frequency of communication			–0.063***	0.029	–0.064***	0.030			–0.019***	0.005	–0.023***	0.006
Frequency of macro news			–0.002	0.003	–0.001	0.003			0.000	0.002	0.000	0.002
Size of communication effects					0.284	0.291					–0.061	0.069
Size of macro news effects					–0.330**	0.140					0.236	0.129
Committee decisions and communication												
Interest rate change last meeting					–0.011	0.012					–0.037***	0.006
Inflation report (MPC)					–0.006	0.010						
Number of observations	84		84		84		94		94		94	
Likelihood ratio chi^2	3.62		10.07		17.58		11.22		27.41		48.03	

Note

Using the tobit model (equation 2), the table shows the marginal effects (as defined in equation (3)) of a change in the independent variables x_t with regard to the observable variable y_t, i.e. the standard deviation of survey responses regarding the expected level of policy rates. Positive parameter estimates do therefore imply lower predictability of monetary policy decisions. The independent variables x_t are defined as explained in the text.

***, **, * indicate significance at the 1%, 5% and 10% levels, respectively.

policy committees about the subsequent decision but about the path of future monetary policy. Hence an assessment of communication also needs to take into account the effects of communication on the understanding of market participants about interest rates in the medium to long run.

Table 7.6 shows how our explanatory variables affect the heterogeneity of responses regarding interest-rate levels at longer horizons. Overall, results point in the same direction as for the other tests for the ECB: more dispersed communication among Governing Council members raises the disagreement among the central bank watchers, whereas more frequent communication helps to reduce it. For the Bank of England, however, no effect is discernible. Disagreement among central bank watchers about the future path of interest rates in the United Kingdom seems to be mainly affected by macroeconomic news: the more dispersed the message coming from the release of macroeconomic announcement, the more disagreement about where interest rates are heading. Furthermore, by analogy to the communication effects discussed so far, controlling for their dispersion, more frequent macroeconomic news allow for a better assessment of the future path of interest rates, as disagreement among forecasters shrinks in response to an increasing number of macro signals.

Finally, the control for the forecast horizon is extremely important. Not surprisingly, we find that the further out interest-rate levels need to be assessed, the more disagreement there is among the survey respondents.

Overall, the results indicate that communication dispersion induces more disagreement about where interest rates are heading, in the short run for both central banks, in the medium run only for the ECB. Moreover, more active communication tends to lower disagreement. Again, this effect is present at the short forecasting horizon for the Bank of England and the ECB, at the medium horizon only for the ECB.

6 Conclusions

How should central banks communicate? This question is of fundamental importance for central banks as communication has become a key instrument for the conduct and implementation of monetary policy over the last ten to 15 years. The chapter focuses on one key aspect of this question, and one that remains highly controversial as the views by Bernanke (2004) and Issing (1999, 2005) reveal: should central banks communicate in a collegial manner, by conveying the consensus or majority view of the committee, or in an individualistic way, by stressing and providing the diversity of views among the committee members and with those of the committee as a whole? Moreover, how much information should central banks provide, and in particular how actively should they communicate with markets and the wider public?

The objective of this chapter has been to answer these questions by analysing and comparing communication by the Bank of England and the ECB. We have used different benchmarks, or normative dimensions, for assessing the effectiveness of communication and its dispersion: the effect of communication

Table 7.6 Explaining the heterogeneity in long-horizon forecasts of policy rates

	Bank of England						*European Central Bank*					
	(1)		*(2)*		*(3)*		*(1)*		*(2)*		*(3)*	
	Coef.	*Std err.*	*Coef.*	*Std err.*	*Coef.*	*Std err.*	*Coef.*	*Std err.*	*Coef.*	*Std err.*	*Coef.*	*Std err.*
Communication dispersion												
Among committee members	–0.098	0.139	–0.144	0.863	–0.026	0.882	0.211**	0.089	0.462***	0.202	0.645***	0.227
With committee releases	–0.013	0.376	–0.151	0.359	–0.162	0.362	0.322	0.298	0.323	0.294	0.400	0.286
Market uncertainty												
Macro view dispersion	0.036	0.051	0.112*	0.055	0.123**	0.058	0.048*	0.026	0.037	0.028	0.035	0.027
Pre-event interest rate volatility			0.051	0.045	0.057	0.052			–0.025	0.019	–0.017	0.019
Frequency and size												
Frequency of communication			0.004	0.076	–0.013	0.078			–0.023	0.014	–0.036**	0.016
Frequency of macro news			–0.024***	0.009	–0.023**	0.009			0.010	0.007	0.012*	0.006
Size of communication effects					0.892	0.896					0.311	0.193
Size of macro news effects					–0.323	0.337					–0.960**	0.379
Committee decisions and communication												
Interest rate change last meeting					–0.004	0.030					0.006	0.031
Inflation report (MPC)					0.019	0.027						
Forecast horizon												
Months to the forecasted decision	0.030***	0.002	0.030***	0.002	0.030***	0.002	0.023***	0.001	0.023***	0.001	0.024***	0.001
Number of observations	84		84		84		97		97		97	
Likelihood ratio chi^2	154.36		163.93		165.64		150.51		155.98		161.83	

Note
Using the tobit model (equation 2), the table shows the marginal effects (as defined in equation (3)) of a change in the independent variables x_t with regard to the observable variable y_t, i.e. the standard deviation of survey responses regarding the expected level of policy rates. Positive parameter estimates do therefore imply lower predictability of monetary policy decisions. The independent variables x_t are defined as explained in the text.
***, **, * indicate significance at the 1%, 5% and 10% levels, respectively.

dispersion on the predictability of subsequent monetary policy decisions as measured by the market consensus, and on the disagreement about subsequent policy decisions and the future path of interest rates among forecasters. With these, we capture several, but not all goals of central bank communication, as also the improvement of the market's understanding of the policy strategy and the reaction of a central bank to shocks are important objectives of communication (Woodford, 2005). However, evaluating communication strategies with regard to the latter objectives is beyond the scope of this chapter.

A first key result of the chapter is that communication that is dispersed and conveys not a single committee view but a variety of views on monetary policy inclinations reduces the predictability of decisions and worsens the ability of market participants to understand the future path of monetary policy. A second key result is that more communication (always controlling for the amount of dispersion involved) tends to improve the market's understanding of monetary policy along all the dimensions we have analysed.

The findings of the chapter provide a clear policy message. Overall, it is the collegiality of views on policy inclinations that appear to enhance the effectiveness of central bank communication. Communicating the diversity of views lowers the market's ability to predict the subsequent policy decision as well as its ability to anticipate the path of future interest rates. Moreover, it appears beneficial to communicate with the markets in the preparation of a decision, as a higher intensity of communication also seems to improve the predictability of policy decisions.

Notes

1 We thank Terhi Jokipii for excellent research assistance, and Reuters and Standard and Poor's for providing some of the data series. We are grateful to the participants at the 2005 NBER Summer Institute's Workshop on Monetary Economics, the 2006 Annual Meeting of the American Economic Association, and the Bundesbank/Bank of Finland conference on 'Designing Central Banks', in particular Athanasios Orphanides and Jakob de Haan. We have benefited substantially from and would like to thank, without implicating them, a number of central banking colleagues at the Federal Reserve, the Bank of England and the ECB and the Eurosystem for numerous discussions, insights and suggestions. This chapter presents the authors' personal opinions and does not necessarily reflect the views of the European Central Bank.

2 Note that this implies a relatively small sample size of 84 observations for the Bank of England and 97 for the ECB.

3 An alternative measure tested is the simple standard deviation across statements in each inter-meeting period. This dispersion measure is very similar to the dispersion measure of equation (1), and the empirical results are almost identical. These results are available upon request.

4 This survey-based measure has been shown to be an efficient and unbiased proxy for the surprise component of monetary policy decisions (Ehrmann and Fratzscher, 2005).

5 It is important to note that the requested forecast horizon differs substantially, both across central banks on average (it amounts to 13 months for the ECB and 16 months for the Bank of England), and across the individual survey for each central bank (ranging from one to 23 months), such that we will need to control for the distance between the survey and the forecast level of interest rates in our analysis.

6 In line with this reasoning, Bauer *et al.* (2006) find that the immediate release of FOMC decisions since 1994 has led to more synchronised private-sector forecasts of future economic conditions, while they find only little evidence that this change in communication policy has brought down the magnitude of common forecast errors.
7 The set of macro news comprises GDP, earnings, industrial production, manufacturing production, M4, PPI, RPIX, retail sales, trade balance and unemployment for the United Kingdom; euro-area business confidence and consumer confidence, German Ifo business climate, industrial production, PPI, retail sales, trade balance, unemployment, CPI and GDP for the euro area. We use the surprise component within each macroeconomic announcement, by subtracting a survey-based expectation measure (obtained from MMS International) from the actually released figure.
8 The results for communication dispersion with the committee are not shown for reasons of brevity.

References

Amato, J.D., S. Morris and H.S. Shin (2002) 'Communication and Monetary Policy'. *Oxford Review of Economic Policy*, 18 (4), 495–503.

Bauer, A., R. Eisenbeis, D. Waggoner and T. Zha (2006) 'Transparency, Expectations, and Forecasts'. *Federal Reserve Bank of Atlanta Economic Review*, 91 (1), 1–25.

Bernanke, B. (2004) 'Fedspeak'. Remarks at the Meetings of the American Economic Association, San Diego, California, 3 January 2004. Available online: www.federalreserve.govboarddocs/speeches/2004/200401032/default.htm.

Blinder, A. (2007) 'Monetary Policy by Committee: Why and How?'. *European Journal of Political Economy*, 23 (1), 106–123.

Blinder, A. and J. Morgan (2005) 'Are Two Heads Better Than One? Monetary Policy by Committee'. *Journal of Money, Credit and Banking*, 37 (5), 798–811.

Ehrmann, M. and M. Fratzscher (2005) 'Equal Size, Equal Role? Interest Rate Interdependence between the Euro Area and the United States'. *Economic Journal*, 115, 930–950, October.

Ehrmann, M. and M. Fratzscher (2007) 'Communication and Decision-Making by Central Bank Committees: Different Strategies, Same Effectiveness?'. *Journal of Money, Credit and Banking*, 39 (2–3), 509–41.

Gerlach, S. (2007) 'Interest Rate Setting by the ECB, 1999–2006: Words and Deeds'. *International Journal of Central Banking*, 3 (3), 1–45.

Guthrie, G. and J. Wright (2000) 'Open Mouth Operations'. *Journal of Monetary Economics*, 46, 489–516.

Heinemann, F. and K. Ullrich (2007) 'Does it Pay to Watch Central Bankers' Lips? The Information Content of ECB Wording'. *Swiss Journal of Economics and Statistics*, 143 (2), 155–185.

Holsti, O. (1969) *Content Analysis for Social Sciences and Humanities*. Reading, MA: Addison-Wesley.

Honore, B. and L. Hu (2003) 'Estimation of Cross Sectional and Panel Data Censored Regression Models with Endogeneity'. Mimeo: Princeton University.

Issing, O. (1999) 'The Eurosystem: Transparent and Accountable, or "Willem in Euroland"'. *Journal of Common Market Studies*, 37 (3), 503–519.

Issing, O. (2005) 'Communication, Transparency, Accountability – Monetary Policy in the Twenty-First Century'. *Federal Reserve Bank of St. Louis Review*, 87 (2), 65–83.

Jansen, D.-J. and J. de Haan (2005) 'Is a Word to the Wise Indeed Enough? ECB Statements and the Predictability of Interest Rate Decisions'. DNB Working Paper No. 75.

Jansen, D.-J. and J. de Haan (2006) 'Look Who's Talking: ECB Communication during the First Years of EMU'. *International Journal of Finance and Economics*, 11 (3), 219–228.

Jansen, D.-J. and J. de Haan (in press) 'The Communication Policy of the ECB: An Assessment'. *Review of International Organizations*.

Kahneman, D. (2003) 'Maps of Bounded Rationality: Psychology for Behavioral Economics'. *American Economic Review*, 93 (5), 1449–1475.

Kohn, D.L. and B.P. Sack (2004) 'Central Bank Talk: Does it Matter and Why?'. In Bank of Canada (ed.), *Macroeconomics, Monetary Policy, and Financial Stability*. Ottawa: Bank of Canada, pp. 175–206.

Lombardelli, C., J. Proudman and J. Talbot (2005) 'Committees Versus Individuals: An Experimental Analysis of Monetary Policy Decision Making'. *International Journal of Central Banking*, 1 (1), 181–205.

Mihov, I. and A. Sibert (2006) 'Credibility and Flexibility with Independent Monetary Policy Committees'. *Journal of Money, Credit and Banking*, 38 (1), 23–46.

Mishkin, F.S. (2004) 'Can Central Bank Transparency Go too Far?'. In C. Kent and S. Guttmann (eds), *The Future of Inflation Targeting*, Sydney: Reserve Bank of Australia, pp. 48–65.

Morris, S. and H.S. Shin (2002) 'Social Value of Public Information'. *American Economic Review*, 92 (5), 1521–1534.

Reinhart, V. and B. Sack (2006) 'Grading the Federal Open Market Committee's Communications'. Mimeo, Federal Reserve Board of Governors, January.

Sibert, A. (2003) 'Monetary Policy Committees: Individual and Collective Reputations'. *Review of Economic Studies*, 70, 649–666.

Svensson, L. (2006) 'Social Value of Public Information: Morris and Shin (2002) Is Actually Pro Transparency, Not Con'. *American Economic Review*, 96 (1), 448–451.

Winkler, B. (2002) 'Which Kind of Transparency? On the Need for Effective Communication in Monetary-Policy Making'. *ifo Studien*, 48 (3), 401–427.

Woodford, M. (2005) 'Central-Bank Communication and Policy Effectiveness'. In *The Greenspan Era: Lessons for the Future*. Kansas City, MO: Federal Reserve Bank of Kansas City, pp. 399–474.

COMMENTS BY JAKOB DE HAAN

Many central banks have become remarkably more transparent in recent decades, putting a much larger weight on their communication with the public nowadays than they used to do. No doubt, the requirement for greater accountability of independent central banks was an important trigger for this increased transparency. As central banks have become more independent over time, they have to pay closer attention to explaining what they do and what underlies their decisions.

However, there is also a growing literature suggesting that communication may support monetary policy making. First, communication may be used to guide private-sector expectations. As such, it may play an important role in improving the effectiveness of policy and, in the end, the economy's overall performance. In an intervention at the 2005 Jackson Hole conference, Jean-Claude Trichet even states:

> under some conditions the central bank can regain control of private expectations without necessarily changing interest rates, but by being visibly and credibly 'alert', explaining and stressing its commitment to maintaining inflation at levels consistent with the price stability objective. The threat to act will be more effective the more credible the central bank has been over time in actually delivering price stability, as defined quantitatively.

Second, communication may be used to reduce noise in financial markets. Greater disclosure and clarity over policy may lead to greater predictability of central bank actions, which, in turn, reduces uncertainty in financial markets. There is a strongly held belief among central bankers nowadays that a high degree of predictability is important. As Poole (2001, p. 9) put it: 'The presumption must be that market participants make more efficient decisions ... when markets can correctly predict central bank actions.'

In a series of papers, Ehrmann and Fratzscher have analysed to what extent central bank communications affect various asset markets. In this chapter, they examine whether communication by the ECB and the Bank of England affect the extent to which financial market participants are able to predict policy decisions correctly. Their main conclusion is that *more active* as well as *more consistent* communication of the policy inclination by committee members improves the predictability of monetary policy decisions significantly, and reduces the disagreement among forecasters, both about policy decisions in the short run as well as about the future path of interest rates.

In a parallel research project with David-Jan Jansen on the communication policy of the ECB, I have also examined the impact of communication dispersion on the predictability of policy decisions. This offers the opportunity to check for the sensitivity of the conclusions of Ehrmann and Fratzscher, as we use a different source, have more categories, perhaps a different coding and another sample period.

Whereas Ehrmann and Fratzscher use statements by ECB officials as reported by Reuters, our analysis is based on a content analysis of reports from the newswire, Bloomberg. We have collected reports on comments by leading euro-area central bankers, such as members of the ECB's Executive Board and the presidents of national central banks.[1] Whereas Ehrmann and Fratzscher focus on the policy inclination, we examine ECB statements on the main refinancing rate, the outlook for euro-area inflation and the outlook for euro-area economic growth. On each topic, we classify every comment on a tertiary scale (−1, 0, +1). For example, statements suggesting a tightening of monetary policy are coded +1, whereas statements hinting at interest-rate cuts are coded −1. We measure dispersion in communication by computing the standard deviation of the coded statements. The event window is always equal to the period between two subsequent ECB interest-rate meetings. Our sample period is 6 May 1999 to 2 May 2002 and thus is shorter than that of Ehrmann and Fratzscher.

We study the effects of inconsistent communication using three characteristics of the survey data. First, we examine whether the absolute difference between the actual decision and the mean of the expectations from the Reuters poll of forecasters is positively related to dispersion in communication. Second, we study whether the percentage of incorrect predictions in the Reuters poll is positively related to dispersion. Finally, we examine whether the standard deviation of the expected interest rates is positively related to dispersion.

In all three cases, we rely on a tobit specification to account for the fact that the dependent variables are censored. In the first and third case, the censoring is at the value zero, in the second case, the dependent variable is censored at zero and one. Finally, we account for the fact that communication is not the only factor that influences predictability. We do this by using the standard deviation of a daily series of one-month Euribor rates in the week before the one in which the interest-rate decision is made to control for macroeconomic uncertainty.

Table 7.7 shows tobit estimation results where the dependent variable is either the absolute prediction error (column 1), the fraction of incorrect predictions (column 2) or the standard deviation of expected interest rates (column 3). We find evidence that dispersion in ECB statements (measured as the standard deviation of the coded statements) is significantly related to the predictability of decisions. In particular, we find that dispersed views on the inflation outlook are negatively related to predictability. In contrast to Ehrmann and Fratzscher, we do not find evidence that the frequency of communication affects the predictability of ECB interest-rate decisions.

Our results support the general conclusion of Ehrmann and Fratzscher that communication dispersion hampers the predictability of policy decisions. So central bankers speak better with one voice.

Table 7.7 Dispersion in ECB communication and the predictability of interest rate decisions

	Dependent variable:		
	(1) Absolute prediction error	*(2) Fraction of incorrect predictions*	*(3) Standard deviation of expected rates*
Dispersion in comments on:			
Main refinancing rate	–0.02 (0.06)	–0.08 (0.23)	0.00 (0.04)
Euro area inflation	0.08** (0.04)	0.36** (0.17)	0.10*** (0.03)
Euro area economic growth	0.02 (0.03)	0.04 (0.14)	0.01 (0.03)
Frequency of communication	0.05 (0.03)	0.19 (0.14)	0.03 (0.02)
Standard deviation one-month Euribor	0.98 (0.67)	4.12 (2.77)	0.83 (0.54)
Constant	–0.09*** (0.04)	–0.38** (0.15)	–0.06** (0.03)
Chi^2 LR-test	14.4**	14.3**	20.9***
Number of observations	65	65	65
Percentage of censored observations	41.5	43.1	41.5

Notes
Standard errors in parenthesis. */**/*** denotes significance at the 10/5/1% level. The sample period is 6 May 1999 to 2 May 2002. All results use robust Huber-White standard errors.

Note

1 The dataset is described in more detail in Jansen and De Haan (2005).

References

Jansen, D. and J. De Haan (2005) 'Talking Heads: The Effects of ECB Statements on the Euro-Dollar Exchange Rate'. *Journal of International Money and Finance*, 24 (2), 343–361.

Poole, W. (2001) 'Expectations'. *Federal Reserve Bank of St. Louis Review*, 83 (1), 1–10.

Trichet, J.C. (2005) 'Monetary Policy and 'Credible Alertness'. Intervention at the Panel Discussion 'Monetary Policy Strategies: A Central Bank Panel', at the Symposium sponsored by the Federal Reserve Bank of Kansas City, Jackson Hole, Wyoming, 27 August 2005. Available online: www.ecb.int/press/key/date/2005/html/sp050827.en.html.

8 Achieving financial stability with cross-border banking in an EU perspective

Mattias Persson

A banking failure could severely affect the functioning of the financial system and generate substantial costs both in large nominal terms and, ultimately, in the form of loss of output in the real economy. It is not easy to assess the costs of a banking crisis, but some attempts have been made. Hoggarth *et al.* (2002) estimated the cumulative output losses of a banking failure to between 15 and 20 per cent. The average fiscal costs of resolving a banking crisis is estimated to be approximately 13 per cent of GDP (empirical analysis of 40 banking crisis episodes) in the study by Honohan and Klingbiel (2003). The Nordic banking crisis in the early 1990s is estimated to have had a fiscal cost of approximately 8 per cent of GDP. Hence, even if estimates vary it is clear that costs could be substantial.

Cross-border banking and global crisis resolution is certainly a very timely topic. A financial turmoil may quickly become a worldwide concern. Today, there are about 50 cross-border banking groups, of which more than 20 banks have substantial cross-border activity in Europe. A failure in any of these banks would not only be costly but also pose new challenges for authorities and supervisors responsible for financial stability. This problem will remain as long as the regulatory framework, supervision, crisis management and crisis resolution continue to be as internationally uncoordinated as they are today.

Two important lessons can be drawn from the development of the financial markets. First, crises will be costly and thus weaken economic growth. Second, financial crises can have clear cross-border implications. Such a changing environment causes constant challenges both to the functioning and stability of the financial system. This chapter presents today's challenges and future solutions on how to achieve financial stability with cross-border banking. It starts with a section that describes the pros and cons of cross-border financial integration. The main focus will be on European banks but described arguments are, of course, also applicable to a wider international framework. Taking a broad view of cross-border banking, the following section is devoted to the challenges facing authorities in order to secure financial stability with increasing international exposures. The chapter continues with a discussion on how to move forward from today's framework and ends with a conclusion.

Financial integration is positive for the economy

Previously, fragmentation was an excellent comprehensive term when it came to explaining European financial markets; every country had its own rules, institutions and practice for the financial sector. Naturally, variations reflected the special needs of every country. However, with the opening up for integration, banks are now able to reap the benefits arising from increased cross-border activity.

Several factors have been driving the cross-border consolidation. First, financial institutions, particularly large banks, have profited from much easier access to a wider range of markets. This is above all important if the home market is mature. Hence, strong economic growth together with less-developed financial markets in Eastern Europe has certainly acted as a catalyst for the recent cross-border development.

Second, economies of scale and scope are increasing, the larger the market and the better the technology. Technological developments, such as Internet banking and standardisation of instruments, such as credit derivatives, have increased the economies of scale. Third, the massive efforts to create a proper internal market in the EU have resulted in an endeavour to make supervisory methods more uniform. However, such changes are still in their infancy and have not yet resulted in larger regulatory relaxation for most European cross-border banks. Fourth, a larger market and a wider variety of financial tools offer banks an increased opportunity to reduce their common exposure to shocks, by adopting their own individual business strategies. Hence, banks are able to choose their own risk levels and diversify risk according to their needs and undertakings. Similarly, banks can rely on enlarged investment opportunities across activities and borders to improve the expected returns for the same amount of risk. Fifth, the introduction of the euro has facilitated free movement of capital between countries as well as reducing exchange risk between cross-border banks.

Firms and consumers have also reaped benefits from cross-border integration as bank competition has increased the retail services offered by banks. Economies of scale, profits and greater competition not only result in a wider range of investment and financing services but also in more efficient pricing of these services. With that, expanding SMEs, for example, could be expected to gain better access to risk capital and incur lower financing costs, in the same way that a more evolved and integrated market for corporate bonds has led to a lower cost of capital for large companies. Furthermore, both firms and consumers would benefit from lower borrowing costs, a broader range of financial services and better opportunities to diversify their own individual risks. All these efficiency gains could be expected to boost economic growth and help to increase employment in Europe.

Researchers have tried to quantify the efficiency gains from a more integrated European financial market. Guiso *et al.* (2004) present a study of the relation between financial integration and growth. This study showed that European manufacturing firms would be able to boost growth by 0.6–0.7 percentage points a year if they had the same access to financing services as their American counterparts. Another study concluded that increased integration could lead to a long-term rise in real GDP of around 1.1 percentage points and to a 0.5 percentage point higher employment rate with deeper and more liquid securities markets.[1]

Globalisation and the banking industry

Banks have a long tradition of international activities but these have primarily been limited to funding, wholesale markets and servicing large corporations. Additionally, many nationally oriented banks have also had offices in large financial centres such as London and New York. However, the difference now being witnessed by increased integration is how mergers and expansions have created international banks that also target retail customers and SMEs. This introduces potential systemic cross-border importance for these banks in several countries.

In the light of the potential for considerable welfare gains, financial integration has indeed resulted in increased cross-border banking (see Figure 8.1). Today, more than 20 banks have considerable operations in a number of countries. To mention just a few: Unicredit Group has a market share of at least 5 per cent (in terms of total assets) in Italy, Germany, Austria, Bulgaria, the Czech

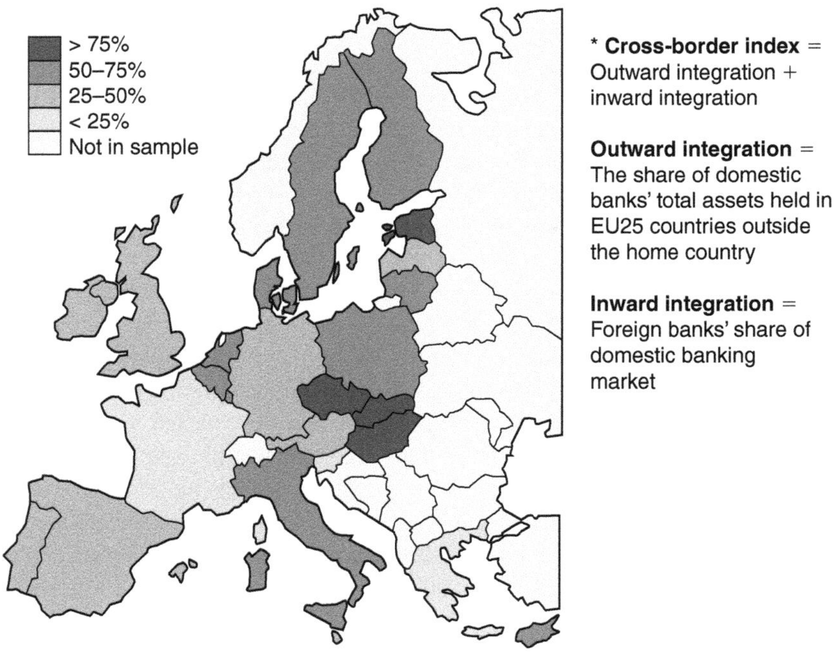

Figure 8.1 Cross-border integration of the banking sector, EU25 countries, year-end 2005* (source: ECB/BSC, Working Group on Banking Development, November 2006).

Republic, Hungary, Poland, Luxembourg, Slovenia and Slovakia.[2] Fortis and ING are major players in the Benelux countries. Barclays and Grupo Santander are important in Spain and the United Kingdom while Erste bank and KBC have considerable operations in Central Europe.[3]

In a historical context, cross-border acquisitions started relatively early in the Nordic and Benelux countries compared with the rest of Europe.[4] As a result of their expansion the four largest Swedish banks, Handelsbanken, Nordea, SEB and Swedbank, now have Northern Europe as their home market. In fact, more than half of the combined assets in these banks are located abroad. In the case of the Nordea Group, which has operations in Denmark, Finland and Norway as well as Sweden, the foreign share amounts to no less than three-quarters.

To sum up, integration and cross-border banking have clearly enhanced the diversification options for banks and improved their resilience to idiosyncratic shocks. As both banks and consumers are expected to benefit from such a process this development is expected to speed up further in the future.

Negative externalities cause instability

However, integration is not without problems. While integration of the financial system is important for economic growth, it also contains inborn instabilities and negative externalities. First, there is a trade off on systemic risk. On the one hand, banks' risk profiles may improve through a greater pool of assets. Better scope for diversification helps banks to handle and diversify risks in loan portfolios. On the other hand, in an integrated market banks are becoming more similar over time and face risks that are more and more the same. This may reduce the benefits of cross-country diversification (De Nicolò and Kwast, 2002; Schröder and Schüler, 2003; Brasili and Vulpes, 2005; Hawkesby *et al.*, 2005). Economic theory cannot say which of the cross-border effects comes out as a winner in a public perspective, however.

A second and very closely related problem is the probability of contagion via the exposure channel and the information channel. The exposure channel refers to a bank's insolvency problem leading to a chain reaction of bank failures in other locations (mainly from real exposures in the interbank market). The second channel concerns how information about one insolvent bank can quickly develop into a general belief that other banks are also having problems.[5] In the worst case, such a rumour or misunderstanding could result in unfavourable adjustments of contracts with other partners and depositor bank runs.

The empirical analyses also show ambiguous results for risk exposures. Amihud *et al.* (2002) argue that cross-border bank mergers do not change the common risk of acquiring banks in any significant way.[6] Instead, whether an acquirer's risk rises or falls seems highly idiosyncratic.

However, the arguments by De Nicolò and Tieman (2006) point in the other direction. In their analysis they find no evidence of a decline in a common risk profile for European banks and insurance companies between 1990 and 2004. In fact, even though individual risk profiles may enhance diversification, *sets* of risk profiles have converged and consequently increased the aggregate risk to both common real and financial shocks. This finding is further strengthened by Schüler's (2002) empirical findings on increased interdependencies and systemic risk potential in European banks during the last 15 years.[7] These results suggest conclusively that integration will not necessarily result in unambiguously positive effects on financial stability.

Challenges for cross-border banking

In response to an integrated financial market and increased number of cross-border retail banks, regulations have become either global (Basle, IAIS, IOSCO) or regional (EU) to make sure of their effectiveness on an international playing field. However, enforcement of these regulations is still rooted in supervisors and authorities using national jurisdictions for legal enforcement (Herring and Litan, 1994). The challenges arising from cross-border cooperation are thus of main concern for national regulators.

A need for efficient regulation

One of the most important challenges from integration is how national authorities must work together to achieve efficiency and stability within an integrated regulatory system. The nature of this challenge is twofold as it becomes, on the one hand, a question of how we can design a legal framework that is flexible enough to fit all countries reasonably well and, on the other hand, how to achieve a sufficiently efficient financial framework.

Regulation is needed at both a national and international level to ensure a stable financial system and adequate consumer protection. However, it should only be used when there is a clear case of market failure and when the benefit of the regulation exceeds its cost to society.[8] Two main motives are usually presented as a basis for banking regulation: the need to protect the economy against systemic shocks and the need for consumer protection. Protection against systemic risk aims to protect the financial system against serious shocks, such as a banking crisis, while the purpose of consumer protection is to protect the individual consumer against various types of exploitation.[9] However, a possible market failure should only be considered a necessary (but not sufficient) condition for regulation. It is also necessary for the regulation's overall benefit to be greater than the cost it entails.

Today, international regulation faces a trade off between a harmonised book of rules (CEBS is currently working to promote the convergence of supervisory rules and practices in the EU) and the cost of overly detailed or inadequate regulation. One of the main regulatory concerns for supervisors and regulatory authorities is, thus, to find a framework that does not impose costly overregulation or national discretion that might hamper financial development.

Most national authorities are convinced that national discretions are valuable and take pride when they are included in the final drafts. However, with such a nationalistic approach there is a clear risk of ending up with the worst of two worlds – very detailed rules internationally and loads of discretions on the national level. This could make it increasingly difficult for the private sector to predict the rules of the game of any new regulation and, hence, undermine private market incentives that limit banking failures and systemic risk.

Supervision and the home-country principle

Information sharing among all authorities involved in a cross-border banking group is also a delicate concern. In the Nordic and Baltic countries, there are six banking groups with significant cross-border activities.[10] The regulatory contacts of these groups include seven supervisors and eight central banks.[11] It is consequently not far-fetched to argue that information sharing will be complicated and slow in such a setting. Cross-border banks may also choose to concentrate different operations in different countries. Extensive information sharing between authorities is then needed to get the full picture of any banking group's total risk. In principle, supervisors of the parent bank should have a full overview of the group but in a crisis, positions may quickly change and complicate international information gathering. A frequent element in the regulatory debate is consequently how we should divide tasks, power and responsibility among countries when it comes to cross-border supervision.

The established EU home-country principle divides the responsibility among supervisors. In short, it specifies that a home country is responsible for regulation and supervision of its national institutions regardless of the location of branches. At the same time, financial stability questions will still be the concern of national authorities. In the case of a group, this means that the home country is responsible for supervising the entire group on a consolidated basis, while the host countries are responsible for their respective subsidiary banks and deposits.

This structure has several dimensions. First, national interests may lead to a home-country bias where domestic institutions are favoured. Second, differences between national regulatory and supervisory regimes may lead to regulatory arbitrage (Kane, 1977). Third, monitoring and supervision may be impaired by the entry of foreign branches or subsidiaries.[12] In the case of a branch structure, host-country authorities tend to lose power to supervise and regulate. Essentially, a host-country authority has to rely on the home country for information on the solvency of the branch while it is politically accountable for its own financial stability. In contrast, regulation and supervision for subsidiaries lie with the countries in which they are chartered. However, because the home country is responsible for the consolidated supervision of the parent banking entity, it may still be difficult to obtain information that reflects the true risk position of a subsidiary. An example of such a situation would be if the parent is experiencing financial difficulties or if the subsidiary is operationally dependent for management or operational support on the parent or other subsidiaries.

Thus, to all intents and purposes, the set-up of the home-country principle is not designed for a fully integrated market. Countries such as New Zealand and Canada have chosen to address this problem by additional restrictions on the operations of foreign branches.[13] The EU, on the other hand, has not considered restrictions as a possible solution, as the benefits from increased integration are considered too important.[14] Consequently, increased harmonisation and removal of barriers is high on the agenda for achieving a competitive European single market. However, as just described, at present this implies a wide gap between legal powers and mandates on the one hand and de facto abilities and responsibilities on the other. Power over branches and subsidiaries are given to the parent bank's home country and it might be unable or unwilling to use them.[15] In turn, host countries are losing powers that they have been willing to use.

The legal distinction between a branch and a subsidiary is also becoming increasingly blurred with banking groups now beginning to organise themselves along business lines instead of legal entities.[16] As the division between branches and subsidiaries within international groups is fading in operational terms, the gap between cross-border banking groups and the national-based responsibilities and supervision of authorities is increasing (Schoenmaker and Oosterloo, 2006). In other words, the operational difference between a group and a company is likely to be very small while the legal and taxation effects may be substantial.

The perception of these problems is likely to induce policy makers to protect their national interests through ring-fencing assets. However, attempts to engage in ring-fencing may be of little value. With assets now being in electronic form they are more easily transferred; in particular between branch entities. Furthermore, ring-fencing could be directly harmful to crisis management. A ban of asset transfers in what appears to be an insolvent subsidiary may in fact cause the failure of the parent bank, which in total had all the vital functions necessary for its subsidiaries' daily business. At best, the main benefit from such a ban may be to establish a legal claim to assets that would otherwise be settled in courts or in negotiations. Such processes would add to the negative externalities as they are not only difficult and expensive but also time-consuming (Eisenbeis, 2006). Either way, the result may be a suboptimal resolution of the crisis, proving more costly for all the countries involved.

Crisis management and conflicts of interest

Another important challenge is the conflicts of interest. In a figurative sense, conflicts may appear at two different levels. First, there may be conflicts within national borders among supervisors, regulators and other authorities. The core argument for increased cooperation on this topic is how banking supervisory functions and crisis management are interrelated. It is not possible to move on one of these without the other (Goodhart, 2004). Naturally, as the number of parties involved increases, the larger the probability that interests in crisis management and resolution diverge. Second, in adding an international dimension to these coordination problems we risk ending up with a complex structure with too many parties with their own national interests. Thus the problem is that supervisors and authorities may have different incentives and act in their own national interests, as pointed out by Bollard (2005).

In general, conflicts of interest occur once the cost of crisis resolution differs between countries. In the case of a cross-border bank with branches in other countries, conflicts of interest certainly concern the question of how far the taxpayers in the home country are willing to go in order to bail out depositors in a host country. This could lead to substantial cross-border transfers. If the reconstruction is successful, the money spent may eventually be recovered by the authorities in the home country. However, this could take considerable time, and a typical requirement is not to bet the taxpayers' money on the wrong horse. Hence, policy makers and taxpayers may be very reluctant to take on such risks in another country. Furthermore, national interests in crisis management may lead to agency problems where countries are reluctant to help banks in other member states even though originating from cross-border externalities caused by financial institutions in their own jurisdiction (Schoenmaker and Osterloo, 2005).

Realising the large costs involved, no country may want to take full responsibility for managing and resolving a crisis. Hence, policy makers will dedicate much effort to take up a position *ex ante* that is favourable in any future negotiations on national responsibility and crisis resolution. The conflicts of interest will thus have a negative impact on the incentives to share information and the conflicts of interest will further aggravate the problems of information sharing displayed in the previous section.

Solving a cross-border crisis will ultimately lead to negotiations. The larger the banking group, the more countries involved and the more important the bank is to the financial system in a country, the higher the stakes for the individual country and the tougher the negotiations. Hence, any cross-border negotiation may be both time constrained and costly and delaying tactics are likely to be common.[17] In fact, measures may be taken too late or not at all. In the worst case, this is a recipe for becoming a widespread systemic event unless there are prior agreements. With the present supervisory set-up there is a considerable risk that the conflicts of interest will add to the time necessary to achieve a joint assessment. And time is a scarce resource, especially in crisis management.

Differences in deposit guarantee schemes

Suboptimal crisis management may also be driven by differences in deposit guarantee schemes (DGS). A DGS is a vital part of the safety net for banks, with deposits being insured in the event of a bank default; depositors are protected from losses and banks reduce their risk of a bank run. Hence, these insurance schemes not only act as consumer protection but also play an important role for financial stability. Yet, despite this important role in the financial safety net, their differences and accompanying effects on cross-border banking is often overlooked in the financial stability debate.

The European Deposit Guarantee Schemes Directive (94/19/EC), which was established in 1994, was an attempt to balance the fact that not all member states had any deposit insurance schemes in place and that those already in use differed greatly. With the hope that schemes would be harmonised over time this directive provided not only the basic features of an acceptable insurance coverage but also set out how deposits should be covered. Specifically, the deposit insurance should cover at least the first 20,000 euros in anyone's account and responsibility should be divided according to the home and host principle.[18]

However, in the light of increasing cross-border activities it is far from radical to conclude that this directive of minimum requirements was not designed for a fully integrated market.[19] In fact, it seems rather to constitute a potential breeding ground for financial instability. First, there is a reason to be concerned about the structure of these systems. At present, a country is not limited to only one DGS but may have more than one scheme for different types of institutions. The terms and details of these schemes are not prescribed by the directive but left to the discretion of each individual member country. These include account coverage, level, ownership, funding, establishment of reserve funds and government support. Second, countries differ greatly in their treatment of troubled institutions and creditors as well as in their efficiency of resolving insolvent banks at a minimum cost to the host country.[20] In general, funds are designed so that deficits in the fund are financed by the banks from future fees. However, these financing schemes are rarely sufficient in the case of a large bank default. In such an event depositors would have to rely on governmental interventions that eventually would hit the taxpayers in one way or another.[21]

As cross-border banking proceeds, differences between schemes may be magnified and complicate the search for a joint solution. Equally important, DGS may generate significant costs and cost shifting when a cross-border banking crisis needs to be resolved. As it stands today, governments would have to intervene for larger systemic problems and this again raises the important question of how far taxpayers are willing to go in order to bail out depositors in countries other than their own.[22]

With increased cross-border banking the patchwork set of deposit insurance schemes not only increases the number of authorities involved but also the number of scheme-related negotiations needed in supervision, crisis management and crisis resolution. Ultimately, differences in the roles and DGS may lead to coordination problems for crisis management. The variations in roles and intervention even among the Nordic countries are substantial. In Norway and Denmark, the DGS can under certain circumstances act as a provider of financial support in public administration, either to allow a bank to continue its operations or to facilitate a merger. In Sweden and Finland the DGS has only a pay-box function.

Differences in approaches to bankruptcy resolution and priority of claims also differ among the countries. In Sweden, the DGS can only pay out after a court has declared the bank in bankruptcy. On the contrary, in Denmark, Finland and Norway the guarantee can be activated by suspension of payments or bankruptcy. In the case of suspension of payments, the guarantee is activated by the supervisor in Finland and Norway, while Denmark leaves room for an independent decision by the DGS board. Hence, the outcome of a cross-border banking failure will be dependent on the bank's home country. In some countries it may be the supervisor that controls the bank, possibly seeking a merger solution or a DGS for public administration, while in other counties the owners remain in control for a much longer period. Going forward, the different scope and levels of the DGS, coupled with ambiguous approaches to controlling systemic risk, seems fraught when taken together with both agency and conflicts of interest problems (Kane, 2003).

Conflicts on burden sharing and crisis resolution

Another important concern is how large variations in the roles of the DGS may complicate burden sharing. Some of the coordination issues are likely to be addressed in *ex ante* agreements. However, in order to ensure that owners take the first loss and that the private sector contributes to the resolution, governments may also rely on suboptimal ad hoc negotiations. In a cross-border setting, Frexias (2003) shows that such *ex post* negotiations lead to under-provision of recapitalisations as countries generally understate their share of the problem.[23]

To avoid *ex post* negotiations one could opt for a burden-sharing formula according to some keys (such as relative GDP size, ECB capital ratio and bank assets). The most important question for regulators in elaborating such a process is what procedures to use when deciding on these keys. An example of this difficult balance is to decide whether keys should be fixed or take into account the geographic spread of a bank's business. To achieve the latter countries would have to agree upon uniform standards for assessing a bank's relevance to the financial system of a country. In a constantly changing banking landscape this could turn out to be a very tricky task.

Also, if governments take a direct role in the crisis management, the differences between DGSs complicate crisis management. Even if a DGS may not be the first usable solution in a large cross-border banking failure, the usage of a DGS has to be included as part of the alternative costs in crisis resolution. The more insolvent an institution is before it is legally closed, the greater are the losses to the insurance funds and to those who have to refinance them. In Denmark, Norway and Finland insolvency assessments by the supervisor automatically lead to an activation of the DGS. In Sweden, they do not. This difference exposes the host-country insurance funds to regulatory risks as the burden-sharing resolution process partly depends on the activation procedures of the home country.

The uncertainty of burden sharing seems to slow down authorities' ability and willingness to act in a crisis. On top of this, there is always the possibility that strained banks will search for the most favourable support among the countries involved. Such competitive distortions may undermine financial stability by provoking higher risk taking by banks. Further, if depositors are protected by a guarantee, they will punish their bank less for risk-taking behaviour and thus, reducing market discipline (Merton, 1977).

Differences in insurance-system design may also affect international depositor decisions on the placements of their funds (Huizinga and Nicodeme, 2002).

In a cross-border setting, conflicts of interest may further complicate the matter and it is also possible that the authorities in a host country may refer its depositors to the home-country authorities, without taking any responsibility. As already argued in the section on conflicts of interest, this raises the important question of the willingness of home-country taxpayers to bail out the depositors in a host country.

As argued by Stern and Feldman (2004), a systemic bank is regarded as one that is 'too big to fail'. However, with cross-border banking it may also be the case that a bank in some sense is 'too big to save'. Today, there is an apparent risk that the responsibility will fall solely on the country that is most affected by the crisis. Without cooperation and explicit rules we cannot reap the benefits from internationalisation. Instead, every risk of a banking failure is reduced to a non-cooperative game where every country tries to minimise its own contribution rather than minimising the total costs. Such behaviour resembles at best a chicken race and at worse a Prisoners' dilemma. However, irrespective of the game, all players tend to end up losing.

Alternatives for the supervision of international groups

As just outlined, there are many challenges to overcome in developing a framework that can meet both the need for financial stability and continued financial integration.

First, there is an apparent need for better information sharing, cooperation and coordination between authorities in different countries. A well-established routine for information collection and distribution fosters both confidence and trust among supervisors. One way to facilitate such cooperation in times of crisis is to set up different memoranda of understanding (MoU). The 2005 EU-wide MoU on cooperation and increased information sharing among finance ministries, central banks and Banking Supervisory Authorities is such an example. Additionally, a number of bilateral and regional MoU has also been agreed upon. All MoUs are important tools in establishing contact networks and a common language, which would be helpful in a crisis.[24] However, because of their lack of a binding legal status they are hardly sufficient for further development of the handling of cross-border banking. Furthermore, practical issues such as that, in the extreme, there may be up to 81 separate entities involved in agreeing a joint assessment, do not speak for the MoUs as an optimal long-run solution. Instead, they should be considered as a first step, and later as a complement, in facilitating international monitoring and supervision.

Second, there is a need for common rules and less national discretion when implementing EU directives. Too much gold-plating leaves room for individual interpretations and solutions. Hence, a basic principle in the regulatory process should always be to question national solutions.

With the establishment of the Lamfalussy process, EU members have put great emphasis on smoothing the process for making new legislation and for improving its quality.[25] Today, attention has turned increasingly to implementation and to the goal of supervisory convergence in the EU and the role of the three Level 3 supervisory networks.[26] At this level, the committees make sure that the common legislation is uniform. However, doubts have been raised about the extent to which the Lamfalussy approach is really achieving its preset goals, and the present allocation of supervisory responsibilities for international groups is being challenged.

Future alternatives for supervision

Given that the present achievements still require an increasing degree of convergence in supervisory practices and cooperation it is likely that we have to look for future alternatives for supervision. Today, the current system may be acceptable but far from optimal.

The first consideration to put forward in the supervisory debate is whether to opt for 'regulatory competition' or a 'harmonisation of laws' in the regulatory framework on financial crises management and resolution.

Competition between regulators may, first of all, increase the possibility that the implemented jurisdiction will offer the best set of laws (Tiebout, 1956). Furthermore, legislative competition may also bring overall benefits by improving the understanding of the effects of alternative regulation to similar problems.

However, as presented throughout this chapter, the challenges with increased competition among regulators in cross-border banking are many: *ex ante*, many regulators and different regulatory regimes weaken supervision and obstruct early intervention; *ex post*, inconsistent and uncoordinated competition among resolution authorities heightens legal uncertainty and undermines an efficient regulatory playing field. Hence, cross-border banks will be directly affected by an increased regulatory burden stemming from the costs entailed by continuous updates and understanding of all the national legal variations.

Furthermore, given that banking crises are uncommon, the risks of lax regulation and supervision cannot be ignored. All the more so as the difficulty of discounting future costs from a potential financial crisis may result in short-sightedness. Ultimately, such an ineffective crisis management and uncoordinated supervision with nationalistic financial interests could even result in a 'race to the bottom' (e.g. Stigler, 1971; Markusen *et al.*, 1993, 1995). Additional downsides such as increased transaction costs and the risk of losing scale economy profits also speak in favour of continuous harmonised regulation and supervision.

A harmonisation of laws is, however, nuanced by nature and four alternatives for supervision may be presented as solutions to the challenges just explored (cf. Schoenmaker and Oosterloo, 2005).[27] The first two options assume a national mandate with or without some form of cooperation while the others assume a European mandate and jurisdiction.

The first solution has close points of similarity to the current system as it proposes to use supervisory colleges. The idea is to create specific standing committees for each individual cross-border banking group with representatives from the relevant supervisors. Today, the Level 3 operational networks of the Committee of European Banking Supervisors (CEBS) can be considered as a first step in this direction. However, although this is a good start, this supervisory framework could quickly become very complex and scattered. Not only could there be considerable debate on which supervisors to include in which college but also that colleges could differ in their supervision of banks. There is also a risk that, in order to achieve consensus between committee members, guidelines end up being based on the lowest common denominator. Even a mix of current practices is a possible outcome. However, this does not imply the creation of an efficient supervisor. Additionally, there is yet no effective mechanism to ensure that agreed guidelines are enforced on the national level.

A second solution is to appoint the home country as the lead supervisor with full responsibility for the EU-wide operations, both branches and subsidiaries. This option implies that the home supervisor keep its national mandate as well as being the consolidated supervisor. In this case, the home-country supervisor is responsible for information gathering, approving capital and liquidity allocation, and approving and formulating joint assessments of the cross-border institutions. Furthermore, the home-country authorities have the responsibilities for managing and resolving the crisis for the whole banking group. With increasing emphasis on consolidated supervision, this seems to be where Europe is heading at present.[28]

The lead supervisor solution ranks high in enhancing efficiency through vertical convergence. However, this model is not without flaws. A general problem is that it does poorly with respect to financial stability. A national mandate neither leads nor encourages a supervisor to incorporate cross-border externalities of a banking failure in its decision making. Hence, a lead supervisor model does not solve the dilemma of giving one country the mandate and opportunity to act, while letting the other country hold on to its responsibility for financial stability. The accountability problem also remains as the impact of a failure or crisis may create mismatched incentives and conflicts of interests. Additionally, a lead supervision model could also affect the level playing field for cross-border banking groups.

Weighing the pros and cons of the lead supervisor model leads us to conclude that it will work best for banks with limited cross-border activities that are insignificant to the host country. Consequently, with a growing importance of cross-border banking it does not present a long-lasting solution to the challenges of the current system.

A third solution and a possible stride forward is then to opt for an extension of the lead supervisor model by giving the home country a European mandate. Such a mandate would require the home country to take the other countries concerned into account in its assessments and decisions. It is, however, not clear how such a solution would work in practice as it would have to consider further appropriate levels of (de)centralisation, geographical reach, financial integration, deposit insurance schemes and fiscal mechanisms.

In order not to be too detailed only a few brief comments are given on these problems. First, a European mandate causes a delicate trade off between the benefits of financial supervision being executed at the local level and dealing with cross-border externalities. Centralisation of supervision may be desirable for financial stability where there is extensive cross-border banking. In this case, one could think of a system of 'European Financial Supervisors' working closely together with the national level (Schoenmaker, 2003; Vives, 2001). Such a system could, for example, develop from the Level 3 committees in the Lamfalussy approach. However, any European mandate would call for continuous work to achieve a well-functioning Single Market. In particular, legal and taxation systems, now rooted at a national level, would need to be further harmonised (Dermine, 2003).

The fourth and last example on how to move forward with supervision and crisis resolution is the supra-national solution. In this case a common international body with a European mandate conducts all supervision of cross-border activities. Advantages of setting up a new agency are that it can be transnational from the start and set up principles for equitable treatment of the partner countries and burden-sharing, should there be a cost. This will increase the effectiveness of supervision and reduce the regulatory burdens for firms in substantial cross-border activities.[29]

In a European context, such a body would imply the creation of a European Organisation for Financial Supervision (EOFS). Aligned with the EU principle of subsidiarity, a centralised supervisory system like EOFS is only necessary for major cross-border institutions. Remaining banking activity, such as small national banks and banks active in a few countries, could use a similar structure to what we have today. Supervisory colleges should also be used to deepen cross-border cooperation at the regional level.

One can argue that it would be next to impossible to expect countries to give up parts of their sovereignty and maybe it is, at least in the immediate near future. However, as soon as we look further ahead it is definitely a more realistic solution. A framework for regulatory cooperation already exists today. And, existing MoUs show that supervisory cooperation is possible and already in place (even though they are not legally binding).

Of course, the creation of the EOFS is a long-term project that requires a long and flexible development process. Thus, in its first phase the EOFS needs to function more like a non-regulatory central bank than a traditional supervisor. Initially, the powers of the EOFS should be limited and the main focus should be on gathering information on the different cross-border groups. This collection process would probably take place in collaboration with the national authorities. Then, with the information acquired, the EOFS should produce a unified assessment and oversee the activities and risks of these banking groups. All other powers, such as licensing, regulations and intervention would still remain the responsibility of the national supervisors.

If it is successful and proves its merits, the role of the EOFS can gradually be extended. However, continuous movement from being a renowned speaking partner to full supervisory powers will require a high level of operational independency and integrity for the EOFS. It should be a separate agency and neither national authorities nor other European bodies, such as the Commission and the ECB, should be part of its organisational structure. This independence could be achieved by making sure that the EOFS is established directly by all member states and with the obligation to report directly to the European Parliament.

At first glance, this proposal may seem very similar to our current set-up with a consolidated supervisory model and Level 3 committees such as CEBS. However, even though tasks overlap there are at least two important differences. First, even if a consolidated supervisor is responsible for the group it still answers to the home-land constituents. Second, CEBS is more of a regulator than a supervisor, as the main task of CEBS is to advise the Commission and work to harmonise supervision, rules and practices.

It could also be argued that the largest threat to a supra-national body such as the EOFS is time and money. The EOFS is a long-term project that requires all member states to strive towards the same goal. This could, of course, be a tricky task if supervisors and authorities in both home and host countries continue to operate according to their own interests. Nevertheless, the European Union has good precedents for establishing a new joint organisation. First, we have done this before. The European Monetary Institute, the forerunner to the ECB, is a good example on this matter. Second, we are aware of the fact that things do take time. One of the underlying long-term principles in the EU is that integration can not be introduced too hastily. The forecast is therefore that we have every possibility to achieve a solution which brings us closer to more common and convergent EU supervision.

Conclusion

The European banking landscape is constantly changing and ongoing financial integration gives rise to increased cross-border penetration of inter-bank markets and payment systems. Today, a number of major European banks have expanded by acquiring banks abroad.

Increased cross-border banking has positive effects on the economy overall, as it substantially enhances efficiency, reduces risk exposures, and thereby contributes to economic growth. However, it also raises questions of what to do about the supervisory structures. Above all, a number of challenges that concern the organisation of supervision and crisis management have to be resolved.

This chapter argues that the present system design is likely to result in high costs that offset the efficiency benefits of cross-border banking. To that end, financial integration includes more aspects than just how to design supervisory structures for cross-border institutions. For example, questions on how to establish proper arrangements for deposit guarantee schemes also need to be considered in the same context.

To date, little has been done to tackle the potential dangers of the current structure and a cross-border banking failure may consequently threaten financial stability in more than one country. Hence, to provide a more efficient structure, supervisors should adapt to market developments and not the other way around.

Several solutions are presented in this chapter but arguments are favouring a single point of contact for all supervision, crisis management and crisis resolution.

So far, the ongoing work on financial stability can build on today's institutional arrangements. However, given the acceleration in the dynamic of integration, this solution is unlikely to result in a sufficient degree of convergence in supervisory practices and cooperation among supervisors in the long run. Instead, a long-term solution will require regulators to show courage and devotion to finding new ways to tackle the negative externalities a crisis would involve. By implementing a European body such as the EOFS, we approach a solution that not only mitigates but also eliminates many of the inherent challenges of the present system. Still, considering that financial integration is not limited by European borders we have to bring forward the challenges in a global context. So even if it is difficult to propose a similar solution at a global level it should still be in everyone's interest to move towards enhanced cooperation between supervisory authorities.

Thus, it is only when the regulatory framework starts matching the actual structures of the financial market, that we can truly minimise the expected social costs of financial crises. And, given that the process towards a common supranational body will be a demanding and gradual process we need to start now. It would be highly unfortunate if the appropriate measures have to be put in place after a major financial crisis arrives.

Notes

1 Quantification of the Macro-Economic Impact of Integration of EU Financial Markets: Final Report to The European Commission – Directorate-General for the Internal Market, London Economics, November 2002.

2 All data on cross-border banking market shares are presented as year-end 2005 figures.

3 Predominantly in Hungary, the Czech Republic and Slovakia.

4 The aftermath of the banking crisis in the early 1990s was certainly one important reason for this new path. After a tough consolidation process the only way ahead for the remaining banks was to search for new markets in other locations. Furthermore, consolidation had increased the size of these banks so they were able to compete in the international market.

5 Of course, imperfect information accentuates such an event (De Bandt and Hartmann, 2000).

6 Data on mergers and acquisitions between 1985 and 1998.

7 Schüler (2002) only investigates the contagion channel for systemic risk. Hence, when an initial shock causes one bank to fail and this leads to the failure of other banks.

8 A market failure occurs when those trading in the market have no incentive to ensure that prices and quantities correspond to those on a free and competitive market. Different types of market failure may arise from negative externalities, public good consumption, asymmetric information, imperfect competition and natural monopolies. For a more detailed discussion on the need for regulation see 'Economic Reasons for Regulation in the Financial Sector' in the Riksbank's Financial Stability Report 1/2005.

9 With systemic risk a key market failure is negative externalities arising from an information failure (Mishkin, 1995). An information failure of this sort may result in adverse selection and moral hazard.

10 These banks are: Nordea, SEB, Swedbank, SHB, Danske Bank and Kaupting.

11 The Bank of Lithuania also has supervisory responsibility.

12 At an aggregate level cross-border development in the EU 15 Member States is equally divided between branches and subsidiaries. Expanding cross-border banks preferred branches (51 per cent) to subsidiaries (49 per cent) in 2005. However, figures hide significant differences both between member states and inside countries and across institutions. An example of such a difference is Unicredit. In 2003, Unicredit had 70.7 per cent of their assets in branches in the EU15. In 2005, they changed their branch development in this area to 8 per cent.

13 New Zealand basically prohibits foreign branches by requiring that every systemically important bank is an own legal entity. Canada had a similar law until 1999. Today, a foreign branch structure is allowed but accompanied by substantial restrictions.

14 See Financial Stability Report 1/2007 for further details on this argument.

15 Schüler (2002) argues that there may be incentive conflicts between home and hosts as home-country regulators might want to disguise or delay information about a poorly performing branch. Supervisory conflicts may also be deepened when the systemic relevance of banks differs between countries.

16 This type of concentration may lead banks to reap benefits from both specialisation and scale.

17 Brouwer *et al.* (2003), for example, argue for authorities to 'buy time' by offering financial help to failing banks in an event of a crisis. However, they do not present how this should be solved beyond the ELA given by central banks and even this solution run the risk of ending up in a negotiation process where both national and international interests may diverge.

18 The deposit insurance should also exclude coverage of inter-bank deposits and may exclude other liabilities at the discretion of the national government. The directive also allows for co-insurance of liabilities. Depositors in branches in countries other than the home country may be covered by the host country as its option.

19 Note that cross-border retail banking was still in its infancy at the time so potential cross-border problems were not given high priority in the shaping of the directive.

20 See Eisenbeis and Kaufman (2006) for more details on these differences.

21 Governments could either lend money to the DGS or provide direct compensation to depositors on behalf of the fund.

22 No DGS is adapted to address a troubled institution in any of the major cross-border groups.

23 Such a scenario would lead to a possible free-rider problem where countries that do not sign up to burden sharing would nevertheless profit from it, as the stability of the European financial system is a public good.

24 Mayes and Vesala (1998) argue that the sharing of home/host responsibilities during the movement towards a single market is possible partly because of MoUs on information sharing. Opinions on this matter are, however, diverging and Mayes (2006) argues, for example, that predetermined responsibility and obligations in a MoU may still cause agency problems and conflicts once a cross-border crisis arrives.

25 Although these were implemented for the banking sector in 2003, the legislative process has long been considered too slow and too stiff to deal with the rapid changes in the financial sector adequately. Four regulatory levels are now included in the regulatory process.

26 CESR, CEIOPS and CEBS.

27 Schoenmaker and Oosterloo (2005) also present a fifth solution based on a host supervisory structure with a national mandate. However, as this solution greatly resembles autarky I am of the opinion that this is not a credible solution for the development of a European Single Market.

28 The European Financial Services Round Table (EFR, 2004) has argued for a lead supervisory solution to provide a more coherent supervisory framework in the EU.

The supervisory process should also include supervisory colleges with home-country supervisors as they have a better understanding of the local market. However, as the powers of the home supervisor in such colleges are not binding, actual involvement of host authorities becomes very limited in practice.

29 Schüler and Heinemann (2005) have estimated substantial cost-efficiency gains with a European supervisor. Assuming that all economies of scale profits can be realised an EU supervisor could reduce institutional supervisory staff (in terms of labour costs) by an approximate 15 per cent.

References

Amihud, Y., DeLong, G.L. and Saunders, A. (2002) The Effects of Cross-Border Bank Mergers on Bank Risk Value, *Journal of International Money and Finance*, 21, 857–877.

Bollard, A. (2005) Being a Responsible Host: Supervising Foreign-Owned Banks, in D.D. Evanoff and G.G. Kaufman (eds), *Systemic Financial Crises: Resolving Large Bank Insolvencies*, World Scientific, Singapore, pp. 3–16.

Brasili, A. and Vulpes, G. (2005) *Co-movement in EU Banks' Fragility: A Dynamic Factor Model Approach*, Working Paper.

Brouwer, H., Hebbink, G. and Wesseling, S. (2003) A European Approach to Banking Crises, in D. Mayes and A. Liuksila (eds), *Who Pays for Bank Insolvency?*, Palgrave, Basingstoke, pp. 205–221.

De Bandt, O. and Hartmann, P. (2000) *Systemic Risk: A Survey*, ECB Working Paper, No. 35.

De Nicolò, M. and Kwast, G. (2002) Systemic Risk and Financial Consolidation: Are They Related?, *Journal of Banking and Finance*, 26, 861–880.

De Nicolò, M. and Tieman, A. (2006) *Economic Integration and Financial Stability: A European Perspective*, IMF Working Paper.

Dermine, J. (2003) Banking in Europe: Past, Present and Future, in V. Gaspar, P. Hartmann and O. Sleijpen (eds), *The Transformation of the European Financial System*, ECB, Frankfurt, pp. 31–96.

Eisenbeis, R. (2006) *Home Country versus Cross-Border Negative Externalities in Large Banking Organization Failures and How to Avoid Them*, Federal Reserve Bank of Atlanta, Working Paper 2006-18.

Eisenbeis, R. and Kaufman, G. (2006) *Cross-Border Banking: Challenges for Deposit Insurance and Financial Stability in the European Union*, Federal Reserve Bank of Atlanta, Working Paper 2006-15.

European Commission (2002) *Quantification of the Macro-Economic Impact of Integration of EU Financial Markets: Final Report to the European Commission*, Directorate-General for the Internal Market, London Economics.

European Financial Services Round Table (2004) *Towards a Lead Supervisor for Cross Border Financial Institutions in the European Union*, Brussels.

Frexias, X. (2003) Crisis Management in Europe, in J. Kremers, D. Schoenmaker and P.J. Wierts (eds), *Financial Supervision in Europe*, Edward Elgar, Cheltenham, pp. 102–119.

Goodhart, C. (2004) *Some New Directions for Financial Stability*, Per Jacobson Lecture, Bank for International Settlements, Basle.

Guiso, L., Jappelli, T., Padula, M. and Pagano, M. (2004) *Financial Market Integration and Economic growth in the EU*, Centre for Economic Policy Research, CEPR Discussion Paper Series, No. 4395.

Hawkesby, C., Marsh, I. and Stevens, I. (2005) *Comovements in the Prices of Securities Issued by Large Complex Financial Institutions*, Bank of England Working Paper, No. 256.

Herring, R. and Litan, R. (1994) *Financial Regulation in a Global Economy*, Brookings Institution, Washington, DC.

Hoggarth, G., Reis, R., Saporta, V. and Street, T. (2002), Costs of Banking System Instability: Some Empirical Evidence, *Journal of Banking and Finance*, 26, 825–855.

Honohan, P. and Klingbiel, D. (2003) The Fiscal Cost Implications of an Accommodating Approach to Banking Crises, *Journal of Banking and Finance*, 26, 825–855.

Huizinga, H. and Nicodeme, G. (2002) *Deposit Insurance and International Bank Deposits*, European Commission Economic Papers, No. 164.

Hupkes, E. (2003) Learning Lessons and Implementing a New Approach to Bank Insolvency Resolution in Switzerland, in D. Mayes and A. Liuksila (eds), *Who Pays for Bank Insolvency?*, Palgrave, Basingstoke, pp. 224–271.

Kane, E. (1977) Good Intentions and Unintended Evil: The Case Against Selective Credit Allocation, *Journal of Money, Credit and Banking*, 9, 55–69.

Kane, E. (2003) What Kind of Multinational Deposit-Insurance Arrangements Might Best Enhance World Welfare?, *Pacific-Basin Finance Journal*, 11, 413–428.

Markusen, J., Morey, E. and Olewiler, N. (1993) Environmental Policy When Market Structure and Plant Locations are Endogenous, *Journal of Environmental Economics and Management*, 24, 69–86.

Markusen, J., Morey, E. and Olewiler, N. (1995) Competition in Regional Environmental Policies When Plant Locations are Endogenous, *Journal of Public Economics*, 56, 55–77.

Mayes, D. (2006) Financial Stability in a World of Cross-Border Banking: Nordic and Antipodean Solutions to the Problem of Responsibility Without Power, *Journal of Banking Regulation*, 8, 20–39.

Mayes, D. and Vesala, J. (1998) *On the Problems of Home Country Control*, Bank of Finland, Working Paper.

Merton, R. (1977) An Analytical Derivation of the Cost of Deposit Insurance and Loan Guarantees, *Journal of Banking and Finance*, 1, 3–11.

Mishkin, F. (1995) Comment on Systemic Risk, in G. Kaufman (ed.), *Banking, Financial Markets and Systemic Risk*, Greenwich, CT: JAI Press, pp. 31–45.

Schoenmaker, D. (2003) *Financial Supervision: From National to European?*, Amsterdam: NIBE-SVV.

Schoenmaker, D. and Oosterloo, S. (2005) Financial Supervision in an Integrating Europe: Measuring Cross-Border Externalities, *International Finance*, 8, 1–27.

Schoenmaker, D. and Oosterloo, S. (2006) Financial Supervision in Europe: Do We Need a New Architecture?, *Cahier Comte Boël 12*, European League for Economic Cooperation, Brussels.

Schröder, M. and Schüler, M. (2003) *Systemic Risk in European Banking – Evidence from Bivariate GARCH Models*, ZEW Discussion Paper 2003-11.

Schüler, M. (2002) The Threat of Systemic Risk in European Banking, *Quarterly Journal of Business and Economics*, 41, 145–165.

Schüler, M. and Heinemann, F. (2005) *The Costs of Supervisory Fragmentation in Europe*, ZEW Discussion Paper 05-01.

Stern, G. and Feldman, R. (2004) *Too Big to Fail: The Hazards of Big Bank Bailouts*, Brookings Institution, Washington, DC.

Stigler, G. (1971) The Economics Theory of Regulation, *Bell Journal of Economics*, 2 (1), 3–21.

Sveriges Riksbank (2005) *Financial Stability Report*, 1/2005, Stockholm.
Sveriges Riksbank (2007) *Financial Stability Report*, 1/2007, Stockholm.
Tiebout, C. (1956) A Pure Theory of Local Expenditure, *Journal of Political Economy*, 64, 416–424.
Vives, X. (2001) Restructuring Financial Regulation in the European Monetary Union, *Journal of Financial Services Research*, 19, 57–82.

COMMENTS BY GEOFFREY WOOD

This is a most useful chapter on an important subject. In these comments I first set out what I see as the main arguments and conclusions of the chapter, and then touch on some minor points of disagreement and interpretation before turning to my two main concerns. These concerns are first that the chapter risks confusing feasibility (and feasibility only under optimistic assumptions at that) with usefulness; and second, that by neglecting the importance of bank closure rules Dr Persson makes the problems he addresses appear more difficult than they actually are.

The chapter is prompted by the increased internationalisation of banking. Banks have become much more internationally diversified in their activities, not necessarily covering more countries but certainly carrying out many more activities than was the case even quite recently in the countries in which they have a presence. This brings all sorts of efficiency benefits through increased banking competition, but it also brings an increased risk of cross-border spread of bank failures and banking crises. Our present system for preventing such events, and for handling them should they happen, is unsatisfactory, as it is based on nation states and in principle downplays or ignores cross-border problems. Dr Persson considers a range of proposals to deal with this. He concludes that we must create a European body, a 'European Organisation of Financial Supervisors' (EOFS) to deal with these cross border issues, for 'it is only when the regulatory framework starts matching the actual structure of the financial market that we can truly minimise the expected social costs of financial crises.'

Minor matters

In this section I consider some differences (disagreements is in general too strong a word) with Dr Persson, and where I would qualify what he says at points in his chapter not central to his conclusions.

First, in thinking what to do about banking instability we must be careful not to overstate its costs. This is not to deny that these can be substantial. But we should remember that the estimates Dr Persson quotes are not only imprecise, as he recognises, but have an upward bias. The reason for this bias is that banking crises generally occur at the end of booms, and these booms are often associated with the kind of banking-sector carelessness that, the moment times become less good, leads to banking problems. Without the risks banks ran (and got away with) in the boom there would have been no boom, or at the least a smaller boom. As the banking problems are a consequence of bank risk taking which amplified the previous boom, some of the benefits of the boom should be offset against the costs of the crash.

Dr Persson also suggests that 'financial crises will be costly and thus weaken economic growth'. If by growth he means the long-term trend his statement is not self-evidently true.

He says that 'the introduction of the Euro has facilitated the free movement of capital between countries'. Maybe it has, but there is some evidence that exchange-rate flexibility does not impede international capital flows (Mills and Wood, 1993). That it has 'reduced exchange risk between cross-border banks' does seem likely, however.

For the effects of 'financial market integration' on welfare he quotes two radically different estimates – one says that 'European manufacturing firms would be able to boost growth by 0.6–0.7 percentage points a year' and the other that there could be a 'long-term rise in real GDP of around 1.1 percentage points'. Not only are these two numbers wildly different, the former being a change to a permanently higher rate of growth, but surely the former is implausibly large. Not only is it a big change for a mature and developed economy, but it would make the EU accelerate ever more above the United States. The reason that is implausible is that the benefits supposedly come from having a capital market rather more like that of the United States.[1]

We also need to consider rather carefully the meaning of market integration. It is easy for an economist to think of that as measured very easily – convergence of prices shows more integration. But that, as George Stigler (1967) pointed out, is at best too simple and quite possibly is wrong. A movement closer together of prices can be associated with a looser relationship between changes in prices. The example that Stigler gave was of narrower cross-country interest-rate spreads being asserted to show increased capital market integration, whereas all they actually showed was reduced costs of transmitting information. So it is actually important to consider both how we can measure capital market integration, and how we can demonstrate that it is happening in the eurozone. Dr Persson does neither of these things.

And finally in this section I note two important omissions. The kind of cross-border banking that concerns Dr Persson is perhaps new in the EU, but it is certainly not new. British banks for many years conducted their business across the British Empire. How to handle financial crises would be hard to learn from that experience, for there was no crisis to learn from – but it would be worth seeing what could be learned about crisis prevention. Further, capital markets can be closely connected with no cross-border banking at all. They can be integrated through, for example, bond markets. Note as an example the close connection between movements in US and UK bond yields in the late nineteenth century.

Challenges with cross-border banking

This section of his chapter starts by urging the need for an 'integrated regulatory system'. Now we need to think carefully. There are (at least) two distinct aspects of cross-border banking. One is competition, the other stability. Why might 'integrated' regulation contribute to the latter? Whether it contributes to or impedes the former is not central to Dr Persson's arguments, but there are a few remarks on this below.

His arguments for integrated regulation are not compelling. He says that without it we might end up with detailed rules internationally and much national discretion. That he says is bad. The first part may be, but national discretion surely allows regulatory competition. That can be desirable if it prevents regulatory excess – and it does not necessarily lead to the fabled 'race to the bottom', for customers of banks are surely interested in how sound their banks are likely to be. An example of how important these effects can be is the introduction, after Enron, of Sarbanes-Oxley in the United States. This is widely regarded as having diverted much business to the London markets, and there is no evidence that London market regulation was eased to attract such business. The example of Sarbanes-Oxley is now frequently used to show the dangers of burdensome regulation.

The home-country principle is criticised, likely to dilute regulatory powers as banks no longer have an obvious 'home' in any business sense but retain one only in law. For example, a bank's home could be Luxembourg but most of its business could be in France. But does that matter?

It matters if a supervisory authority may need to muster capital to inject into a troubled bank. Conflicts of interest may arise in a crisis, he suggests, as a result of the costs of 'managing and resolving a crisis'. There will be attempts to dodge responsibility. This will, he argues, and surely correctly, slow down the response to a problem and thus quite likely increase the costs of solving it.

So there may be a source of problems there. It is, though, important not to overstate these problems. Indeed, I will argue in the concluding section of these comments that these problems may be kept to a close to trivial level.

Moving on to deposit insurance ('deposit guarantee schemes' in the term of the chapter): national differences are criticised as being a 'potential breeding ground for financial instability'. National differences may affect competition, especially in the eurozone where there is one currency and different means of financing the schemes. But how do national differences promote instability? Badly designed schemes do – we saw that in the United Kingdom with the problems surrounding the Northern Rock debacle – but schemes can be different without all but one being bad. Certainly there are crucial core features – speed of payout and certainty of what is covered, for example – but beyond that differences might well be appropriate for different national banking structures.

In the light of these concerns, what does he propose? He examines in turn a supervisory college, a lead supervisor and a common European supervisory body. Allowing competition among supervisors he dismisses. As remarked above, his arguments dismissing competition are not compelling. What about the approaches in which he sees merit? Supervisory colleges would comprise 'specific standing committees for each individual cross-border banking group'. Some of his objections do not seem to me persuasive – that colleges could supervise different banks differently does not seem self-evidently wrong to me – but his crucial objection is surely correct: there is no mechanism to ensure national enforcement of such international decisions.

He looks on the concept of a lead supervisor with more favour. In this system the home country would be responsible for the 'EU-wide' operations. But as he acknowledges, surely correctly, this is a neat and efficient system which is best designed for handling banks with modest cross-border activity, and of no great significance in any country except its home one. For such a system would be inclined to downplay problems outside home, and the incentive to put up with reputational damage would be outweighed only if the costs of dealing with problems originating outside home were modest.

In view of the limited benefits of that system he ends up advocating a common European supervisory body – a supra-national system. If Europe were the whole world then this scheme might be worth supporting. But as it is not, the scheme is not. If the problem is as important as he claims, his scheme is inadequate; and if his solution is adequate, the problem cannot be all that important.

Any significant bank in the EU does extensive business outside the EU also. Accordingly, EU-wide coordination would be helpful only for banks of modest size. Even then, would the political will necessary to give up national control of national budgets, and under some circumstances give an international body unlimited access to these national budgets, be readily mustered? It seems unlikely. Accordingly, the chances of getting such an international body going in any meaningful way are slight. Happily, that need not matter.

What is the international problem?

The difficulty if an international bank runs into difficulties is that it may be necessary to keep the bank going so as to preserve core banking functions. The bank may be in difficulties through shortage of liquidity or through shortage of capital. I deal first with shortage of liquidity.

Under these circumstances it is essential to have clear, but strictly limited, procedures for the provision of financial support, for letting any bank in liquidity difficulties fail can create both inefficiency and systemic problems.

Inefficiency arises because the refusal to provide short-term liquidity, to an institution that cannot obtain credit from the private sector, threatens insolvency. If this cannot be quickly resolved by the private-sector arrangements, for example a takeover or a recapitalisation, then the resulting reorganisation of the bank can lead to substantial loss of value. Systemic problems arise because the failure to provide short-term support can lead to an impact on other financial institutions; this could be in the form of loss of confidence among uninsured depositors, or increases in spreads in interbank markets, for example.

Such support can, however, be kept to amounts trivial relative to the budget of even a small country. It must be provided on strict terms. It must be provided against collateral, enough collateral and of sufficient quality so that there is no risk of credit loss arising from the support operation. This collateral could include loans or non-standard securities, but the valuations of these must be conservative. Second, it must be provided at a penalty cost above market rates for collateralised borrowing, so that the provision of government liquidity is not a liquidity subsidy. Somehow this borrowing must not attract stigma, despite attracting penalty; perhaps a way to achieve this would be a system of money market operations where banks are transacting very frequently with the central bank. Finally, the support must be strictly limited in duration, with a requirement for transfer of control from shareholders to the financial authorities after a defined period, which could reasonably be about three months.

If the bank is in difficulties through shortage of capital then capital is needed immediately; but in fact capital may be needed even when the original problem was, as in the case of Northern Rock in the United Kingdom in 2007/2008, a shortage of liquidity.

Which country is to provide the capital? That is a big problem – if big sums are involved. But big sums do not have to be involved. This desirable outcome can be achieved if prompt closure rules are in operation. Such a scheme could take the following form.

Intervention in a bank, in which shareholders lose both ownership and control rights, would have to take place in either of two circumstances:

1 When a maximum period of three months of liquidity support operation has passed;
2 When net worth declines below some minimum level(s), short of balance-sheet insolvency; this might correspond to the usual Basle requirement on risk-weighted capitalisation with intervention at the tier 1 4%; but there might in addition be a simpler requirement to intervene based on unweighted leverage (equity as a proportion of total assets).

There are a number of different approaches to such intervention, including:

- Operating the bank as a going concern, but with cash-flow subsidy from the deposit insurance fund, with a view to preparing it for a private-sector sale. Shareholders can then be reimbursed if the proceeds of this sale exceed the amounted needed to reimburse the fund.
- Transferring deposits to another financial institution, together with cash from the deposit insurance fund.
- Reorganising and selling bank assets and then paying out liability holders, with the deposit insurance fund first in the queue and the shareholders last.
- Transferring deposits, together with performing assets, to a 'bridge bank' (requiring an injection of funds from the deposit insurance fund), and preparing this bank for sale. The deposit insurance fund then acquires a claim

on remaining non-performing assets, with shareholders receiving payment only if these eventually realise more than the transfer from the deposit insurance fund.

If we had an effective prompt-closure scheme, why would there be any need at all for bank support and thus possibly for capital? This is still required because prompt closure, of the kind mandated, for example, by the US FDICIA, is always based on accounting measures such as net worth. Where there are substantial off-balance-sheet problems (as was the case for Northern Rock, for example), the first sign of difficulties is likely to be a withdrawal of wholesale funding, but it is not then necessarily appropriate for the authorities to move the bank directly into the closure regime.

Accordingly, what it is important to agree on is not national burden sharing and supervision arrangements, but prompt-closure rules. These are desirable for many reasons, but in the present context they can reduce the costs associated with stabilising a troubled bank to a level such that national disputes would be about small sums.

Internationalisation and competition

Internationalisation of banking should increase banking competition. Unfortunately this can be impeded not only by diverse national regulations but also by harmonised ones. Diverse regulations could be biased against new entrants; harmonised ones could, as a result of the lack of regulatory competition harmonisation inevitably produces, lead to stifling of efficiency in banking. Which is the lesser evil? Surely it is diversity in regulation. The reason is that diversity would lead only to bias against new (foreign) entrants if there were no fear of retaliation. There might be some circumstances, as with the optimum tariff, where even allowing for retaliation need not lead us back to a desirable outcome; but the existence of such possibilities is yet to be demonstrated in the area of regulation.

Conclusion

The internationalisation of banking has not necessarily increased the integration of financial markets, but it surely has increased competition, and on those grounds alone it is desirable. As Dr Persson points out, this internationalisation brings problems if a bank gets into trouble. These problems in principle appear to require international agreement on a matter on which agreement is unlikely – ready access to other countries' budgets. But if we concentrate not on trying to achieve that but on achieving agreement on a regime of prompt bank closure, while the problem would remain it would be sufficiently small as to be manageable.

Dr Persson has identified a real problem, but he has sought to cure it in the wrong way. Rather than attacking the problem directly the patient should be on a regime such that the problem never gets serious.

Note

1 It should be remembered that the faster growth rate of the United States as compared to, for example, France is largely explained (in an accounting sense) by faster population growth.

References

Mills, Terry C. and Wood, Geoffrey (1993) 'Does the Exchange Rate Regime Matter?', *Federal Reserve Bank of St. Louis Review*, 75, 4 (July/August), 3–20.

Stigler, George J. (1967) 'Imperfections in the Capital Market', *Journal of Political Economy*, 75, 3 (June), 287–292.

9 What kinds of research in central banks?

Jan Marc Berk, Már Guðmundsson, Loretta J. Mester, Øyvind Eitrheim and Jan F. Qvigstad

THE EXPERIENCE OF DE NEDERLANDSCHE BANK – *JAN MARC BERK*[1]

1 Introduction

Most people would associate central banks with two things, the issuance of bank notes and formulation of policy. The policy dimension of course differs between central banks, although most of them have tasks related to achieving and maintaining price and financial stability. Probably less widely known is the fact that most central banks also have a research function. In a number of countries including the Netherlands, this is in contrast to the natural counterparts of central banks in the national public policy arena, such as ministries. In part this is due to the fact that central banks are independent and relatively more distant from the day-to-day political pressures, which allows them to study economic problems in depth and objectively, and publish freely the results of these studies. But central banks have no monopoly in this respect, as these studies could also be produced by academia. The primary reason for performing research in a central bank is that it improves the quality of its policies. The purpose of this contribution is to share with you some of my thoughts on the research function of a central bank. These thoughts are a reflection of the experiences of a relatively small national central bank operating in the European System of Central Banks.[2] This perspective highlights something that in my mind is crucial: the design of the research function of a central bank should be a reflection of its corporate strategy. This strategy is generally directed towards achieving a certain desired positioning of the central bank in society. The point I want to make here is that different central banks may want to make different strategic choices, and this will have a consequence for their organisation, including that of research. One size does not necessarily fit all.[3]

After discussing the role of research in a central bank in the next section, Section 3 identifies important research areas for central banks. Section 4 then turns to the issue of how to assess the quality of central bank research. Section 5 concludes.

2 Research in a policy institution

In the Dutch case, the above-mentioned corporate strategy was clear at the outset, that is at the start of EMU: De Nederlandsche Bank (DNB) wants to be recognised as a knowledge-intensive institution, that derives its influence – within as well as outside the Eurosystem – mainly from the quality of its arguments. This requires a strong research function. Its output should be judged along two dimensions. First there is what I define as internal relevance, meaning that research must be directed towards issues relevant for the primary central banking tasks. The second dimension, what I would call the external relevance of research, implies that research output should be of high academic quality, using the standards that apply to academia.

Good policy advice today requires research performed yesterday. And the quality of today's research will determine the quality of policy tomorrow. This is why DNB decided against outsourcing the research function. Moreover, although we stimulate and foster collaboration with outside researchers, and frequently invite them in the context of our lecture series and visiting scholar programme, the emphasis is on research produced by our own staff. In this way the potential for synergies between research and policy is maximised.

Notwithstanding the synergetic benefits that can arise from conducting research in a policy institution, there also exists a certain tension between the two. This tension arises because the nature of the production processes of policy preparation and research differ to some extent. On the one hand, research is a time-consuming process that requires a long-term perspective. Policy work including current analysis ,on the other hand, has a much shorter horizon, and is an activity that is relatively difficult to plan – the work is in large part determined by the current policy agenda, which may be both uncertain and to some extent exogenous. These differences imply that there is a risk of research being crowded out by policy work. This is an important reason why some central banks, including DNB until a few years ago, organise policy and research functions in separate entities. This comes at the cost of interaction between both areas. A few years ago, we at DNB decided to move to a more hybrid set-up that preserves the organisational independence of research (a safeguard against crowding out of research) and at the same time stimulates further cross-fertilisation of ideas and improves the quality of both research and policy analysis. This is achieved via internal secondments, where economists working in the policy areas are, for a specific research project during a specified period of time, seconded to the research area. After completion of the project, which often is conducted in collaboration with the 'resident' researcher, the economist returns to the policy area. As the quality criteria applied to these projects are identical to the ones applied to research conducted by resident researchers of the research area (see Section 4), we impose certain professional requirements on policy economists wanting to qualify for these internal secondments, such as having a PhD.

3 Areas for research in central banks

Research enhances the quality of central bank policies. In my view, this philosophy holds for all central banking tasks, not only those related to monetary policy. De Nederlandsche Bank is responsible for safeguarding financial stability. More particularly, DNB contributes to defining and implementing the single monetary policy of the countries which have introduced the euro, promotes the smooth operation of the payment system, and supervises financial institutions and the financial sector. So the research efforts of DNB should relate to the fields of supervision (of *all* financial institutions), payment systems, financial stability and economics. The research programme of DNB reflects this. We consider topics in the field of financial stability, payment systems, pension and insurance economics to be relatively underdeveloped. So, without suggesting abandoning research in the 'traditional' money-macro field, we actively stimulate programmes in the former areas. This generally is a bottom-up procedure in that researchers, in close collaboration with the policy areas, identify and formulate individual projects. However, for some researchers, this entails broadening their agendas with some elements of directed research. But it is our experience at DNB that central bank researchers in general do not object to a certain amount of directed research. In fact, in the recruitment process, most candidates explicitly mention the possibility of doing policy-relevant research as an attractive feature of being a central bank researcher. Moreover, while directed research implies some cost for the researcher (becoming acquainted with a new field entails an investment in human capital characterised by some gestation lag), the potential benefits are substantial. This is because these areas are relatively under-researched. High-quality research in these fields therefore readily captures the eye of journal editors.

The research programme of DNB (see www.dnb.nl) thus is organised around a limited number of themes in order to maintain focus. Each theme is composed of a number of projects. Only those proposals that meet criteria for internal and external relevance are accepted (i.e. incorporated into the programme). That is, a project should be clearly connected to one of the core tasks of the institution (internal relevance) and publishable in refereed international journals (external relevance). Collaboration (between persons in a business area, between business areas and between institutions) is actively stimulated. So are joined appointments of our researchers with universities.

4 Assessing the quality of central bank research

The objectives for the research area of DNB are laid down in a balanced scorecard, which is formulated by the Board and senior management. Involvement of the Board is of crucial importance, as it ensures that (future) research plans are aligned with the strategic goals of the institution. To give an example, DNB in 2004 merged with the Dutch supervisory agency for pension funds and insurance companies. The Board held the view that a research programme in the field of pension and insurance economics should be developed, in order to increase our understanding of the pension and insurance sectors.

The balanced scorecard for the research area of DNB follows a general-to-specific approach. That is, the Board formulates the general strategic objectives, and senior management subsequently translates these into deliverables for business units and, ultimately, individual researchers. Objectives and deliverables are linked and quantified using key performance indicators. These indicators are expressed along both the internal and external dimensions I defined above.

In line with the balanced scorecard for research as a whole, individual researchers will be judged in terms of their academic output and in terms of their ability to translate their research into implications for the fulfilment of the core tasks of the institution. Rankings of central banks in terms of the quality of their research are provided elsewhere, see, for example, Eijffinger *et al.* (2002, 2003), Angelini (2002), Jondeau and Pagès (2003) and St-Amant *et al.* (2005). Below I discuss the strategy of DNB behind the assessment of the quality of central bank research.

The academic output of researchers consists of working papers, that is research in progress, and publications in academic outlets such as journals and books. The difference in the stage of the life cycle of both products is reflected in the quality requirements. Working papers should have the potential to be published in a high-quality journal. To determine this potential, the working paper should be subjected to the usual intellectual scrutiny by peers in the form of presentations in seminars and conferences. So we expect our researchers to organise their own opposition, via participation in seminars and conferences and by performing referee duties for academic journals. But these working papers are not an end in themselves; they are a vehicle to elicit discussion, to organise opposition. The solicited comments improve the quality of the research and increase the likelihood of the work being published in academic journals.

The quality of DNB academic publications is ascertained by applying standards that are currently in use in academia. See Kalaitzidakis *et al.* (2001), Palacios-Huerta and Volij (2004) and Kodrzycki and Yu (2005) for recent discussions on the pros and cons of various measures and rankings. Our measurement system follows the existing literature by recognising that not all journals are of the same academic quality. In addition, journals differ in terms of areas covered, which in turn are not equally relevant for a central bank. We therefore use a ranking of economic journals combined with a points system. Researchers can earn credits, based on the quality of the journal in which their paper is published. This quality assessment of journals[4] is based on rankings used by Dutch graduate schools as part of their selection process of research fellows, supplemented with top-tier journals (selected by using so-called impact factors calculated from citation indices by the Institute for Scientific Information)[5] in fields which are close to the core tasks of DNB (these fields would include accountancy, finance, insurance and actuarial science).

Assessing the internal relevance of central bank research is more difficult. In my view, the researcher is internally relevant when he or she is recognised as being the expert in a particular area and therefore should participate in policy discussions that relate to that area. That means a couple of things for the researcher. First of all, he or she should investigate topics that become or remain topical for the institution after the research is completed. So the researcher should definitely be 'ahead of the curve'. Second, his or her expertise should be recognised outside the research area. This means that the researcher must be a skilled communicator, with the ability to translate his or her results to be effective in front of an audience of relatively uninformed people. And finally, the researcher should be able to actively participate in the policy debate. This participation can take various forms. It may, for example, include articles written by researchers in policy or other official central bank outlets, such as Quarterly or Monthly Bulletins. It may also include seminar-style presentations of researchers to the Board, in which policy implications of research would be discussed. Another example would be for researchers to act as consultants in internal policy debates. And last but not least, it would include researchers influencing future policy agendas by formulating and conducting relevant projects today.

5 Concluding observations

It is important to stress what internal relevance of research does *not* mean. It does not mean that the researcher is also routinely involved in day-to-day policy work. That leads to crowding out of research by policy work. And it certainly does not mean that research should aim to confirm certain policy priors. Research in a central bank should be goal dependent, but instrument independent. By that I mean that the researcher does not have complete freedom to determine his own research agenda. The areas that research is supposed to cover are part of the strategic choices made by the institution. But once the main research areas are determined, the researcher should have the freedom to conduct the research in the way he or she sees fit. Moreover, the conclusions from research should be determined only by the analysis performed (and not by policy), and the quality of the research is determined by its academic content.

The experience of DNB indicates that letting policy and research interact in a way that is beneficial to both is a process that takes time. This is because researchers and policy economists must learn to speak the same language. The former should be able to make the implications of their work clear in non-technical terms. The latter should be able to (re)formulate their policy questions in such a way that research can translate them into research objectives. It also takes time, because of the long gestation periods involved in getting papers published in refereed academic journals. So, the quality improvement of research itself will only be visible after a number of years. Moreover, research will by definition remain a risky endeavour – the high rejection rates of top-tier academic journals are a testimony to that. Although we acknowledge these facts, we at DNB clearly see the benefits of our research policy. The execution of core central banking tasks benefits from the most recent academic insights, brought to the institution by the brightest researchers that are attracted to the central bank by its reputation of fostering high-quality research, aimed at publications in the best journals. Positive externalities will therefore arise, both in recruitment and in fostering a reputation among stakeholders of the central bank as a knowledge-intensive institution.

However, there is no room for complacency. To ensure that the research effort and strategy of DNB remains focused and on a par with (inter)national academic standards, we regularly commission external visitations of the research area. In these visitations, independent external academics and other outside experts assess and benchmark the research efforts of De Nederlandsche Bank.

Notes

1 Constructive comments by Job Swank are gratefully acknowledged.
2 See DNB (2000) for details.
3 See Goodfriend (1999) for an account of the experience of the US Federal Reserve System. The point is that the role of regional central banks in a monetary union, including the question of whether or not to specialise, is their strategic choice and not exogenous.
4 The list also includes a quality assessment of publishing houses for evaluating academic books published by central bank researchers.
5 See http://scientific.thomson.com/isi for details.

References

Angelini, P. (2002) 'Small is Beautiful but Large is Not to Be Belittled', *European Journal of Political Economy*, 19 (4), 901–903.

DNB (2000) 'The Role of a National Central Bank in the Single European Monetary Policy', *Quarterly Bulletin March 2000*, De Nederlandsche Bank.

Eijffinger, S.C.W., de Haan, J. and Koedijk, K. (2002) 'Small is Beautiful: Measuring the Research Input and Output of European Central Banks', *European Journal of Political Economy*, 18 (2), 365–374.

Eijffinger, S.C.W., de Haan, J. and Koedijk, K. (2003) 'Small is Beautiful but Large is Not to Be Belittled: A Reply', *European Journal of Political Economy*, 19 (4), 905–907.

Goodfriend, M. (1999) 'The Role of a Regional Bank in a System of Central Banks', *Carnegie-Rochester Conference Series on Public Policy*, 51 (1), 51–71.

Jondeau, E. and Pagès, H. (2003) 'Benchmarking Research in European Central Banks', mimeo, Banque de France (presented at workshop on central bank efficiency, Sveriges Riksbank, Stockholm, May 2003).

Kalaitzidakis, P., Mamuneas, P. and Stengos, T. (2001) 'Rankings of Academic Journals and Institutions in Economics', Discussion Paper 2001-10, Department of Economics, University of Cyprus.

Kodrzycki, Y. and Yu, P.D. (2005) 'New Approaches to Ranking Economics Journals', Working Paper 05-12, Federal Reserve Bank of Boston.

Palacios-Huerta, I. and Volij, O. (2004) 'The Measurement of Intellectual Influence', *Econometrica*, 72 (3), 963–977.

St-Amant, P., Tkacz, G., Guérard-Langlois, A. and Morel, L. (2005) 'Quantity, Quality and Relevance: Central Bank Research, 1990–2003', Working Paper no. 2005-37, Bank of Canada.

THE RATIONALE AND ORGANISATION OF RESEARCH IN CENTRAL BANKS – *MÁR GUÐMUNDSSON*[1]

Why do central banks need research?

We are asked the question: what kind of research should be done in central banks? However, that begs two questions: what is research, and what is a central bank? You might consider the second question silly; we all know what a central bank is! However, as Amartya Sen has demonstrated so well in a recent book (Sen, 2006), individuals tend to have multiple identities and I think that the same might apply to institutions, at least up to a point. Central banks are hybrids of the public sector and the market and operate at the crossroads of public policy, market activity and academic research – which, in my view, is one of the reasons that it can be so stimulating to work in a central bank. This mixture has implications for the kind of research that is of interest to central banks. In particular, it must meet the following two criteria:

1 It should serve a public purpose, i.e. have policy relevance.
2 It should be of high quality and be able to withstand the scrutiny of academic standards.

But back to the question: what is research? In the most general sense, research is a rigorous analysis of phenomena or policy issues, using logical reasoning and investigation of evidence and data. Although I hope that all central bank activity is permeated by research in this sense, the definition is too broad to be useful in defining the activity that we usually call research in central banks and which has important resource and governance aspects. A narrower definition would add references to an existing body of theory and the testing of predictions generated by theory against data and other evidence, using sound statistical methods. This implies that the research has to meet academic standards and, at least potentially, be publishable in refereed journals. However, even if research output meets this standard, it does not have to take this form. It could be a working paper, or even, as is sometimes the case at the BIS, a meeting document.

It is important to note that the above definition is not restricted to economic research. Although the bulk of research used by central banks is in the realm of economics, one can easily make the argument that central banks also need research that draws on history, law and political science, for example.

Central banks are heavy consumers of research – probably more so than, for example, ministries of finance. I can think of at least four reasons for this:

1 Monetary policy is a repeated game. Central banks take frequent policy actions. These give rise to responses in the economy that lend themselves to systematic study and thus to a refinement of future policy decisions.
2 Many trade offs in the area of monetary policy seem to be stable enough to be candidates for systematic investigation (e.g. unemployment and inflation).

3. Central banks in democratic societies communicate through the strength of their arguments rather than their raw political power. Arguments based on quality research are more compelling.
4. Related to this, grounding central bank actions in quality research helps to enhance their credibility and to preserve and enhance central bank independence. This also applies to the standing of the central bank vis-à-vis the government.

Many of these points would, *mutatis mutandis,* apply to other governmental entities, some of which consume more research than central banks. However, the relevant comparison is with policy decisions of governments, especially when the frequency of decisions is lower and ill-defined trade offs are prevalent. Governments have political mandates to take such decisions and they can, at least up to a point, do so more through the force of their power than through the strength of their arguments.

Where should research be located?

Using and making reference to research is one thing. Producing it in-house is another. However, the facts speak clearly about the revealed preference of central bankers. There has been a marked increase in in-house central bank research in at least the last decade and a half. This can be seen in the number of research staff, the number of publications by central bank staff and the number of conferences they hold. St-Amant *et al.* (2005) provide some figures: among the over 30 central banks (including all the major ones) in their survey, the number of researchers increased by 113 per cent between 1990 and 2003 and the number of working papers published by these central banks increased by 50 per cent between 1999 and 2003. We can also see this increase on the central bank research hub on the BIS website (www.bis.org/cbhub/index.htm). The final example I mention is the publication of the *International Journal of Central Banking* by the global central bank community.

What then are the arguments for having research in-house rather than simply consuming what the academic community produces, or hiring contractors, e.g. academics, on a part-time basis when the output of the academic community is not deemed to be sufficient? I can think of a few (see also Trichet, 2007):

- To recognise the potential relevance of external research for policy making and translate academic research into policy-relevant research.
- To serve as a more general two-way interface between central banks and the academic community.
- To provide the policy process with research output that is not readily available at universities or research institutes.
- To assist in the recruitment of 'the best and the brightest' to the operational sides of central banks. Central banks might, for this purpose, have to hire PhDs interested in their own research early in their career. We can look at this as long-term hiring costs with side benefits.

There is an additional, compelling reason for keeping some research in-house in central banks. The fads and fashion of academia can sometimes lead it grossly astray into the wilderness of irrelevance. In those cases, policy-relevant research has to be conducted in other places. It can even go so far as to be a case of preserving the existing stock of knowledge of policy-relevant research through such episodes. Don Kohn (2004) mentions an important such example: 'In fact, Board staff, like monks in the Middle Ages, kept policy research alive through the dark night that initially settled on academic analysis of monetary policy following the Lucas critique and real-business-cycle theory.'

But the above points do not tell us how much is enough and I guess this will remain an open question. In addition, there are hybrid forms to be considered. Central banks seem to be increasingly hiring external researchers either on a temporary basis through visiting research programmes or on an ad hoc basis. Some fund research institutes to which they can then have access.

In addition to the issue of the degree to which research should be done inside central banks, there is the question of where in the central banking community research efforts should be located. There are different levels: (1) national central banks, (2) federal central banks, (3) regional organisations, and (4) international organisations. In my view, one successful initiative that transcends the different levels of the central banking community mentioned above is the spreading of research networks. The ECB has made successful use of such networks, and the BIS Asian Office has organised two successful networks under the auspices of the BIS Asian Research Programme (see www.bis.org/about/arnetworks/index.htm).

Organisation of in-house research

In-house research raises several issues in terms of dedication, resources, evaluation, governance and the relationship with academia. A key issue is how, on the one hand, to create the necessary time and resources for research and, on the other, to engage the best minds with important policy issues and operational matters. There is as yet no single model that has prevailed in this connection. Some organise research separately (e.g. the ECB), with or without regular rotation, some mix research with their operational and policy departments (e.g. the BoE) and some request that researchers split their time between dedicated policy work and free research and competition of ideas (e.g. the US Fed).

The optimal mix of policy work and free research is probably both state and time dependent. Thus, for the ECB it was imperative as a new central bank to establish a strong track record in this area early on. At the same time, the risk of operational work crowding out research was potentially significant in its build-up phase. When central banks have matured and stabilised, other considerations may become more important, such as the need for strong cross-fertilisation between policy work and research.

Small central banks with limited resources may also find it difficult, if not impossible, to separate research from other work. That tended to be the case at the Central Bank of Iceland, where I was the chief economist for a decade, and the synergies turned out to be strong. However, the Internet, research networks and data access provided by international organisations have radically improved the conditions for conducting research in small central banks.

The BIS provides an interesting hybrid in this regard. The economists are split between those that provide policy-oriented analytical work for meetings of governors and other central bank officials, and those that do policy-relevant research for publication. But the split is far from pure: those that do analytical work for meetings also do research for publication, and those that mostly focus on research for publications also do, from time to time, analytical work for meetings. The split is about 70–30 in each case. On top of that, we try to promote mobility between the two functions. Finally, in order to further facilitate cross-fertilisation, we place those working on both sides on macroeconomic and monetary issues on the same floor, and those working on financial market and stability issues together on another floor.

Economic research of the type needed by central banks is resource-intensive. It requires access to extensive databases, IT support, library services and networking. Let me focus on the data.

Much of the early research efforts in central banks were associated with compiling and analysing data in order to be better able to monitor macroeconomic developments (see, for instance, Kohn, 2004). The data are still crucial. Thus a significant amount of fruitful research is conducted on the basis of in-house specialised data sets of the particular institutions. A good example of this is the BIS, where a lot of research of has been directed at using the BIS international financial statistics (see www.bis.org/statistics/index.htm).

Cooperation with academia

I mentioned above how central banks and academia have sometimes gone in different directions. Central banks can live with that for a while but it has costs. Most progress has been made when the two are in step. Part of the success of monetary policy in the past decade or so has been due to the cross-fertilisation that has occurred between the central banking community and academia. It eventually resulted in a consensus on the goal of monetary policy and a rudimentary model of how it all works: called either the New Keynesian model or New Neoclassical Synthesis, partly depending on from which side of the fence one came to the consensus (see Goodfriend, 2007 for an excellent summary of how the current consensus on monetary policy was achieved).

However, a lot remains to be done, not least in the realm of financial stability analysis and the interaction between monetary policy and financial stability. It is therefore important to maintain strong cooperation between central banks and academia. Both sides realise this, as we can see in the composition of conferences such as the one that generated this book.

Note

1 Views expressed are those of the author and do not necessarily reflect those of the BIS. I thank David Archer, Andy Filardo and Allen Frankel for helpful suggestions.

References

Goodfriend, Marvin (2007) 'How the World Achieved Consensus on Monetary Policy', *Journal of Economic Perspectives*, 21 (4), Fall, 47–68.

Kohn, Donald L. (2004) 'Research at the Federal Reserve Board: The Contributions of Henderson, Porter, and Tinsley', remarks at the Federal Reserve Board Models and Monetary Policy Conference, Washington, DC, 26 March. Available online: www.federalreserve.gov/boarddocs/speeches/2004/200403262/default.htm.

Sen, Amartya (2006) *Identity and Violence: The Illusion of Destiny*, Penguin, London.

St-Amant, Pierre, Greg Tkacz, Annie Guérard-Langlois and Louis Morel (2005) 'Quantity, Quality, and Relevance: Central Bank Research, 1990–2003', Bank of Canada Working Paper 2005-37, December.

Trichet, Jean-Claude (2007) 'The Role of Research in Central Banks and at the ECB', speech at the ceremony for the Award of the Germán Bernácer Prize, Madrid, 21 May.

WHAT KIND OF RESEARCH SHOULD CENTRAL BANKS DO? – *LORETTA J. MESTER*[1]

First, let me thank the organisers for putting together such an interesting conference and for inviting me to contribute to this panel on what kind of research central banks should be doing. The panel is very well designed. We have a representative from an institution that helps coordinate and foster cooperation among central banks, and representatives from three different central banks with three different designs.

I'd like to focus my comments on what I believe is the important role of research within a central bank setting. I will speak about mature central banks, once they are past any start-up phase. Of course, my experience within the Federal Reserve System is going to inform my views, but I hope what I'm going to say is broadly applicable to central banks around the world. I am – as I'm sure you are – very curious to learn the differences and similarities among the panelists' views.

Fiscal responsibility

First, let me set some context. It is important to recognise that the central bank is funded with public money. In the United States, while the Fed is not under the budget and appropriations process of other government agencies, it returns its surplus to the US Treasury each year. This means the Fed and other central banks need to be fiscally responsible and efficient with what they do with their funding, and that all of the banks' various functions and operations have to be done in support of the banks' given responsibilities.

Regarding a central bank's research initiatives, it is important to recognise that the Fed (and other central banks) cannot be think tanks. Rather, the research mission must be done in support of the central bank's key goals. I note that the responsibilities of a central bank can vary across countries, in particular, with regard to the central bank's role in banking supervision and financial services.

In the United States, the Federal Reserve has responsibility for setting monetary policy to achieve and maintain price stability and maximum sustainable growth. It also is responsible for ensuring and maintaining the stability of the financial system and containing systemic risk that can arise in financial markets. These are responsibilities the Fed shares with other central banks. But unlike some central banks, the Fed plays a role in supervising and regulating banking institutions to ensure the safety and soundness of the banking and financial system and to protect the credit rights of consumers. And the Federal Reserve, through its Federal Reserve Banks, also provides financial services to depository institutions and to the government.

The research mission of a central bank should be to provide a strong scientific foundation – both theoretical and empirical – to support central bank policy making in its designated areas of responsibility.

Long-term research versus short-term policy analysis

I firmly believe that longer-term economic research informs policy making, yielding better outcomes. I can point to many examples. In the monetary policy arena, these would include the important ideas of rational expectations and time inconsistency, the role of central bank independence, and the implementation of a numerical definition of price stability – indeed some of these topics were covered in this conference. In the financial stability arena, work on capital requirements, risk-modelling, moral hazard and prompt corrective action was important in formulating better policy.

There is a tension between the shorter-term focus of policy briefings and current analysis driven by the meeting schedule, and longer-term research. The gains from shorter-term analyses useful for the next policy meeting are obvious. But the payoff from longer-term research is not as immediate. Similarly, the opportunity costs of briefings and current analyses in taking time away from long-term research and in disrupting progress on the research agenda are not easily measured. But this long-term research is necessary – it forms the basis for better policy making.

It is not always obvious what the next major policy issue will be. And research takes time. If you wait until the issue is apparent, you will be without good research on which to base decisions. A case in point is the current problems created by the housing and mortgage markets in the United States. The Fed was well-served by the fact that, over the years, it had developed a body of research on the transmission of housing price shocks and asset bubbles to the macroeconomy and appropriate policy responses. It had a body of work on financial markets and financial innovation, including sub-prime mortgages, securitisation and asset-backed commercial paper. Even so, there are many things that are not known and need more study. But having the body of work and having researchers with expertise on these issues on whom to call were an immense and essential help in working through various policy options and in forecasting future economic outcomes.

Research autonomy

I think central banks are better served by allowing substantial autonomy to researchers in setting their research agendas. This is not to say that central banks should not ask economists on staff to do analyses on topics of specific interest, or to offer incentives for particular areas of research. But this is different from directing a person's research agenda.

I believe research driven from the top down does not end up being that productive for several reasons. First, good research takes a long time and requires perseverance; if the person isn't genuinely interested in the area, he or she is unlikely to invest the energy needed to produce good work and to develop the research agenda – remember, we are not talking about piece work but rather a longer-term body of work. Second, the topic that might be of interest today is not necessarily the topic that will be of most interest in a year or two. Directed research would tend to yield shorter-term analyses and not the well-thought-out agendas that enhance policy decision making over the long term. Third, as part of management, I'm loath to think that I know better than the researchers what constitutes an interesting direction in which to take research. I might feel competent to make such decisions about my own field of financial intermediation, but I don't necessarily think I can or should make them about other fields. Finally, I think it is important to remember that our responsibility is not only to support current policy makers but also *future* policy makers. This means we should allow our economists opportunities to develop their human capital and to explore research ideas that are not perceived as necessarily currently relevant or valuable but that might become relevant in the future. We need to ensure the research mission serves the long-lived institution.

That is not to say that all research is a go at a central bank. Instead, I think the central bank's preferences over fields should be reflected at the time of *hiring* economists; i.e. I think the central bank is better served by hiring economists with interests in the fields the central bank wants to support and then allowing them significant autonomy over their research agendas.

I note that this is not as freewheeling as it might sound. Remember, researchers don't like to work in isolation. They will self-select out of the central bank if there are not fellow researchers there with common interests. Also, good researchers' own interests tend to reflect the environment in which they are working. Being exposed to policy issues will inform their research. This does not occur only in central banks. Think of finance departments that hire people with PhDs in economics – over time, these economists start to look like their colleagues, working on issues of more interest to finance departments than to economics departments.

Specialisation

The Fed's policy work covers macroeconomics and monetary policy, financial system stability and bank regulation, and payments. Since policy making across these fields needs to be supported by sound research, we need to hire in a broad number of fields, although there is certainly scope for specialisation.

Within the Federal Reserve System, the Board of Governors does not have many researchers working in the areas of regional economics, but the Reserve Banks tend to have an economist or two working in this area given the Banks' regional presence and their need to gather and interpret information on the regional economy. Reserve Banks may choose to develop expertise in an area related to their region or of particular interest to their President. For example, given the Philadelphia Fed's location near Delaware's credit card industry, our previous President developed and our current President continues to support the Bank's expertise in consumer payments. The Philadelphia Fed also runs the Survey of Professional Forecasters and Livingston Survey, and we provide real-time data on the macro economy to the public for research and current analysis. Work done at several of the Banks on banking to lower-income individuals, which recently became an important part of the discussion of macroeconomic policy, was not done within the Bank's research departments but became quite important during the recent financial disruptions. Fields of strength can also occur naturally if an economist with a strong reputation attracts others with similar interests.

But specialisation can go too far. I believe there is value in having some overlap across the staffs of the regional Federal Reserve Banks and the Board of Governors in the topics they analyse. One strength of the Reserve Bank system is that it allows for a diversity of views among policy makers. The policy process (both monetary policy and regulatory policy) fosters consensus building but permits differences of opinion to be aired. Indeed, the airing of such differences can play a role in effective communication. (E.g. at the last FOMC meeting, there was a dissenting vote for no change instead of the 25-basis-point cut that was made. The public interpreted this, as well as the statement language, as saying that further rate cuts were not a sure thing, and the market's expectations were revised.)

Certainly, a regional Reserve Bank would want to have researchers that can help support the Bank's president in formulating his or her policy views. But this duplication also serves an important role in helping to spur innovative thinking and avoiding 'group think' on policy issues. These researchers are able to investigate alternative views. The diversification of research in the regional Reserve Bank system allows a variety of analytical perspectives to be brought to bear on policy. This is valuable given the state of economic science – there is not one right answer to many policy questions.

In-house research versus consultants

But does the longer-term research have to be done in-house? Couldn't the central bank rely on outside consultants? My answer is no. I don't think this would be a successful model because I firmly believe there are *synergies between research and policy making*. It is important for central bank policy makers to have researchers in-house so that the researchers are exposed to and are thinking about important policy issues as they formulate their research agendas. I think it is important for researchers to be engaged in the policy process so that these synergies can be exploited – good researchers are in a position to know which of the many advances in economic science are most relevant for the policy mission.

For this reason, I am not in favour of a sharp separation between the research and policy staffs within a central bank – *provided* top management recognises the importance of ensuring that researchers receive long uninterrupted periods of time (not just days here and there) to devote to their research agendas, and provided that newly minted PhDs are given time to establish their research agendas. I believe that this exposure to policy is one of the things that attract good researchers to a central bank.

It would be very difficult to exploit the synergies between policy and research if research were delegated to consultants. Consultants cannot be involved in the policy process because of confidentiality, and their interests typically lie elsewhere. Moreover, multiple interactions between researchers and policy decision makers and a close working relationship between the two are needed to get a mutual understanding of issues. This would be difficult to achieve with outside consultants.

That is not to say that consultants do not have a role to play. Most central banks invite in visiting scholars or consultants. These scholars interact with staff economists, sharing their research and offering opinions on the staff's research efforts. This can lead to co-authorships, which benefit the central bank by increasing the number of scholars working on issues relevant to central banking. Visiting scholars also are a conduit through which the central bank can enhance its reputation – which is important for increasing the public's confidence in central bank policy making. Indeed, having research departments in central banks more outwardly focused, more engaged with the economics profession via seminar and conference participation, not only enhances the central bank economists' research but also helps enhance the central bank's reputation and the public's confidence in the central bank's policy making, which makes that policy more effective.

Public education mission

One of the things we have learned from research on monetary policy is the important role of expectations in the effect of policy on the economy. By anchoring inflation expectations, monetary policy helps sustain economic growth. Its ability to influence expectations depends on the central bank's ability to convey to the public its objectives, its methods for achieving those objectives, and its commitment to those objectives. Thus, monetary policy transparency and communication are important.

Certainly, monetary policy statements and the minutes of policy meetings are an important component of that communication. But non-technical papers published by central bank economists can help the central bank educate the public about relevant economic issues and thereby raise the effectiveness of its monetary and regulatory policies. Thus, these are important outputs of central banks, but these in-house publications are not the way to evaluate central bank research.

Criteria for evaluating central bank research

Over the 20 years that I've been at the Fed, there has been an important change in focus from inward to outward. I believe this change was informed by economic research on the importance of central bank credibility and public confidence in central bank policy making. The institution's inward focus was rationalised by saying that the issues we investigated were highly specialised and confidential. Working papers were published but not necessarily publicised.

But this caused two problems. First, it was difficult to benefit from the critiques and suggestions of other researchers outside the central bank. Thus, the research was likely not as good as it could be. Second, it was difficult to convey to the public that the research on which policy was based was first rate. This is important to the extent that policy effectiveness is enhanced when the public has confidence in the policy and to the extent that the central bank is held accountable for its actions.

To create this confidence, it is important for central bank research to be vetted by the economics profession. That means playing by the academic rules of the profession, and that means certification by publication in academic journals. The outside publication process and the necessary precursors of giving a paper in seminars and at conferences actually *improve* the research. Moreover, it conveys in a verifiable way that the research is high quality – that it passes the market test. I know of no more efficient way to do this.

Some argue that some topics that the central bank is interested in are not the 'sexiest' in terms of academic interest. I believe that may have been truer in the past than it is now. Several good journals recognise the value of policy-related research; some even specialise in central bank policy issues (e.g. the *International Journal of Central Banking* and the *Journal of Financial Stability*).

Moreover, exposure of central bank research to the profession, via seminars and conferences and with visiting scholars at the central bank, can increase the interest of outside researchers in issues relevant to central banking. This helps raise the amount of good work being done, and also helps to ensure a flow of *new* researchers into the area, since academic economists train students and guide dissertations.

Similarly, central bank economists with strong publication records can ultimately be invited to serve as editors of journals, and thereby have a larger influence on the field.

Of course, these are long-run gains. But I think it serves the central bank well to remember the long run and the important contributions long-run research has made to good policy making.

Note

1 The views expressed here are those of the author and do not necessarily reflect those of the Federal Reserve Bank of Philadelphia or of the Federal Reserve System.

DESIGNING RESEARCH IN CENTRAL BANKS – *ØYVIND EITRHEIM AND JAN F. QVIGSTAD*

When designing research in central banks, a starting point could be to ask what our 'end product' is. What do we deliver to the general public? The answer is: *The interest rate decision.* The interest rate setting is our *raison d'être.*
But when setting the interest rate, *the decision maker would have in mind, implicitly or explicitly, a forward-looking interest rate path.* We and other central banks publish the interest rate path, others do not. We want to put aside the question of publishing and just assume that the decision makers have an interest rate path in mind.

The graph of the interest rate path describes how we have *organised the work* among the 60–70 economists that we have at our disposal for monetary policy.

We need to estimate the (unknown) current state of the economy – the so-called 'nowcasting'. In this process we need to have an opinion on what the output gap is, what underlying inflation is, what the current real interest rate is and so forth. The economists that focus on the *nowcasting* are organised in a special group. Some of the techniques they use are technically quite advanced.

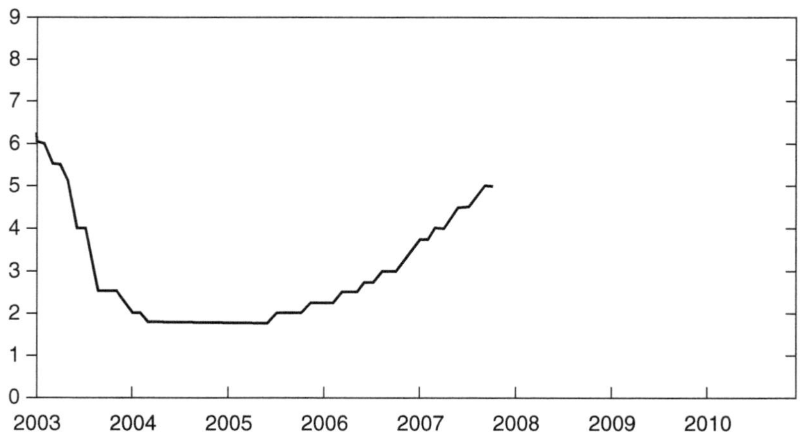

Figure 9.1 It is all about deciding on interest rates.

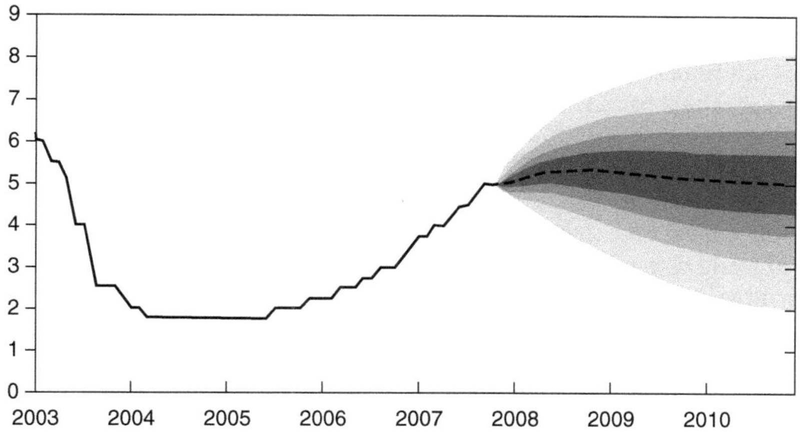

Figure 9.2 An interest rate path.

The economists that are engaged in helping the Board find an *'interest rate path that looks good'* are organised in another group. It requires some skills in order to minimise loss functions within a DSGE model under commitment!

There are also a group of economists that have a special responsibility for *communication*, i.e. drafting press releases, the monetary policy report (which used to be called the Inflation Report) and speeches and so on.

You cannot only decide on the interest rate, you have to also 'do it'. You need *market operations* supplying liquidity to the market to make sure that the money market is close to the signal rate. This is not trivial work. We were reminded of that on Thursday 9 August 2007 and the days thereafter. It is not a one-way street from the policy maker's decision on the interest rate to market operations. We use market information gathered from the market operations intensively when deciding on the interest rate. Market operations are considered an integral part of monetary policy in our bank.

We have to make decisions at the Board meetings even if there are a lot of things we do not know. What really is the output gap, what do we mean by the concept, what is the underlying inflation, should we look at the sticky prices, what is the present real interest rate, the neutral rate? The list of questions is endless. So it is quite obvious that *we need research.* We have to try to move our knowledge frontier forward a bit, step by step, each interest rate meeting.

We need research in all senses of the word. We need practical research that gives answers next week and we need *academic research* that is published in the international academic journals and yields practical results usually with a long time lag, if ever.

Recognising that we are a small central bank and the only one in the country, we adhere to the following *guiding principles* for policy research activities in the bank:

- Look to mainstream academic theory.
- Aim for central banking best practice.
- Expose yourself to regular external examinations. (But be careful only to pick academics. Make sure that the committee also includes someone from another central bank.)

Hence, we look internationally: You do not have to be so smart if you are good at learning from others.

So, *why bother with own academic research*? The research we do will only be 1/*N* of world research where *N* is a large number! The answer is that if we are to learn from others, we need 'translators', 'importers' and 'evaluators'. We have also learnt that we have to contribute in order to get in touch with the world.

Norges Bank Monetary Policy employs 60–70 economists, of whom 15–20 are research economists with PhDs. Approximately half of the PhDs do academic research. Research includes theoretical and empirical research.

In order to be successful in academic research we need to *publish in international refereed journals*.

It is acknowledged that the work of individual researchers has to be strongly *motivated by the interests of the researcher himself*. So 'putty' turns to 'clay' when you *hire*. The research strategy must be formulated by the Bank leadership. We say that we do monetary policy. But that leaves quite a lot of room for variety. We do research in mathematical algorithms for solving the optimal interest rate path. We do theory, empirical research and so on. However, academic research need not be mainstream or directly relevant for policy today. For example, research on inflation targeting in the years of fixed exchange rates was valuable indeed. Also, it is important to acknowledge that academic research is a risky sport. It is impossible to know *ex ante* what research projects will yield valuable insights in the future. An important part of research activities is to promote and contribute *to international networking*.

To obtain high-quality interaction with the economists doing current policy analyses geared towards setting the interest rate, researchers need to have *at least one 'friend'* among these.

As part of a commitment to internationalisation, quite a few of the economists are temporarily abroad, at universities or working for other central banks. We need to understand the ideas and implement them. We have also started to hire economists from abroad. We go for *internationalisation*. Our working language will be English – at least for the researchers.

In our experience, the typical employee is part of a dual-career household that tend to be very *fertile*. We have to adjust our working practices to the fact that both parents want to continue to work after childbirth. We do not really care where the work is done, at home or at the bank. We only care about the results. Modern technology with Internet is very helpful in this regard.

Closeness to the decision making is a clear advantage of being *a small central bank*. The distance from a good idea to implemented policy may not be so long.

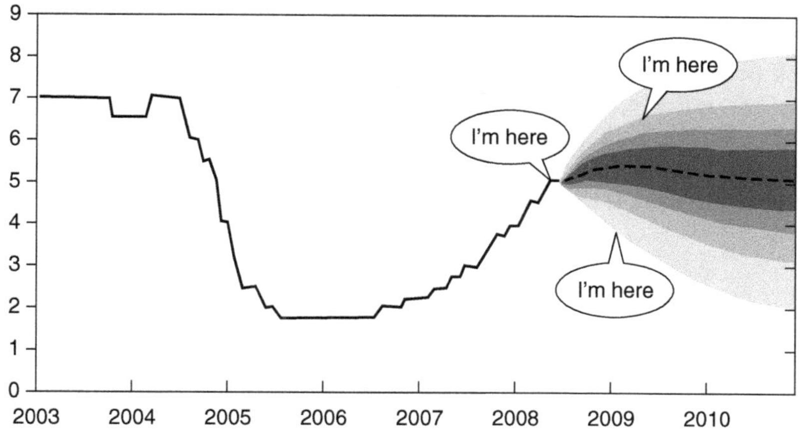

Figure 9.3 The beauty of being small.

Employees at small central banks may have a strong sense of accountability. At Norges Bank Monetary Policy, all economists, as well as the academic researchers, are asked to advise on the interest rate before interest rate meetings.

We think a good test of any organisation is to ask a random person: *Why are you here?* What are you actually doing relative to the current policy decision? You should also ask the academic researcher this question.

Some years ago Adrian Pagan was asked by the Bank of England to examine their research on models. He described the *trade-off between theory coherency and data coherency* which we need to factor into the analysis of monetary policy alternatives; ranging from assessing the current situation (nowcasting), through medium-term forecasting to long-run (steady-state) equilibrium. This dilemma can be referred to as the Pagan dilemma.

Years of participation-by-observation in Executive Board meetings has convinced us that *the challenge of presenting analysis of the current situation and policy alternatives for the decision-making body should be taken very seriously.* The idea of framing these issues in a way which provides sufficient discipline

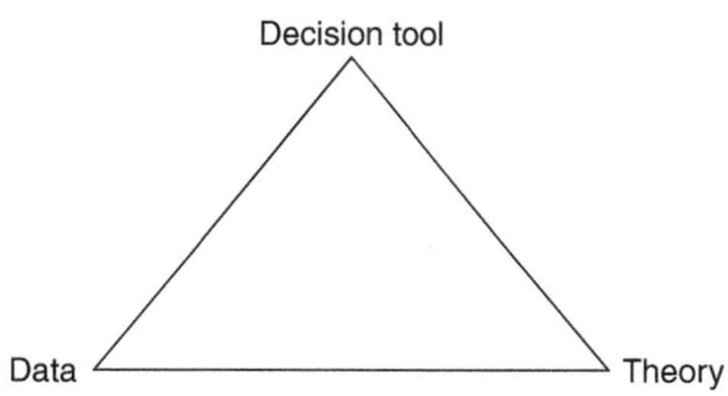

Figure 9.4 The dilemma.

without limiting the discussion and which informs the Executive Board on the degree of time consistency of their current policy alternatives is important. If models and research is not geared towards being applicable for the Board, the fall-back position of the Board is to throw out the models and resort to 'free thinking'. So research, models and analytical work in central banks should be designed with the goal of being useful for decisions! So the Pagan two-dimensional dilemmas have a third dilemma. So our contribution is perhaps to demonstrate that there is a third dimension to the Pagan dilemma.

Index

For Product Safety Concerns and Information please contact our EU
representative GPSR@taylorandfrancis.com
Taylor & Francis Verlag GmbH, Kaufingerstraße 24, 80331 München, Germany

www.ingramcontent.com/pod-product-compliance
Ingram Content Group UK Ltd.
Pitfield, Milton Keynes, MK11 3LW, UK
UKHW020011200926
475702UK00014B/1819
9780415696548